The Problem of
CRIME

Crime, Order and Social Control Course Team

The Open University

Mandy Anton	*Graphic Designer*
Sally Baker	*Subject Librarian, Education and Social Sciences*
Hilary Canneaux	*Course Manager*
John Clarke	*Professor of Social Policy*
Jonathan Davies	*Graphic Design Co-ordinator*
Margaret Dickens	*Print Buying Co-ordinator*
Clive Emsley	*Professor of History, Arts*
Janis Gilbert	*Graphic Artist*
Peggotty Graham	*Staff Tutor, Social Sciences*
Fiona Harris	*Editor, Social Sciences*
Celia Hart	*Picture Researcher*
Gordon Hughes	*Lecturer in Social Policy*
Liz Freeman	*Book Trade Department*
Nicole Jones	*Course Secretary*
Mary Langan	*Senior Lecturer in Social Policy*
Patti Langton	*Producer, BBC/OUPC*
Eugene McLaughlin	*Senior Lecturer in Criminology and Social Policy*
John Muncie	*Senior Lecturer in Criminology and Social Policy (Course Team Chair)*
Doreen Pendlebury	*Course Secretary*
Winifred Power	*Editor, Social Sciences*
Roger Sapsford	*Reader in Psychology, University of Teesside*
Esther Saraga	*Staff Tutor, Social Sciences*
Mercia Seminara	*Producer, BBC/OUPC*
Richard Skellington	*Project Officer, Social Sciences*
Alison Tucker	*Producer, BBC/OUPC*
Emma Wheeler	*Project Control*
Chris Wooldridge	*Editor, Social Sciences*

Consultant Authors

Sean Damer	*Honorary Research Fellow, University of Glasgow*
Loraine Gelsthorpe	*Lecturer in Criminology, University of Cambridge*
Paul Gordon	*Academic Consultant, London*
Victor Jupp	*Head of Sociology, University of Northumbria*
Jim Sharpe	*Professor of History, University of York*
Richard Sparks	*Professor of Criminology, University of Keele*
Sandra Walklate	*Professor of Sociology, Manchester Metropolitan University*
Louise Westmarland	*Lecturer in Criminology, Scarman Centre, University of Leicester*

External Assessors and Examiners

Pat Carlen	*Professor of Criminology, University of Bath (Course Assessor: 1st editions)*
Victor Jupp	*Head of Sociology, University of Northumbria (Book Assessor)*
Tony Jefferson	*Professor of Criminology, University of Keele (Course Assessor: 2nd editions)*
Ken Pease	*Professor of Criminology, University of Huddersfield (Course Examiner)*
Sandra Walklate	*Professor of Sociology, Manchester Metropolitan University (Course Examiner)*

Tutor Panel

Tom Burden	*Policy Research Unit, Leeds Metropolitan University*
Hilary Hiram	*School of Law, University of Glasgow*
Marilyn Woolfson	*Open University Associate Lecturer, London*

The Problem of CRIME

Edited by

John Muncie and Eugene McLaughlin

SAGE Publications
London • Thousand Oaks • New Delhi

in association with

The Open
University

This book is the first in a series published by Sage Publications in association with
The Open University.

The Problem of Crime
edited by John Muncie and Eugene McLaughlin

Controlling Crime
edited by Eugene McLaughlin and John Muncie

Criminological Perspectives: A Reader
edited by John Muncie, Eugene McLaughlin and Mary Langan

The books are part of The Open University course D315 *Crime, Order and Social Control.*
Details of this and other Open University courses can be obtained from the Call Centre, PO Box 724,
The Open University, Milton Keynes MK7 6ZS, United Kingdom: tel. +44(0) 1908-653231,
e-mail ces-gen@open.ac.uk. Alternatively, you may visit The Open University website at
http://www.open.ac.uk where you can learn more about the wide range of courses and packs offered
at all levels by The Open University. For availability of other course components, including video- and
audio-cassette materials, contact Open University Worldwide Ltd, The Berrill Building, Walton Hall,
Milton Keynes MK7 6AA, United Kingdom: tel. +44 (0) 1908-858785; fax +44 (0) 1908-858787;
e-mail ouwenq@open.ac.uk; website http://www.ouw.co.uk.

© The Open University 1996, 2001

First published in 1996
Second edition 2001

The opinions expressed are not necessarily those of the Course Team or of The Open University.

SAGE Publications Ltd
6 Bonhill Street
London EC2A 4PU

SAGE Publications Inc
2455 Teller Road
Thousand Oaks
California 91320

SAGE Publications India Pvt Ltd
32, M-Block Market
Greater Kailash – I
New Delhi 110 048

British Library Cataloguing in Publication data
A catalogue record for this book is available from The British Library.

ISBN 0-7619-6970-5
ISBN 0-7619-6971-3 (pbk)

Library of Congress Cataloging-in-Publication data
A catalogue record for this book has been requested.

Edited, designed and typeset by The Open University.

Printed by The Bath Press, Bath.

Contents

Preface

This second edition of *The Problem of Crime* is the first text of three volumes in a series of criminology texts first published by Sage in association with The Open University in 1996. The series, entitled *Crime, Order and Social Control*, explores key issues in the study of crime and criminal justice by examining the diverse and contested nature of crime, the varied formal and informal means designed to effect its control, and the multiplicity of approaches and interpretations that criminologists have brought to bear on this study. Each volume introduces readers to different aspects of the complex bodies of knowledge that make up contemporary criminology. By emphasizing diversity – both in the nature of criminological knowledge and in its object of study – the series engages with stereotypical representations of the extent and causes of crime and of the rationales and practices of criminal justice. Above all, we maintain that the study of crime cannot be divorced from the study of how the social is ordered and reproduced. Definitions of crime, and the ways in which it is understood and responded to, are contingent on the interplay of social, political and economic circumstances.

The main aim of these second editions is to continue to chart and re-conceptualize the parameters of a contemporary criminological imagination. They provide an interdisciplinary overview of 'classic' and current scholarly work in crime, criminal justice and criminology by drawing on the approaches and modes of analysis found in such subjects as sociology, social policy, psychology, socio-legal studies, gender studies, social geography and political science. This again alerts us to the potentially disparate and diverse nature of our subject matter and to ongoing disputes about the 'proper' constitution of the discipline of criminology.

This volume, *The Problem of Crime*, is a critical and comprehensive examination of the complex and multi-faceted ways in which 'crime' is defined and theorized. The second volume, *Controlling Crime*, offers detailed consideration of the changing and expanding parameters of criminal justice. The third, *Criminological Perspectives: A Reader*, narrates and explores the interdisciplinary bodies of knowledge that are constitutive of criminology and is designed as an essential sourcebook for the other volumes. Each is distinctive, not only in its chosen subject matter, but also because, unlike a majority of edited collections, it is primarily intended as a resource to facilitate student understanding of the distinctiveness of criminology as an academic discipline and its relations with other social sciences.

To this end, this volume has been designed as a fully illustrated interactive teaching text. The chapters should be read sequentially, as each builds on those that have gone before, and each concludes with suggestions for further and more in-depth reading. The following features have also been built into the overall structure of the book:

- activities: these are exercises to encourage students to work through the text, in order to test their understanding and develop skills in critical thinking.

- review questions: these are designed to encourage the reader to pause and reflect back on what has just been studied.

- key concepts: concepts that are core to each chapter and central to the study of criminology are highlighted in the margins.

In addition, the majority of chapters include a number of readings – newspaper articles, or extracts from academic books and articles – which are integral to the discussion as it develops and are designed both to encourage self-reflection and to aid in the application of central criminological ideas and concepts to contemporary issues, debates and trends. While each volume in the series is self-contained, there are also a number of references back and forward to the other volumes, and for those readers who wish to use the books for an integrated exploration of issues in crime, criminal justice and criminology, the references to chapters in the other volumes are printed in bold type. The aim of all these features is to help readers to examine more readily the principal arguments not only of each chapter, but of each book and the series as a whole.

The production of this volume – and the series – has been made possible not simply through the work of its editors and chapter authors, but through the collective endeavours of an Open University Course Team. Each chapter has been substantially revised from the first edition whereby content and argument have been updated and teaching strategy modified and refined. In this respect, we are indebted to our consultants, tutor-testers and assessors who have given invaluable advice; a course manager who, against all the odds, has ensured that all our efforts have been co-ordinated and that deadlines have been met; course secretaries who have suffered more than most from being asked to do the impossible; and a supportive team of production editors, designers, graphic artists and media librarians who have made sure that the quality of the first editions has been maintained and enhanced. Gillian Stern and Miranda Nunhofer at Sage have been a constant source of support and encouragement. We thank them all.

John Muncie
(on behalf of The Open University Course Team)

Introduction:
reading 'the problem of crime'

John Muncie and Eugene McLaughlin

Of all the social and economic problems facing a range of contemporary western societies, crime has been cited as 'the most important problem', superceding national security, employment, cost of living, health and poverty. The vast majority still perceive crime to be rising and believe that much of this is violent crime. Despite the attempts of successive governments to 'act tough', public fear and anxiety is unabated. Surveys across a variety of societies indicate that people are afraid of criminal victimization, afraid of strangers and have well-honed notions of risk, danger and safety. Many have lost faith in the ability of the police to protect them and they believe that the criminal justice system prioritizes the rights of offenders over victims. It is one of the key tasks of criminology to address public understanding of the crime problem.

This book is not, however, just an exercise in getting the 'facts' of crime straight. Its starting-point is to recognize that the formal concept of 'crime' is an inherently unstable and shifting index of fear and insecurity. A clear-cut definition of crime is that it refers to behaviours that are a violation of the criminal law, but the law and the discourses surrounding it are continually under contestation and review. What is conceptualized as crime changes over time and circumstance and is rarely consistent across different societies. For example, in specific contexts, killing is murder, in others it is viewed as heroism. Until relatively recently, slavery, non-consensual sexual intercourse within marriage and all forms of execution received official approval. Equally, legal conceptions of crime offer only a partial representation of the misfortunes, dangers, harms, risks and injuries that are a routine part of everyday life. The risk of suffering those misfortunes defined as 'crime' is often negligible compared to the risks associated with workplace injury and avoidable disease. Similarly, we are more likely to suffer accidental injury than theft, yet only the latter is likely to engender insecurity. Hence, crime holds a pivotal position in assessments of personal safety.

Poverty, malnutrition, pollution, medical negligence, breaches of workplace health and safety laws, corporate corruption, state violence, genocide, human rights violations and so on all carry with them more widespread and damaging consequences than most of the behaviours and incidents that are currently constituted through official categories as crime. As a result, during the 1990s it became more common to find instances of social harm, which may or may not be legally proscribed, entering criminological agendas.

It has taken some twenty years of feminist enquiry to have it widely acknowledged that violence, danger and risk lie not just on the streets or in the corridors of power, but in the sanctity of the home. Recognizing male violence and opening up the vexed question of 'violent masculinities' has disrupted the narrow and myopic concerns of much of what traditionally has been understood to be the 'crime problem'. In other areas too we can witness a partial emergence of 'hidden or denied crime' onto a mainstream agenda. The racist murder of

Stephen Lawrence in South London in April 1993 and the unrelenting campaign by his family to expose police and judicial racism had, by the end of the 1990s, catapulted racial violence and hate crime to the forefront of issues to be addressed by law enforcement and community safety agencies. Questions of human rights denial have begun to enter the agenda, not simply through extending conceptions of 'what is crime?' but by recognizing the legal transgressions routinely employed by those wielding political and economic power and their ability to deny or conceal the harms they unleash under the protection of the law. State crime in the form of illegal arms dealings, war crimes and crimes against humanity has been consistent front-page news following successive wars in the Balkans and the establishment of the War Crimes Tribunal in the Hague. A long campaign against the transportation of live animals from Britain to Europe has drawn the issue of animal rights into a crime discourse, as has a recognition of the culpable negligence of tobacco and food companies in knowingly marketing unsafe and life-threatening substances. It has also become increasingly likely to find numerous aspects of social policy (housing policy and youth homelessness), environmental policy (road building and pollution) and global economic policy (third-world debt, the arms trade and corporate greed) being described within a crime discourse.

As a result, notions of 'incivility', 'disorder', 'malpractice', 'risk' and 'violation' are all beginning to move from the margins to the centre of criminal-justice policy formulation. In themselves, these 'new' emergent sites – emanating from all sides of the political spectrum – alert us to the ongoing struggle over what is, and what should be, the proper constitution of 'crime'. For example, for realist criminologies, the identification and control of 'incivility' is a clear priority whilst for critical criminologies the redefinition of corporate and state malpractice as crime foresees how such perpetrators might face the same (or enhanced) criminal justice consequences as those endured by 'ordinary criminals'.

It must also be noted that in the same moment that there have been campaigns for the state to intervene legislatively to apply the criminal sanction or to intensify the sanction across a variety of potential harms and risks; other campaigns have been mounted demanding that the state becomes less intrusive and allow citizens to reach their own solutions to problems. This is most notable in the campaigns for the legalization or decriminalization of victimless crimes. This double movement is played out in a variety of mass media settings, and it is this that has normalized 'crime talk' in everyday life.

This book not only recognizes these deepenings of the criminological agenda, but illustrates how the study of crime is in a process of continual reconstruction. As a result, we are less concerned with trying to unravel specific causes and more with examining the diverse and expanding 'sites' in which crime and harm are constructed, experienced and understood. From our insistence that the concept of 'crime' is not self-evident and should not be taken for granted, a number of key issues arise:

- Should we study crime as a form of behaviour or as a type of legal sanction?
- Is there any behaviour that is intrinsically criminal?
- Why and how are certain behaviours, at certain times, criminalized?
- What is the relationship between crime and the social?

■ Why is crime such a potent signifier?

■ What are the interpretative repertoires that construct and authorize dominant definitions of crime?

The title of this book has a double meaning. The 'problem of crime' is not only a matter of the harms, injuries and risks that crime inflicts, it is also a matter of the limited and limiting nature of any debate which talks about 'crime' as if its meaning is self-evident. All the chapters explore questions of how and why it is not simply crime (as behaviour) but also 'crime' (as a conceptual category) that make up the 'problem of crime'. The point can be illustrated simply enough by noting how 'crime' denotes pain and fear, but it is also pleasure, fascination, drama and even glamour. It is typically portrayed as pathological, but also appears to be one of the most characteristic and enduring features of social order. Consequently, 'crime' attracts multiple and contradictory meanings and emotional reactions. It is only by revealing how it comes to find expression at particular moments in particular sites that we can begin to move to a more informed analysis of exactly how the 'problem of crime' is framed and constituted.

The Problem of Crime interrogates seven discursive sites of crime. The opening chapter begins this process by asking the seemingly straightforward questions: What is crime? How extensive is crime? How serious is crime? When subjected to sustained analysis, none of these questions is capable of delivering unequivocal and incontestable answers. Much depends on how 'crime' is defined. If we restrict ourselves to a legal definition and rely on official statistical measures of recorded crime, a common-sense picture emerges of crime being closely correlated with a particular age (the young), a particular gender (male), and a particular social position (low socio-economic). However, if we define 'crime' as an ideological construction – the means by which only a small and specific selection of social harms are criminalized – then we are forced to confront the uncomfortable notion not only that crime is widespread, but that it is practised at all levels in the social formation. Expanding the concept of 'crime' in this way reveals that law-breaking is not the preserve of working-class young men, but is prevalent in some of our most cherished institutions – the nuclear family, the democratic state, the global economy. As John Muncie makes clear, 'crime' is a problem, not simply in its damaging consequences, but also in the way in which the 'problem of crime' is commonly understood and conceptualized. Above all, the constitution of crime is never self-evident; it remains a controversial and contested concept in its own right.

In trying to unravel the meaning of 'crime', there are dangers, too, in continually locating it within the discourse of a 'problem'. In Chapter 2, John Clarke explores how crime is not just something to be feared, but is also a major source of popular entertainment, amusement and diversion. By focusing on how crime and its detection are *represented* in different types of detective novel, the chapter underlines the point that our knowledge of crime is also significantly affected by particular sets of definitions, interpretations and images that circulate widely in the media and fictional entertainment. Moreover, detective novels are not simply stories of criminals, victims and 'whodunit', they also tell stories about the relationship between types of crime and types of social order – ranging from familial murders in English country houses to the rank corruption of the American underworld. The social orders imagined in the novel provide us with different ways of seeing crime and the social relationships in which it is enmeshed. Rather than crime being simply an object of repulsion, the study of fictional representations reveals how it can also be an object of fascination and seduction. This ambiguity is a telling reminder of the extent to which we are capable of finding pleasure in the morbid and gratification in the 'unthinkable'.

Chapter 3 details another important point of entry into the study of crime: namely, research into social history. History is important not simply as a consequence of our curiosity about the past, but because it reveals that crime is not a fixed and universal phenomenon. It changes through time. More significantly, as Jim Sharpe reveals, what a society defines as 'crime' depends on social, political and economic factors that are specific to particular societies at particular stages of their development. By focusing on how transformations in the definition and control of crime occurred in English society in the eighteenth and early nineteenth centuries, it becomes possible to extend our understanding of crime as something historically relative and context-bound. Above all, the chapter alerts us to the idea that the frames of reference through which we so readily understand and make sense of crime – such as notions of a criminal class and the juvenile delinquent – are relatively recent in origin and are the product of particular sets of economic, political and ideological relations. Moreover, studying the history of crime and punishment reminds us that our current ways of thinking about these problems are not the only ways that are understandable and defensible.

Chapter 4 focuses on the familiar site of the city as a place of crime and disorder. However, it is designed not simply to describe such elements, but to account for the emergence and perseverance of particular sets of images that have helped to cement the notion that the city is intrinsically a dangerous place. By tracing the tension between representations of progress and danger, from the mid nineteenth century through to visions of the twenty-first century city, Peggotty Graham and John Clarke note how ideas of crime have tended to circulate continually through such peculiarly urban images as the 'dangerous classes', the 'casual poor', the 'social residuum', the 'disorganized', the 'slum family', the 'underclass', the 'rioter' and so on. Woven throughout the chapter is the idea of struggle – struggle not simply about the causes of crime, but struggle about the city as an arrangement of space, and struggle over who has rights of access to its shifting configurations of public and private places. Questions of crime and criminalization are always at the centre of such disputes because every attempt to change the social and spatial organization of a city poses key questions for social order. What sort of social order is envisaged in urban reform, renewal and reconstruction? How are challenges to such order conflated with images of undesirability and criminality? Above all, Chapter 4 notes how the obsession with the city as a dangerous place forms an enduring element of the public debate about crime. However, the focus of such debate rarely stretches further than a concern for such problems as street crime and vandalism. As a result, the city–crime couplet typically produces a peculiarly one-dimensional view of the problem of crime.

The remaining three chapters of the book concentrate on various 'sites' of crime which have until recently been absent from political and public debate. Chapter 5 focuses on crimes of violence and abuse in the domestic sphere; Chapter 6 explores how corporate 'crime' has, in no small measure, been traditionally considered as a legitimate and respectable element of competitive market economies; and Chapter 7 examines the nature and extent of violence in society as expressed not only in political challenges to state authority, but also in the state's own monopoly on the use of legitimate force. Collectively, they develop a broader understanding of the problem of crime by revealing the significance of the 'presence of absences' – how everyday assumptions about crime are implicitly framed through a partial and narrow vision of crime's extent and meaning. These final chapters bring questions that have long remained on the margins of the crime debate into the centre of a criminological agenda.

In Chapter 5, Esther Saraga addresses the key questions of to what extent, and why, crime is characteristically defined as a public phenomenon. The implications of such a definition for understanding instances of violence and abuse in the home are discussed, in particular noting how the family occupies an ambiguous position in contemporary crime discourse. In contrast to the public world of the city, the family is often viewed as a private place of safety and protection. Yet, on the other hand, the family is also seen as fragile, at risk of breakdown and as the breeding ground for adult crime. In short, the family is typically viewed as both the cause and the cure of crime. However, both of these dominant public images fail to acknowledge how familial relationships themselves can also contribute to fear and danger, particularly for women, children and older people. Ongoing campaigns to bring instances of domestic violence and child abuse into the centre of public debate once more underline the extent to which the concept of 'crime' is inherently unstable and contestable.

Chapter 6 also moves beyond the sorts of offences that commonly engage the police and the courts to consider a range of property and personal offences committed by financiers and business people, by corporations and small firms and by employees, entrepreneurs and professionals. Whilst 'ordinary crime' appears easily recognizable, these offences often seem remote, complex or obscure and, as a result, have tended to attract a somewhat more ambivalent response from law-enforcement agencies and academic analysts. By focusing on the parallels between legitimate and illegitimate dealings within a competitive and free-market economy, Gordon Hughes and Mary Langan reveal not only the extent of corporate crime and its links to organized crime, but also limitations of the law, means of detection and punishment in bringing the economically powerful to 'justice'.

Chapter 7 continues to address questions of power and crime, but focuses on issues of political violence, terrorism and crimes of the state. Eugene McLaughlin confronts the many issues of why, when and how certain political movements and nations states come to be defined as 'terrorist', whilst others seem able to wield a monopoly of violence with impunity. Again, such questions force us to move beyond traditional criminological agendas and into a world occupied by human rights violations, war crimes, torture and genocide. Such 'political' crimes clearly have potentially more damaging social consequences than those behaviours that are commonly considered to be 'criminal', yet rarely (if ever) do they enter public debate as part of the 'problem of crime'.

By focusing on issues of how the 'problem of crime' is constructed in public, political and academic discourses, and by revealing the significant absences in those discourses, all the chapters in this book are designed to illustrate how the concept of 'crime' is not as self-evident as we might be led to believe. This is why we advocate a problematic of crime that does not necessarily depend on pre-existing over-determined categorizations. Our proposed problematic requires a constant re-assessment of the contradictory and shifting ways in which 'crime' is constituted within and constitutive of 'the social' at any given moment.

CHAPTER I

The Construction and Deconstruction of Crime

by John Muncie

Contents

1   Introduction

Crime appears to be a constant source of social concern. Escalating levels of insecurity, fear of violence, the threat of public disorder, rioting, household burglary, children out of control, new forms of terrorism, football hooligans, 'mindless vandals' and a growth in all manner of anti-social behaviours are but a few of the enduring images that characterize a society that apparently is drifting further and further into lawlessness. Even if we have no direct experience of crime as offender, victim or criminal justice practitioner, we are continually reminded of its extent and seriousness. 'Law and order' has come to occupy a central position on the agendas of all major political parties in the UK. In political rhetoric, crime is a key signifier of family, community and national decline: a manifestation of some deeper social, cultural and moral malaise. The topic of crime also remains a defining characteristic of what is considered 'news' and newsworthy. All sections of the media rely on crime to fill their news bulletins, documentaries and column inches. Crime is a constant source of fascination. Police, detective and crime stories are part of the staple diet of film making and television programming and are a recurring element of everyday conversation. Indeed, in many ways, law enforcement and criminality lie at the very heart of popular culture. It is perhaps unsurprising, then, that crime, law and order have been consistently ranked high in public opinion polls listing the most crucial matters of concern 'facing Britain today'.

But how far are such concerns and preoccupations warranted? Is society on the verge of imminent collapse? Are we becoming less and less law-abiding? Such questions are usually translated into the perennial obsession with the two interrelated issues of what causes crime and what can be done about it. In the popular imagination, the topic of crime appears as unfathomable as the weather; everyone has an opinion but no-one seems to be able to do much about it. For example, low IQ, illegitimacy, lone parenting, television, unemployment, poverty, affluence, lenient courts, drugs, homelessness, recession, and so on, have all been cited as causes of crime; at the same time, hanging, birching, flogging, segregation, imprisonment, more policing (public, private and self), community service, rehabilitative treatments, shock incarceration, better parenting, improved social amenities, full employment, community-safety initiatives and so on, have all been cited as its remedy. These lists of contradictory claims immediately alert us to some of the complexities and contestations that are intrinsic to the study of crime. However, the obsession with causes and solutions offers a peculiarly partial and short-sighted way of entering into the debate. It assumes that we all know what crime is. Moreover, such 'incessant chatter' is fuelled by a taken-for-granted knowledge that crime is not only a major social problem, but also that it is one of continually growing proportions.

This chapter presents a number of ways in which the 'problem of crime' can be subjected to social scientific inquiry. In particular, it asks:

- What is crime? Which forms of behaviour are (or can be) considered criminal and which not?

- How extensive is crime? How can it be measured? How reliable are statistical indices?

- How serious is crime? From where do notions of seriousness emanate? Are our fears of crime warranted? Is crime a significant feature of living in a 'risk' society?

To ask such questions demands that we distance ourselves critically from a subject matter that retains the power to evoke highly charged and emotional responses. It requires that we subject the concept of crime to a series of deconstructions. This process can be summarized as:

deconstruction

- Breaking down the concept of 'the problem of crime' into its various constituent elements.
- Revealing the internal contradictions and inconsistencies between those elements.
- Undoing 'common-sense' assumptions and, through critical analysis, resituating their place within hierarchies of explanations.
- Acknowledging the wide range of interpretations that can legitimately lay claim to the crime debate.
- Recognizing that the problem of crime defies theoretical resolution and is likely to remain a matter of continual dispute and contestation.

Finally, our intention is not to pursue such deconstruction to the extent that we are incapable of saying anything meaningful about the 'crime problem'; neither is the chapter designed to provide definitive and incontestable answers to the numerous questions raised. Rather, its aim is to *reconstruct* the parameters within which a more reasoned and informed assessment of 'the crime problem' can be gained.

2   Defining crime

What is crime? The *Oxford English Dictionary* states that crime is:

crime

An act punishable by law, as being forbidden by statute or injurious to the public welfare. … An evil or injurious act; an offence, a sin; *esp.* of a grave character.

At first sight, such a definition appears straightforward and uncontroversial: a crime is an illegal act. However, on closer examination things are not so simple. Dictionary definitions neatly avoid complex issues of interpretation by conflating a number of competing meanings. Does crime refer to particular acts and behaviours or to their legal sanction? Is it simply the existence of law that creates crime? What counts as 'injurious', 'sinful' or 'evil'? Who deems some acts to be sinful and evil and others not? Are moral and legal codes inseparable? Are they reflective of any widely held consensus of opinion of the constitution of unlawful activity? Similarly, we could ask what is meant by a 'grave' offence. Grave to whom? Are all crimes grave? Finally, is what counts as crime universal and unchanging, or do societies at different historical moments require different kinds of law, which in turn create new categories of crime?

In short, dictionary definitions pose questions rather than provide answers. To appreciate fully the complexities of the question, 'what is crime?', we need to broaden our enquiry to include some understanding of criminal law, social mores and social order.

2.1   Crime as criminal law violation

The most common and frequently applied definition of crime is that which links it to substantive criminal law. In other words, an act is only a crime when it violates the prevailing legal code of the jurisdiction in which it occurs. Michael and Adler are thus able to argue that the most precise and least ambiguous definition of crime is 'behaviour which is prohibited by the criminal code' (Michael and Adler, 1933, p.5) **[DEFINITION 1]**. Similarly, Williams re-emphasizes the legal foundation of crime by arguing that 'it is essential that one never forgets that no matter how immoral, reprehensible, damaging or dangerous an act is, it is not a crime unless it is made such by the authorities of the State – the legislature and, at least through interpretation, the judges' (Williams, 1994, p.11).

This logic was taken to its extreme by Tappan's argument that: 'Only those are criminals who have been adjudicated as such by the courts. Crime is an intentional act in violation of the criminal law (statutory and case law), committed without defence or excuse and penalized by the state as a felony or misdemeanor' (Tappan, 1947, p.100) **[DEFINITION 2]**. This black letter law approach – that the application of a legal sanction through court processes and practices must be pursued before a crime can be formally established to have occurred – maintains that no act can be considered criminal before and unless a court has meted out some penalty.

black letter law

Again, this may appear clear-cut and uncontroversial, but two important consequences flow from such formulations. First, there would be no crime without criminal law. No behaviour can be considered criminal unless a formal sanction exists to prohibit it. Michael and Adler (1933, p.5) contend that: 'if crime is merely an instance of conduct which is proscribed by the criminal code, it follows that the criminal law is the formal cause of crime'. Second, there would be no crime until an offender is caught, tried, convicted and punished. No behaviour or individual can be considered criminal until formally decided upon by the criminal justice system.

By drawing these lines of argument together, Sutherland and Cressey proposed a definition of crime which (at least up to the 1960s) was adopted by most social scientists and legal scholars:

> Criminal behaviour is behaviour in violation of the criminal law ... it is not a crime unless it is prohibited by the criminal law. The criminal law, in turn, is defined conventionally as a body of specific rules regarding human conduct which have been promulgated by political authority, which apply uniformly to all members of the classes to which the rules refer and which are enforced by punishment administered by the state.
>
> (Sutherland and Cressey, 1924/1970, p.4) **[DEFINITION 3]**

In a similar vein, a number of conditions must be met before an act can be legally defined as a crime:

- The act must be legally prohibited at the time it is committed.
- The perpetrator must have criminal intent (*mens rea*).

- The perpetrator must have acted voluntarily (*actus rea*).
- There must be some legally prescribed punishment for committal of the act.

What this means is that we can only understand crime by identifying the distinctive procedural rules of evidence, burdens and standards of proof and particular forms of trial established within criminal law. It also assumes that people act with free will and should be made responsible for their actions. Yet the argument is circular: criminal law and court procedures claim to respond to crime, yet crime can only be defined by looking to the criminal law itself. Lacey *et al.* suggest that, in order to break out of this impasse and move towards a more adequate answer to the apparently straightforward question, 'what is crime?', 'we must enter upon some broader reflection about how our society comes to define "deviance"; how it comes to be decided which deviance calls for a *legal* response; and what determines that legal response as a criminal as opposed to, or as well as, a civil response' (Lacey *et al.*, 1990, pp.2–3).

Asking such questions moves us away from the traditional assumptions that criminal law constitutes some unitary and discrete category, divorced from questions of social interaction and social order. Rather, they lead inevitably to considerations of the political role of criminal law and to a different set of questions: 'about who has the *power* to define criminal deviance and about the ways in which the legal definition of certain behaviours as criminal operates as an "objective" depoliticized construction of those behaviours as deviant' (Lacey *et al.*, 1990, p.7).

In essence, formal legally based definitions tend to remove law (and thus crime) from the social, political and economic terrain. Moreover, because the social creation of criminal law is not subject to any critical scrutiny, it remains assumed (as we saw in Definition 3) that it is applied equally to all people, and thus reflects the common assent of the majority. In short, it is predicated upon the assumption that criminal law is an expression of widespread public sentiment, that it is a natural outcome of people's views in general, and that it simply reflects a basic consensus on matters of right and wrong held by most, if not all, members of society.

We can identify a number of other issues and consequences that flow from legally based definitions:

- An act can only be considered a 'crime' once it is identified as such by law – thus criminals can only be identified once processed and convicted by the courts. But not all of those who break criminal laws are caught and convicted and many acts that could be considered 'criminal' are rarely prosecuted. The study of criminal behaviour is thus severely hampered, and may be particularly one-dimensional if restricted only to those persons who are convicted of offences.

- The approach neglects the basic issues of *why* and *how* some acts are legislated as criminal, while others may remain subject only to informal control or rebuke.

Crime and law as contested categories: civil rights campaigners mark the enactment of the 1994 Criminal Justice and Public Order Act

- A black letter law approach tends to refer only to the formal constitution and enactment of law and underplays the different ways in which it is enforced. It divorces the criminal process from its social context, masking the ways in which the law is not simply applied by the courts, but is actively made and interpreted by key court personnel (for example, in plea bargaining, the quality of legal representation, and judicial discretion). In turn, this may have important consequences for what kinds of behaviour should be regarded as truly criminal. Are theft and violence more serious than violations of health and safety codes in the work place? Both may be dealt with by the criminal law, but the tendency to view the former as 'real crime' and the latter as 'regulatory offences' may only lead us (unjustifiably?) to exclude these latter behaviours from our legitimate subject matter.

2.2 Crime as violation of moral codes

A black letter law definition of crime has its logic in expediency, since no behaviour can be considered illegal unless a specific statute exists to define it as such. However, some sociologists have argued that, because criminal laws change over time and between different societies, a more 'scientific' and reliable index is needed to separate out the 'criminal' from the 'non-criminal'. For example, Sellin (1938) argued that the concept of crime should be extended beyond legal violations to violations of *moral* and *social* codes. He contended that every society has its own standards of behaviour or 'conduct norms', but that not all these standards are necessarily reflected in law. In this context, terms such as 'deviance', 'non-conformity' and 'anti-social conduct' are preferred to that of 'crime', because the latter is incapable of encompassing all acts of wrong-doing. Accordingly, such diverse activities as income tax avoidance, environmental pollution, insider-trading and sexual promiscuity may be considered legitimate topics for criminological inquiry. Of key significance is that this 'normative' approach does not require any reference to the criminal law at all. As Sellin (1938, p.20) contended, if the study of crime is to attain an objective and scientific status, it should not allow itself to be restricted to the terms and boundaries of enquiry established by legislators. However, while Sellin argued that a universal definition of 'crime' depended on isolating conduct norms that are invariable across all cultural groups, he failed to specify what such universal conduct norms might be. Indeed, given the diversity of human behaviours, moralities and social organizations, it is highly unlikely that any such 'universals' can be found, either inside or outside of the law (Hagan, 1985, p.45).

A similar problem arises when we consider the concept of deviance. **deviance** Although clearly a social, rather than a legal, category, it too suffers from an extreme cultural relativism and is inextricably related to difficulties in establishing what is 'normal'. As Simmons (1969, p.3) found in public responses to the question, 'who's deviant?', the concept can be as readily applied to Christians, pacifists, divorcees, 'know-it-all' professors and the president of the United States as it can to criminals and law-breakers. The partiality of those elements of deviance that are legally proscribed also remain apparent. Sutherland's (1949) research into unethical practices among corporate managers in the USA found that, despite their serious and injurious nature, such practices were often considered non-criminal: as violations of civil, rather than criminal, law. As a result, he argued that crime should be defined not on the basis of criminal law, but on the more abstract notions of 'social injury' and 'social harm'. Thus:

> The essential characteristic of crime is that it is behaviour which is prohibited by the state as an *injury* to the state … The two abstract criteria … as necessary elements in a definition of crime are legal descriptions of an act as *socially harmful* and legal provision of a penalty for the act.
>
> (Sutherland, 1949, p.31, emphasis added) **[DEFINITION 4]**

Sutherland implied that some moral criteria of social injury must be applied before any comprehensive definition of crime can be formulated. However, whether morality has any more an objective status than law also remains disputed.

Subsequent moral 'readings' of crime have been most forcibly put by those on the right of the political spectrum but not confined to them. The American neo-conservative social policy analyst Charles Murray, for example, has maintained that increases in crime are directly the result of a breakdown in family relationships and a growth in illegitimacy (**Murray, 1990**). This is a theme also echoed in New Labour's reforming agenda of the late 1990s. By equating crime with *disorder, nuisance* and the *anti-social*, such an agenda has clear moral overtones. It focuses attention on the 'undesirable' as well as the legally defined 'criminal'. The Audit Commission (1999), for example, argued that legal definitions of crime only capture 'the tip of the iceberg' of the numerous factors that undermine public safety and security (see Figure 1.1).

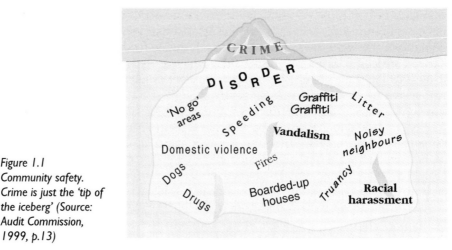

Figure 1.1
Community safety.
Crime is just the 'tip of
the iceberg' (Source:
Audit Commission,
1999, p.13)

ACTIVITY 1.1

Pause now and reflect on the implications that legal and moral definitions might hold for the identification of certain behaviours and acts as criminal. Is there any behaviour that is universally and invariably criminal? Is there any behaviour that is universally and invariably morally wrong?

Behaviours such as taking the life of another, sexual violence and stealing for personal gain may be considered to be particularly heinous and abhorrent. Each though has at sometime also been considered quite legitimate. Criminal laws are never static or permanent features of any society. Customary practices in England – for example, poaching game – only became criminalized through the convergence of new class and power interests in the eighteenth century. Similarly, causing the death of another may be particularly odious, but is almost always viewed as justifiable and sometimes as heroic when practised as a part of warfare and in 'defence of the nation'. In the USA, capital punishment was reinstated by the Supreme Court in 1976. Since then, there have been over 300 state-sponsored executions. The historical and socially relative nature of crime is reasonably easy to establish. The consumption of alcohol in the USA was deemed criminal in the days of prohibition between 1920 and 1932. Now it is considered a legal and respectable social activity. Domestic violence, far from being viewed legally as criminal (or even deviant), has been considered quite legitimate through much of western history. For example, it was not until 1991 that England was brought into line with France, Sweden, the former USSR, Norway, Denmark, Poland and most US and Australian states by the overturning of a 255-year-old ruling that had given husbands immunity from marital rape. What counts legally as crime also varies from one jurisdiction to another, even in similar historical periods. A clear example is that, while in England and Wales a person cannot be considered responsible for their actions before the age of 10, in Scotland such responsibility begins at the age of 8. In France the age of criminal responsibility is 13, in Germany 14 and in Spain 16. In these examples, crime appears not as a fixed object, the same for all societies for all times. Rather, it is a historically and socially specific concept.

As Wilkins (1964, p.46) warns: 'there are no absolute standards. At some time or another, some form of society or another has defined almost all forms of behaviour that we now call "criminal" as desirable for the functioning of that form of society'. The temporal and cultural relativity of 'crime' ensures that 'there is no one behavioural entity which we can call crime, there is no behaviour which is always and everywhere criminal' (Phillipson, 1971, p.5). Similarly, if there are no clear and unambiguous rules to decide which actions should be subject to moral and legal sanction, can it be argued that any consensus exists in society? Can the law or moral codes be relied upon to reveal any such consensus?

2.3 Crime as social construct

A vast array of behaviours have been (or can be) deemed 'deviant' or 'criminal' because they violate legal or normative prescriptions. But there is no common behavioural denominator that ties all of these acts together. Propositions, such as society is based upon a moral consensus or that the criminal law is merely a reflection of that consensus, also remain contentious. The interactionist school of sociology, for example, argues that there is no underlying or enduring consensus in society. Rather, the social order consists of a plurality of social groups each acting in accordance with its own interpretations of reality. Such diversity is as likely to produce conflict as much as consensus. Interpretations of reality are learnt through the ways in which people *perceive* and *react*, either positively or negatively, to the various behaviours of others (Mead, 1934). Thus, with respect to crime, an interactionist position would argue that defining crime with reference to legal or norm-violating actions is seriously limited. Rather, crime is viewed as a consequence of social interaction: that is, as a result of a *negotiated process* that involves the rule-violator, the police, the courts, lawyers and the law-makers who define a person's behaviour as criminal. Behaviour may be *labelled* criminal, but it is not this behaviour in itself that constitutes crime. Rather, behaviour is *criminalized* by a process of social perception and reaction as applied and interpreted by agents of the law. Crime exists only when the label and the law are successfully applied to an individual's behaviour. It is not what people do, but how they are perceived and evaluated by others, that constitutes crime. Whereas law-violation approaches argue that the existence of 'crime' depends on the prior existence of criminal law, interactionism logically contends that, without the *enforcement and enactment* of criminal law (or social reaction to certain behaviours), there would be no crime. As Ditton put it: 'the reaction is constitutive of the criminal (or deviant) act. In fact the reaction *is* the "commission of the act"' (Ditton, 1979, p.20). Just as criminal law is constructed within society, then crime too is a social construction (Hester and Eglin, 1992). **social construction** In this sense, society creates crime because it (or at least those in positions of authority) makes the rules, the infraction of which constitutes crime. As Becker explains, the social construct argument is not so much concerned with locating the causes of crime and deviance in social factors or social situations, but in establishing that:

Social groups create deviance by making the rules whose infraction constitutes deviance, and by applying those rules to particular people and labelling them as outsiders. From this point of view deviance is not a quality of the act a person commits, but rather a consequence of the application by others of rules and sanctions to an 'offender'. The deviant is one to whom that label has been successfully applied; deviant behaviour is behaviour that people so label.

(Becker, 1963, p.9) [DEFINITION 5]

Thus 'crime' has no universal or objective existence, but is relative to the subjective contingencies of social and historical circumstance. This in turn opens up and expands the range of criminological inquiry away from behavioural questions – Why did they do it? –towards *definitional* issues – Why is that rule there? Who created it? In whose interests? How is it enforced? What are the consequences of this enforcement? (Cohen, 1973a, p.623). It implies that we will only come to understand why an action is regarded as criminal by examining both the processes of rule creation and law enforcement. We will not discover 'crime' simply by looking at behaviours, for there is nothing intrinsic to any behaviour that makes it criminal (Phillipson, 1971). We will not discover 'crime' simply by looking at violations of legal statutes. These constitute only one element of rule-breaking, and in themselves are the subjects of social perceptions and interpretations. Similarly, asking the perennial question, 'what makes some people commit crime?', is short-sighted because there cannot be specific kinds of motivation to engage in crime if there are no categories of activities that are inherently criminal (Sharrock, 1984, p.99). In this way, the interactionist approach refutes the notion that criminality is driven by some peculiar motivation or that criminals are a species apart. Rather, it contends that criminality is *ordinary*, *natural* and *widespread* and as a result requires no more explanation than that which might be attached to any 'ordinary' activity. However, what does require explanation is the complex process by which agencies of social control are able to construct a public identification of *certain* people as criminal, and how social reaction and labelling are able to produce and reproduce a recognizable criminal population. A corollary of this, of course, is that the more such labels are applied and enforced, then the greater the chance that more 'crime' will be discovered. In these ways, a social constructionist position continually alerts us to the 'constantly problematic, changing and contested nature of crime and social problems' (Young, 1999, p.40).

2.4 Crime as ideological censure

Conflict-based analyses of the social order have expanded on the basic premise of interactionism – that crime only exists through the labelling of certain behaviours as such – by arguing that it is essential to ground such generalities in specific relations of power and domination. It is not a simple question of interest groups acting in competition with each other (as the interactionists would argue), but of the systematic and consistent empowerment of some groups to the detriment of others. Some Marxist conceptions would, for example, emphasize class divisions in which those who own and control the means of production are in a position to assert their economic and political power by using the law to protect their own interests. Some feminist conceptions would, in contrast, emphasize gender divisions and the discriminatory implications of a patriarchal monopoly of political, economic and legal power. Each stresses the political nature of crime. The law supplies to some people both the authority *and* the means to criminalize the behaviour of others.

<aside>political nature of crime</aside>

Crime can also be viewed as political in the sense that it involves and requires the deployment of *power* to translate legal rules into action, to impose one's will on others and to enforce one's definition of another's behaviour as illegal. The Schwendingers' (1970) argument that current practices of law creation and enforcement are selective and partial is endorsed by Cohen's insistence that 'damage, victimisation, exploitation, theft and destruction when carried out by the powerful are not only not punished, but are not called "crime"' (Cohen, 1973a, p.624). In this way, a conflict-based conception of crime questions the agreed assumptions of legal, behavioural and state definitions because these latter act to confine the criminologist to the established order and to official versions of reality. Characteristically, the concept of 'crime' is viewed not as value free, but as a highly politicized state-constructed category. It has no 'objective' reality other than in the ways in which the state construes 'criminality' for its own ends. Rather, if the signifier of 'crime' is to be retained, it should be equally applied not only to 'ordinary crime' or behaviours that are not typically prosecuted (such as tax avoidance, environmental pollution and government corruption), but also to crimes of the state and mass political killings (such as the Holocaust, the genocide of the East Timorese and the 'ethnic cleansing' in Bosnia and Kosova). Such an approach opens up long-neglected topics for criminological investigation (**Cohen, 1993**). By doing so, the *ideological* nature of what constitutes 'crime' is revealed. For example, until the 1990s, the activities of the African National Congress (ANC) in South Africa or the Palestine Liberation Organization (PLO) in the Middle East were defined as criminal by many Western jurisdictions. Yet without such 'criminality' it is unlikely that the repressive (and equally 'criminal'?) policies of apartheid and armed occupation would have come to be acknowledged internationally. In both cases, this broad criminological agenda would point out how the opposing terms 'terrorist' and 'freedom-fighter' illustrate how notions of 'crime' can also be politically informed and tied to particular political ideologies (this is explored in more depth in Chapter 7).

In developing a Marxist theory of crime and criminal law, **Chambliss (1975, p.152**) argues that acts are defined as criminal only when it is in the interest of the ruling class to define them so. Crime is a reality which exists only as it is created by those in society whose interests are served by its presence. In capitalist societies, 'crime' performs the vital function of diverting the lower classes' attention away from the conditions and source of their exploitation, and enables the bourgeoisie to expand penal law in their efforts to coerce the proletariat into submission. Behaviours are criminalized in order to maintain political control and to counter any perceived threat to the legitimacy of the ruling class (the clearest examples of such a process being the creation of public order offences to curtail political demonstration and trade union legislation to prevent 'wildcat' strikes):

Criminality is simply *not* something that people have or don't have; crime is not something some people do and others don't. Crime is a matter of who can pin the label on whom, and underlying this socio-political process is the structure of social relations determined by the political economy.

(Chambliss, 1975, p.165) [DEFINITION 6]

social censure

Sumner (1990) presents a development of this line of argument which continues to recognize how criminal law (and thus crime) can be a crucial instrument of class power, but also argues that it cannot be simply reduced to class relations and class conflict. He prefers to treat crime and deviance as matters of moral and political judgement – as social censures rooted in particular ideologies. The concept of crime, then, is neither a behavioural nor a legal category, but an expression of particular cultural and political conditions. Neither is 'crime' simply a label, but a generic term to describe a series of 'negative ideological categories with specific historical applications … categories of denunciation or abuse lodged within very complex, historically loaded practical conflicts and moral debates … these negative categories of moral ideology are social censures' (Sumner, 1990, pp.26, 28) **[DEFINITION 7]**.

2.5   Crime as historical invention

Troublesome behaviours have been called 'crimes' (whether or not recognized in law) for so long that the term is habitually used to condemn 'unwanted' or 'undesirable' acts or people. If 'crime' is intrinsically tied to 'criminal law', as various definitions assume, then we only discover the origins of crime in the development of criminal law in the eighteenth century. Up till then, the newly emergent nation states in Europe lacked the resources to invest in the wholesale formulation and enforcement of state law. At the time, many behaviours that are today deemed criminal were governed by civil law and religion. In other words, there was less 'crime' and more 'sin', 'civil wrongs' and 'private disputes'. The terms in which crime might be construed as a problem had not yet been formed (Chapter 3 explores this in more detail).

However, this is not to say that there was no such thing as criminal law. Rather, it was in a slow process of development until its acceleration in the eighteenth century, as particular groups sought to protect their own interests and property. As Hall (1952, p.34) notes, it was not until then that such crimes as receiving stolen property, obtaining goods by false pretences and embezzlement were first legally recognized. He cites the example of the bank teller, who on receiving a £100 deposit at his place of work in 1799, credited it to the customer's account, but then pocketed it. Fortunately for the dishonest teller, he could not be found guilty of any crime: he had not stolen from the bank (they had never *possessed* the money); nor had he stolen from the unlucky customer (who had handed over the sum freely). As a result of this case, the British parliament passed the first embezzlement statute in British law.

Many explanations of the origins of criminal law have pointed to the symbiotic relationship that existed between economic power and the forging of new legislation tailored to protect the unique interests of dominant groups. Chambliss (1964) demonstrates how vagrancy laws find their origins in economic circumstance and class power: originating in 1349, these laws made it a crime to give alms to unemployed people. The law was passed following a chronic labour shortage experienced by landowners as a consequence of the Black Death of 1348. The traditional custom of migratory and free labour was criminalized in order to ensure an abundant supply of local, cheap labour. Agricultural labourers could no longer move from county to county to seek higher wages. Once the labour market was full, the laws fell into disuse, but were revived in 1530 to protect the interests of the new mercantile class. The emphasis shifted to controlling the movement of 'rogues' and 'vagabonds' in order to reduce the risk of robberies of commercial goods while in transit. By 1743, a person could be liable for prosecution if unable to give a 'good account of themselves'. The legislation was designed to serve the interests of powerful interest groups who needed a stable and static workforce to fill the fields and the emergent factories.

Hall's (1952) study of the 1473 Theft Act again highlights the role of economic power in the criminalization of customary or common-law practices. Prior to the Act, the notion of trespass was an integral element of the charge of theft. A consequence of this was that persons hired to transport goods who subsequently absconded with the goods could not be charged with a crime. The protection of property by trust seemed to have been satisfactory during the Middle Ages when the economy was dominated by feudalism and commercial exchange through barter. With the development of merchant-trading companies in the fifteenth century and the break-up of feudal estates by a mercantile and commercial complex, the emerging institutions required a new rule. The self-interest of an economically empowered minority was thus able to dictate the rewriting of theft law.

criminalization

Galliher's (1989, p.151) examination of the history of American colonies also supports the contention that powerful groups create law to protect their own interests. He notes how, originally, the concept of crime was closely linked to the Puritan concept of sin: court records up to the 1800s reveal that the term 'crime', if used at all, referred to personal depravity. The records also show that most prosecutions were for 'fornication', 'violation of the Sabbath' and 'adultery'. Offenders could be found in all social classes. However, by the nineteenth century, the concern had shifted from worries about the preservation of *morality* to the protection of *property*, which necessitated the formulation of precise criminal laws. New forms of private land ownership, economic depression and unemployment accelerated the rate of convictions for property offences. It is perhaps unsurprising that criminal records began to show that offenders were clustered amongst the urban poor (as records do today). The function of law in these instances appears to have been the protection of the interests of property owners and the criminalization of non-owners. Criminal law is dictated by particular economic and political interests.

From such analyses, 'crime' has been defined as 'human conduct that is created by authorised agents in a politically organised society' and used to describe 'behaviours that conflict with the interests of the segments of the society that have the power to shape public policy' (Quinney, 1970, pp.15–16) **[DEFINITION 8]**. This definition suggests that the identification and delineation of 'crime' is an inherently political process. The law (and thus crime) is created and applied by those who have the power to translate their private interests into public policy. Criminal law is coercive and partial, its political neutrality a myth. Developing this line of argument, De Haan claims that 'crime' is an ideological concept which 'serves to maintain political power relations; justifies inequality and serves to distract public attention from more serious problems and injustices' (**De Haan, 1991, p.207**) **[DEFINITION 9]**. In a similar vein, the historian, E.P. Thompson (1975, p.194), has asserted that 'crime' is a disabling and moralistic category. To restrict the analysis of crime to those definitions constructed by property owners and the state can only hinder accurate historical research and produce pre-given moral interpretations.

2.6   Crime as social harm

In section 2.2 we noted that Sutherland's (1949) pathbreaking study of corporate malpractices led to a recognition among criminologists of the need to move beyond legally defined conceptions of crime if the existence of other more damaging forms of 'injury' or 'social harm' are to be recognized and incorporated into the criminological agenda. By the 1970s, the critical criminologists, the Schwendingers, for example, expanded the list of potentially injurious practices to include the systematic violation of basic human rights. Working within a theoretical tradition which maintains that capitalist and imperialist social orders (and their state practices) contain their own criminogenic tendencies, they promoted a definition of crime based on a conception of the denial of basic fundamental human rights:

> The abrogation of these rights certainly limits the individual's chance to fulfil himself in many spheres of life. It can be stated that individuals who deny these rights to others are criminal. Likewise social relationships and social systems which regularly cause the abrogation of these rights are also criminal. If the terms imperialism, racism, sexism and poverty are abbreviated signs for theories of social relationships or social systems which cause the systematic abrogation of basic rights, then imperialism, racism, sexism and poverty can be called crimes.
>
> (Schwendinger and Schwendinger, 1970, p.148) **[DEFINITION 10]**

And in the 1990s, a whole range of 'injurious practices' or 'non-crimes' such as the failure to enforce health and safety standards at work, the deliberate marketing of known faulty products, the 'culpable negligence' of tobacco and food companies knowingly promoting unsafe and life-threatening substances, the international dumping of toxic waste, the abuse involved in the transportation of live animals, the extent of violence in the home or the systematic flaunting of export controls to certain countries by arms manufacturers not only came to enter public idiom as 'crime', but also began to be taken seriously by academic criminologists. What all such cases reveal is that a legal concept of 'crime' is not only partial but that many of the most harmful acts are actually supported by the law (Tifft, 1994/5). They also suggest that victimization is far more prevalent and widespread than official definitions would have us believe.

social harm   To tackle such partiality, some authors have begun to place 'crime' within a broader context of social harm in which the visible and the obscured, the legally recognized and the legally sanctioned can be included in a comprehensive, continuous and integrated vision of criminal and harmful acts (see Figure 1.2). Henry and Milovanovic (1996, p.116), for example, work within a broad conception of 'crime' as the 'power to deny others': 'crime is the expression of some agency's energy to make a difference on others and it is the exclusion of those others who in the instant are rendered powerless to maintain and express their humanity' **[DEFINITION 11]**. For others, given the vast diversity of behaviours or acts that

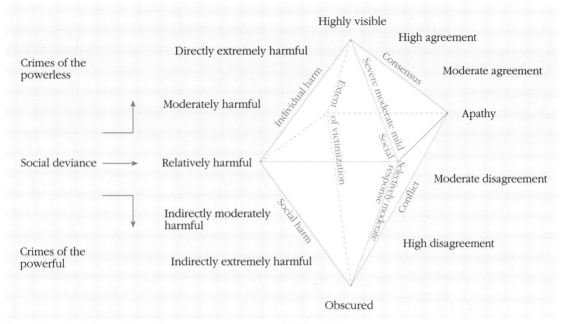

Figure 1.2 The Prism of Crime (Source: Henry and Lanier, 1998, p.622)

have been (or can be) considered 'criminal', there remains no sense in retaining the concept of 'crime' at all. **Hulsman (1986, p.71)**, for example, has argued that 'crime has no ontological reality. Crime is not the *object* but the *product* of criminal policy.' He prefers to work with the less emotionally charged concepts of 'trouble', 'problematic situation' and 'undesirable occurrence'. In a similar vein, **De Haan (1991, p.208)** contends that 'what we need is not a better theory of crime, but a more powerful critique of crime.' Again, this requires an alternative series of conceptualizations: 'unfortunate events'; 'more or less serious troubles'; 'conflicts which can result in suffering, harm or damage'. The key point is that 'crime' can never be defined in any consistent or conclusive manner. 'What is crime?' will always remain 'essentially contested'.

In harm-based definitions, the concept of 'crime' remains important only in so far as it alerts us to relations of power embedded in social orders that generate a whole series of social problems for their populations, but of which only a selected few are considered worthy of criminal sanction. A conception of crime without a conception of power is meaningless. The power to render certain harmful acts visible and define them as 'crime', while maintaining the invisibility of others (or defining them as beyond criminal sanction) lies at the heart of the problem of working within notions of 'the problem of crime'. Far from protecting members of society, the criminal law often seems to immunize those with power and influence and, in the process, protects those who generate the most serious social harms from legal sanction (Tifft, 1994/5, p.10). Legal notions of 'crime' do seem to provide a peculiarly blinkered vision of the range of misfortunes, dangers, harms, risks and injuries that are a routine part of everyday life. If the criminological intent is to reveal such misfortunes, risks and harms, then the concept of 'crime' has to be rejected as its sole justification and object of inquiry: in this sense criminology needs to be thoroughly decriminalized (Muncie, 2000). Any number of damaging events are far more serious than those that make up the 'crime problem'. Moreover, many of those incidents (such as petty theft, shoplifting, recreational drug-use, vandalism, brawls, anti-social behaviour) that are commonly accepted as criminal would not seem to score particularly high on a scale of serious harm. And yet it is often these 'minor' events that take up much of the time and preoccupation of law-enforcement agencies and the criminal justice system. Conversely, the risk of suffering many of those crimes defined by the state as 'serious', such as murder and armed robbery, would seem negligible compared to such everyday risks as workplace injury and avoidable disease. Similarly, the risk of homicide is far less than that of terminal disease or of being struck by lightning and we are more likely to suffer accidental injury than theft. So why are we generally more fearful of crime than other equally or more pertinent threats to our personal safety?

ACTIVITY 1.2

The preceding text has outlined 11 definitions of 'crime'. Some of these share the same assumptions about the inseparability of crime and law; others place more emphasis on social categories such as deviance; others move beyond behavioural issues to focus almost entirely on questions of meaning. Look back over the definitions in section 2, and any notes you have made on them, and consider the following questions in relation to each definition:

- Does the definition assume a particular model of society? If it does, is that society deemed consensual, pluralist or conflictual?
- Can 'crime' be explained through value-free means and measures? Or is it always relative to social and historical circumstances?
- What is the relationship between what can be considered 'crime' and criminal law?
- What is the relationship between criminal law and social order?
- What are the advantages and limitations of viewing 'crime' as (a) a legal concept; (b) a behavioural concept; (c) a socio-politically constructed concept or (d) a social harm?

Definitions of crime are neither objectively right nor wrong: they do, however, point out the elusive and the contested nature of our subject matter. The strength of explanations based on criminal-law prescriptions is that they provide an objective criteria by which 'crime' can be reliably identified: 'crime' is whatever the law deems to be illegal at particular times and in particular jurisdictions. Such a definition does, nevertheless, bind us to state-generated notions of law-breaking. It narrows our attention to formulations enshrined in legal statutes, and, while it may assume a greater objectivity, it overlooks the fact that 'the law' itself is deeply problematic, as a site of struggle, dispute, construction and contestation. In addition, a legal-based definition systematically excludes notions of harm, deviance, anti-social conduct, injustices and rule-breaking. We lose sight of how and why it is only *certain* behaviours that come to be considered deviant and how and why it is only *some* harmful practices that are ultimately subject to criminal sanction. In short, we lose sight of 'crime' as a forever shifting concept, as a morally and politically loaded term, or as something constructed through social processes and social censures.

Importantly, the various conceptions of crime appear to be generated from competing accounts of the social order. If that order is considered consensual (as we discussed in sections 2.1 and 2.2), 'crime' can be defined as the infraction of

social order

legal, moral or conduct norms. When the social order is considered pluralist or conflict based (as we showed in sections 2.3 and 2.4), 'crime' refers not to particular behaviours, but to the social and political processes whereby those actions are subjected to criminalization. Accordingly, it can be argued that any definition of crime rests on prior assumptions about the nature of social order and how that order is conceived and maintained. Indeed, this has led some to argue that crime only comes to be a problem when order is a problem. Our key problematic then may not be 'crime', but the 'struggle around order and the products it produces among which are crime and criminal justice' (Shearing, 1989, p.178).

3   Counting crime

The most widely used and commonly accepted measures of the extent of crime are the series of statistical data recorded by the police, courts and prisons. Most countries collect annual data, which are basically a count of the volume of *particular categories* of crime as recorded by the police. In the US, data is submitted by local police departments to the FBI and published as *Uniform Crime Reports*. In the UK, similar statistics are produced by the Home Office (*Criminal Statistics England and Wales* and the biannual *Statistical Bulletins*), the Scottish Office (*Recorded Crime in Scotland*) and the Northern Ireland Office (*Commentary of Northern Ireland Crime Statistics*). Each includes data on offences (from which trends in crime over time are charted) and on offenders who have eventually been found guilty or cautioned (from which details of the sex and age of offenders are derived).

The first national crime statistics were produced in France in the early nineteenth century (see **Quetelet, 1842**). In England and Wales, crimes recorded by the police have been published since 1876 and in the US since 1930. Both of these latter countries have witnessed a dramatic rise in the crime rate since the mid-1950s with the only sustained fall occurring in the mid- to late 1990s. A similar long-term upward trend has been a feature of most western democracies, with the notable exception of Switzerland (Maguire, 1997, p.159). In England and Wales, for example, the total number of notifiable offences increased from half a million in 1955 to nearing five and a half million in 1992 (see Figure 1.3).

UK Began collecting stats

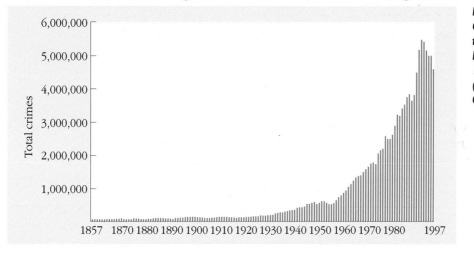

Figure 1.3
Crimes recorded by the police in England and Wales, 1857–1997 (Source: Home Office, 1999, p.2)

Breaking down this overall rate into *offence groups* reveals that the 'crime problem' is predominantly one of crimes against property (theft, burglary, criminal damage) and above all theft of, or from, vehicles. Crimes of violence appear small in comparison (Figure 1.4 gives the breakdown of offences in England and Wales for 1997). The data on *offenders* highlights that their numbers are dramatically lower than the total number of offences recorded. For example, in 1998, approximately half a million people were either cautioned or sentenced in England and Wales; the total crime recorded, however, was over five million offences. While some of this disparity may be attributable to people committing more than one offence, in the majority of cases nothing is officially known about those responsible (Maguire, 1997, p.173; Coleman and Moynihan 1997, p.43). The data on 'known offenders', however, produces a picture of the 'typical offender': in 1998, over 80 per cent of offenders were male and almost a half under the age of 21. Further data on social characteristics is not collected by the police or courts, but surveys of prison populations in England and Wales (e.g. Walmsley *et al.*, 1992; White, 1999) have found disproportionate numbers of prisoners from minority ethnic groups and from those who are unemployed or in unskilled and partly skilled occupations.

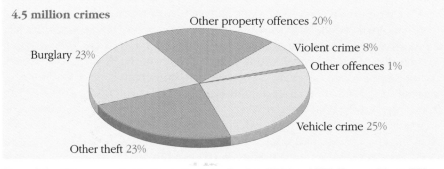

Figure 1.4 *Crimes recorded by the police in England and Wales, 1997 (Source: Home Office, 1999, p.4)*

This basic data is now regularly added to by nationwide victim surveys. In 1972, the US Bureau of the Census began collecting information about rates of victimization by asking random samples of the population to recall crimes committed against them in the past year. In 1982, Britain followed this lead with its own *British Crime Survey* (BCS). By the late 1990s, it had produced seven reports. Both in the USA and in Britain, it was consistently revealed that only about 50 per cent of crime is in fact reported to the police. This suggests that the official statistics may then only be the tip of an iceberg. In spite of this, such raw figures of the 'crime problem' are often used to make the following assumptions:

- Crime is soaring out of control. Moreover, it is a relatively recent (a post-1960) phenomenon.

- The present can be contrasted with a relatively trouble-free past (for example, the 1950s, 1930s, Victorian/Edwardian England).

- Crime is the preserve of young and working-class men among whom those from minority ethnic backgrounds also predominate.

- The 'crime problem' is overwhelmingly one of property crime (theft and burglary).

These assumptions, however, represent only one possible reading of the crime data. Quinney and Wildeman (1977, p.97) suggest that at least three interpretations can be drawn from the data. First, an *orthodox approach* to statistical measures would contend that the data reflect a growing wilful and conscious choice of individuals to violate the legal or moral consensus. Official statistics are thus more or less actual measures of the level of offending. The concentration of crime amongst minority ethnic groups and the lower classes reflects their weaker and more tenuous commitment to the social order. Second, an *interactionist approach*, on the other hand, would argue that, as not all the crimes occurring in a population are reported or recorded, then what is counted as crime merely reflects what, where and when the law-enforcement agencies decide to target. In this respect, crime rates are accurate measures, but only of the activities, priorities and labelling processes of official agencies. Third, a *structural conflict approach* would present a somewhat different argument: that official statistics do not measure crime as such, but reflect the ability of dominant groups to achieve their rule through the consent or coercion of the 'subordinate'. Escalating crime rates are thus an expression of a failure to achieve consensus, of increasing social division and inequality, and of an increased willingness on the part of the state to achieve its dominance through criminalization, coercion, oppression and persecution.

As we shall see below, the official criminal statistics do not provide any straightforward answers to the questions of: How much crime? How many criminals? How many victims? The 'true facts' of crime are probably unknowable. They depend not only on what we define as crime, but also on the *validity* of statistical measures, no matter how they are produced.

3.1 Criminal statistics as social and organizational products

Even if we adopt an orthodox position on statistics, the best that can be said of official crime statistics is that they do not measure the true extent of crime in society, but rather the extent of reported and recorded crime. Although most academic analysts, the media, politicians and the public rely on official statistics as 'hard facts', the first and most paramount 'fact' is that they are both partial and subjectively constructed. There are a number of reasons for this:

1   The official statistics do not include offences recorded by those police forces which are outside of Home Office responsibility, such as the British Transport Police, Ministry of Defence Police and UK Atomic Energy Authority Police. Since 1989 these agencies have collectively recorded about 80,000 offences per year (Maguire, 1997, p.149). Official statistics also provide an inaccurate picture because many crimes such as tax evasion (recorded by the Inland Revenue) and VAT evasion (recorded by Customs and Excise) will only appear in official criminal records if they are subsequently brought to court. As **Box (1983, p.13)** argues, such offences may be more personally and economically damaging than those that make up official depictions of crime, but they are generally rendered invisible as the number of eventual prosecutions is low.

reported crime

2 Crime statistics are based on those crimes reported to, and subsequently recorded by, the police. However, while the police detect some crime themselves, in the main they depend on the general public or victims to bring crime to their notice. Maguire (1997) notes that public reporting is the source of 80 per cent of all recorded crime. But some offences may not be reported because of ignorance that a crime has been committed (for example, tax evasion, computer fraud); there appears to be no victim (for example, certain drugs offences, prostitution, sexual offences between consenting adults, illegal abortion); the victim is powerless (for example, child abuse); ambivalence towards or distrust of the police (for example, certain youth cultures); the offence may be considered trivial (for example, thefts from work, vandalism, minor shoplifting, brawls); the victim may be concerned that the offence will not be taken seriously (for example, some cases of rape); or the victim has no faith that the police will act to protect his or her interests (for example, racial intimidation and harassment). Victim surveys, such as the BCS, have suggested that in fact only about a half of known crime is reported. Thefts of vehicles and burglaries with loss are generally reported; vandalism, theft from the person and attempted motor vehicle theft less so. The main reasons given for not reporting a crime to the police were that victims felt they were not serious enough or that the police would be unable to take any effective action. However, not all unreported crime is trivial. Some involves substantial loss or injury. Comparing BCS and police statistics in 1992, it was found that only 48 per cent of violent incidents and only 40 per cent of robbery and theft from the person were reported (Mayhew and Maung, 1992, p.6). Burglary with loss and auto theft, on the other hand, had an almost 100 per cent rate of reportage.

3 A wide range of personal and social factors is likely to affect both whether an incident is perceived as criminal and whether the observer then decides to report the incident to the police. Box concludes that: 'an offence was more likely to be reported to the police if the suspect apprehended by the complainant … was a member of the less privileged section of society; the closer the psychological and social identification of the complainant and the suspect, the less likely the former was to report the offence' (Box, 1981, p.176). Similarly, Stevens and Willis (1979) and Shah and Pease (1992) note that ethnic factors help to determine both the victim's decision to report a crime and the police decision to record it. In particular, they suggest that, in assaults when no injury is afflicted, the incident is more likely to be reported if it was committed by a non-white rather than a white suspect. Such discrepancies once more underline the proposition that measurements of crime rest initially and critically on the extent to which the public perceives and interprets behaviour as 'criminal' (Walker, 1983, p.292).

4 An 'increase in crime' may in fact be because more crime is *reported*, rather than because more crime is *committed*. The 1992 BCS, for instance, explains an increase in the reporting of certain offences (for example, car theft and burglary with loss) from 1981 to 1991 with reference to increases in telephone ownership and wider ownership of house-contents and car-insurance policies. Discrepancies between survey and police statistics can indeed alter

our perception of the 'crime problem' radically. In Bottomley and Pease's (1986, pp.22–3) attempt to account for a nationwide burglary prevention campaign mounted in 1982, they note that, while the number of *recorded* burglaries increased by 50 per cent between 1971 and 1981, data from General Household Surveys concluded that there was almost no change. They contend that one reason for this discrepancy may be the increased availability of 'new for old' insurance policies at this time, which increased the amounts claimed and also the incentive for fraudulent claiming. Since 1981, burglary, as reported by BCS respondents, has risen broadly in line with recorded crime figures, but similar recorded increases in violent crime and vandalism are not confirmed by the survey data. This may be because the police choose to record some offences as vandalism while the BCS classifies them as attempted burglary, or, where there is an option for classification – between, say, wounding and common assault – the police may choose the more serious.

5   Not all offences reported are recorded as offences by the police. The amount of resources available to the police and courts is limited and thus subjective and/or administrative decisions are made concerning which crimes to act against. It is only recorded crime which enters the official statistics. As Walker   **recorded crime** (1983, p.286) notes, although the police have a statutory obligation to record crimes, considerable discretion remains about whether an offence is considered sufficiently serious to warrant their attention. Violent disputes between neighbours or members of a family may, for example, be classified as 'domestic – advice given', with the result that the alleged 'offence' goes unrecorded. Similarly, how a recorded offence is classified by the police – as 'theft from a person' or 'robbery', as 'burglary, no loss' or 'vandalism', as 'wounding' or 'common assault', for instance – will affect the rate at which certain crimes appear to be committed. Problems inherent in recording, and variations due to local police 'targeting', will also colour our understanding of the extent of particular crimes. Williams (1994, p.49) cites a clear example of these effects: in 1932, London's commissioner of police ruled that cases classified as 'suspected stolen' should be redesignated as either 'lost property' or 'stolen'. The result was that recorded thefts increased by over 300 per cent in a year! Similarly, Lea and Young recall how an 108-fold increase in the figures for 'homosexual importuning' in Manchester between 1958 and 1963 had 'a great deal to do with the predilections of the Chief Constable and very little to do with the changing desires of gay men' (Lea and Young, 1984, pp.15–16).

6   Changes in law enforcement and in what the law counts as crime also preclude much meaningful discussion over the extent of historical increases and decreases in crime. Legislative changes may mean that existing categories are redefined, thus rendering any historical comparison meaningless. Pearson (1983, p.216), for example, notes how successive pieces of legislation governing the treatment of young people in the early twentieth century (for instance, the formation of specific juvenile courts by the 1908 Children Act and the incorporation of welfare-based principles in the 1933 Children and Young Persons Act) encouraged law-enforcement agencies

to proceed with a significant number of cases which previously might have been dealt with informally. Increasing the likelihood of bringing young people before the courts, however, also produces a sharp increase in committals, creating the impression of successive 'crime waves' and 'crime explosions'. More recently, the use of formal cautions in the 1970s, rather than unregistered cautioning, did not simply divert

> work away from the courts – as was its intention – but added substantially to the volume of recorded crime and recorded police activity. Among boys under 14 years of age, the increased use of the formal caution is enough to account for the whole of the increase in recorded crime for this age-group during the 1970s.
>
> (Pearson, 1983, p.217)

Similarly, Rohrer notes how some increases in crime can be artificially constructed solely by economic and administrative circumstance:

> Inflation provides a perfect example of one distortion of crime trends. The law is not index linked and so acts of criminal damage, officially defined as damage exceeding £20 in value, have shot up from 17,000 in 1969 to 124,000 in 1977. Inflation has shifted many thousands of previously trivial incidents of damage into the more serious crime bracket.
>
> (Rohrer, 1982, p.6)

Pearson elaborates further on this process by recording how, after 1977, the distinction between minor and major criminal damage was abandoned in favour of a classification of all as 'known crimes'. This resulted in an apparent doubling of vandalism in one year: 'adding at a single stroke a sixth of a million indictable offences to the criminal records … or four times the *total* number of criminal convictions in 1900' (Pearson, 1983, pp.217–18).

7   Changes in police practices, priorities and politics will also have a dramatic effect on such headline statistics as 'crimes recorded by the police'. What is remarkable about long-term historical trends in crime rates (see Figure 1.3) is their consistently low level during the nineteenth and early twentieth century followed by a consistent doubling in every decade (except the 1950s) until the 1990s. Did society suddenly become less law-abiding after the First World War? From his analysis of police inspectorate and committee reports of the time, Taylor (1998) argues that the increases in crime between 1914 and 1960 can be largely accounted for by senior police officers 'playing the crime card' in order to improve their establishment. By recording large numbers of minor property offences which were traditionally 'cuffed' (not recorded), chief constables were able to persuade their police authorities to increase funding. The crime rate is then more a reflection of police lobbying and politics than of criminal behaviour. This is a process that Taylor traces back to the police strike of 1918. Following the strike, wages were increased but this in turn led to pressure to cut police numbers. The provincial police forces fought back by raising their crime statistics in order to move crime and policing further up the political agenda. As a result, during the 1920s, crime rose by about 65 per cent throughout England and Wales except in London (where the Metropolitan police remained under direct Home Office control) where the rate remained static. In the same

way, Taylor casts doubt on the common wisdom that the fall in crime in the 1950s was the result of social stability and the consolidation of the welfare state. Rather, he notes how successive years of police agitation on pay and recruitment were eventually realized in increased pay awards in 1951, 1952 and 1954. Each of these years were followed by decreases in the crime rate. When further pay claims were not realized following the 1955 general election, the crime rate rose dramatically (and continued to do so until the 1990s when performance targets on crime reduction and clear-up rates were first introduced).

8   The implications of such an analysis are far reaching. As well as exposing the fallacy of historical comparison, it also undermines any definitive (though widely held) notion that 'things are getting progressively worse' and that 'if we could only recover the past our troubles would be over'. Indeed, in a series of backward glances through English social history, Pearson illustrates how images of a more peaceful and orderly past (against which the present can be unfavourably compared) fail to stand up to close scrutiny. Drawing on the popular idioms of '20 years ago' and 'in my day', he shows how, 20 years before the moral outrage surrounding the 1981 riots, similar fears centred on the lawlessness of the Teddy Boys; in the inter-war years the 'folk devils' were football rowdyism and the demoralizing influence of the American cinema. At the turn of the century the term 'hooligan' emerged as a media description of street gangs in south London, only later to be generically applied to similar gangs such as the Peaky Blinders in Birmingham, the Scuttlers in Manchester and the Redskins in Glasgow. Victorian England, meanwhile, was 'plagued' by the garrotters of the 1860s and the street urchins of the 1840s, as well as numerous instances of riot. All these phenomena attracted the (now familiar) official charges of historical decline, excessive leniency of the law and moral degeneracy, yet each illustrates how understandings of the present are coloured by an idealistic historical romanticism (see Extract 1.1)

9   The deeper we delve into the processes of criminal justice and the more we rely on prosecution, court and prison statistics, the more we reduce our chances of saying anything straightforward about the nature and extent of crime. Self-evidently, changes in the number of arrests, trials and sentences may not represent actual changes in the amount of crime, but rather changes in the *capacity* of the criminal justice system to process individual cases. Increases or decreases in the number of police, judges, courtrooms and prison places will inevitably affect these statistics: 'There is no doubt about it: more police, more judges and more prisons appear to have a nearly infinite capacity to increase the amount of officially recorded crime' (Galliher, 1989, p.119). This is partly because there is a constant unlimited well of unrecorded criminal and disorderly misbehaviour that can be tapped when and if the political will and the resources for law enforcement are sufficiently activated. It is also because a huge potential exists to perceive and redefine actions as 'crimes' as the technological ability to implement forms of mass surveillance increases.

Extract 1.1 Pearson: 'Painting by numbers'

Criminal statistics are notoriously unreliable as measures of the actual extent of criminal activity, to such a degree that it is not unknown for historians to discount them altogether [Tobias, 1972]. The reason for their notoriety is that they are complicated by a number of factors other than real changes in levels of crime. The growing size of the police force and its supporting apparatus is the most obvious and general factor. Changes in the routines of law enforcement, the increased mobility of the police, changes in what the law counts as crime, fluctuations in the vigour with which the law is applied, and shifts in public attitudes and tolerance – these must all be counted within the hidden dimensions of the manufacture of crime figures.

To take just one example of where a naive reading of official crime statistics will lead us, Chief Constable James Anderton in his 'Crime Top Growth Industry' speech of 1978 pointed to the apparently disturbing fact that 'crimes recorded in England and Wales in 1900 stood at 77,934;

by 1976 that figure had reached 2,135,713'. 'In the same period', he added for good measure, 'convictions rose from 45,259 to 415,471' [*The Guardian, The Daily Telegraph*, 26 April 1978]. It is all too obvious what conclusion Mr Anderton would like us to arrive at. But having spent a little time among the disorderly streets of the early 1900s – the home of the original Hooligans – what sense can we possibly make of these numbers? ...

What is usually known as the 'dark figure' of crime – illegalities that go unnoticed, or ignored, or unreported, or unrecorded – is such an imponderable that all statements about movements in the levels of crime (whether up or down) are largely a matter of guesswork. We neither know with any useful degree of certainty what proportion of the 'dark figure' is reflected in the crime statistics, nor how this proportion might fluctuate across time. The only certainty is that the crime statistics are but a pale shadow of the total volume of illegalities

'Garrotters' lying in wait in a London square, 1863

Football violence at Perry Barr, 1888

'Bloody Sunday', St Martin's Lane/ Trafalgar Square, London, 1887

imates of the size of the 'black economy', for example, ggest that it dwarfs conventional theft; and more nerally some informed guesses put the proportion of ne revealed by official sources as low as 15 per cent dzinowicz and King, 1977, p.49]. But there is no way reliably counting on the size of this 'dark figure' and nce no way of making sure-footed judgements about ether movements in recorded crime reflect actual erations in criminal activity; or shifts in public erance; or changes in policing; or some messy rmutation of any of these factors. Statements about ing crime (or about falling crime) can neither be garded as true nor false in this strict sense. Instead, must regard them as logically *undecidable*. That is, less we totally disregard these long-standing and ep-rooted controversies about the interpretation of me statistics and accept a naive view of them as aightforward reflections of criminal activities.

If we reject these myths of numerical certainty, as I we must, then the strictly regulated operations of rational thought can only supply us with a quicksand of indecision when we attempt to strike comparisons of the state of lawlessness in different historical times. The only guarantee is that the continually mounting crime figure cannot be used to lend some objective status to feelings of historical decline. Computer-assisted quantum-leaps in the crime rate, while they certainly reflect massive changes in the scope and organization of policing, tell us nothing much worth knowing about the historical realities of crime and violence.

References

Radzinowicz, L. and King, J. (1977) *The Growth of Crime*, Hamilton.

Tobias, J.J. (1972) *Crime and Industrial Society in the Nineteenth Century*, Penguin.

(Pearson, 1983, pp.213, 218–19)

As Christie argues, 'this new situation, with an unlimited reservoir of acts which can be defined as crimes, also creates unlimited possibilities for warfare against all sorts of unwanted acts' (Christie, 1993, p.22). As such, increases in police resources and staffing will almost inevitably lead to a statistical rise in crime, just as the expansion of prison-building programmes will create more prisoners, or the creation of new legislation will criminalize ever wider sections of the population (for example, the powers of the 1994 Criminal Justice Act which criminalized squatting, New Age Travellers, hunt saboteurs, 'rave' parties and 'mass trespass' or the 1998 Crime and Disorder Act which targeted 'anti-social' behaviour).

The least reliable statistics to depend upon in attempts to answer the questions, 'who is likely to be criminal?' and 'what offences are the most prevalent?' are statistics of known offenders: those collected by the courts and the prisons. These statistics can be revealing about trends in sentencing practices, but are meaningless in understanding trends in crime. The history of a crime, from the time it becomes known to the police through to it being taken seriously, recorded and proceeded with – arrest, prosecution, conviction and sentence – reflects a myriad of public perceptions, professional judgements, judicial discretions and sentencing policies (see *The Guardian*, 27 November 1993, reproduced below).

Such processes have been well documented in relation to race. In England and Wales, Afro-Caribbeans are significantly more likely than whites to be stopped by the police, even when factors such as age and employment are controlled; their arrest rate is higher, in court they are more likely to be remanded in custody before conviction, and average sentence length is higher despite fewer previous convictions (Hood, 1993; Fitzgerald, 1993; Hudson, 1989; Walker, 1987) (see the CRE poster reproduced below).

As Chambliss has remarked, this is the end result of the concentration of law enforcement on *particular* offences and within *particular* sections of the population:

> Persons are arrested, tried and sentenced who can offer the fewest rewards for nonenforcement of the laws and who can be processed without creating any undue strain for the organisations which comprise the legal system ... The lower class person is (i) more likely to be scrutinised and therefore to be observed in any violation of the law, (ii) more likely to be arrested if discovered under suspicious circumstances, (iii) more likely to spend the time between arrest and trial in jail, (iv) more likely to come to trial, (v) more likely to be found guilty, and (vi) if found guilty, more likely to receive harsh punishment than his middle or upper class counterpart.
>
> (Chambliss, 1969, p.84)

Levittating the laws

ITEM: According to Home Office research, 40 per cent of people found guilty of theft of under £200 are sent to prison by the Crown Courts.

ITEM: A pregnant mother was this week sentenced to five days imprisonment for failing to come up with a £55 penalty for not paying her television licence. She was only saved from jail when two solicitors had a whip-round to pay the fine.

ITEM: Yesterday Roger Levitt, founder of the Levitt Group, which crashed in 1990 owing £34 million and who ploughed nearly £900,000 belonging to Frederick Forsyth, the author, into his doomed business instead of buying bonds, walked free. Mr Levitt, who admitted lying to the City watchdog body to keep his debt-ridden company afloat, was ordered to serve 180 hours community service – though whether anyone would want this discredited fraudster anywhere near them, even on community service, remains to be seen.

There are, of course, as there always are on these occasions, excuses. Earlier this week Mr Levitt and his former managing director and right-hand man, Mark Reed, unexpectedly pleaded guilty to fraudulent trading. This undoubtedly saved a lot of public money in a trial which was expected to last at least four months. And, of course, the authorities weighed the chances of securing a conviction – never certain in complicated City cases tried before juries – against the public resources which would inevitably be devoured. Mr Justice Laws, a highly regarded judge, described Levitt's acts as 'thoroughly and markedly dishonest'. He said: 'Actions of this kind must tend to subvert the efficacy of the regulatory bodies which have so important a role to play in keeping up standards in the financial services industry. The court has no option but to take a serious view of these offences.' He added that he felt a community service order was 'most suitable' punishment and 'commensurate' with what he had done. What Mr Levitt had admitted was extremely serious. In a failed bid to keep trading, bogus documentation was handed to Fimbra, the City's financial regulator, when it began investigating the Levitt Group shortly before it crashed in December 1990 with debts of £34 million. But, apart from anything else Mr Levitt may or may not have done, if lying on this scale to the City regulator only carries a penalty of community service (plus loss of directorships for seven years) then what message is this sending to everyone else in the City?

If the worst that can befall you for hood-winking the regulator is working in the community (which enlightened City folk surely ought to be doing anyway) then maybe the Serious Fraud Office should pack up shop or be merged with some of the community action programmes. What the pregnant woman sentenced to prison for failing to pay her television licence makes of all this can only be guessed at. But to the average person, unversed in the niceties of plea bargaining, the sight of Mr Levitt walking free (as long as he remembers to pay his TV licence) is further proof that there is one law for the rich and one for the poor. The whole episode stinks, stinks, stinks.

(*The Guardian*, 27 November 1993, p.24)

CRIMINAL ISN'T IT?

A 1992 survey of Midlands crown courts revealed that some ethnic minorities are receiving longer prison sentences. On average, up to 9 months longer than white people for the same crimes. If this is typical, it leads to one simple and rather alarming conclusion.

The criminal justice system is heavily weighted against some ethnic minorities.

Sadly other similar investigations seem to bear this out.

Blacks and Asians are more likely to be charged than cautioned.

They are more likely to be refused bail.

Ethnic minorities are also more likely to be stopped by the police than whites.

(In one London borough Black people are four times more likely to be stopped by the police than whites.)

Mark a British born Afro-Caribbean is a case in point.

'I had never been involved or in trouble with the police before.

They said – "I'm talking to you jungle bunnie." I felt like it went on for hours and hours. I knew what he was trying to do, he was trying to coax me into causing trouble, start a fight, so he could have an excuse to arrest me.'

Contrary to what some people might think, minorities are more often the victims of crime than the perpetrators.

Black and Asian people are more likely than whites to be the victims of violence against the person and property.

And yet the stereotypical image of Black people is as aggressors.

It's a terrible slur on the vast majority of ethnic minorities in Britain who are law abiding contributors to society.

Moreover when Blacks and Asians are charged with a criminal offence, the courtroom ritual is quite daunting.

They are likely to be faced with a predominantly white institution.

From white judges and lawyers to white clerks of the courtroom.

(Out of 2,887 judges in England and Wales, only 32 are from ethnic minorities.)

The chances are they might not see a black face on the jury either.

They have to endure uncomfortable and humiliating displays of ignorance about their culture and lives.

It's a small wonder they find it difficult to co-operate with the system.

This then confirms the stereotypes of people who are alienated, hostile and aggressive to authority.

At the Commission for Racial Equality we believe there is hope.

We were set up in 1976 by the Race Relations Act to eliminate every kind of racial discrimination.

The CRE is an independent body funded by an annual Home Office grant.

The 1976 Race Relations Act quite simply states that people should not be discriminated against on the ground of colour, race or national origin.

It makes discrimination unlawful in jobs, training, housing and education.

The irony is it doesn't cover certain areas of the criminal justice process.

This basically means if you have been discriminated against in the justice process it is not possible to bring a complaint against a police officer or a judge under the Race Relations Act.

Clearly the Act should apply to these and many other similar institutions.

But the CRE are working to put an end to discrimination on how people are treated by the police force and other organisations and are working with the Association of Chief Police Officers to this end.

Secondly, we are influencing the judicial process to eliminate any kind of discrimination within their own system.

The judiciary is now undertaking training courses on racial equality issues and are planning to monitor sentencing trends to eradicate racial bias.

But what can you do?

If you feel you have been racially abused or harassed by a police officer, or if you feel you have been denied your rights and treated harshly because of your race or colour, complain.

Write to the superintendent at the station where the offending officer works.

Or, if you think you may have been unfairly discriminated against by the court system, complain.

Write to the Lord Chancellor's office.

You may be entitled to legal aid.

You could also apply to the CRE or contact your local Racial Equality Council for assistance and guidance.

We're not advocating special treatment for Britain's ethnic minorities.

(That would be positive discrimination, which is not allowed under our legislation.)

White or Black, if a person is found guilty of a criminal offence it's only right they should be justly punished.

Our criminal justice system is seen as being one of the best in the world.

It's something we can all be proud of.

But growing evidence suggests a more even handed approach is needed.

The sooner we can address these fundamental imbalances, the fairer the system will be for everyone.

If you're concerned about race issues, write to your MP and say so, or if you'd like a copy of the CRE report this advert was based on, write to the address below.

Prejudice and bigotry are passed from one generation to the next.

We have a simple choice, either take this opportunity to set an example, or ignore the problem altogether.

But that truly would be criminal.

Commission for Racial Equality

CRE Communications Section Elliot House 10–12 Allington Street London SW1E 5EH

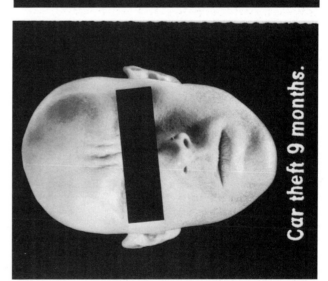

Car theft 9 months.

Car theft 1½ years.

ACTIVITY 1.3

The process whereby an incident or behaviour may or may not be registered as an official statistic is illustrated in Table 1.1, where the example of illegal drug-use is used to show how 'official data are social products' (Box, 1981, p.208). How well do you think this process applies to other incidents that are liable to criminalization? Are there any crimes to which the 'social construction of official statistics' argument is more difficult to apply? Make some notes to record your responses to such questions.

Table 1.1   Factors affecting the criminal processing of an incident

Event	Factors
Marijuana smoking	
Reported to the police?	• Country where incident takes place
	• Visibility: public or private space?
	• Public ignorance or support for sub-cultural norms
	• Notions of seriousness in eyes of observer
	• Victimless offence?
	• Social status of perpetrators
Recorded by the police?	• Social status of reporter
	• Gravity as defined by the police
	• Presence of 'law and order' campaigns
	• Chief constable directives
Individual detected and apprehended?	• Police resources and time available
	• Nature of evidence
	• Possibility of successful arrest
Arrest?	• Inter-organization obligations
	• Stereotypical notions of criminals
	• Behaviour and attributes of suspect
	• 'Dramaturgical' skills of suspect
Court?	• Past record of suspect
	• 'Normal' or 'abnormal' crime?
	• Quality of legal representation
	• Personal appearance in court
	• Nature of plea
	• Magistrates or crown court
Sentence?	• Previous sentences
	• Notions of 'persistent' offending
	• Closeness of status of judge to that of offender

Collectively, such processes of data collection inevitably mean that notions of crime waves and of perpetual increases in offending have to be interpreted with extreme caution. Nevertheless, the picture they create of crime, criminals and offending remains one of the key means through which academic, political, media and public knowledge is gained. The statistics cannot be dismissed as simply meaningless: they provide valuable insights into police and court definitions of crime and the operation of social, legal and organizational constraints and priorities. They cannot, however, be expected to aid our understanding of the 'independent entity of crime', for, as Lea and Young acknowledge, 'by its nature no such fact exists' (Lea and Young, 1984, p.15). Consequently, statistics remain ripe ingredients for media interpretation and political manipulation. It is only through being employed within a variety of discourses that they come to have meaning. Here are some examples:

- The 1982 British Crime Survey revealed a rate of 250 burglaries per 10,000 households in England and Wales in 1981. This rate, though, can be expressed in a variety of ways depending on the intended message the user wishes to put across:
  (a) a burglary every minute throughout the country;
  (b) a one-in-forty likelihood of being burgled in a year;
  (c) the likelihood of being burgled once in every 40 years.

- In March 1982, the Metropolitan Police released the annual crime figures for the London area. The occasion was chosen to issue a press release that concentrated on the smallest category of crime: the 3 per cent of offences constituting 'robbery and other violent theft'. These had risen by 34 per cent from 13,984 in 1980 to 18,763 in 1981. The figure included 5,889 cases which were described as 'street robbery of personal property'. Although these amounted to only 0.9 per cent of all recorded offences, they attracted extensive media interest because 'street robbery of personal property' is what is popularly known as 'mugging'. These particular statistics were also for the first time officially classified according to the race of the offender and they suggested that some 55 per cent of offenders were black. What is noteworthy is that no such descriptions of the other 97 per cent of offences were offered. Consequently, the *Daily Mail* of 11 March 1982 could latch on to the headline: 'Black Crime: The Alarming Figures'.

- Statistical sources can be used in quite contradictory ways to support or disclaim the view that the UK is on an ever-increasing crime spiral. Following the release of crime figures for the London Metropolitan area in February 1980, the *London Evening News* (28 February) could claim on its *front* page: 'London Violence Growing', while the *Evening Standard* of the same day declared on *page 5*: 'London Is Winning the Crime War'. Both papers were 'right', although they provided totally opposing impressions of the 'crime problem'. Serious crime as a whole (as recorded by the police) had decreased by 2 per cent, while various categories within this – for example, assaults – had risen by 12 per cent.

- Crime statistics can be used selectively or summarily dismissed by politicians, depending on their ability to confirm or deny ideological preferences. In 1993, the home secretary chose the occasion of the release of Home Office statistics, which revealed a marked *fall* in the number of juvenile convictions and cautions between 1981 and 1991, to claim that the figures were 'next to useless'. Rather, he maintained that juvenile offending was on the rise, but that much was going unrecorded because of a rise in the 1980s of informal police cautioning (*The Independent*, 25 February 1993, p.3). Responding to the prevailing image of a 'hard core of young persistent offenders', the home secretary was simultaneously planning to expand the secure accommodation network for offenders aged under 15.

Revealed: how police fiddle crime figures

By Nick Davies

Police forces across the country have been taking part in a huge fiddle in which they have pretended to detect tens of thousands of crimes and have wiped from the records a mass of other petty crimes, a Guardian investigation has revealed.

The fiddle has left an uncountable number of crime victims cheated of justice while criminals have been allowed to escape unpunished. Senior officers, most of whom claim to be unaware of the malpractice within their forces, have benefited from crime figures which credit them with a bogus success. Home Secretaries have repeatedly claimed false glory.

The investigation by the Guardian, with Channel 4's Dispatches programme, has obtained detailed evidence of the malpractice in one force, Nottinghamshire, in the mid-1990s. Officers repeatedly persuaded criminals to 'write off' lists of offences, regardless of whether or not they had committed them.

In some cases the crimes were pure fiction, invented simply so that they could be listed as detected. The criminals were virtually guaranteed that they would not be prosecuted. Some of them were rewarded with day trips out of prison, free meals and visits to girlfriends. The evidence also shows that Nottinghamshire officers were routinely 'cuffing' petty crimes and recording incidents in such a way that they disappeared from official records.

In a single year Nottinghamshire officers 'lost' 9,175 incidents, the vast majority of which should have been recorded as crimes. This left their victims bereft of police attention but cut the rate of recorded crime in the county by more than 6 per cent.

The former chief constable of South Yorkshire, Richard Wells, told the Guardian: 'It would be a brave chief constable who said, "It doesn't go on here." I don't think you could be on the same planet and not be aware that it is an issue for all police forces.'

He said he felt passionate about the malpractice. 'Everybody is cheated, and it is absolutely pointless.'

The editor of Police Review, Gary Mason, calculated, on the basis of his daily contact with detectives around the country, that three quarters of the police forces in Britain were probably involved in the abuse.

The Home Office is investigating what it calls 'statistical variations' in police work.

Police officers have said that the fiddle has been part of police work for 30 years but has recently been boosted by the Home Office decision to set performance targets for police.

In the past two years, individual officers have been suspended for the malpractice in the West Midlands, Devon and Cornwall, and Lincolnshire, but the case of Nottinghamshire for the first time proves that the abuse has been taking place on a force-wide scale.

The evidence emerged after the most senior operational detective in the county lodged a formal complaint that his entire senior command was guilty of 'organisational dishonesty'. In 1997 his complaint was investigated by the chief constable of Bedfordshire, Michael O'Byrne, who cleared the senior officers of corruption but found evidence of malpractice throughout the force.

Mr O'Byrne found that during the mid-1990s, in their efforts to satisfy their senior commanders' thirst for better figures, Nottinghamshire officers had pretended to detect numerous offences of shoplifting, car theft and burglary, sometimes using children of only 10 and 11 to record bogus admissions. Other officers had logged phoney detections for serious offences such as rapes and sexual assaults on children. Repeatedly, the real offenders had been allowed to escape and crime victims had been conned.

'The true picture of recorded and detected crime,' he concluded, 'was being suppressed and distorted.'

Despite the scathing conclusions of the Bedfordshire report and the detailed examples of dishonesty, the Nottinghamshire police and the county's police authority made public statements which suggested the force had been cleared.

The assistant clerk to the Nottinghamshire police authority, Steve Jackson, told us explicitly that Bedfordshire had found no evidence of any malpractice by any officer of any rank.

He went on to claim that Bedfordshire had made no recommendations for change. In truth, they made 59, as a result of which Nottinghamshire police have produced a new policy.

(The Guardian, 18 March 1999)

■ At the end of September 1994, crime figures showed the biggest fall in recorded crime in England and Wales for 40 years. Indeed, reductions in property crime continued for the next five years. This might make it appear that the home secretary, who had announced a 27-point plan for tackling crime in the previous year, had been successful. However, police and statistical analysts have subsequently suggested that such decreases were a myth, created in the main by non-recording and the re-classifying of certain offences (for example 'actual bodily harm' as 'common assault'; 'attempted burglary' as 'minor damage'). It has been argued that this practice was encouraged by performance indicators introduced in 1992 to improve clear-up rates and detection rates. It led to widespread 'cuffing' in order to reduce crime to politically acceptable levels (see *The Guardian*, 18 March 1999 reproduced opposite).

■ A centrepiece of New Labour's crime-reduction programme has been a crackdown on drug-use. A direct connection between addiction and crime is widely assumed: at the 1999 Labour Party conference, a controversial mandatory drug testing of all those arrested was announced. The prime minister and home secretary claimed that 61 per cent of those arrested had illegal drugs in their system. However, detailed analysis of such a bald and alarming statistic revealed that the most common drugs used were alcohol and cannabis, which were not heavily implicated in acquisitive crime. Heroin users were found to be at a significant, but much lower, 18 per cent of all arrestees (*The Guardian*, 29 November 1999).

3.2 Hidden crime

As criminologists began to acknowledge that there is no reliable statistical measure of the extent of crime, they were led to admit the widespread existence of hidden crime. Radzinowicz and King (1977), for example, suggested that only about 15 per cent of all crimes committed in England and Wales were recorded officially. Given the inadequacies of official statistics, criminologists have turned to other methods. For example, the extent of crime can be assessed by self-report studies (where people are asked to list crimes they have committed) or is now (as we noted in section 3.1) regularly 'measured' by victim surveys such as the BCS (where victims recall crimes committed against them). Both of these sources of course may also be seriously flawed because of interviewer bias, low response rates, the unwillingness of respondents to admit their criminality or a reluctance to accept a victim status. Nevertheless, they do provide useful points of comparison with Home Office statistics, in particular through their ability to reveal the wide extent of some 'invisible' crimes which have no official record. As a result, the first BCS concluded that, for every offence recorded, four were committed (Hough and Mayhew, 1983). The seventh survey (Mirrlees-Black *et al.*, 1998) indicated that 56 per cent of crime was not *reported* and that only 24 per cent of comparable BCS crimes were *recorded* by the police (see Table 1.2).

Table 1.2 also shows that, according to police records, between 1981 and 1997, the crime rate rose by 67 per cent, while the BCS data suggest a rise of 56 per cent. Both, however, for the first time did record a *fall* in the crime rate

hidden crime

Table 1.2   Comparison of British Crime Survey and crimes recorded by the police, 1981–97

	1997 police	1997 BCS	Per cent BCS	Per cent recorded of reported	Per cent recorded of all BCS	Per cent change 1995–97		Per cent change 1981–97	
						police	BCS	police	BCS
Vandalism	443	2,917	26	58	15	-4	-15	121	7
All comparable property theft (acquisitive crime)	1,751	6,261	50	56	28	-17	-15	51	99
Burglary	519	1,639	64	49	32	-19	-7	48	119
Attempts & no loss	140	976	50	29	14	-17	-0.1	90	160
With loss	379	664	85	67	57	-20	-15	37	77
All vehicle thefts	1,022	3,483	47	62	29	-15	-19	57	99
Theft from vehicle	552	2,164	43	59	25	-16	-14	63	68
Theft of vehicle	316	375	97	87	84	-21	-25	10	31
Attempted thefts	154	943	37	44	16	3	-27	447	425
Bicycle theft	151	549	64	43	27	-18	-17	19	154
Theft from the person	60	590	35	29	10	-4	-12	71	36
All comparable violence	256	1,022	49	51	25	11	-13	150	53
Wounding	205	714	45	63	29	18	-17	143	41
Robbery	52	307	57	30	17	-11	-2	183	89
All comparable	2,450	10,199	44	54	24	-12	-15	67	56

Source: Mirrlees-Black *et al.*, 1998, p.26

between 1995 and 1997 although subsequent police records for 1999 suggested that this may be shortlived. Surveys of victimization in particular localities (for example, Islington in London) have tended to uncover even higher rates than those reported to the BCS, particularly incidents of burglary and vandalism. In addition, local surveys brought to light the extent of offences which until 1996 were omitted from BCS data, such as domestic violence, sexual abuse, threats and assaults (Crawford *et al.*, 1990 and Chapter 5 explore this further). Nevertheless, both corporate crime and victims, such as businesses, shops and public services, remain infrequent objects of all forms of study.

Most self-report studies have been directed at young people. Likewise, they have revealed that offending is more common than official statistics suggest and that, in all probability, law-breaking is a widespread phenomenon, practised by most, if not all, of the population at some time in their lives. In Graham and Bowling's (1995) sample of over 1,700 under-25-year-olds, a half of males and a third of females admitted to having committed an offence at some time in their lives. Jungar-Tas's (1994) international study of five European countries confirmed that up to 90 per cent of young people have been offenders in their lifetime. Rutter and Giller's (1983, p.27) summary of delinquency self-report research found that, *inter alia*, 82 per cent of respondents admitted breaking windows of empty houses, 70 per cent had stolen from a shop and almost no-one admitted that they had *never* committed an offence. Risk of prosecution ranged from 8 per cent (shoplifting) to 60 per cent (breaking and entering). Significantly, and in contrast to dominant statistical and public perceptions, middle-class children were just as likely to be involved in crime as their working-class counterparts – a conclusion also reached through interviews with 4,000 11- to 15-year-olds in Edinburgh in the early 1990s (Anderson *et al.*, 1994). This latter study also noted how young people face serious problems as *victims* of crime, but again this was underreported either to parents or the police.

Indeed, the widespread nature of offending is fairly easy to establish. Taking stationery or other goods from office/work, using a firm's telephone for personal calls, taking 'souvenirs' from pubs/hotels, overestimating expenses and keeping money found in the street, for example, all constitute theft, capable of attracting up to a £5,000 fine and/or six months imprisonment, prosecution in a magistrates court (as of 1999). Such offending (yours and mine?) is not automatically synonymous with being criminal. A majority of us presumably lack criminal status, but only because our offences have remained excused, undetected, ignored or gone unreported. And while we may justify our actions as insignificant, collectively the economic and social ramifications of such behaviour may be far from trivial. For example, in 1972 it was estimated that £225–£300 million worth of goods would 'disappear' that year from shops, offices and factories. Similarly, the Grosvenor House Hotel in London wanted to trace the disappearance of 10,000 teaspoons and 40,000 napkins! (*Daily Mail*, 31 May 1972.) In 1992–3 the report, *Retail Crime Costs*, estimated that employees were responsible for a quarter of thefts from shops and stores, amounting to £554 million, while a Social Market Foundation report in 1999 reckoned that, overall, the hidden economy – activities not made known to the tax authorities – was running at £50 billion a year or around 20 per cent of annual gross domestic product (*The Guardian*, 5 July 1999). The question is: where do we draw the line? Where does 'respectability' end and 'criminality' begin?

3.3   Institutionalized crime

While definitional issues ensure that the 'reality of crime' is always open to dispute (as we saw in section 2), there are also numerous reasons why certain incidents, even when they are prima facie infractions of the law, remain invisible and thus absent from law-and-order statistics and debates. Jupp, Davies and Francis (1999, p.5) list these as:

- *no knowledge*, e.g., workers in hazardous industries may see themselves as being in a dangerous job rather than as victims of the failure to implement health and safety codes;

- *no statistics*, e.g., official statistics focus predominantly on 'street-level' crime and give a poor reflection of state, corporate, green or cyber crime;

- *no theory and no research*, e.g., criminology as a discipline has traditionally focused on conventional crime, and youth crime in particular, and promoted theories of individual and family pathology that may appear to have little relevance to understanding other transgressions, such as corporate corruption;

- *no control*, e.g., the globalization of corporate crime between nation states precludes any possibility of detection and prevention;

- *no politics, no panic*, e.g., political rhetoric continues to focus on individual and street-level crime as *the* source of the 'crime' problem. As a result, corporations and businesses are generally not made responsible for the fatal 'accidents' or environmental pollution that they cause.

Research into 'crime at work', for example, has revealed that fiddling of stocks and sales returns is not only an established part of such jobs as catering, bread sales and milk delivery – a 'legitimate commerce' – but that it is also necessary for the smooth running of the companies involved, acting as a supplement to low wages and often allowed for in wage negotiations. The 'basic structural and normative similarity' between fiddling and legitimate business practice means that the fiddler, far from being vilified, is likely to attract an 'ambiguous (but generally) benevolent societal reaction' (Ditton, 1977, p.173). Crime in this context is an institutionalized practice. A 'hidden' economy co-exists with the 'legitimate' economy, each dependent on the other for goods and resources. Fiddling in the provision of professional services by doctors, surgeons, pharmacists, lawyers and business executives has also been shown to be widespread and 'normative' (Henry, 1978). Here, 'offences' include charging for unnecessary work, use of fictitious or overvalued collateral and tax violations.

hidden economy

Indeed, white-collar crimes are probably far more numerous and more costly than recorded crime, but they seldom come to the attention of law-enforcement agencies. Sutherland's pioneering work in the 1930s effectively destroyed the notion of criminality as an exclusively lower-class phenomenon. Using records of administrative commissions, he showed that the senior executives of the 70 largest industrial corporations in the USA had consistently violated the law with regard to trade restraint, misrepresentation in advertising, infringement of patent rights and unfair labour practices (Sutherland, 1949). Such 'legitimate rackets' are likely to be more economically significant than all the robberies, thefts and acts of larceny put together. In the USA in 1965, for example, the Federal Bureau of Investigation (FBI) estimated that some $284 million were lost in burglaries. This, however, paled into insignificance when compared to the estimated $9 *billion* of which the wealthiest 1 per cent of the American population defrauded their tax department in the same year (Pearce, 1976, pp.77–8). Similarly, Snider (1993) estimates the annual cost of street crime in the USA to be $4 billion, or 'much less than 5 per cent of the take from corporate crime'. In the deregulated markets of the 1980s, corporate crime came to be described as the 'fastest growing in Britain' (see *The Guardian 2*, 1 July 1993, reproduced opposite).

Crime in the City

Alex Brummer

Three decades ago, on August 8, 1963, an audacious group of British gangsters etched their names into folklore when they stole £2.5 million – the equivalent of £25 million at today's prices – from the Glasgow–London mail train and received 30-year jail sentences for their trouble. But by the standards of the late 20th century, when the most daring crimes are of a more cerebral kind and the proceeds start in the tens-of millions and can reach the billions, the Great Train Robbery looks modest.

Clearly, men in grey suits with grand jobs in public companies – from whose ranks Britain's biggest criminals are often drawn today – do not conjure up the Wild West images which endowed the train robbers. Yet the sums looted from company coffers, pension funds and bank accounts in recent years, by executives with all the trappings of power, have been enormous by the standards of regular criminality. Robert Maxwell, arguably the biggest crook ever to sit at the top of a group of public companies, robbed his workers of some £500 millions of their life savings and could still look them in the eye.

Asil Nadir, whose case has become a political *cause célèbre* this summer, took investors on an astonishing roller-coaster ride. In a decade at the head of Polly Peck, where the riches were founded in the unglamorous trade of fruit packaging, Nadir took the company's shares from 8p each to £35 at their peak in 1983. In the process he made millionaires of investors who had put just £1,000 into his company. But the growth in the business and the huge profits were a chimera.

At the last count the administrators, charged with making as much recovery as possible for shareholders and creditors, found that £450 million had gone walkabout through a series of complex offshore banking arrangements with a complexity that made Hampton Court Maze look linear.

At the Bank of Commerce & Credit International, described by the Governor of the Bank of England, Robin Leigh-Pemberton, as the most fraudulent bank in the history of finance, directors siphoned off billions of pounds. They left a hole which has been estimated by some experts as being in the region of $10 billion. Such a sum would be all but impossible to stash away in a farm house.

But contemporary fraud is not just about men such as Peter Clowes, now serving a jail term, who made away with almost £100 million of elderly people's money, or the more complex financial shenanigans which earned the Guinness defendants Ernest Saunders, Gerald Ronson and Anthony Parnes a stretch at Ford Open Prison. It is a burgeoning business, which is growing so fast that it is almost impossible for the lumbering criminal justice system to keep up with it.

New figures produced this week by the management consultants KPMG show that in the first four months of this year alone some £571 million of new financial fraud was reported. This compares with £671 million in the whole of 1992. The new wave of financial fraudsters are not the modest or grubby clerks of the kind portrayed in Arthur Hailey's novels which sold so well in the 1970s. Most of them are right at the very top of their professions – company directors or chief executives – and drawn from the high achievement age group of 41–50 years old. They are the glitzy figures of Oliver Stone's film Wall Street. None of these fraudsters is content with fiddling his expenses.

(The Guardian 2, 1 July 1993, p.2)

The crimes of the powerful are not simply crimes against property. In 1978, four people died following a hoist accident at a power-station in Kent. The Health and Safety Commission subsequently identified the cause of the accident as the company's neglect of safety equipment. In the late 1970s, the Chemie Grunenthal company of Germany had criminal charges brought against it for deliberately falsifying the test data on the drug thalidomide. Eight thousand pregnant women around the Western world had, in the meantime, given birth to deformed babies (Box, 1983). During the 1970s, 106 fatalities occurred in the North Sea oil industry, many of which were due to the operation of lower safety standards offshore when the rush for oil, with the blessing of successive British governments, placed profit before safety (Carson, 1981). Reports into the successive transport disasters in the 1980s and 1990s (Zeebruge, 1987, 187 deaths; Kings Cross, 1987, 31 deaths; Clapham, 1988, 35 deaths; Southall, 1997, 7 deaths; Paddington, 1999, 32 deaths) have consistently exposed the failure of company directors and companies to take safety issues seriously. Box (1983, p.28) estimates a ratio of 7:1 regarding deaths from occupational accidents and diseases, and deaths recorded as homicide.

Given the nature of much corporate and safety crime, these cases stand only as examples of what is arguably a widespread practice (Slapper and Tombs, 1999). Corporate crime is relatively invisible and thus infrequently reported to, or detected by, the legal authorities. It is rarely the subject of a sustained public 'moral outrage' despite the economic costs. Box attributes the relative impunity of corporate crime not just to invisibility, but to various ideological mechanisms whereby the pursuit of profit is supported irrespective of its human costs:

> Executives are able to violate the law without feeling guilt or denting their respectable self image ... corporate officials are both mystified as to their own crime and misdirected as to the distribution of crime in general. Both mystification and misdirection preserve the appearance of corporate respectability and help keep invisible to themselves and others the underlying ugly reality of corporate crime.
>
> (Box, 1983, p.57)

These demonstrations of the extensiveness of crime may suggest and encourage such populisms as 'everyone is at it', but such a view tends to disregard the different opportunities for 'crime' available in different workplaces. A hidden economy analysis tends to cut across the issues of opportunity for crime, and type and extent of crime, by collapsing *all* crimes at or involving work into a homogeneous category. Not only does this deny the quantitative differences in out-of-market dealing, but it fails to recognize the qualitative differences in the work context which allow such opportunities. What is also disguised by this position is the existence of a hierarchy of acceptability within the full range of property crime. While tax avoidance (as opposed to evasion), for example, may be considered a legitimate business activity, social-security fiddling is regarded as a form of social malaise (Cook, 1989).

Chambliss develops this argument further and contends that the state itself is frequently implicated in the organization and committal of criminal acts. By this, he refers not simply to questions of dubious morality or the denial of human rights, but to historical and current institutionalized state practices involving 'complicity in piracy, smuggling, assassinations, criminal conspiracies ... and diverting funds in ways prohibited by law (e.g. illegal campaign contributions, selling arms to countries prohibited by law and supporting terrorist activities)' (Chambliss, 1989, p.184; Chambliss, 1999). Some of the more infamous examples would include the Watergate scandals of 1973 in the USA; the bombing of the Greenpeace ship, *The Rainbow Warrior*, by the French secret service in New Zealand in 1985; and the 1993 'arms for Iraq' allegations in England (Chapter 7 examines this further).

However, it is precisely these forms of 'respectable' crime that rarely feature in either the official statistics or victimization surveys. Despite the seriousness of some instances of white-collar, corporate and state crime (many involving enormous sums of money and resulting in widespread human suffering), the subject has rarely been at the head of the 'problem of crime' agenda. Since the late 1960s, the growth of multinationals operating beyond the limits of national control, the rise of consumer protection movements, and the threat of more dangerous forms of pollution have, however, increased its public visibility (this is discussed further in Chapter 6). Nevertheless, the belief that property crime (theft, robbery) is mainly a lower-class phenomenon retains its potency.

Property crimes – as Sutherland suggested in 1949 – are rooted in the very structure of society. However, only a small and specific section of the population is consistently singled out as a matter of social concern. Similarly, it is only from the analysis of such 'specific sections' that the vast majority of criminological theories purporting to uncover the causes of crime have been constructed. As mentioned earlier, most academic and public 'theories' about the causes of crime depend on the picture painted by official statistics. Because such statistics consistently report strong correlations between offending and young, male and low-income sections of the population, it is to these particular groups that most academic research and public outrage is directed. For example, **Braithwaite's (1989)** list of 'thirteen powerful associations' (which he argues every criminological theory is bound to address), while undoubtedly having some validity, also allows statistical indices to set the research agenda (see Table 1.3).

Table 1.3   Thirteen powerful associations

1   Crime is committed disproportionately by males
2   Crime is committed disproportionately by 15- to 25-year-olds
3   Crime is committed disproportionately by unmarried people
4   Crime is committed disproportionately by people living in large cities
5   Crime is committed disproportionately by people who have experienced high residential mobility and who live in areas characterized by high residential mobility
6   Young people who are strongly attached to their school are less likely to engage in crime
7   Young people who have high educational and occupational aspirations are less likely to engage in crime
8   Young people who do poorly at school are more likely to engage in crime
9   Young people who are strongly attached to their parents are less likely to engage in crime
10 Young people who have friendships with criminals are more likely to engage in crime themselves
11 People who believe strongly in the importance of complying with the law are less likely to violate the law
12 Being at the bottom of the class structure increases rates of offending for all types of crime apart from white-collar crime
13 Crime rates have been increasing in most countries since the Second World War

Source: based on Braithwaite, 1989, pp.44–50

In the process, street crime tends to be elevated as a more serious cause for concern than corporate crime; street violence more than domestic violence; and welfare-benefit fraud more than income tax evasion. Common-sense 'theories' that single out poor parenting, low IQ, educational underachievement, lone-parent families, youth peer-group pressure, and so on, as key determinants of crime are readily applied to the former, but rarely (if ever) to the latter. Most criminological theory, then, tends to exacerbate the partial and distorted view of crime, constructed in the first instance by the statistical measures.

4 Representations of crime

Media discourse is saturated with crime. Crime consumes an enormous amount of media space as both entertainment and news. Whether it be TV cop shows, crime novels, docudramas, newspaper articles, comics, documentaries or 'real-life' reconstructions, crime, criminality and criminal justice appear to have an endless capacity to tap not only into public fear but also public fascination (as we will see in Chapter 2). Much of our information about the nature and extent of crime comes to us via the secondary source of the media. We should expect then, that as 'distributors of social knowledge', they play a significant role in our perception and understanding of the boundaries between order and disorder (Surette, 1998, p.11). But despite the powerful 'commonsense' view that news media merely provide the *facts* of a process in which crime occurs, police apprehend criminals and courts punish them, the relationship between crime and media reportage is far from simple.

4.1 News values and institutional sources

Since at least the mid-1880s, crime news has been a staple diet of the popular press. Roshier (1973) found that, between 1938 and 1967, an average of 4 per cent of total news space was devoted to crime. It is a percentage nonetheless that increased significantly in the 1980s and 1990s. Williams and Dickinson's (1993) analysis of ten national dailies in 1989 put the figure at almost 13 per cent and Reiner (1997) reports that data from the *Daily Mirror* and *The Times* between 1945 and 1991 show a rise from an average of 8 per cent to 21 per cent. It is probably no coincidence that law and order has also grown as a significant political issue during this time.

But while the amount of crime news has increased, the *type* of crime reported has been remarkably constant. Since Davis's (1952) pioneering research in Colorado, comparisons of crime news and crime statistics have produced consistent results. For example, studies of the provincial press by Ditton and Duffy (1983) in Strathclyde and Smith (1984) in Birmingham both revealed that newspapers distort the 'official' picture of crimes known to and recorded by the police. In Strathclyde, an over-reporting of crimes involving violence and sex was so significant that during March 1981 such crimes constituted only 2.4 per cent of reported incidence yet occupied 45.8 per cent of newspaper coverage (Ditton and Duffy, 1983, p.164). In Birmingham, personal offences such as robbery and assault accounted for less than 6 per cent of known crimes but occupied 52.7 per cent of the space devoted to crime stories (Smith, 1984, p.290). Smith also reported biases in the media's identification of 'key criminal areas' of a city, although they did not have the highest reported crime rate, and a tendency to link issues of race with crime. The first research of crime news in all of the national dailies in Britain in the late 1980s similarly found that newspapers regularly devoted over 60 per cent of the space given to crime reporting to stories dealing with cases of personal violence even though they only constituted some 6 per cent of crimes reported by victims (Williams and Dickinson, 1993, p.40).

Clearly, while newspapers do inform the public, they can also help to create a public awareness that is substantially different from any 'reality' contained in victim surveys or in the official statistics (Smith, 1984, p.293). For example, Young (1974) noted that the type of information that the mass media select and disseminate to the public is coloured throughout by notions of newsworthiness. He argued that, rather than providing a pure reflection of the social world, 'newspapers select events which

are *atypical*, present them in a *stereotypical* fashion and contrast t
backcloth of normality which is *overtypical*' (Young, 1974, p.241). T
then usually depicted as violent, immoral and a threat to an other
social order. Crime – despite its ubiquity – is presented in a way in that
breaches our 'normal' expectations about the world.

It is a function of the media to search continually for the 'new',
and the dramatic. This is what makes 'news'. Chibnall (1977, p.77) no
of informal rules of relevancy which govern the professional imperative
journalism: (a) visible and spectacular acts (b) sexual or political conn
graphic presentation (d) individual pathology and (e) deterrence and
According to Chibnall, press reports cannot simply be a reflection of
because two key processes always intervene: *selection* – which aspect
to report, and which to omit; and *presentation* – choosing what sort of headline,
language, imagery, photograph and typography to use. As he argues, the violence **news values**
most likely to receive coverage in the press is indeed that which involves sudden
injury to 'innocent others', especially in public places. Concern with such violence
has typified newspaper accounts throughout the past 50 years, bolstered by such
media labels as 'cosh boys', 'bullyboy skinheads', 'vandals', 'muggers', 'hooligans',
'joyriders', 'blood-crazed mobs', 'rampaging thugs'. The concentration on these
forms in media and public discourse reinforces limited concepts of crime and
violence. Domestic violence, unsafe working conditions, pollution of the
environment and the mental violence involved in repetitive jobs are all cited by
Chibnall as phenomena that have caused equal suffering but have received less
sustained press attention because they do not conform to the criteria of 'spectacular
newsworthiness' (Chibnall, 1977, p.78). The same applies to white-collar crime,
corporate corruption, state violence and the systematic denial of human rights.

One case stands out as worthy of critical reflection. Female criminality is almost
always depicted and described in different terms to that of male. Partly because of
women's under-representation in statistical measures and partly because of
stereotypes regarding 'proper' gender roles, the female criminal is regarded as
transgressing not only the law, but also sex-role norms. In short, she is likely to be
considered as 'doubly deviant'. As Hutter and Williams (1981, p.23) argue, female
deviancy is characteristically portrayed by media and judicial authorities as unnatural
or abnormal, behaviour to which the stereotypes of 'mad' or 'sad' are more readily
applied than that of 'bad'. Female behaviour tends to attract a restricted range of
media typifications, revolving around the sexually based dichotomies of chaste/
unchaste, virgin/whore and Madonna/Magdalene (see *The Sun*, 7 July 1992, and
Daily Star, 10 December 1994). Heidensohn notes how the image of the witch
remains at the top of a 'pyramid of related images of deviant women as especially
evil, depraved and monstrous' (Heidensohn, 1985, p.92). For example, while
prostitutes are depicted as *sexual* deviants, as *fallen* women, their male clients are
at worst viewed as misguided (or simply propelled into their actions because of
unloving wives and/or mothers). Men and male sexuality are not seen to be the
problem; the blame tends to rest with the female. Since 'true femininity' is assumed
to preclude 'improper' behaviour, another recurring image is the denigration of
deviant women as 'masculine'. Above all, there is no male equivalent for notions
of 'the slag', 'the whore' or 'the witch'. Conversely, media reports of violence against
women tend to reproduce a woman-blaming ideology – 'she asked for it'; 'she
made me do it'. It has also been argued that the celebration of famous murderers,
such as Jack the Ripper, reveals the media's voyeuristic pose and a 'failure to take
femicide seriously' (Radford and Russell, 1992, p.353).

By James Lewthwaite

It was bride Alison Shaughnessy's day of joy.

But standing among her wedding guests was her bridegroom's secret lover who was to murder her in a knife frenzy, the Old Bailey heard yesterday.

Michelle Taylor, 21, … stabbed Alison 54 times, a jury was told.

WAIT

She hatched a murder plot with her sister Lisa, 18, because she was 'completely infatuated' with Alison's husband, prosecutor John Nutting said.

The pair had been making love at least twice a week before the wedding and continued even after it, he said.

Pretty bank clerk Alison, suspected nothing, even when husband John, 29, invited Michelle to their wedding in Ireland and paid for her fare and hotel bill.

But 11 months later Michelle used a knife five inches long and an inch wide to kill her love rival in her home in Battersea, South West London, Mr Nutting said.

(*The Sun*, 7 July 1992, p.1)

Convicted of murder in July 1992 and sentenced to life imprisonment, Michelle and Lisa Taylor were subsequently acquitted on appeal in June 1993. The appeal judge ruled that press publicity had prejudiced their chances of a fair trial. In December 1994 the sisters won the right to a review of their case to bring contempt proceedings against the tabloid press, including The Sun. Their appeal to the House of Lords was subsequently refused in August 1995

The abductor of Abbie Humphries in 1994 was placed on probation with the condition that she receive treatment at a psychiatric hospital, on the grounds that the kidnap was 'deliberate but not premeditated'

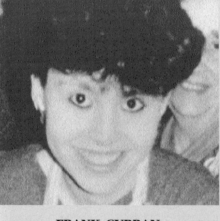

YOU'RE MAD NOT BAD

Abbie snatch nurse is freed

FRANK CURRAN

Baby snatcher Julie Kelley, who put newborn Abbie Humphries' parents through a 15-day nightmare, walked free yesterday.

The abductor smiled as she left the dock after a judge put her on probation, telling her she was 'more mad rather than bad.'

He ruled that Kelley should receive treatment at a mental hospital after her own baby is born in three weeks.

There were gasps of amazement when the verdict was returned at Nottingham Crown Court where Mr Justice Laws told Kelley she had put Abbie's parents through 'dreadful torture.'

But Abbie's forgiving mother Karen said yesterday she felt no malice towards her kidnapper.

Dream

Karen, 33, added at home in Sherwood, Nottingham: 'I don't blame Julie – we've put it all behind us like it was a bad dream.'

Kelley, her head bowed, had been told by the judge: 'It is hard to imagine the extent of the agony of Abbie Humphries' parents during that fortnight.

'They did not know if they would ever see her again.

'You were not completely mentally ill and you were under no delusions as to the nature of your act.'

Mr Laws said the kidnap was 'deliberate but not premeditated – although the consequences were horrific'.

The court heard that dental nurse Kelley faked a pregnancy after boyfriend Leigh Gilbert dumped her.

The 23-year-old car mechanic took her back when she told him he was the father.

William Everard, QC, prosecuting, said Kelley kept up the elaborate hoax in a bid to save her relationship with Gilbert.

She moved into his home where a bedroom was turned into a nursery.

Kelley padded her abdomen, feigned morning sickness and pretended to make trips to her GP and an ante-natal clinic.

(*Daily Star*, 10 December 1994, p.1)

The ready application of stereotypes is a characteristic feature of most crime reporting. Crime tends to be depicted in terms of a basic confrontation between the symbolic forces of good and evil. Complex social events are collapsed into simplistic questions of right and wrong. The intricate history and consequences of an event necessary to provide a fuller and more complex picture are rarely provided, or only at a later date when the terms of debate have already been set. Hall *et al.* (1975) conclude that crime reports tend to undo the complexities of crime by constructing a number of easy categories into which each type of crime can be placed (see Extract 1.2).

Extract 1.2 Hall *et al.*: 'The complexities of crime'

Though criminology has long aspired to the condition of a science, the fact is that explanations of crime are powerfully and massively overlaid by lay ideologies. These ideological frameworks set whole *chains* of explanations in motion; whole families of criminal types and categories are set going, which knit together, while appearing to unravel, the enigma of crime and its causation. Here one often finds the *complexities* of crime … 'classified out' into the genetic, or the psychopathic, or the environmental, or the sociological, or the psychiatric – or the socially disorganized and undersocialized 'explanations'. To each cluster of explanations is attached an appropriate typology of the criminal: the under-chromosomed, the unregenerated evil, the criminally insane, the deprived, the sick, the weak, the mother-deprived, criminal type. To each is often also attached its chain of motivations: the irrational, the driven, the neurotic, the search for kicks, the congenitally wicked, motive. To each, often also belongs the appropriate social setting or scene: the back street, or multiply deprived working-class area; the bomb site; the high-rise block and the unused telephone kiosk; the football end; the drug scene or hippie pad … No doubt something of the truth lurks and hovers within and between these stereotyped and clustered maps of meaning. But they are rarely pressed through in depth and detail to the difficult and complex but necessary social connections which they index. Sometimes, after a parade of 'explorations and explanations', the argument is dissolved ideologically: into one of the great Public Images – Inner City Slum, Family whose Mother went out to work, etc. – which bring the account conveniently to 'an end', if not to a resolution. …

The media provide the bridge or link between crime and the public anxiety or concern about crime. There is, of course, a widespread and growing anxiety about crime and its upward movement. But, over and above what we know of rising crime either from reported crime, or from the offered interpretations of the criminal statistics, there has been also the closely related phenomenon of a public 'moral panic' about rising crime: on the one hand panics about *certain specific* crimes which connect with troubling public issues (for example, race, drugs, pornography, youth) or, on the other hand, panics about the highly generalized but nameless unspecified 'tide' or 'epidemic' of crime itself. These 'panics' have grown in intensity and number through the post-war years; they clearly reflect very deep-seated public anxieties and uncertainties; but they are distinguished, above all, by four things: (1) the *discrepancy* between the scale of the known facts and the depth, intensity and escalation of the public perception and response; (2) the focusing of these 'panics' around key social themes and social groups (for example, black people) or social categories (for example, drugs offenders); (3) the way each 'panic' feeds off and spirals with *other* concerns which are mapped into it, or in some other way, identified with it; (4) the way in which 'moral panics' issue into control crusades and 'law and order' campaigns.

(Hall *et al.*, 1975, pp.13–15)

primary definers

It is important to remember, too, that the news media have little *direct* access to crime. The majority of crime stories come to them via the police, the courts and the Home Office. These agencies of crime control are the primary definers and sources of crime news. This means that they are in a position to provide initial definitions of crime and locate them within the context of a continuing crime problem. The credibility of their definitions is in turn enhanced by their 'official' and 'institutional' standing. The regular access of control institutions to media reportage is both open and 'acceptable'. They are the institutions in the frontline of crime control – they have an everyday knowledge of the 'fight against crime'. It therefore appears quite 'natural' that they should be the main source of news about crime: 'Law is among the dominant institutions entwined with the mass media. The people and organisations in the institution of law join with mass media operatives in constituting a deviance-defining elite that perpetually articulates morality and justice in all other social institutions' (Ericson, 1991, p.223). Media, crime and criminal justice have become intricately intertwined.

As Chibnall (1977, p.49) argues, crime stories have historically been the bread and butter of popular journalism. From the nineteenth century on, a tradition of sensational crime reporting in the Sunday newspapers, the *Police Gazette* and the *Illustrated Police News* developed. Stories were initially dependent on court cases, but as popular journalism expanded in the twentieth century, information about the earlier, and potentially more sensational, aspects of criminal proceedings became highly sought after. As a consequence, the press came to rely increasingly on one major institutional source – the police. Reporters' increased contact with the police gradually became more informal and their role more secure and autonomous. In 1945, these specialist journalists formed the Crime Reporters' Association in order to improve press–police relations. And from the 1970s, the police have also had considerable success in elevating themselves as authoritative political advisers, not only on the implementation of crime control, but also on matters of criminal-justice policy

Police remove a box, supposedly containing the remains of the victims of alleged serial killer Frederick West, from 25 Cromwell Street in 1994. Several newspapers carried the picture on their front pages. However, there were no human remains in the box at all. The police agreed to stage the scene after pressure from a section of the press corps

and reform. Under the guidance of Sir Robert Mark, then Commissioner of the Metropolitan Police, a new and more 'open' press-relations policy was instituted, in which press conferences and direct communication between editors and senior police officers have become commonplace.

This shift from a defensive to a proactive posture is such that 'the police now view the news media as part of the policing apparatus of society' (Schlesinger and Tumber, 1994, p.107): a role underlined since the mid-1980s by the advent of such television programmes as *Crimestoppers* (ITV), *Crime Monthly* (LWT) and *Crimewatch UK* (BBC), where viewers are mobilized to help the police with the aid of dramatic reconstructions of various incidents. Anonymous informing, once a disparaged social behaviour, has been transformed into a normalized and legitimate civic act (Surette, 1998, p.12). Murder, armed robbery with violence and sexual crime are the staple items of coverage; fraud and corporate crime notable absences. Schlesinger and Tumber (1994, p.268) note that in such 'documentary reconstructions', the police have 'complete control over access to evidence and a determining voice over the possible uses to which this might be put'. (*Crimewatch UK* regularly attracts 11 million viewers, many more than that of the national nightly news.)

This is not to argue that journalists and broadcasters are incapable of presenting views that are controversial or unacceptable to established politicians or the control agencies, but it does suggest that in the majority of cases their accounts are grounded in the agendas set, and interpretations provided, by these primary sources. These interpretations are in turn dependent largely on the rate of reported crime, the focused and organized police response to certain crimes, and the reports of Home Office statisticians reliant on police records (as we saw in section 3.1). As a result, media and official definitions of crime are likely to be partial *and* reflective of institutional constraints and demands. They do not simply reflect social reality, but define it in a particular way, subsequently influencing the quality of public or lay opinions. In analysing this effect, Hall *et al.* (1975) proposed replacing the 'everyday' public assumption that crime → apprehension → crime report, with the more complex model shown in Figure 1.5 below.

Hall *et al.*'s model suggests that popular images about crime are 'popular' only in so far as they are consequences of information provided by official sources (with a vested interest in crime control), and by media sources (with a vested interest in maintaining news values). Such observations are not unique to the British media. Marsh's (1991) comparative analysis found a striking similarity amongst newspapers worldwide, in types of crime reported, lack of

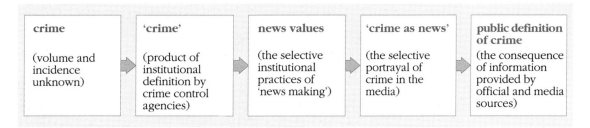

crime	'crime'	news values	'crime as news'	public definition of crime
(volume and incidence unknown)	(product of institutional definition by crime control agencies)	(the selective institutional practices of 'news making')	(the selective portrayal of crime in the media)	(the consequence of information provided by official and media sources)

Figure 1.5   (Source: Hall et al., 1975, p.2)

discussion of crime causation and in their presentation of false images of the effectiveness of the police and courts in detecting and punishing criminals.

However, it has also been argued that the media do not necessarily adopt a unitary approach to crime news. Important degrees of emphasis appear between the quality, mid market and tabloid press and between the national dailies and television news. Schlesinger, Tumber and Murdock's (1991) research, for example, found that the tabloids are more likely to feature violent crime, while television gives more attention to offences relating to public order, to the justice system and to the state. Roshier's (1973) analysis also found that it is not only the dramatic and exceptional that is considered newsworthy by the press. Rather, incidents of petty theft when coupled with 'a personality' or 'whimsical circumstances' also feature strongly, usually in the inside pages as a reliable form of trivial, light entertainment.

Detailed analysis of the production of crime news in the 1980s and 1990s has also maintained that the media is not hegemonic but the site of different group interests (Ericson, 1991; Schlesinger and Tumber, 1994; Sparks, 1992; McLaughlin and Murji, 2000). Increasingly, pressure groups, penal-reform organizations and civil-liberties groups have gained access to the news media and have become ever more sophisticated in designing their own media strategies, to which the established law-enforcement agencies have been forced to respond. Such oppositional and alternative entries into the policy agenda process may indeed lead us to query conceptions of all-powerful 'primary definers'. Schlesinger, Tumber and Murdock's (1991, p.413) analysis, for example, found that while the quality newspapers tended to 'source' judges, lawyers and court officials, similar weight was also given to members of lobby and pressure groups. In the tabloids, law-enforcement agencies were again prioritized but not at the expense of victims, suspects' relatives and criminals. Such diversity, however, may mask continuing inequalities in media access, and in particular may not be able to withstand the dramatic and political purchase of certain mediatized events. As Roshier (1973) acknowledges, in certain events such as drug-use and football hooliganism in the 1960s, a noticeable tendency to dramatize offence seriousness and publicize 'get tough' responses emerges. Nowhere was such unanimity more clearly seen than in the media reaction to the murder of two-year-old Jamie Bulger in 1993. This particular murder by two ten-year-olds was to become a watershed in media and political responses to crime, and youth crime in particular, and not simply because of its apparent brutality. The Bulger case had at least three related consequences. Firstly, it initiated a reconsideration of the social construction of ten-year-olds as 'demons' rather than as 'innocents'. Secondly, it coalesced with, and helped to mobilize, a moral panic not only about crime but also about anti-social behaviour. Thirdly, it legitimized a hardening of political and judicial attitudes to offenders in general, which came to characterize much of the 1990s (Muncie, 1999). As Figure 1.6 shows, despite a renewed emphasis on crime prevention and restorative justice promoted by New Labour since 1997, the numbers in custody have grown consistently since that pivotal moment in 1993.

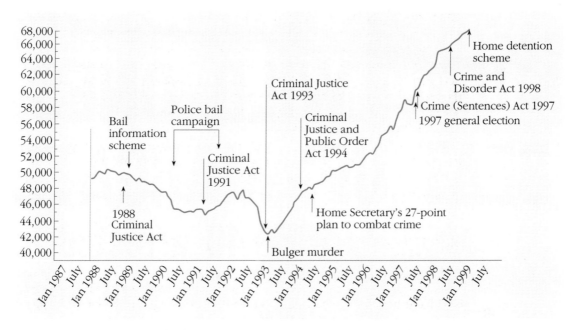

Figure 1.6 Prison population and policy interventions, 1987–1999 (Source: adapted from Wilson and Ashton, 1998, Figure 2, p.17)

4.2 The sociology of moral panics

Since the 1960s, the concept of moral panic has been used by sociologists and criminologists to describe public reactions (or, perhaps more pertinently, *media* and *political* reactions) to mugging, soccer violence, social security 'scroungers', child abuse, vandalism, drug-use, student militancy, 'spectacular' youth sub-cultures, street crime, permissiveness, 'bail bandits' and lone parents.

    The first systematic empirical study of a moral panic in the UK was Stanley Cohen's research on the social reaction to the Mods and Rockers disturbances of 1964 (Cohen, 1973b). Over the Easter bank holiday weekend that year, groups of working-class youths arrived in the seaside resort of Clacton - the traditional meeting place for holidaying youths from the East End of London. Easter 1964 was cold and wet, and shopkeepers were irritated by the lack of business. The facilities and amusements for young people were strictly limited, whose boredom was fanned by rumours of café owners refusing to serve some of them. Eventually, scuffles between groups of youths broke out, windows were broken, beach huts vandalized, and those on scooters and bikes roared up and down the promenade.

    Such events were by no means new. Pearson's (1983) study of hooliganism in British history, as we saw in section 3.1, noted comparable disturbances in the 'lawlessness' of the Teddy Boys in the 1950s and in a series of clashes between police and East End youths (the first 'hooligans') during the August bank holiday celebrations in London in 1898. However, the events of Easter 1964 were to

moral panic

51

Daily Mirror

3d. Monday, May 18, 1964 No. 18,788

After Clacton.. a new battlefield

WILD ONES 'BEAT UP' MARGATE

40 arrested in all-day clashes

THE Wild Ones —self-styled Mods and Rockers —picked the Kent resort of Margate to beat up for Whitsun.

All day yesterday the rival teenagers fought and smashed their way around the town.

They clashed with police, who went into action with truncheons drawn.

When it got dark, about 800 Mods were parading around Margate. Two hundred Rockers were lurking in a quiet corner of the town.

Blood

At least forty youths had been arrested. And there was blood on the sand.

Most of the Mods had arrived on scooters bristling with headlights and badges.

Most of the leather-jacketed Rockers had roared into town on shiny motor-cycles.

Many of the teenagers turned up late on Saturday night. They got down to the wrecking and smashing right away.

At 10.30 yesterday morning, the big battle broke out—as 500 Mods attacked 100 Rockers. Six policemen stepped in, truncheons waving — and both mobs turned on them.

Shouting

Then the Mods streamed across to the huge Dreamland amusement centre, knocking over people as they went. They marched among the pintables, chanting, shouting and clapping hands.

Police trapped about 100 Mods in the car park. But 300 others charged the gates and freed them. Soon after that, raging Mods swarmed along Margate's High-street.

Five youths burst into a cafe, swept food on to the floor, grabbed a chair and stormed out.

Then the Mods set about

breaking windows of shops, pubs, houses and flats.

Later, the rival gangs again faced each other on the crowded beach, but there were only isolated outbreaks of fighting.

Late last night, one group of youths set fire to a pile of deckchairs on the beach, then sang and danced around the bonfire.

A twelve-strong squad of policemen surrounded the youths. Some officers questioned the youngsters,

MIRROR REPORTER

while others put out the fire with sand.

At Brighton last night, hundreds of Mods roamed the sea front hunting for Rockers and breaking windows.

Practically all of Brighton's police force was on duty and more than 100 officers rushed to the seafront cinema where gangs of Mods were attacking a dozen Rockers.

The Rockers, bruised and shaken, escaped on their motor bikes.

Girls behind the Wild Ones— Page 4. Charge of the Mods at Margate—Centre Pages.

BLACK EYE A constable with a black eye and a sergeant who has lost his helmet carry a youth away to a police car. —*Picture by Mirror cameraman Alisdair Macdonald.*

THE GIRLS FIGHT IT OUT A girl Mod and a girl Rocker stage a hair-pulling battle outside Margate Station, while their friends stand looking on. The fight lasted about three minutes, with the girls rolling over and over on the ground.

Daily Mirror, *front page, 18 May 1964: headline 'Wild Ones "Beat Up" Margate'*

receive the full vent of front-page outrage in the national press. The media spoke of a 'day of terror', of youngsters who had beaten up an entire town; of a community invaded by a mob 'hell-bent on destruction'. The youths were presented as being engaged in a confrontation between two easily recognizable rival gangs. They were described as affluent young people who deliberately caused trouble by acting aggressively towards local residents and by destroying a great deal of public property.

Cohen's research, however, found no evidence of any structured gangs. He showed that, even at the time, the groups were not polarized within a Mod–Rocker distinction. Rivalries were more likely to have been built around regional identities. Motorbike or scooter owners were a minority. The young were not particularly affluent – in the main being unskilled or semi-skilled manual workers. Above all, Cohen argued, the total amount of serious violence and vandalism was minimal. The typical offence throughout was not assault or malicious damage, but threatening behaviour. A few days after the event, a journalist was forced to admit that the affair had been 'a little over-reported' (Cohen, 1973b, p.31).

By then, though, the media reaction had set in train a series of interrelated responses. First, it initiated a wider public concern that obliged the police to step up their surveillance. The result was more frequent arrests, court cases and heavy fines, which appeared to confirm the validity of the initial media reaction. Second, by emphasizing the antagonism between two groups, and their stylistic differences, the youths were encouraged to place themselves in one of the opposing camps. This polarization cemented the original image and produced more clashes in several other seaside resorts on subsequent bank holidays. Third, the continuing disturbances attracted more news coverage, increased police activity and furthered public concern.

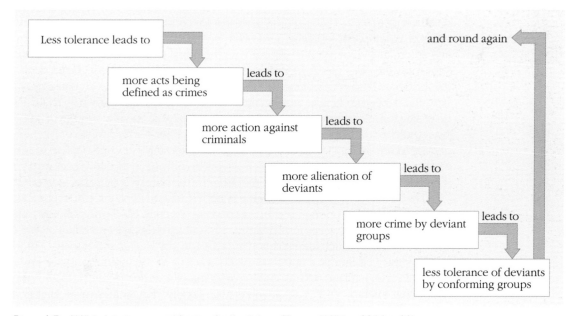

Figure 1.7 Wilkins' deviancy amplification feedback loop (Source: Wilkins, 1964, p.90)

deviancy amplification

Wilkins's model demonstrates how a deviancy amplification spiral can be set in motion (see Figure 1.7). The media's distortion of the initial events in 1964 resulted in an amplification of youthful deviance both in perceived *and* real terms. Youths began to identify with the label attached to them and as a result believed themselves to be more deviant and separate from the rest of society. They had been singled out as society's 'folk devils' and acted out that role accordingly in subsequent years.

The moral panic thesis not only helps us to identify instances of media exaggeration and distortion, but also maintains that selective reporting and police targeting can *create* crime waves and social problems. The media can stir up public indignation and engineer concern about certain types of behaviour even when there is nothing new about that behaviour or when its real threat is minimal. The press can play a role in orchestrating the concern they have helped to create and, through a process of 'repetitive retribution', they are also capable of making a significant impact on major policy decisions (Sanders and Lyon, 1995).

Cohen (1973b) also addressed the question of why this process should have occurred at all in the 1960s. He argued that we need to place such reactions in their socio-historical context. The mid-1960s was the time of a supposedly new permissiveness, the beginnings of a Swinging London, a rise in working-class youth spending power, the onslaught of a new consumerism, and the decline of traditional working-class communities. It was, above all, a time of rapid social change. For Cohen, the ensuing public anxiety and uncertainty were resolved by identifying certain social groups as scapegoats or 'folk devils'. They became the visual symbols of what was wrong with society. In the meantime, the more intractable and structural problems to do with relative deprivation and a restricted opportunity structure could be overlooked and passed by. The public gaze was fixed on the symptoms rather than on the causes of social unrest.

Throughout the 1970s, youth was to play a central part in this scapegoating and diversionary process. Hall *et al.* (1978) reused the concept of moral panic to identify a series of 'major social problems' to do with permissiveness, vandals, student radicals and so on, that culminated in 1972–3 with the moral panic of 'mugging'. Hall *et al.* show how the news media, working with images from the New York ghetto, defined the incidence of street robberies by youth in Britain's inner cities as an outbreak of a new and dangerous kind of violent crime. What was previously known as 'snatching' or 'getting rolled' was now redefined as 'mugging'. Hall *et al.* trace the way this definition was employed to justify, not only a new category of crime, but also punitive sentencing and the fostering of an image of a generalized breakdown of law and order in society. Furthermore, as the panic developed, mugging became defined almost exclusively as a problem with black youth, who in turn became the primary folk devils.

The notion of moral panic is central to both studies in explaining how particular sections of youth (working-class/black) become identified as worthy of police and judicial attention. However, in adopting a conflict-based definition of criminalization, the implications of such identification are extended by Hall *et al.* For them, a moral panic is the first link in a spiral of events leading to the maintenance of law in society by a legitimized rule through coercion and the general exercise of authority. While that interactionist position refers to a 'society' that creates rules, Hall *et al.* locate moral panic in terms of a 'crisis of hegemony' and of a 'state' that has the power to criminalize. The re-defining of the historically recurring event of street crime as a mugging created the *impression* of a crime wave and provided government with the justification to introduce repressive legislation which ultimately came to affect the quality of life of the vast majority of the population.

Extract 1.3 Scraton and Chadwick: 'The politics of criminalization'

Criminalization, the application of the criminal label to an identifiable social category, is dependent on *how* certain acts are labelled and on *who* has the power to label, and is directly limited to the political economy of marginalization. The power to criminalize is not derived necessarily in consensus politics but it carries with it the ideologies associated with marginalization and it is within these portrayals that certain actions are named, contained and regulated. This is a powerful process because it mobilizes popular approval and legitimacy in support of powerful interests within the state. As Hillyard's (1987) discussion of Northern Ireland illustrates clearly, public support is more likely to be achieved for state intervention against 'criminal' acts than for the repression or suppression of a 'political' cause. Further, even where no purposeful political intention is involved, the process of criminalization can divert attention from the social or political dynamics of a movement and specify its 'criminal' potential. If black youth is portrayed exclusively as 'muggers' (Hall *et al.*, 1978) there will be less tolerance of organized campaigns which emphasize that they have legitimate political and economic grievances (Gilroy, 1987). The marginalization of women who campaign for rights or for peace and the questioning of their sexuality is a further example of the process by which meaningful and informed political action can be undermined, de-legitimized and criminalized (Chadwick and Little, 1987; Young, 1990). Fundamental to the criminalization thesis is the proposition that while political motives are downplayed, the degree of *violence* involved is emphasized. In industrial relations, for example, it is the violence of the pickets which is pinpointed (Scraton and Thomas, 1985; Fine and Millar, 1985; Beynon, 1985), rather than the importance, for the success of a strike, of preventing supplies getting through to a factory. The preoccupation with the 'violence' of political opposition makes it easier to mobilize popular support for measures of containment.

In many of these examples, 'criminalization' is a process which has been employed to underpin the repressive or control functions of the state. ... Married to the process of marginalization, through which identifiable groups systematically and structurally become peripheral to the core relations of the political economy, criminalization offers a strong analytical construct. Taken together these theses provide the foundations to critical analyses of the state, the rule of law and social conflict in advanced capitalist society.

References

Beynon, H. (1985) *Digging Deeper: Issues in the Miners' Strike*, London, Verso.

Chadwick, K. and Little, C. (1987) 'The criminalization of women', in Scraton (1987).

Fine, B. and Millar, R. (eds) (1985) *Policing the Miners' Strike*, London, Lawrence and Wishart.

Gilroy, P. (1987) *There Ain't No Black in the Union Jack*, London, Hutchinson.

Hall, S. *et al.* (1978) *Policing the Crisis*, London, Macmillan.

Hillyard, P. (1987) 'The normalization of special powers: from Northern Ireland to Britain', in Scraton (1987).

Scraton, P. (ed.) (1987) *Law, Order and the Authoritarian State*, Milton Keynes, Open University Press.

Scraton, P. and Thomas, P. (1985) *The State v The People: Lessons from the Coal Dispute* (*Journal of Law and Society*, special issue), Oxford, Blackwell.

Young, A. (1990) *Femininity in Dissent*, London, Routledge.

(Scraton and Chadwick, 1991, pp.172–3)

For example, as was evident by the late 1970s, the enunciation of authoritarian populist policies, if repeated often enough, comes to form the terrain of any debate concerned with issues of law and order. As (Hall, 1978, p.34) succinctly put it in writing about football hooliganism: 'the tendency is increased to deal with any problem, first by simplifying its causes, second by stigmatising those involved, third by whipping up public feeling and fourth by stamping hard on it from above'. Moral panics thus form part of a sensitizing and legitimizing process for solidifying moral boundaries, identifying 'enemies within', strengthening the powers of state control and enabling law and order to be promoted without cognizance of the social divisions and conflicts that produce deviance and political dissent. For Sim *et al.* (1987, p.60) this process reached its apogee in the Thatcher administration of the 1980s with new forms of surveillance, regulation and control in all areas of social policy, welfare and criminal justice. Industrial conflicts, feminist activism, the peace movement and all manner of social protest and alternative life-styles became subject to a process of criminalization. In many respects, political dissent was marginalized and redefined as criminal activity (see Extract 1.3).

However, by the mid-1980s, the theoretical integrity of the concept of moral panic came to be seriously questioned. By then, the term was widely used by the media as a means through which daily events could be sensationalized and brought to public attention: 'moral panic' became a normalized rhetoric, rather than an exceptional, emergency intervention. McRobbie and Thornton (1995) are persuasive in their argument that moral panic, far from being an unwanted label attached to certain youth cultural pursuits, became something to be actively pursued. In the late 1980s, the global domination of acid-house and rave music rested in no small part on record-company and consumer-industry marketing of a new 'dangerous' subcultural activity. Moreover, the assumption of the original moral panic thesis that the demonizing of certain groups actively placed them further outside of society must be examined in the light of the way in which such groups increasingly gained access to the news media and created their own niche media for promotional purposes. The growing prevalence of lobbies, pressure groups and commercial interests shifted the concern about isolated moral panics into an 'endless debate' about deviance, difference and national identity (McRobbie and Thornton 1995, pp.571–3). As Figure 1.8 shows, by the 1990s, moral panics were more likely to be continually contested categories rather than automatically received as evidence of a growing moral malaise.

left realism

From a criminological point of view, a substantive critical evaluation of the moral panic thesis has also come from a left-realist perspective in understanding crime and deviance. This maintains that it is both unrealistic and naively idealist to suggest that the problem of, say, youth disorder or street crime is merely a problem of miscategorization and concomitant moral panics (**Young, 1986**). However exaggerated and distorted the images of crime are in the media, the *reality* of crime can be, and often is, one of human suffering and disaster. As such, it needs to be 'taken seriously' and not simply dismissed as a media construction. So, while the left-realist position might sympathize with Cohen's notion of crime as a metaphor for wider social change, it maintains that it is a metaphor rooted in reality. That 'reality' is taken to be a growing public fear of crime, a recognition that crime is a problem, and an acknowledgement of the damaging effects of crime, particularly within inner-city and other working-class communities. To this extent, left realism moves away from notions of social construction and back to definitions of crime as violations of legal codes. Lea and Young (1984) maintain that certain crimes, such as the high rate of burglaries, sexual and racial attacks, are part of the 'real problems' facing working-class neighbourhoods. It is thus myopic and politically naive to dismiss crime as a ruling-class mystification, or as something that is simply 'created' by the state and its agencies. However, as a result, left realism deliberately shifts the focus

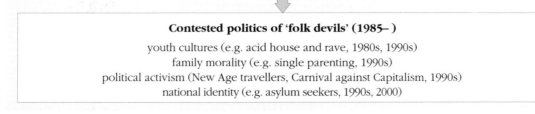

Discrete moral panics (1955–65)

Teddy Boys, 1950s
Mods and Rockers, early 1960s

More diffuse moral panics (1966–70)

permissiveness; drugs; pornography; student radicalism

youth violence; skinheads; football hooligans

'radical' trade unionism

Generalized climate of hostility to 'marginal' groups and racial minorities (1971–)

street crime (e.g. mugging, early 1970s; joyriders, early 1990s)
political violence (e.g. IRA, 1970s, 1980s)
trade union militancy (e.g. 'red scare', 1974; miners' strikes, 1974, 1985)
welfare liberalism (e.g. social security 'scroungers', 1974)
drugs (e.g. glue-sniffing, 1982; heroin, 1985; crack, 1992)
family morality (e.g. abortion, 1980; homosexuality, 1986; child abuse, 1974, 1987; satanic abuse, 1990;
video nasties, 1993)
black youth (e.g. inner-city disturbances, 1980, 1981, 1985)
sub-cultures (e.g. punk, 1976; football hooligans, 1970s, 1980s, 2000)
feminism (e.g. Greenham Common protests, 1980)
national identity (e.g. immigration, 1970s)

Contested politics of 'folk devils' (1985–)

youth cultures (e.g. acid house and rave, 1980s, 1990s)
family morality (e.g. single parenting, 1990s)
political activism (New Age travellers, Carnival against Capitalism, 1990s)
national identity (e.g. asylum seekers, 1990s, 2000)

Figure 1.8   A chronology of moral panics (Source: based on Muncie, 1987, p.45)

away from developing analyses of power, law, the state and corporate crime towards establishing an accurate policy-orientated working-class victimology.

The problem, of course, is in charting a path which neither adopts a romanticist and idealist position (which might argue that crime is illusory and that the 'real' victim is the offender) nor falls into a position that celebrates moral panic and sees state violence as ubiquitous. Indeed, Gilroy (1987) has accused left realism of 'accepting' state-generated definitions of crime (particularly in relation to the question of race) and official pictures of the extent and seriousness of crime rates, and, by doing so, of implicitly providing more armour for an authoritarian law-and-order position (Sim *et al.*, 1987, pp.39–46). A key issue remains, though: while it may be morally acceptable (for some) to cite concern about single parenting and youthful exuberance as instances of moral panic, can the same be said of racial violence, rape and domestic violence? (This is discussed in more depth in Chapter 5.)

4.3   Risk and fear of crime

The 1982 British Crime Survey was the first UK survey to suggest that *fear* of crime was as great a problem as crime itself. The survey asked: 'What sorts of crime do you worry about most?' The percentages of 'worried' respondents mentioning particular types of crime were: vehicle theft, 1 per cent, vandalism, 4 per cent, assault, 16 per cent, sexual attacks, 25 per cent, mugging, 34 per cent and burglary, 44 per cent. Surprisingly, fear of crime appears to have an inverse relationship with statistical occurrence. In other words, according to the BCS, people are concerned most about those crimes which they are *least likely to experience*. Those who felt least safe were notably women, older people and those living in the inner cities. People in manual occupations were consistently more fearful than those in non-manual, and those living alone more than those living with others (Hough and Mayhew, 1983, p.23). The BCS data showed, however, that, frequently, it was those who felt most unsafe who had the lowest risk of becoming victims. Conversely, young men expressed the least fear, yet young, working-class inner-city males were the most likely to be victimized. The discrepancy was marked for fear and actual risk of 'street crime' (as we see in Table 1.4 below).

fear and risk

Table 1.4   Fear and risk of street crime

		Percentage feeling very 'unsafe'	Percentage of victims of 'street crime'
Men			
	16–30	1	7.7
	31–60	4	1.6
	61+	7	0.6
Women			
	16–30	16	2.8
	31–60	35	1.4
	61+	37	1.2

Note: percentages represent responses to the question: 'How safe do you feel walking alone in this area after dark?' Weighted data; unweighted $n = 10,905$.

Source: Hough and Mayhew, 1983, Table 5, p.25

The 1984 BCS similarly concluded that people tend to hold exaggerated estimates of the risks of becoming victims of such crimes as burglary, mugging and rape. One in nine women under 30, for instance, thought it likely or fairly likely that they would be raped in the next year; one in six people thought it likely they would be mugged; 53 per cent believed burglary to be the most prevalent crime in their area (Hough and Mayhew, 1985, p.38). However, most people were found to have an accurate idea of the *relative* risks of some crime. For example, while concern consistently outweighed occurrence, those most at risk of burglary – people living in multiracial areas and poor council estates – reported the highest levels of anxiety. On the other hand, respondents living in rural and high-income areas had both the lowest occurrence and lowest fear of property crime.

Such data raise the issue of irrational/rational fears and the degree to which public concern and policy should be analysed as panic or as reasonable responses to actual problems. The left-realist position has maintained that public experience of crime, particularly in the inner city, has generated a rational and well-founded fear. Young, for example, argued that: 'ascribing irrationality to women is based on ignoring that much crime against women, such as domestic violence, is concealed in the official figures, that women are less tolerant of violence and that they experience harassment on a level unknown to most men' (Young, 1992, p.50). Such analysis is, in the main, based on data gathered from local crime surveys. While the first BCS was only able to report one attempted rape nationally, the locally based Islington Crime Survey found that 20 per cent of women knew someone who had been sexually assaulted in the previous 12 months (Jones *et al.*, 1986). This has been confirmed by much sexual-violence victimization research. A study in Leeds revealed that 59 per cent of women had experienced some form of sexual violence in the previous year; while a study in Wandsworth, London, found the rate to be as high as 76 per cent (Hanmer and Saunders, 1984; Radford, 1987). In this respect, the BCS findings – that a third of women admitted not going out at night due to fear of crime – cannot be explained away as 'irrational'. Similarly, the fear expressed by older people may well be rational in reflecting their relative physical disadvantage and vulnerability. The lack of fear expressed by young males may, in any event, simply reflect a masculine bravado prevalent in a male-defined society. Crawford *et al.* (1990) maintain that fear does indeed accord to people's real-life circumstances. Such issues are complicated further because the data supplied by any victim survey rest crucially on the precise wording of the questions asked and the way in which particular offences are categorized.

Fear cannot, however, be simply accounted for with reference to the likelihood of actual victimization. Rather, it may be generated by any number of personal, cultural or environmental factors. Box *et al.* (1988), for example, argue that 'incivilities' such as loud parties, 'street corner' rowdyism, boarded-up houses, subway graffiti, and broken windows may all signify a neighbourhood that is disorderly and threatening. They conclude that fear depends on an interactive complex of vulnerability, environmental conditions, personal knowledge of crime, confidence (or lack of) in the police, perceptions of personal risk and offence seriousness. For Taylor (1999), 'fear of crime' is but one element of a generalized reality of political, cultural and economic insecurity that has come to characterize modern free market societies. Homeless and other excluded populations are increasingly perceived as the 'other' and are set apart through the development of 'fortress' and 'drawbridge' mentalities. Fear, it is argued, is extraneous, generated by factors other than risk of crime *per se*. Not least of these is the symbolic purchase of certain people, spaces and places as inherently dangerous (this is examined further in Chapter 4).

Attempts to measure the impact of the mass media in promoting fear have generally found that readers of those newspapers that report crime in the most dramatic and salient fashion also have the highest levels of fear of crime. Moreover, the majority of people attribute their knowledge of the risk of crime to information received from television and press reports (Williams and Dickinson, 1993; Surette, 1998). Some strong parallels have also been found between media biases and public misperceptions. Using data from the 1996 British Crime Survey, Hough and Roberts (1998) found that, while the national recorded crime rate *fell* by 8 per cent between 1993 and 1996, 96 per cent of the public believed rates to have risen or stayed the same. When asked how much crime involves violence, 78 per cent of those surveyed replied 30 per cent or more – Home Office statistics record it at just 6 per cent. Conversely, substantial underestimates were routinely made about the extent to which the courts use custodial sentences for convicted offenders. A view, not that dissimilar to that propagated by most of the media, emerges from public perceptions of a continually spiralling crime rate and an over-lenient criminal justice system. Neither could be further from the truth. Indeed, this study implicates the media directly for such public misunderstanding: 'media news values militate against balanced coverage. Erratic court sentences make news and sensible ones do not. As a result large segments of the population are exposed to a steady stream of unrepresentative stories about sentencing incompetence' (Hough and Roberts, 1998, p.x, and see *The Guardian*, 6 January 1998 reproduced opposite). Nevertheless, a left-realist perspective maintains that 'in inner city areas mass media coverage of crime tends to reinforce what people already know', and that 'crime is a product of inner city reality and government policy, not a figment of some editor's imagination' (Crawford *et al.*, 1990, pp.76–7) (see Extract 1.4 below).

Extract 1.4 Young: 'Crime really is a problem'

Crime is not an activity of latter day Robin Hoods – the vast majority of working-class crime is directed within the working class. It is intra-class *not* inter-class in its nature. Similarly, despite the mass media predilection for focusing on inter-racial crime, it is overwhelmingly intra-racial. Crimes of violence, for example, are by and large one poor person hitting another poor person – and in almost half of these instances it is a man hitting his wife or lover.

This is not to deny the impact of crimes of the powerful or indeed of the social problems created by capitalism which are perfectly legal. Rather, left realism notes that the working class is a victim of crime from all directions. It notes that the more vulnerable a person is economically and socially the more likely it is that *both* working-class and white-collar crime will occur against them; that one sort of crime tends to compound another, as does one social problem another. Furthermore, it notes that crime is a potent symbol of the anti-social nature of capitalism and is the most immediate way in which people experience other problems, such as unemployment or competitive individualism.

Realism starts from problems as people experience them. It takes seriously the complaints of women [with regard to] the dangers of being in public places at night, it takes note of the fears of the elderly with regard to burglary, it acknowledges the widespread occurrence of domestic violence and racist attacks. It does not ignore the fears of the vulnerable nor recontextualize them out of existence by putting them into a perspective which abounds with abstractions such as the 'average citizen' bereft of class or gender. It is only too aware of the systematic concealment and ignorance of crimes against the least powerful. Yet it does not take these fears at face value – it pinpoints their rational kernel but it is also aware of the forces towards irrationality.

Realism is not empiricism. Crime and deviance are prime sites of moral anxiety and tension in a society which is fraught with real inequalities and injustices. Criminals can quite easily become folk devils onto which are projected such feelings of unfairness. But there is a rational core to the fear of crime just as there is a rational core to the anxieties which distort it. Realism argues with popular consciousness in its attempts to separate out reality from fantasy. But it does not deny that crime is a problem. Indeed, if there were no rational core the media would have no power of leverage to the public consciousness. Crime becomes a metaphor but it is a metaphor rooted in reality.

(Young, 1986, pp.23–4)

Crime 'crisis' based on myth

Ministers accused of playing to gallery

By Alan Travis, Home Affairs Editor

Public ignorance about law and order is widespread and lies at the heart of a crisis of confidence in Britain's courts and judges, according to a Home Office study published yesterday.

The authoritative British Crime Survey says that politicians have been wrong to 'play to the gallery' by basing their criminal justice policies during the 1990s on jailing more and more people to feed the public's mistaken appetite for tougher punishments.

'These findings should warn politicians away from populist responses to crime. They show that a populist sentencing policy will not actually achieve much in the long run. It will not actually change public perceptions,' said the report's co-author, Professor Michael Hough.

The key findings from the BCS's Attitudes to Punishment study show that, despite more than five years of 'prison works' and 'get tough' policies from the former Conservative Home Secretary Michael Howard, there still exists a crisis of public confidence in the courts that needs tackling urgently.

The study discloses for the first time the scale of public ignorance on this key issue. It says the majority of the public is wrong to believe that recorded crime is rising dramatically, that a large proportion of crime is violent, and that judges are handing out sentences which are far too lenient.

The BCS study, based on interviews with more than 16,000 people in 1996, shows that the public seriously underestimates just how severe the courts are when it comes to sending people to prison.

It says this ignorance of crime and sentencing is contributing to widespread public cynicism about law and order. The problem is compounded by the absence of easily accessible figures showing the 'going rate' for any particular crime.

'Those who were most likely to underestimate the courts' use of imprisonment had lower educational attainment than others, were likely to be older and were more likely to read the tabloid newspapers,' says the survey.

'Women were more likely than men to underestimate the proportion of convicted rapists sent to prison, and owner-occupiers more likely than others to underestimate the use of imprisonment for burglars.'

The report says that when asked about sentencing in general people tend to think of the worst kind of offenders but when presented with the facts of an actual case tend to be far less punitive.

The study blames the media for such a large public misunderstanding of what goes on in the courts.

'News values mitigate against balanced coverage,' it says. 'Erratic court sentences make news; sensible ones do not. As a result large parts of the population are exposed to a steady stream of misleading stories about sentencing incompetence.'

However, the authors of the survey say part of the solution lies in the hands of the judges and the rest of the criminal justice system.

They say that the public has a very jaundiced view of judges, with more than a third believing they do a poor job. This compares with much higher levels of confidence in the police, the prison service and magistrates.

The report scathingly concludes that judges may not be unique in continuing to use 18th-century trappings of pomp and ritual to sustain their authority, but that it is about time they started using late 20th-century communication techniques to let the public know about sentencing practice if they are to combat public cynicism.

The Home Secretary, Jack Straw, said he intended that new sentencing guidelines would be published by the Court of Appeal for all the main offences but that everybody, including politicians, judges, lawyers and the media, had a responsibility to present a more accurate picture of crime.

He said newspapers and television had an understandable role in highlighting vivid crimes but that those offences were only a small proportion of the total.

The Home Office would consult the media and judges over a new public awareness campaign.

'Only when crime and the criminal justice system is presented in the correct context will the public begin to regain confidence in the justice it delivers,' he said.

Mr Straw added that he had already proposed that the courts should spell out exactly how long criminals would spend behind bars at the time when they are sentenced.

Crime facts and fiction

- Recorded crime has fallen by 8 per cent in recent years. Some 75 per cent of people think it is going up.
- Only 6 per cent of crimes are violent or sexual. Most people think violent crime accounts for more than one-third of all crimes.
- The British murder rate is going down. There were 681 homicides in 1996 – 10 per cent fewer than in 1995.
- Convicted criminals are increasingly likely to be sent to jail: 79,100 were imprisoned in 1995, compared with 58,400 in 1993.
- Serious offenders are jailed. More than 90 per cent of convicted robbers and 97 per cent of rapists go to prison.
- Young children are no more likely to be killed by a stranger than they were in the past. Seven children a year have been killed over the past 20 years.
- Women are three times less likely than men to be attacked by a stranger.
- The elderly are at less risk from violent crime than the young. Those aged under 29 are 13 times more likely to be mugged than a pensioner.
- Forty per cent of men in Britain have a criminal record for a non-motoring offence by the time they reach the age of 40.

(*The Guardian*, 6 January 1998)

The issue of media effects on perceptions of crime remains controversial. Increasingly, it is acknowledged that media representations are unlikely to be received passively, but rather interpreted by an 'active audience' as but one element in their lived experience (Livingstone, 1996; Ericson, 1991; Roshier, 1973). But that 'active audience', as Osborne (1995) reminds us, increasingly lives in a media-saturated world. Trying to isolate a *specific* media effect may be particularly problematic when the boundaries between drama and reality are becoming more and more blurred and when the parameters of 'lived experience' are harder to define. As such, the exact extent to which news media actually affect attitudes, beliefs and policies is likely to remain unresolved (Surette, 1998).

The questions of how fear is constituted, experienced and constructed also remain controversial. Sparks (1992), for example, questions the left-realist assertion that fear of crime, no matter the circumstances, is always rational and should be taken seriously. The ability of survey respondents to estimate risk, he argues, is more likely to be governed by 'uncertainty' than any 'known probabilities'. The measurements of risk and fear via surveys are likely to be complex and uneven given the 'inherent scope for discrepancy between what criminal events mean at the moment of their commission and what they stand for once they have entered the widening circles of punishment, retribution, reporting, rhetoric and rebuttal, election platforms and the multitude of communicative exchanges which compose the public sphere' (Sparks, 1992, pp.13–14). Fear of crime, as a mode of perception, then, may not necessarily be either rational or irrational, but reflective of a range of diffuse anxieties about one's position and identity in the world. In other words, the issue of fear always involves the problems of representation, interpretation and meaning. While victims of crime may be more fearful as a result of direct experience, the vast majority of the public's contact with crime is indirect and 'learnt' through a variety of 'readings' of neighbourhood conditions, media information, personal conversations, and unique biographies. Moreover, the issue is clouded through being construed in a partial and limiting fashion. Hollway and Jefferson (1997, p.264) suggest that 'fear of crime' can hold a sense of reassurance. It continually reconstitutes the criminal as knowable (local kids), crime prevention as a personal decision and actionable (lock all doors), and criminality as readily identifiable (the 'other', not oneself). The 'fear of crime thesis' also remains most developed in relation to certain forms of street crime. It concentrates more on unpredictable violence than on those forms which are normalized as in domestic violence, or where victimization is indirect and dispersed, as in corporate crime (Walklate, 1995, p.78; Downes, 1988, p.182).

The key issue thus may not be whether 'fear of crime' has any rational basis, but rather how far its emotiveness as a topic, and the general fascination the public holds for 'all things criminal', can be (or is) used for ulterior, ideological and political motives.

ACTIVITY 1.4

Look back over the preceding discussion in sections 3 and 4 and Extracts 1.3 and 1.4, and draw up a list of the relative strengths and weaknesses of the competing accounts of crime offered by the moral panic and the left-realist positions. In particular, you should take note of how each offers a different *definition* of crime, and focuses its analysis on (or ignores) different aspects of the 'crime problem'.

5 Conclusion: crime as a problem and the problem of 'crime'

This chapter has explored the complexities involved not only in what can and should be considered as crime, but also in measurements and assessments of its extent and seriousness. There are no easy answers to be gained. We may be tempted to conclude that, given the high profile of crime, as news and as drama, all we are dealing with is a never-ending and self-fulfilling series of social and organizational constructions. Yet few who have been the victims of abuse, personal loss or violent attack are likely to be reassured by such an argument. While some advocates of a moral panic position might campaign for limitations in recourse to the criminal law in dealing with certain social harms, others argue for an extension of the law's reach to afford some protection to systematically oppressed populations (for example racial violence, domestic violence and homophobic violence). Arguments for decriminalization stand uneasily against those that advocate a broadening of definitions of crime. For the former, 'crime' acts to simplify and mystify complex social conflicts; for the latter, the delineation of certain practices as 'crime' remains one of the few ways in which otherwise ignored social problems can achieve social visibility and public acknowledgement.

Part of the problem in establishing the reality of crime does seem to lie in the concept of 'crime' itself. It implies a unity to what are a vast array of diverse behaviours, events and legal sanctions. Rather, this chapter has shown how the elusive nature of our subject matter can only begin to be captured by subjecting it to a series of *deconstructions* – revealing how the concept becomes active only through the variable meanings attached to it in specific political and socio-historical contexts and through the diverse 'voices' of the media, civil servants, the public, criminal justice professionals, politicians, victims and pressure groups. 'Crime' clearly takes on different meanings for different social audiences. It is frequently depicted as a 'problem', yet it is also one of the most enduring and 'normalized' aspects of modern society. Its 'reality' is assumed, but its existence depends upon the prior formulation of criminal law. As a result, it might also be tempting to abandon use of the concept altogether. It is of such emotional charge and historical variance to have little analytical validity. Yet such a position would leave us peculiarly stranded and unable to enter into what remains, whether we are aware of it or not, a recurrent and contested issue in our everyday lives. Nevertheless, as a governing principle, we should refer not to '*the* crime problem' singular, but to a diverse and complex array of 'crimes' and harms. As De Haan argues:

> disputes about the proper use of the concept of crime will be endless precisely because contending positions can be sustained by perfectly respectable arguments and evidence. This does not mean falling into a total and undiscriminating relativism, as good reasons can always be given for the claim that one interpretation of the concept enables one to see further and deeper than another.
>
> (De Haan, 1990, p.154)

Accordingly, what this chapter advocates is a critical *reconstruction* of crime – by revealing how 'crime' is not as simple a concept as might be first presumed; that it has numerous contexts and consequences; and that it remains a site of legal, political and moral contestation. By exploring these ideas in more detail, we might be better placed to make some measured judgement, not only of 'the problem of crime', but of the nature of a social order which, while consistently producing and reproducing that problem, remains selective and partial in delineating which social harms are to be deemed 'criminal' and which are not.

Review questions

- Why is crime a contested concept?
- Does a concept of 'social harm' hold any advantage over that of 'crime'?
- What can be learnt about crime by studying crime statistics?
- What does the study of crime tell us about the nature of social order?
- To what extent do the media inform and misinform us about the nature and extent of crime?

Further reading

There are a growing number but still relatively few texts which begin by problematizing the concept of 'crime' itself. The American textbooks by Quinney and Wildeman (1977) and Beirne and Messerschmidt (1999) do, however, provide a critical introduction, as do Lacey *et al.* (1990) on the concept of 'criminal law'. The competing definitions offered by Tappan (1947), **Becker (1963)** and **Chambliss (1975)** continue to offer some valuable insights. Regularly updated information on crime and criminal justice can be found on the Home Office website at http://www.homeoffice.gov.uk. A thorough account of the production and interpretation of crime data is provided by Coleman and Moynihan (1996) and Maguire (1997). A similar job is done on crime and the media by Schlesinger and Tumber (1994) and Surette (1998). Issues surrounding women and crime are introduced in Heidensohn (1985) and the gender and crime debate is reviewed in Walklate (1995). **Box (1983)** and Pearson (1983) still provide some of the most accessible means through which many of our taken-for-granted images of crime can be jolted out of their 'common-sense' and nostalgic complacency.

References

Anderson, S., Kinsey, R., Loader, I. and Smith, C. (1994) *Cautionary Tales: Young People, Crime and Policing in Edinburgh*, Aldershot, Avebury.

Audit Commission (1999) *Safety in Numbers: Promoting Community Safety*, London, Audit Commission.

Becker, H. (1963) *Outsiders: Studies in the Sociology of Deviance*, New York, Free Press. (Extract reprinted as 'Outsiders' in Muncie *et al.*, 1996.)

Beirne, P. and Messerschmidt, J. (1999) *Criminology*, 3rd edn, Boulder Co., Westview.

Bottomley, K. and Pease, K. (1986) *Crime and Punishment: Interpreting the Data*, Milton Keynes, Open University Press.

Box, S. (1981) *Deviance, Reality and Society*, 2nd edn, London, Holt, Rinehart and Winston.

Box, S. (1983) *Power, Crime and Mystification*, London, Tavistock. (Extract reprinted as 'Crime, power and ideological mystification' in Muncie *et al.*, 1996.)

Box, S., Hale, C. and Andrews, G. (1988) 'Explaining fear of crime', *British Journal of Criminology*, vol.28, no.3, pp.340–56.

Braithwaite, J. (1989) *Crime, Shame and Reintegration*, Cambridge and New York, Cambridge University Press. (Extract reprinted as 'Reintegrative shaming' in Muncie *et al.*, 1996.)

Carson, W.G. (1981) *The Other Price of British Oil*, Oxford, Martin Robertson.

Chambliss, W.J. (1964) 'A sociological analysis of the law of vagrancy', *Social Problems*, no.12, pp.67–77.

Chambliss, W.J. (1969) *Crime and the Legal Process*, New York, McGraw-Hill.

Chambliss, W.J. (1975) 'Toward a political economy of crime', *Theory and Society*, vol.2, pp.149–70. (Extract reprinted in Muncie *et al.*, 1996.)

Chambliss, W.J. (1989) 'State organised crime', *Criminology*, vol.27, no.2, pp.183–208.

Chambliss, W.J. (1999) *Power, Politics and Crime*, Boulder, Colorado, Westview.

Chibnall, S. (1977) *Law and Order News*, London, Tavistock.

Christie, N. (1993) *Crime Control as Industry*, London, Routledge.

Cohen, S. (1973a) 'The failures of criminology', *The Listener*, 8 November.

Cohen, S. (1973b) *Folk Devils and Moral Panics: The Creation of the Mods and Rockers*, London, Paladin.

Cohen, S. (1993) 'Human rights and crimes of the state: the culture of denial', *Australian and New Zealand Journal of Criminology*, vol.26, no.1, pp.98–114. (Extract reprinted in Muncie *et al.*, 1996.)

Coleman, C. and Moynihan, J. (1996) *Understanding Crime Data*, Buckingham, Open University Press.

Cook, D. (1989) *Rich Law; Poor Law*, Buckingham, Open University Press.

Crawford, A., Jones, T., Woodhouse, T. and Young, J. (1990) *Second Islington Crime Survey*, Middlesex Polytechnic.

Davis, J. (1952) 'Crime news in Colorado newspapers', *American Journal of Sociology*, vol.57, pp.325–30.

De Haan, W. (1990) *The Politics of Redress*, London, Unwin Hyman.

De Haan, W. (1991) 'Abolitionism and crime control: a contradiction in terms', in Stenson and Cowell (1991). (Extract reprinted as 'Abolitionism and crime control' in Muncie *et al.*, 1996.)

Ditton, J. (1977) *Part-Time Crime*, London, Macmillan.

Ditton, J. (1979) *Contrology: Beyond the New Criminology*, London, Macmillan.

Ditton, J. and Duffy, J. (1983) 'Bias in the newspaper reporting of crime news', *British Journal of Criminology*, vol.23, no.2, pp.159–65.

Downes, D. (1988) 'Crime and social control in Britain', *British Journal of Criminology*, vol.28, no.2, pp.45–57.

Ericson, R.V. (1991) 'Mass media, crime, law and justice', *British Journal of Criminology*, vol.31, no.3, pp.219–49.

Fitzgerald, M. (1993) *Ethnic Minorities and the Criminal Justice System*, Royal Commission on Criminal Justice, Research Study no.20, London, HMSO.

Galliher, J.F. (1989) *Criminology: Human Rights, Criminal Law and Crime*, Englewood Cliffs, NJ, Prentice-Hall.

Gilroy, P. (1987) *There Ain't No Black in the Union Jack*, London, Hutchinson.

Graham, J. and Bowling, B. (1995) *Young People and Crime*, Home Office Research Study no.145, London, HMSO.

Hagan, J. (1985) *Modern Criminology*, New York, McGraw-Hill.

Hall, J. (1952) *Theft, Law and Society*, Indianapolis, IN, Bobs-Merrill.

Hall, S. (1978) 'The treatment of football hooliganism in the press', in Ingham, R. (ed.) *Football Hooliganism*, London, Inter-Action.

Hall, S., Clarke, J., Critcher, C., Jefferson, T. and Roberts, B. (1975) *Newsmaking and Crime*, Paper presented to NACRO Conference on Crime and the Media, Birmingham, Centre for Contemporary Cultural Studies, University of Birmingham.

Hall, S., Critcher, C., Jefferson, T., Clarke, J. and Roberts, B. (1978) *Policing the Crisis*, London, Macmillan.

Hanmer, J. and Saunders, S. (1984) *Well-Founded Fears*, London, Macmillan.

Heidensohn, F. (1985) *Women and Crime*, London, Macmillan.

Henry, S. (1978) *The Hidden Economy*, Oxford, Martin Robertson.

Henry, S. and Milovanovic, D. (1996) *Constitutive Criminology*, London, Sage.

Henry, S. and Lanier, M.M. (1998) 'The prism of crime: arguments for an "integrated definition of crime"', *Justice Quarterly*, vol.15, no.4, pp.609–27.

Hester, S. and Eglin, P. (1992) *A Sociology of Crime*, London, Routledge.

Hollway, W. and Jefferson, T. (1997) 'The Risk Society in an age of anxiety: situating fear of crime', *British Journal of Sociology*, vol.48, no.2, pp.255–66.

Home Office (2000) http://www.homeoffice.gov.uk [accessed 1 August 2000].

Home Office (1999) *Digest 4: Information on the Criminal Justice System in England and Wales*, Home Office Research and Statistics Department, London, HMSO.

Hood, R. (1993) *Race and Sentencing*, Oxford, Oxford University Press.

Hough, M. and Mayhew, P. (1983) *The British Crime Survey: First Report*, Home Office Research Study no.16, London, HMSO.

Hough, M. and Mayhew, P. (1985) *Taking Account of Crime: Findings from the Second British Crime Survey*, Home Office Research Study no.85, London, HMSO.

Hough, M. and Roberts, J. (1998) *Attitudes to Punishment*, Home Office Research Study no.179, London, HMSO.

Hudson, B. (1989) 'Discrimination and disparity', *New Community*, vol.16, no.1, pp.23–34.

Hulsman, L. (1986) 'Critical criminology and the concept of crime', *Contemporary Crises*, vol.10, no.1, pp.63–80. (Extract reprinted in Muncie *et al.*, 1996.)

Hutter, B. and Williams, G. (1981) *Controlling Women: The Normal and the Deviant*, London, Croom Helm.

Jones, T., Maclean, B. and Young, J. (1986) *The Islington Crime Survey*, Aldershot, Gower.

Jungar-Tas, J., Terlouw, G.-J., and Hein, M.W. (1994) *Delinquent Behaviour Among Young People in the Western World: First Results of the International Self Report Delinquency Study*, Amsterdam, Kugler.

Jupp, V., Davies, P. and Francis, P. (1999) 'The features of invisible crimes', in Davies, P., Francis, P. and Jupp, V. (eds) *Invisible Crimes*, Basingstoke, Macmillan.

Lacey, N., Wells, C. and Meure, D. (1990) *Reconstructing Criminal Law*, London, Weidenfeld and Nicolson.

Lea, J. and Young, J. (1984) *What Is To Be Done About Law and Order?*, Harmondsworth, Penguin.

Livingstone, S. (1996) 'On the continuing problem of media effects', in Curran, J. and Gurevitch, M. (eds), *Mass Media and Society*, London, Arnold.

Maguire, M. (1997) 'Crime statistics, patterns and trends: changing perceptions and their implications', in Maguire, M., Morgan, R. and Reiner, R., *The Oxford Handbook of Criminology*, 2nd edn, Oxford, Clarendon.

Marsh, H.L. (1991) 'A comparative analysis of crime coverage in newspapers in the United States and other countries from 1960 to 1989', *Journal of Criminal Justice*, vol.19, no.1, pp.67–79.

Mayhew, P. and Maung, N.A. (1992) *Surveying Crime: Findings from the 1992 British Crime Survey*, Home Office Research and Statistics Department, Research Findings no.2, London, HMSO.

Mayhew, P., Elliott, D. and Dowds, L. (1989) *The 1988 British Crime Survey*, Home Office Research Study no.111, London, HMSO.

Mayhew, P., Mirrlees-Black, C. and Maung, N.A. (1994) *Trends in Crime: Findings from the 1994 British Crime Survey*, Home Office Research and Statistics Department, Research Findings no.14, London, HMSO.

McLaughlin, E. and Murji, K. (2000) 'Re-reading all about it: news media coverage of racial violence', in May, M., Brunsden, E. and Page, R. (eds), *Social Problems in Social Policy*, Oxford, Blackwell.

McRobbie, A. and Thornton, S. (1995) 'Rethinking moral panic for multi-mediated social worlds', *British Journal of Sociology*, vol.46, no.4, pp.559–74.

Mead, G.H. (1934) *Mind, Self and Society*, Chicago, Chicago University Press.

Michael, J. and Adler, M. (1933) *Crime, Law and Social Science*, New York, Harcourt, Brace Jovanovich.

Mirrlees-Black, C., Budd, T., Partridge, S. and Mayhew, P. (1998) *The 1998 British Crime Survey*, Home Office Statistical Bulletin, issue 21/98, London, HMSO.

Muncie, J. (1987) 'Much ado about nothing? The sociology of moral panics', *Social Studies Review*, vol.3, no.2, pp.42–7.

Muncie, J. (1999) *Youth and Crime: A Critical Introduction*, London, Sage.

Muncie, J. (2000) 'Decriminalising criminology', in Lewis, G., Gewirtz, S. and Clarke, J. (eds) *Rethinking Social Policy*, London, Sage.

Muncie, J., McLaughlin, E. and Langan, M. (eds) (1996) *Criminological Perspectives: A Reader*, London, Sage in association with The Open University.

Murray, C. (1990) *The Emerging British Underclass*, London, Institute of Economic Affairs. (Extract reprinted as 'The Underclass' in Muncie *et al.*, 1996.)

Northern Ireland Office (1993) *Crime and the Community*, Belfast, HMSO.

Osborne, R. (1995) 'Crime and the media: from media studies to postmodernism', in Kidd-Hewitt, D. and Osborne, R. (eds) *Crime and the Media*, London, Pluto.

Pearce, F. (1976) *Crimes of the Powerful*, London, Pluto.

Pearson, G. (1983) *Hooligan: A History of Respectable Fears*, London, Macmillan.

Phillipson, M. (1971) *Sociological Aspects of Crime and Delinquency*, London, Routledge and Kegan Paul.

Quetelet, A. (1842) *A Treatise on Man*, Edinburgh, Chambers. (Extract reprinted as 'Of the development of the propensity to crime' in Muncie *et al.*, 1996.)

Quinney, R. (1970) *The Social Reality of Crime*, Boston, MA, Little Brown.

Quinney, R. and Wildeman, J. (1977) *The Problem of Crime*, 2nd edn, New York, Harper and Row.

Radford, J. (1987) 'Policing male violence', in Hanmer, J. and Maynard, M. (eds) *Women, Violence and Social Control*, London, Macmillan.

Radford, J. and Russell, D. (eds) (1992) *Femicide*, Buckingham, Open University Press.

Radzinowicz, I. and King, J. (1977) *The Growth of Crime*, London, Hamish Hamilton.

Reiner, R. (1997) 'Media made criminality: the representation of crime in the mass media', in Maguire, M., Morgan, R. and Reiner, R. (eds) *The Oxford Handbook of Criminology*, 2nd edn, Oxford, Clarendon.

Rohrer, R. (1982) 'Lost in the myths of crime', *New Statesman*, 22 January.

Roshier, B. (1973) 'The selection of crime news by the press', in Cohen, S. and Young, J. (eds) *The Manufacture of News*, London, Constable.

Rutter, M. and Giller, H. (1983) *Juvenile Delinquency: Trends and Perspectives*, New York, Guilford.

Sanders, C.R. and Lyon, E. (1995) 'Repetitive retribution: media images and the cultural construction of criminal justice', in Ferrell, J. and Sanders, C. (eds) *Cultural Criminology*, Boston, Mass., NE University Press.

Schlesinger, P. and Tumber, H. (1994) *Reporting Crime: The Media Politics of Criminal Justice*, Oxford, Clarendon Press.

Schlesinger, P., Tumber, H. and Murdock, G. (1991) 'The media politics of crime and criminal justice', *British Journal of Sociology*, vol.42, no.3, pp.397–420.

Schwendinger, H. and Schwendinger, J. (1970) 'Defenders of order or guardians of human rights?', *Issues in Criminology*, vol.5, no.2, pp.123–57.

Scraton, P. and Chadwick, K. (1991) 'The theoretical and political priorities of critical criminology', in Stenson and Cowell (1991). (Extract reprinted in Muncie *et al.*, 1996.)

Sellin, T. (1938) *Culture, Conflict and Crime*, New York, Social Science Research Council.

Shah, R. and Pease, K. (1992) 'Crime, race and reporting to the police', *Howard Journal*, vol.31, no.3, pp.192–9.

Sharrock, W. (1984) 'The social realities of deviance', in Anderson, R.J. and Sharrock, W. (eds) *Applied Sociological Perspectives*, London, Allen and Unwin.

Shearing, C. (1989) 'Decriminalising criminology', *Canadian Journal of Criminology*, vol.31, no.2, pp.169–78.

Sim, J., Scraton, P. and Gordon, P. (1987) 'Crime, the state and critical analysis', in Scraton, P. (ed.) *Law, Order and the Authoritarian State*, Buckingham, Open University Press.

Simmons, J.L. (1969) *Deviants*, Berkeley, CA, Glendessary Press.

Slapper, G. and Tombs, S. (1999) *Corporate Crime*, London, Longman.

Smith, S.J. (1984) 'Crime in the news', *British Journal of Criminology*, vol.24, no.3, pp.289–95.

Snider, L. (1993) 'The politics of corporate crime control', in Pearce, F. and Woodiwiss, M. (eds) *Global Crime Connections*, London, Macmillan.

Sparks, R. (1992) *Television and the Drama of Crime*, Buckingham, Open University Press.

Stenson, K. and Cowell, D. (eds) (1991) *The Politics of Crime Control*, London, Sage.

Stevens, P. and Willis, C. (1979) *Race, Crime and Arrests*, Home Office Research Study no.58, London, HMSO.

Sumner, C. (ed.) (1990) *Censure, Politics and Criminal Justice*, Buckingham, Open University Press.

Surette, R. (1998) *Media, Crime and Criminal Justice*, Belmont, CA, West/Wadsworth.

Sutherland, E. (1949) *White Collar Crime*, New York, Dryden Press.

Sutherland, E. and Cressey, D. (1924/1970) *Criminology*, 8th edn, Philadelphia, PA, Lippincott.

Tappan, P.W. (1947) 'Who is the criminal?', *American Sociological Review*, vol.12, pp.96–102.

Taylor, H. (1998) 'The politics of the rising crime statistics of England and Wales 1914–1960', *Crime, History and Societies*, vol.2, no.1, pp.5–28.

Taylor, I. (1999) *Crime in Context*, Cambridge, Polity.

Thompson, E.P. (1975) *Whigs and Hunters*, London, Allen Lane.

Tifft, L. (1994/5) 'Social harm definitions of crime', *The Critical Criminologist*, vol.6, no.3, pp.9–13.

Walmsley, R., Howard, L. and White, S. (1992) *The National Prison Survey 1991*, Home Office Research Study no.128, London, HMSO.

Walker, M.A. (1983) 'Some problems in interpreting statistics relating to crime', *Journal of the Royal Statistical Society, Series A*, no.146, part 3, pp.282–93.

Walker, M.A. (1987) 'Interpreting race and crime statistics', *Journal of the Royal Statistical Society, Series A*, no.150, part 1, pp.39–56.

Walklate, S. (1995) *Gender and Crime: An Introduction*, Hemel Hempstead, Prentice Hall/Harvester Wheatsheaf.

White, P. (1999) *The Prison Population in 1998: A Statistical Review*, Home Office Research, Development and Statistics Directorate, Research Findings no.94, London, HMSO.

Wilkins, L. (1964) *Social Deviance*, London, Tavistock.

Williams, K.S. (1994) *Textbook on Criminology*, 2nd edn, London, Blackstone.

Williams, P. and Dickinson, J. (1993) 'Fear of crime: read all about it?', *British Journal of Criminology*, vol.33, no.1, pp.33–56.

Wilson, D. and Ashton, J. (1998) *What Everyone in Britain Should Know about Crime and Punishment*, London, Blackstone.

Young, J. (1974) 'Mass media, drugs and deviance', in Rock, P. and McKintosh, M. (eds) *Deviance and Social Control*, London, Tavistock.

Young, J. (1986) 'The failure of criminology: the need for a radical realism', in Matthews, R. and Young, J. (eds) *Confronting Crime*, London, Sage. (Extract reprinted in Muncie *et al.*, 1996.)

Young, J. (1992) 'Ten points of realism', in Young, J. and Matthews, R. (eds) *Rethinking Criminology: The Realist Debate*, London, Sage.

Young, J. (1999) *The Exclusive Society*, London, Sage.

CHAPTER 2

The Pleasures of Crime: Interrogating the Detective Story

by John Clarke

Contents

1   Introduction

Our society is saturated by images – or representations – of crime. It is, as John Muncie indicated in the preceding chapter, a staple focus of news-reporting and documentary or investigative journalism. However, its presence in reportage of various kinds is still outweighed by the huge range of fictional representations of crime that circulate in television drama, films, and books. There is a profound paradox in this role of crime as entertainment. How do we make sense of a popular culture that is drenched in crime (and the artificial blood of its victims) in a society that is apparently increasingly fearful and concerned about the 'crime problem'? Crime provides a constant source of fascination, pleasure and entertainment. Can this be a form of escapism from a world dominated by the problem of crime? Are we reassured by fictional representations of crime, in which Poirot – or the other embodiments of Law, Order and Justice – make everything come out right in the end? Are we, on the contrary, fascinated by the chance to play with the 'dark side' – to imagine crime as the evil within or the underside of social life – without real danger? Are we able to enjoy crime in these fictional forms because we can 'tell the difference' between entertainment and reality? If so, we are also prone to constant worries about those who we suspect cannot tell the difference – and are prone to being led astray by bad entertainments (ranging from murder ballads in the eighteenth century to horror videos in the late twentieth). As Jeff Ferrell (1998) has argued, one of the recurrent intersections between crime and popular culture is that popular culture is itself frequently 'criminalized', subject to political and legal interventions because of its (supposed) contribution to social, moral and political disorders.

Each of these views about crime-as-entertainment rests on a notion that the forms and content of popular culture reflect a popular psychology. We are 'fascinated' by crime; or we are 'two-faced' in our response to crime, both condemning it and wanting to see more. Alternatively, we can distinguish between fact and fiction (though some cannot). Yet again, we are reassured and reinforced in our sense of what is right by the sight of the villain getting his or her just deserts. Such explanations of the place of crime in popular culture are hardly satisfying. They rely on a circular argument (there is a lot of fictional crime because we are fascinated by it. How do we know we are fascinated by it? Because there is a lot of fictional crime). These explanations are also ahistorical, implying an unchanging popular psychology. But the forms and content of fictional representations of crime are not unchanging: they vary through time (and between societies). This chapter will explore issues about the place of crime in popular culture in a rather different way – by dealing with them as **representation** representations that are part of the processes of producing, circulating and consuming 'meanings' within society. Crime fictions form part of what Ferrell (1998, p.80) calls the 'swirl of symbolism, imagery and meaning' that flows around us and through which we engage in making sense of our social world for ourselves. We may know about crime through a range of processes: personal experience, professional experience, our networks and milieux, reportage and stories. But all of these are mediated by this 'swirl of symbolism, imagery and meaning'. Even those directly engaged in the business of crime and crime control are exposed to, and consume, these fictional representations – some even contribute to the production of them. Crime fictions may be 'only entertainment' (Dyer, 1992), but they both draw on and add to the repertoire of images, ideas and meanings that are available to us about crime.

Within the bounds of this chapter, it will be impossible to explore the entire range of fictional representations of crime, so we will focus on one type of fiction – the detective story. This will allow us to examine the shifting imaginings of crime that can be discovered in this genre. This narrower focus will also make it possible to tease out some of the connections between these imaginings of crime and the contested and changing representations of the social orders within which these crimes are placed. The concept of genre highlights the characteristic features that distinguish a particular type of fiction from others (such as romance, science fiction, situation comedy, action drama and so on). Christine Gledhill has described genre as referring to 'the way individual fictions can be grouped together in terms of similar plots, stereotypes, settings, theses, style, emotional affects and so on' (1997, p.351). The detective story is one such genre. As we will see, there are similarities of plot (the solution of a problem by a hero/ine); there are stereotypes (the butler, the femme fatale); there are – some – common settings (from the English village to urban-industrial America). But if genres mark out these conventions – the patterns of similarity that make a fiction recognizable as a detective story – they are also marked by internal variation, as particular authors produce their distinctive version. Gledhill talks about this as the intersection of standardization and differentiation. The creators of films, TV programmes and novels use the detective story genre to simplify the process of producing a work of fiction and to engage with audiences (those who consume detective stories). But, Gledhill says, 'genre production is equally about differentiation – managing product differentiation to maximize, and appeal to, different audiences and to keep tabs on changing audiences'. Such differentiation combines 'the pleasure of recognition, along with the frisson of the new' (1997, p.355).

Genre provides a setting and a framework for such differentiation and in this chapter we will explore some of the diverse and divergent ways of imagining crime and social order through the detective story. Within the genre, this chapter will be focusing on detective novels, rather than film or television forms of detective story. There are two main reasons for this choice. The first, and more technical one, is that it is simpler to reproduce extracts from written texts in this print format and simpler to analyse them. Certainly, much of the analysis in this chapter is equally relevant to other formats, but dealing with film and TV forms would also require attention to visual composition, styles and dynamics. Secondly, and more significantly in cultural terms, the detective *novel* is the form in which more diverse or differentiated imaginings of crime and detection have been produced. The final qualification about this chapter is that it aims neither to tell the history of the detective story nor to provide a reader's guide to consuming them. It treats the genre as one setting in which different changing and contested imaginings of crime and its social significance take place. They may be 'only entertainment', but even fictional representations add to the stock of images and meanings about crime that are available to us. Even though we know they are 'only stories', they are part of our social reality – the stuff of conversation and reflection, and the source of both pleasures and profits.

2   It happens in the best of families: the classic English mystery

In an English village, a murder is discovered, probably in a large country house in which are assembled a variety of relatives, friends and business partners of the deceased. Within the next 200 pages, we will have discovered that almost everyone present had either the opportunity or the motive to do away with the victim. In the final chapters, the detective will review the conditions, characters and clues and reveal that only one combination of these can point to the identity of the murderer – the one 'whodunit'.

In this 'mystery' format, the puzzling-through of the clues is the organizing principle of the genre. But the puzzle needs to be played out in a social context that is peopled with characters – however thinly drawn some of these may be. The classic mystery represents 'crime' through images of specific social settings and social types.

In the murder mystery, crime is represented as an event which takes place **class structure** in the upper reaches of an English class structure. To be more accurate, *the crime that matters* takes place in this setting. Other crimes may be going on elsewhere and may distract the attention of the police, but the crime which is intended to hold our attention – the murder which provides the impetus of the **hierarchy of** plot – takes place here. The 'mystery' rests on an implicit hierarchy of crime in **crime** which murder is the most serious. This hierarchy intersects with the social ranking of the class structure, so that the primary victim is usually of high social status. It is one of the members of this milieu who dies and the other members of the milieu who fall under suspicion. Lest there be any doubt, crime writers are at pains to rule out the possibility of the 'mysterious stranger' and to turn attention inwards to the intimate circle of suspects.

In generic terms, such limitations are functional for the purposes of plotting. They constrain attention and direct us and the author to concentrate on the minutiae of the clues and characters. But they also create an imagined and distinctive social world – grand houses, the trappings of wealth and social demeanour – to which we are admitted as 'spectators'. We are invited to participate in the complex imagery of social class and status distinctions. Crime is centred in its upper reaches, among the country aristocrats, stockbrokers, old families clustered alongside nouveau riche businessmen and entrepreneurs. This stratum of wealth is seen as being supported by two other distinctive social groups. One is the old professional class: doctors (whether country GPs or Harley Street specialists) and solicitors (a vital role given the centrality of the laws of inheritance). The other group is composed of those in domestic service – butlers, maids and gardeners, for example. These loyal retainers people the world of the murder mystery, but mainly as testimony to the wealth and standing of the principal characters.

This is, of course, an *imaginary* England, both in the general sense that it is a fiction and in the particular sense that it is selectively imagined. It obscures about three-quarters of the real inter-war population – the mass of the working and lower middle classes leading their lives in urban settings. They are not part of the social milieu of the mystery, although they may occasionally be glimpsed going about their business in the margins of the story (through the window of a train or taxi). This imaginary nature of the country – what Watson (1979) calls 'Mayhem Parva' – can also be glimpsed geographically. The England of the Golden Age detective story is a strange composite of London and the rural counties. The countryside is represented by the 'English village', which is dominated physically and socially by the 'big house':

> At a window overlooking a garden in Kent, Brian Page sat amid a clutter of open books at a writing table, and felt a strong distaste for work. Through both windows the late July sunlight turned the floor of the room to gold. The somnolent heat brought out the odour of old wood and old books … .
>
> Beyond his garden wall, past the inn of the Bull and Butcher, the road wound for some quarter of a mile between orchards. It passed the gates of Farnleigh Court, whose thin clusters of chimneys Page could see above rifts in the trees, and then ascended past the wood poetically known as Hanging Chart … .
>
> There was, Brian Page thought lazily, almost too much excitement in Mallingford village.
>
> (From the opening of J.D. Carr, *The Crooked Hinge*, 1964)

Even London is a city partially imagined. The London of the Golden Age detective story finds its limits in the combination of the grand houses, clubs and hotels of the West End with occasional glimpses of respectable suburbia. The East End hovers in the background – providing a sense of 'otherness' which occasionally surfaces in the form of cheery cockneys or troublesome roughs. But, like the rest of urbanized and proletarianized Britain, it cannot play a central part in this imaginary social order. The distance between the late nineteenth-century detective story (such as Conan Doyle's Sherlock Holmes novels) and its inter-war counterpart can in some ways be measured by this changing place of the East End. In the late nineteenth century, it was the imagined haunt of crime – represented as a dangerous place, filled by swirling fogs and nameless threats, an uneasy mixture of social groups (its indigenous working class, its mobile seafaring population) and vibrant with exotic promise (music halls, drugs, prostitution). By the 1920s and 1930s, the London of the detective story rarely extends further east than the stockbrokers' and bankers' offices of the City.

The social order that is represented in the classic mystery seems to me to be self-confidently imperial. It registers the place of the 'best of British' – the upper classes – and the novels are at pains to delineate their world, their accomplishments, their property, their accommodation and their eating habits. It is difficult to ignore the intense round of breakfast, luncheon, tea, dinner and occasional cold supper that punctuates the solving of the mystery and provides a rhythm to the investigation – as well as providing convenient meeting points for all suspects, who are forced to stomach multiple courses while worrying about which of the others is the murderer. The hierarchies of status, demeanour and appropriate deference are lovingly observed: everyone knowing their place and behaving accordingly. This order is intermittently and marginally disrupted by someone who reveals a lack of social graces: a nouveau riche 'upstart' or a 'foreigner'. Such 'foreigners', for the most part, provide the means of demonstrating the unselfconscious superiority of the 'British race' – whether they be 'brash' Americans, 'mysterious' middle-Europeans or 'excitable' Latins (Watson, 1979, chapters 9 and 10). They are not often the villains but they will certainly behave badly. Such juxtapositions are characteristic forms of representation: the 'normal' is constructed and defined in relation to the 'other'.

There is, though, a paradox in the way that this social order is imagined and represented in the English mystery. On the one hand, it is self-confident, powerful and well respected. On the other, its members keep killing one another – and when one of them is murdered, there is a long queue of likely candidates for the role of the chief suspect. They may maintain an equable veneer of self-confidence in public, but in private, it seems, they hate one another with considerable intensity. In this form of the genre, crime is not a product of the dangerous world 'out there', but the effect of intimate relationships going wrong.

2.1 Familiar motives: the why of the whodunit

The setting of crime in the murder mystery is the family – or at least the domestic milieu inhabited by the relatives and friends of the victim. The murder and its investigation reveal a tangled web of motivation in which all or most of the cast of characters are implicated in patterns of hostility towards the victim. However much any particular detective may lean towards the 'scientific method' of detection and be concerned with physical evidence, the *generic* investigation comes to focus on the characters, feelings and patterns of relationship between victim and suspects. What is drawn out for us is the shape of familiar motives – love, money, revenge – which are represented as the most potent and most fundamental features of these family lives. Who hated or feared whom, and why, are the focus of the classic English mystery and these patterns are to be found at their most intense in the familial world. Even money, the most *apparently* impersonal of the 'classic' motives, is a focus for family feelings since the laws of property and inheritance bind people in complex and conflictual relationships. Many an apparently marginal character has been 'revealed' as the murderer through the disentangling of forgotten blood relationships or complex patterns of inheritance.

As a consequence, much of the *narrative* in the mystery involves the detective teasing out how people *really* felt about the victim from beneath the conventional poses and attitudes which they originally strike: the 'tear-stained widow' looking forward to a new relationship, the 'devastated son' anticipating release from a tyrannical father, or the 'meek governess' preparing to use her new inheritance to lead a full and active life. In this familial milieu, we discover a sharp contrast between the surface appearances of convention and normality – wifely devotion, filial piety and genteel servitude – and the real passions which burn underneath. The family in the mystery story is a profoundly unhealthy place and the detective performs the role of analyst bringing the repressed feelings and tensions out into the open. Through recurring conversations with the main characters, the detective manages to reveal that which up to now has been concealed. The problem for the detective is not in performing this role – all of them seem to possess the analyst's skill to get people talking about themselves – but in accomplishing the act of distinguishing those emotions and relationships which are merely dysfunctional from those which are dangerous and have led to the murderous impulse.

In the closing chapters of Agatha Christie's *Five Little Pigs* (1959), Hercule Poirot picks over a 16-year-old murder, demonstrating how things said at the time have been misinterpreted because they are not being heard in the context of the 'real' characters and motives of those who said them:

Poirot (David Suchet): the extraordinary detective?

> Poirot did not allow himself to be angered. He said 'You say we all know what happened. You speak without reflection. The accepted version of the facts is not necessarily the true one. On the face of it, for instance, you, Mr Blake, disliked Caroline Crale. That is the accepted version of your attitude. But any one with the least flair for psychology can perceive at once that the exact opposite was the truth. You were always violently attracted towards Caroline Crale. You resented the fact, and tried to conquer it by steadfastly telling yourself her defects and reiterating your dislike …'.
>
> …'There is always a danger of accepting facts as proved which are nothing of the kind. Let us take the situation at Alderbury. A very old situation. Two women and one man. We have taken it for granted that Amyas Crale intended to leave his wife for the other woman. But I suggest to you now that he never intended to do anything of the kind …'.
>
> (Agatha Christie, *Five Little Pigs*, 1959, pp.173, 183)

It is in this context that we discover something else about the upper classes who inhabit the world of the whodunit. With few exceptions, they are represented as social actors who maintain a social mask and play their roles. They are skilled performers who are continually engaged in the activity described by Erving Goffman (1959) as 'the presentation of self'. We are invited to watch the detective's struggle to remove the masks and to reveal the *real* person behind. This performance – this acting of roles – seems to be a class-specific form of behaviour. It is as though the upper-class concern with manners and demeanour has produced an instinctive self-concealment, a preoccupation with how the self is managed and presented. The stability of this imagined social order is seen as being maintained through the management of appearances. Agatha Christie's *At Bertram's Hotel* (1968) both exemplifies and uses this concern with maintaining a public face (see Extract 2.1 overleaf). The fact that these appearances are too good to be true is one of the central features of the story. It is, in fact, a hotel run by villains who find its 'respectable façade' a great help in carrying out their real business. But it is *not* the motive for murder. Once again, this is to be found in tangled family relationships.

presentation of self

Extract 2.1 Christie: 'The problem of appearances'

In the heart of the West End, there are many quiet pockets, unknown to almost all but taxi drivers who traverse them with expert knowledge, and arrive triumphantly thereby at Park Lane, Berkeley Square or South Audley Street.

If you turn off on an unpretentious street from the Park, and turn left and right once or twice, you will find yourself in a quiet street with Bertram's Hotel on the right hand side. Bertram's Hotel has been there a long time. During the war, houses were demolished on the right of it, and a little farther down on the left of it, but Bertram's itself remained unscathed. Naturally it could not escape being, as house agents would say, scratched, bruised and marked, but by the expenditure of only a reasonable amount of money it was restored to its original condition. By 1955 it looked precisely as it had looked in 1939 – dignified, unostentatious, and quietly expensive.

Such was Bertram's, patronized over a long stretch of years by the higher *échelons* of the clergy, dowager ladies of the aristocracy up from the country, girls on their way home for the holidays from expensive finishing schools. ('So few places where a girl can stay alone in London but of course it is *quite* all right at Bertram's. We have stayed there for *years*.')

There had, of course, been many other hotels on the model of Bertram's. Some still existed, but nearly all had felt the wind of change. They had had necessarily to modernize themselves, to cater for a different clientele. Bertram's, too, had had to change, but it had been done so cleverly that it was not at all apparent at the first casual glance.

Outside the steps that led up to the big swing doors stood what at first sight appeared to be no less than a Field Marshal. Gold braid and medal ribbons adorned a broad and manly chest. His deportment was perfect. He received you with tender concern as you emerged with rheumatic difficulty from a taxi or a car, guided you carefully up the steps and piloted you through the silently swinging doorway.

Inside, if this was the first time you had visited Bertram's, you felt, almost with alarm, that you had re-entered a vanished world. Time had gone back. You were in Edwardian England once more.

There was, of course, central heating, but it was not apparent. As there had always been, in the big central lounge, there were two magnificent coal fires; beside them big brass coal scuttles shone in the way they used to shine when Edwardian housemaids polished them, and they were filled with exactly the right sized lumps of coal. There

By comparison, other social groups are treated as being less competent at this sort of self-presentation. It is true that domestic servants maintain a façade of deference, and getting access to below-stairs gossip and information may occasionally be helpful to the detective, but this is never a matter of getting to know who the servants 'really' are. Similarly, the representatives of the lower middle classes may be seen presenting a veneer of respectability, but there is rarely little of interest behind the veneer – and the fact that they can be *seen* doing it is intended to suggest that they are not as skilled in the art of self-presentation exhibited by the upper classes. Finally, we might note that the occasional member of the lower orders who enters such stories may display a degree of natural cunning. If they do, however, it tends to lead them into trouble – for example, making them think they can blackmail the murderer. The consequences of setting 'natural cunning' against the performance skills of the upper classes are a testimony to social superiority being as marked in criminal ability as it is in the distribution of wealth (natural cunning inevitably loses). Otherwise, the lower orders are simply transparent: beacons of goodheartedness (the salt of the earth) in a murky world. They are, for the most part, 'below suspicion'.

These *generic features* of the mystery – the imagined class milieu, the familial setting and the performance skills of the principal characters – may account for one other distinctive feature: the 'extraordinary' detectives who solve these

is a general appearance of rich red velvet and plushy ⌐siness. The arm-chairs were not of this time and age. ⌐ey were well above the level of the floor, so that ⌐eumatic old ladies had not to struggle in an undignified ⌐nner in order to get to their feet. The seats of the chairs ⌐1 not, as in so many modern high-priced arm-chairs, ⌐p half-way between the thigh and the knee, thereby ⌐licting agony on those suffering from arthritis and ⌐atica; and they were not all of a pattern. There were ⌐aight backs and reclining backs, different widths to ⌐commodate the slender and the obese. People of almost ⌐y dimension could find a comfortable chair at Bertram's.

⌐ice it was now the tea hour, the lounge hall was full. ⌐ot that the lounge hall was the only place where you ⌐uld have tea. There was a drawing-room (chintz), a ⌐noking-room (by some hidden influence reserved for ⌐ntlemen only), where the vast chairs were of fine ⌐ather, two writing-rooms, where you could take a ⌐ecial friend and have a cosy little gossip in a quiet ⌐rner – and even write a letter as well if you wanted to. ⌐esides these amenities of the Edwardian age, there were ⌐her retreats, not in any way publicized, but known to ⌐ose who wanted them. There was a double bar, with ⌐o bar attendants, an American barman to make the ⌐mericans feel at home and to provide them with ⌐urbon, rye, and every kind of cocktail, and an English

one to deal with sherries and Pimm's No. 1, and to talk knowledgeably about the runners at Ascot and Newbury to the middle-aged men who stayed at Bertram's for the more serious race meetings. There was also, tucked down a passage, in a secretive way, a television-room for those who asked for it.

But the big entrance lounge was the favourite place for the afternoon tea drinking. The elderly ladies enjoyed seeing who came in and out, recognizing old friends, and commenting unfavourably on how these had aged. There were also American visitors fascinated by seeing the titled English really getting down to their traditional afternoon tea. For afternoon tea was quite a feature of Bertram's.

It was nothing less than splendid. Presiding over the ritual was Henry, a large and magnificent figure, a ripe fifty, avuncular, sympathetic, and with the courtly manners of that long vanished species: the perfect butler. Slim youths performed the actual work under Henry's austere direction. There were large crested silver trays, and Georgian silver teapots. The china, if not actually Rockingham and Davenport, looked like it. The Blind Earl services were particular favourites. The tea was the best Indian, Ceylon, Darjeeling, Lapsang, etc. As for eatables, you could ask for anything you liked – and get it!

(Agatha Christie, *At Bertram's Hotel*, 1968, pp.7–9)

mysteries. The generic features identified so far suggest the 'ordinary policeman' will be doomed to fail from the outset. He (it normally is 'he') possesses neither the social standing necessary to gain access to, nor the social graces to move easily in, this social milieu. Above all, he is not attuned to the arts of performance practised by this social group and is thus unable to accomplish the task of unmasking the murderer. Baffled, intimidated, patronized and ignored, the ordinary policeman can only stand by – more or less helpfully – while the 'extraordinary' detective solves the case.

2.2 'Mon pauvre Japp': the problem of the detective

Given that the ordinary policeman cannot work effectively in this social milieu, the stage is set for someone who can bridge the world of the upper classes and the world of justice. The detective in the mystery is represented as an *ambiguous* figure – inside, but with a certain distance from, the social setting of crime. Predominantly, this role is one occupied by an amateur – or at least, someone who is not a member of the police force. Within this generic code, there are differences between those who are mainly bystanders (Agatha Christie's Miss

Marple) and those who seek out crime (Christie's Poirot, Dorothy Sayer's Lord Peter Wimsey). The occasional extraordinary detective who is also a policeman is also different from the rest of the police – as in the case of Ngaio Marsh's Inspector Roderick Alleyn, who is able to move in the social milieu of the murders that he investigates by virtue of his birth and breeding.

It is their access to the *manners* of the murder milieu that gives such detectives their edge over the ordinary police. Most of the murder mysteries play upon this constructed tension between the dogged, decent, but ultimately wrong, police investigation and the triumph of their extraordinary detective. Each of these has his or her own particular idiosyncrasy or characteristics. Poirot, while possessed of the social graces, is nevertheless a 'foreigner' and liable to be underestimated by English suspects. Miss Marple, meanwhile, is such an apparently familiar figure of this landscape – the elderly lady with a lot of time on her hands – that she is, like Poirot, underestimated, if not ignored. She has also developed the art of social observation to a high level through extensive practice on the inhabitants of St Mary Mead. As Mary Weinkaupf describes her: 'She is a fine actress, and she pretends to be dithery, fluffy and gossipy to disarm people. Though some might call her an "old scandalmonger", she is a fact finder, knitting and talking but mostly listening. People tend to overlook her ...' (Weinkaupf, 1980, pp.37–8).

It is also worth noting that the revelation of 'whodunit' by the detective marks the closure of these narratives. The murder mystery conventionally ends with the solution to the puzzle rather than with the processes of criminal justice – arrest, trial and sentencing. More attention is paid to the removal of the 'problem' and the restoration of the social order of this world than to the wider social and legal processes. If murder happens in 'the best of families', it is also solved and sorted out within that world – the rest of us can only stand by and watch.

pleasure

What might be the pleasures of this generic form? Why has the classic mystery been read so widely (and been so successfully transformed into film and television formats)? We might begin by suggesting that these are not the pleasures of 'realist' fiction. People are unlikely to read them to discover subtle and detailed portrayals of social circumstances or rich character studies. Indeed, the genre makes no claims to such 'realism', or what Gledhill (1997) calls 'cultural verisimilitude'. On the contrary, the imaginary social order of the mystery is *self-consciously imagined*. So, the pleasures of reading are more likely to be *generic* ones – the combination of standardization (or predictability) and difference (or variation). We 'know' (or come to know, as *regular* readers) the patterns, codes and conventions that govern the story in the mystery. Through those codes and conventions, the reader is invited to observe (alongside the detective), see behind the surface appearances (like the detective) and, possibly, solve the mystery (before the detective). The reader thus occupies a *privileged position*, a position of superiority in relation to the participants (and possibly in relation to the detective). Such privilege is, potentially, a powerful source of pleasure. Studies of the mystery have also typically drawn attention to one other source of pleasure or satisfaction. This is the generic structure of *narrative closure* that characterizes the mystery. The elementary form of the narrative is: first, there is order; second, order is disrupted and this is a source of narrative *tension*; third, the source of disruption is discovered and removed, so that, fourth, order is restored. The narrative thus resolves the tension that has been its driving force and this resolution and closure may be a source of cultural or even psychological satisfaction.

But, even though the mystery genre makes no claims to be 'realistic', there may be pleasures for readers in its representation of the imaginary social order. We may enjoy the depiction of a 'golden age', even though we do not believe it ever existed. Indeed, we might view the mystery story as an exercise in fictive nostalgia – the *imagining* of a past (of order, stability and deference) that never was. Even during the inter-war period, the mystery story was already an exercise in this sort of fictive nostalgia – projecting an imagined past into the present. As readers, our relation to this imagined order and the characters who inhabit it may be ambiguous. Do we admire them (because of their status and wealth)? Do we feel superior to them (because we are privileged observers)? Do we take pleasure in them getting their fictional 'come-uppance'?

Let me add one significant qualification to this discussion. It should not be assumed that there is a clear and unproblematic 'we' who all enjoy or respond to the detective story in the same way. There are three ways in which the 'reading public' or 'consumers' of this genre may be differentiated. It may be that there are some social groups (distinguished by class, ethnicity or gender) who consume some sorts of fiction more than others. This chapter, however, will not pursue this sociology of the audience for detective stories. The second distinction concerns possible 'points of identification' between the reader and the individuals and groups represented in the stories. While there may be some lines of 'fit' between the reader's social identity and the social groups that are the focus of the novel, this is not a very tight fit. It is clearly possible to enjoy fictions where one does not share the social identity of the hero(ine) or the main protagonists. Thirdly, there are issues about whether audiences for such fictions can only enjoy them if they share the social assumptions around which the fictions are constructed. While there are clearly pleasures to be gained from shared views of the world, it is also possible to gain pleasures while 'reading against the grain' or from a social/political perspective different from that of the text (Clarke, 1990, see also Ellsworth, 1988).

3   The rank smell of corruption: the arrival of the private eye

Meanwhile, on the other side of the Atlantic, a different type of detective and a different type of detective story were being created – most famously around the person of Raymond Chandler's Philip Marlowe. The 'private eye' novel imagines a different milieu of crime, a different view of crime and a different role for the detective. In contrast with the mystery format, the 'hard-boiled' detective story does lay claim to a sense of social realism in its urban settings, its engagement with 'low life', and its use of everyday language. It offers a form of 'cultural verisimilitude': inviting us to recognize the 'seamy side of life'. Wealth, power and status are still elements – indeed central elements – of these stories, but they function in a different way. They are bound up in a different imaginary social order: a representation of society in which the rich, no matter how hard they may try to insulate themselves in a closed world, nevertheless find that their fortunes (financial and social) are inextricably linked to the wider world of the USA.

In this imagined America, the city is a setting in which money links a variety of social groups – the old rich, businessmen, gangsters, hustlers and con men. Money – and its flows – is seen to bind these people together in symbiotic and unstable patterns of relationships. The city is ripe with the possibility and reality of corruption and moral decay: it is represented as a tangled web of strands connecting apparently separate individuals in a network of power, corruption and crime.

> The strike lasted eight months. Both sides bled plenty. The wobblies had to do their own bleeding. Old Elihu hired gunmen, strike-breakers, national guardsmen, and even parts of the regular army, to do his. When the last skull had been cracked, the last rib kicked in, organized labour in Personville was a used firecracker.
>
> But, said Bill Quint, old Elihu didn't know his Italian history. He won the strike, but he lost his hold on the city and the state. To beat the miners he had to let his hired thugs run wild. When the fight was over he couldn't get rid of them. He had given his city to them and he wasn't strong enough to take it away from them. Personville looked good to them and they took it over.
>
> (Dashiell Hammett, *Red Harvest*, 1975, p.11)

Personville (pronounced 'Poisonville') is probably the most extreme example of the corruption of the social order in the private eye (PI) story, but its premise – the interlocking of 'respectable' wealth and crime – is one which is a generic feature. This amoral order produces a different generic task for the detective. It is not a matter of solving the problem posed by a specific crime (the murder). Rather, it is a moral obligation to rescue someone or something in peril in a social order which is itself disordered. The 'crime' in these novels is not a one-off event which disrupts social stability (as is the English murder) and brings dangerous relationships to light. Instead, 'crime' is represented as inherent in the social order: it is all around – illegal gambling, drug-use, prohibition-breaking, corrupt business-dealing, blackmail and prostitution, as well as murder. Murders certainly happen and may even be the focus of the plot, but the detective is likely to be drawn into the action by a variety of criminal or other 'problems' such as missing persons, kidnapping and blackmail.

disordered social order

Private – or familial – relationships are seen to reflect the *disordered* social order. They, too, are likely to be tangled, corrupt and dangerous – morally unstable. For example, in Raymond Chandler's *The Big Sleep* (1988a) General Sternwood's daughters are embroiled in a web of relationships which involve murder, blackmail, disturbed sexuality, drug-use and theft. Their social connections include gangsters, narcotics peddlers and killers. The boundary between public and private crime collapses while the general struggles to maintain 'traditional virtues' at the same time as colluding with the corrupt world at his door to protect his daughters and his family name.

In most PI novels, this sense of decay and corruption extends to the police as well. They are understood as an integral part of the moral collapse of urban America. At best, they are hamstrung by local politics (and local politics are intimately woven into the web of corruption). Beyond that, they may be brutally incompetent, with a constant hostility towards the 'interfering' private investigator. In the worst cases, they may be constructed as intrinsically corrupt – tied directly into the local economy of business and crime. In this generic form, there is clearly the 'investigative space' for someone who is not beholden to any of these established interests – though they may be forced to deal with them along the way. Equally importantly, PIs are not bound by the legal and bureaucratic rules of law-enforcement agencies – they must make *moral*, rather than legal, choices in pursuit of their mission.

3.1 Reluctant heroes: the PI's code of conduct

The generic PI is neither a gifted amateur nor a professional police officer. He – and historically the PI was a he – is available for hire, but is unlikely to be constrained by the simple contractual framework of 'twenty-five dollars a day and expenses'. Once set to work, he creates his own trajectory through webs of relationships – identifying his own commitments, which may or may not be to the client who has paid his fee. In some cases, he may decide that someone else is more worthy of, or more in need of, his loyalty – even if that person is now dead. It is this sense of commitment – or obligation – rather than the contract which motivates his actions and informs his choices. Hammett's 'Continental Op' is both an exception to this description (because he is employed by an agency) and demonstrates the generic problem of the PI:

> It is into this bottomlessly equivocal, endlessly fraudulent, and brutally acquisitive world that Hammett precipitates the Op. There is nothing glamorous about him. Short, thick-set, balding, between thirty five and forty, he has no name, no home, no personal existence apart from his work. He is, and he regards himself as, 'the hired man' of official and respectable society, who is paid so much per day to clean it up and rescue it from the crooks and thieves who are perpetually threatening to take it over. Yet what he – and the reader – just as perpetually learn is that the respectable society that employs him is itself inveterately vicious, deceitful, culpable, crooked, and degraded.
>
> (Marcus, 1977, p.21)

The PI is necessarily a loner – someone not bound by pre-existing ties of loyalty but available for new attachments and commitments. Nor, given the corrupt social order in which he plies his trade, are there many safe points of anchorage – the occasional journalist or decent policeman who may provide information and assistance – and there is no structural framework of order to which he is attached. Rather, if there is to be any order or any justice in the social milieu in which he works, the detective must create it for himself, by himself. He must impose a moral solution on an amoral world: this is the generic tension that drives the PI narrative.

This detachment is a precondition for the work of the PI. It allows him to see clearly in a world which is complex and where moral judgements have collapsed. He is both cynical and idealistic. His cynicism is a world-weariness, underpinning the laconic, wisecracking and corrosive humour of his conventional style. It underscores his detachment from those he encounters, indicating his distance from conventional evaluations of wealth, power and status. He inhabits a world in which he suspects everyone and trusts no-one. If someone offers him money, it will have strings attached. If a woman makes advances, it will be because she intends to use him. In these ways, the PI is represented as dislocated, alienated from the world in which he lives. But at the same time, he carries the possibility of making things right, of rescuing something of value from this corrupt order. This is the 'romance' of the private eye: in spite of everything, he can, and will, make a difference. But in setting the world – or this particular microcosm of it – to rights, he will not overcome his own alienation. He may rescue the innocent (or at least, the not so guilty) or may avenge the wronged, but the narrative closure of this form will see him return to the office, the bottle of bourbon and the neon sign through the window, knowing that the social order continues to be disordered (Grella, 1980).

For these men, attachments are dangerous. They threaten the PI's capacity to remain detached and cynical observers. This gives women in the classic PI story a profoundly ambiguous identity. Women, especially attractive women, are a problem for the PI. He cannot but succumb to a code of chivalry which suggests that women are inherently more vulnerable than men in this corrupt world and thus in need of a defender or champion. The PI novel is rich in reworked 'knightly' metaphors, often with reference to rusting or tarnished armour. Other things being equal, women are more likely to engage the detective's loyalty and commitment than men. At the same time, women are a threat to detachment, undermining the hard-won capacity for independent thought and action. Worse still, attachment creates the capacity for betrayal and many a PI suffers from the discovery that he has been set up and exploited by a woman. The effect of this view of women in the PI novel is a situation in which the detective moves between the poles of attraction and repulsion.

The classic PI novel works through this constructed tension between the amoral and corrupt world and the isolated moral sense of the detective. The detective must be socially mobile enough to work in a whole variety of urban milieux without becoming contaminated. He will be as at ease (and as cynically distanced) in the homes of the wealthy as he is in the low dives and bars; he will handle gangsters as disrespectfully as he does the police. He will kill, fix evidence, cheat and break and enter – all reluctantly, and all framed by a set of moral obligations which stand above and beyond the categories of the law. He is represented as the moral conscience of America – the 'everyman' figure summoned up by Raymond Chandler's analysis of the detective:

> But down these streets a man must go, a man who is himself not mean, who is neither tarnished nor afraid ... He is the hero, he is everything. He must be a complete man and a common man and yet an unusual man. He must be, to use a rather weathered phrase, a man of honor – by instinct, by inevitability, without thought of it, and without saying it ... .

> He is a relatively poor man or he would not be a detective at all. He is a common man or he could not go among people. He has a sense of character or he would not know his job. He will take no man's money dishonestly and no man's insolence without a due and dispassionate revenge. He is a lonely man and his pride is that you will treat him as a proud man or be very sorry you ever saw him. He talks as the man of his age talks – that is, with rude wit, a lively sense of the grotesque, a distrust of sham and a contempt of pettiness.

> (Raymond Chandler, *The Simple Art of Murder*, 1988b, p.18)

A reluctant hero? Humphrey Bogart as Chandler's Philip Marlowe

However bruised, battered, drunk or in contravention of the law, the PI is made to embody the belief that there is still something beyond the swamp of corruption – some values, ethics and commitments: a not very well articulated vision that there can be something better than that which exists. In the absence of any other source of order, the PI is used to represent a *popular* commitment to decency and justice. He must stand for all the 'little people' who are not part of the centres of power and influence, but whose lives are threatened by their corruption.

What, then, are the reader's pleasures and satisfactions that can be derived from this form of detective story? We might be engaged by its implied realism – the cultural verisimilitude claimed in its settings, its characterization and its use of vernacular language. It is possible that the appeal of such 'realism' works differently for audiences within and beyond the United States. Readers might also find the juxtaposition of amorality and morality rewarding, taking pleasure from the (temporary) triumph of a 'good man'. Some commentators (for example, Marcus, 1997) have pointed to the importance of a 'popular hero' (a 'common man') confronting the forces of wealth, power and corruption. But this view of popular or populist morality does pose a problem about whether the PI can be 'everyman' – or, at least, whether we can all identify with or be represented by this figure. He is, of course, every *man*. The generic form of the PI story is highly structured around gender differentiation. Indeed, many of the male authors explicitly contrasted the masculine virility of such stories with the cosy, 'feminine' form of the mystery (see Chandler, 1988b; and the discussion of these distinctions by Glover and Kaplan, 1992). This is not to say that women readers cannot identify with or take the viewpoint of a male hero: the distinctions between masculine and feminine styles and viewpoints are cultural constructs rather than biological determinants. But it is important to see how this 'everyman' is constructed as a universal figure when, in practice, he is distinctively male, white and heterosexual: a very particular sort of person. This, though, is the generic *norm* and, as we will see in section 5, is one of the focal points around which new forms of generic differentiation are constructed.

4   The policeman's lot is not a happy one

If the PI novel represents one distinctive variant within the detective-story genre, then another has emerged around the changing representation of the police. As Bailey and Hale point out: 'In both classic detective fiction and hard-boiled fiction, the agents of law enforcement are peripheral characters. They are often ineffective, sometimes stupid or (in tough-guy fiction) brutal' (1998, p.9). But since the 1960s, the police have been making a comeback in the world of the detective story. Clearly, this involves a different type of fictional realism – working on the collective understanding that crime is the daily *business* of the police. The imaginary English social order in which gifted amateurs could carry out investigations under the noses or over the heads of humble policemen could hardly be sustained (except as a *pastiche*) in the post-war context. The detective story moved its social milieu to the occupational world of the police investigation where stories are based in police settings, and detection becomes 'professionalized'.

In some variants, the 'mystery' novel does not change much in being scene-shifted to the world of the police. It remains a matter of the detective managing to penetrate masks and motives in order to arrive at a solution, but now the detective is (more or less) supported by the apparatus of organized investigation. However, the focus of our attention is still concentrated on the detective's capacity to uncover the truths beneath the surface appearances (Colin Dexter's Morse, John Harvey's Resnick, Ian Rankin's Rebus). Each detective is likely to have his distinguishing quirks and idiosyncrasies, but the core is the ability to 'get to the bottom' of a mysterious murder. Other variants explore the tensions between the 'good cop' and the occupational world in which he is obliged to function. Here we are closer to the PI form, with the 'loner' having been institutionalized in a police department – and often unhappily so. Here, solutions are accomplished as much in spite of, as because of, the police organization and procedure. Such stories transpose the generic tension between the 'extraordinary detective' and the 'ordinary policeman' to a new setting, this time inside the police itself.

A different variant of the police procedural constructs its narrative around a tension between the 'interior' world of the police and social change in the world beyond it. This might be best described as the 'thin blue line' representation of policing as an activity which stands between civilization and anarchy. The police are seen to embody and personify order but are represented as feeling increasingly isolated from the world beyond the station doors. What is represented here is a growing 'siege mentality' on the part of the police and the density of mutual support and affirmation provided by the occupational culture (see **McLaughlin, 2001**).

Other police procedurals construct a narrative around the flawed processes and practices of policing itself. The Swedish series by Maj Sjöwall and Per Wahlöö presents a critique of the role of policing in sustaining a particular type of social order – Swedish social democracy. Their central characters (Martin Beck and Lennart Kollberg, in particular) exist in a state of permanent disenchantment. They are seen to recognize the interrelationship between crime and wider social problems, but are increasingly frustrated by the nationalized, bureaucratized and paramilitary style of policing in which they are enmeshed. Crimes do take place and do get solved, sometimes even to the detectives' satisfaction. But, more often, the outcomes merely serve to underscore their deepening frustration and alienation. These novels engage self-consciously with other social and political representations of Sweden, particularly its status as a modern, social democratic society. The generic concerns with crime and policing are re-imagined through this engagement with the meanings and symbolism of modern Swedish society. Extract 2.2 below, from *Cop Killer*, deals with the culmination of Kollberg's disaffection from the task of policing.

Some novels have begun to deal in representations of other dimensions of the occupational culture of policing, treating its processes of mutual support and its social density as the source of problems. For some, this is signified through the cultural trajectory of police forces that become alienated from mainstream or 'straight' society, and feel more at home or have more in common with the 'underworld' or criminal sub-cultures:

> 'Thieves and killers,' said Cunningham, his face flushed with anger, 'not cops. Don't put me in the same category with them. It's bad enough I have to work for the same department.' He reached into his pocket for his cigarettes. After offering one to the other man, he stuck one in his mouth, but didn't light it, letting it dangle there as he spoke. 'First we got these animals in LA beating some guy to bloody pulp on videotape for the whole world to see, and now we have our own guys blowing dope dealers away and pocketing the drug money.'
>
> (N.T. Rosenberg, *Mitigating Circumstances*, 1993, p.118)

Others have picked up and used the potential for corruption in representing the impact of other organizations on policing (Masonic lodges or local politics, for example). Yet others have explored the tensions posed for those who do not fit the conventional or generic specification of police officers – black people, gay men, women and lesbians. Each of these social identities (to be discussed in more detail in section 5) draws on new social representations to imagine social closures and social biases in policing which threaten both individual careers and the practice of investigation in a complexly patterned society.

Even within the confines of the police procedural, it is possible to trace a shift from a generic setting organized around an imagined, firmly structured social order, in which all that is required is the clarity of purpose and competence of the investigator, to new images of a more complex, fluid and multi-faceted social order in which conventional wisdoms and moral judgements are profoundly problematic. In such novels, the police do not stand apart from this more complex social order – rather, their power is implicated in such complexities. For instance, the South Yorkshire-set novels of Reginald Hill (for

Extract 2.2 Sjöwall and Wahlöö: 'The detective who can't go on'

Stockholm
November 27, 1973
To: National Police Administration
Subject: Resignation

…

Lennart Kollberg typed slowly, with two fingers. He knew that this letter, which he had thought about for such a long time, had to be considered a formal document, but he didn't want to make it too long-winded. And as far as possible, he tried to keep the tone of it informal.

> After long and careful consideration, I have decided to leave the police force. My reasons are of a personal nature, and yet I would like to try and explain them briefly. Right at the outset, I feel compelled to point out that my decision is in no way a political action, even though many people will see it in that light. To be sure, the police establishment has been increasingly politicized over the last few years, and the police force itself has been exploited for political purposes more and more often. I have observed these developments with considerable alarm, even though I, personally, have managed to avoid coming into contact with this aspect of police activity almost completely.

> Nevertheless, during the twenty-seven years that I have served on the force, its activities, structure, and organization have altered in a manner that has convinced

> me that I am no longer suited to being a policeman – assuming that I ever was. Above all, I find that I cannot feel any sense of solidarity with the kind of organization the police department has become. Consequently, it seems to me that my own best interests and those of the department would be best served by my resignation.

> The question of whether or not the individual policeman should be armed has long struck me as an especially important one. For many years, I have held to the opinion that, under normal circumstances, policemen should not be armed. This applies to uniformed patrolmen as well as to plainclothesmen.

> The great increase in the number of violent crimes over the last decade is, in my opinion, largely due to the fact that policemen invariably carry firearms. It is a known fact, and can be demonstrated with statistics from many other countries, that the incidence of violent crime immediately increases when the police force sets, as it were, a bad example. The events of recent months make it seem more obvious than ever that we can expect our situation to deteriorate even further with regard to violence. This is especially true of Stockholm and other large cities.

> The Police Academy devotes far too little time to providing instruction in psychology. As a result,

example, *Underworld*, 1989) have engaged the problems of policing in the aftermath of the 1984–85 miners' strike, the attraction of a gay sergeant to a young Asian constable, and the impact of local women's groups (often involving Ellie Pascoe, whose husband is one of the main police officers).

Does the 'police procedural' add anything distinctive to the generic pleasures of the detective story? There may be a number of differences that engage readers in this variant of the genre. Firstly, the procedural tends to claim distinctive forms of cultural verisimilitude – about the occupational world and professional practices of policing, and about the interrelationships between policing and the society in which it takes place. Secondly, there are some sorts of narrative tension that are more central to, or significant for, the police procedural. For example, there are tensions in the working relationships; tensions in the relationships between individuals and organizations or hierarchies; tensions in the interconnections between crime, criminals and the police; and tensions in the relationships between the police and the wider social and political institutions. Each of these can be the source of narrative drive and innovation. Thirdly, police procedurals tend to multiply the numbers of, and variations of, the detective as 'everyman'. They may evoke different social positions and identities as the source of dramatic action, different points of view or forms of social and organizational conflict. Fourthly, police procedurals appear particularly well suited to the international spread of the detective story, since most nations have police forces. This shows a combination of generic repetition with national/cultural variation.

policemen lack what is perhaps the most important prerequisite for success in their profession.

The fact that we nevertheless have so-called police psychologists, who are sent out in difficult situations to try and bring the criminal to reason, seems to me to be nothing but an admission of defeat. For psychology cannot be used to camouflage violence. To my way of thinking, this must be one of the simplest and most obvious tenets of the science of psychology.

I would like to emphasize in this connection that for many years I myself have never carried a gun. This has often been a direct violation of orders, but I have never had the feeling that it hampered me in the execution of my duties. On the contrary, being forced to carry arms might have had a strong inhibiting effect, it could have caused accidents, and it could well have led to even poorer contact with persons outside the police force.

What I am trying to say, essentially, is that I cannot continue to be a policeman. It is possible that every society has the police force it deserves, but that is not a thesis I intend to try and develop, at least not here and now.

I find myself confronted with a *fait accompli*. When I joined the police department, I could not have imagined that this profession would undergo the transformation or take on the direction that it has.

After twenty-seven years of service, I find that I am so ashamed of my profession that my conscience will no longer permit me to practice it.

Kollberg rolled the paper up an inch or two and read what he had written. Once he had started, he had the feeling he could have gone on indefinitely.

But this would have to do.

He added two more lines:

I therefore request that this resignation be accepted effective immediately.

Sten Lennart Kollberg.

He folded the sheets of paper and stuffed them into an official plain brown envelope.

Wrote the address.

Threw the letter into his Out basket.

Then he stood up and looked around the room.

Closed the door behind him and went.

Home.

(Maj Sjöwall and Per Wahlöö, *Cop Killer*, 1978, pp.294–7)

Where the 'mystery' is predominantly identified with Britain and the PI with the US, the police-based detective story is more mobile in its settings. While paying attention to the differentiated pleasures of the police procedural, it is important to also remember the wider generic features that it shares with other forms of detective story: the pleasures of repetition and standardization.

5 Back on the mean streets: the 'deviant' detective

The imaginary social orders of the detective story have tended to be thoroughly *conventional* ones, even when the detective has been uncovering its 'underside' – the familial tensions of the English mystery or the corruption of power and wealth in the American PI novel. Nevertheless, the place of particular types of people in these social orders has tended to be generic, reproducing normative or conventional social assumptions. So, we find representations of the finely ordered gradations of class in which everyone knows their place; the gendered divisions of social roles, character and behaviour; the familial structures of age, gender and sexuality; the social architecture of 'race' and ethnicity – ranging from the English novel's suspect 'foreigners' to the subterranean world of black America in the PI story, whose members appear in service roles or as the

gender
sexuality
'race'/ethnicity

indicators of another 'way of life' (clubs, gangs, petty crime, etc.) which lurks in the background of white America. Where the PI was quintessentially 'everyman' in his white, male **heterosexuality**, the development of the detective story genre during the 1970s and 1980s saw the 'eye' change social places with disturbing implications for the representation of social order. The detective has changed gender, 'race' and sexuality and each of these changes produces different representations of and assumptions about crime and its social location and significance.

Glover and Kaplan point to the generic variations that have been constructed by shifting the social place and identity of the detective away from Chandler's 'everyman'. 'This older representation of the public remains and the civic relations that are engaged there have been sharply challenged on several fronts. One thinks immediately of the tactically important "entryism" of feminist crime writers, creatively opening up the discursive landscape for women cops and 'tecs, gay as well as straight, black as well as white' (1992, p.215). Glover and Kaplan's argument, and the language in which it is phrased, draws attention to the *conflictual* or *contested* character of representation – even in the fictional representations that are 'just entertainment'. To displace the universal 'everyman' in detective fiction involves drawing on new representations, associated with and articulated by social and cultural movements. Such representations challenge and attempt to displace conventional (social and generic) assumptions about who can be a detective. In the process, different claims to realism or verisimilitude are implied. These 'deviant' detectives involve claims about alternative, ignored or suppressed 'realities'. They may also imply claims that the social order 'looks different' if it is looked at from a different place.

5.1 'But I was expecting a man'

The generic detective has been predominantly male. In this conventional imagery, the detective story has reproduced wider social representations of the gendered distribution of capabilities and capacities – that men are the natural repositories of 'rational analysis' (as opposed to intuition) and physical action (as opposed to emotional energy). Since most detective stories have relied on one or other of these principles as the basis for resolving problems, the occasional woman detective tends to prove the rule. Jane Marple does not possess Hercule Poirot's 'little grey cells'; rather, she is an 'old biddy' who spends too much time watching people and speculating (if not actually gossiping) about them. Her counterparts appear in minor roles as witnesses in many detective stories – peering out from behind their curtains and keeping tabs on what the neighbours are up to.

In this respect, the creation of a woman detective (whether private or police) is itself a challenge to the conventional social order of the detective story – she is 'out of place' in a world that we have come to see as male. In particular, the imagining of a woman detective opens a set of potential narrative dynamics around the negotiation of a structure of male assumptions about the world, crime and the division between the sexes, from villains, cops, friends and relatives. Anna Lee's experiences with prospective clients at the Brierly Detective Agency in Liza Cody's *Dupe* exemplify this generic shift:

The tea was poured and Beryl left with heavy-footed discretion. Mr Jackson seemed to take note of Anna for the first time.

'And who's this?' he said. 'You assured me over the phone that this business would be confidential.'

'Biscuit?' offered Brierly. 'No?, Ah, yes, forgive me. Mr and Mrs Jackson, this is Miss Lee. Let me assure you again that your affair will be treated in the strictest confidence. All my employees are hand-picked ...'.

'That's as may be.' Jackson was unappeased. 'But this is just a slip of a girl. And it doesn't look to me as if you're taking this too seriously, Mr Brierly.'

'We take all our cases with the utmost seriousness,' Brierly said weightily.

'Miss Lee has spent five years in the police force prior to her employment here, and has subsequently undergone the special training needed for the unique requirements of this organization.'

'Well, she looks a bit young to me,' said Jackson, unwilling to give up his objection.
(Liza Cody, *Dupe*, 1982, p.14)

In many of these novels, the woman detective is represented as having to struggle for the 'right to detect' in the face of individual and institutional prejudice. In this respect, such narratives can draw on a wider stock of representations about gendered inequality in employment and the problems of overcoming it. But the rise of the woman detective is only superficially a demonstration of the claim that 'women can do it, too'. More substantially, it is an exploration of what is *in the way of* women doing it – the blocks and barriers that are placed in the way by a social order which systematically structures and legitimates sexual inequalities. As a consequence, the woman detective is likely to be represented as attentive to particular patterns and relationships – gendered ones, especially – that may be ignored or simply dismissed as 'normal' by her male counterparts. Sara Paretsky's Warshawski, like others, has to struggle to explain why this 'normality' might be problematic:

I hunched a shoulder impatiently. 'The trouble is, Michael, you belong to a crowd where the girls sit on a blanket waiting for the boys to finish talking business and bring them drinks. I like LeAnn and Clara, but they'll never be good friends of mine – it's not the way I act or think or live or – or anything. I think that style – the segregated way you and Ernie and Ron work – it's too much part of you.'
(Sara Paretsky, *Burn Marks*, 1990a, p.48)

Such observations are treated as *mundane* points in these detective stories – they deal in representations of the gendered patterning of everyday life. They underscore the sense of a different '*point of view*' – one that recognizes the socially constructed character of the apparently natural gender dimensions of social order. It is not that crime has changed – although the woman-centred detective story may be more likely to explore issues of physical, emotional and sexual abuse absent from the earlier generations of the crime novel (for example, Barbara Wilson's *Sisters of the Road*, 1986). Nevertheless, blackmail, corporate corruption and murder continue to be staple crimes. What does get changed are the ways in which those crimes are imagined and understood – they are framed by an understanding of the gendered inequalities and dynamics of the social order, and the roles and relationships within it.

Such women detectives are also inclined to be resourceful in unfamiliar as well as familiar ways. In addition to being physically tough and resilient (though with rather more attention to the physical and emotional costs of violence), as well as possessing investigatory skills, the woman detective tends to be 'networked' in different ways from the male detective. Thus, while Paretsky's Warshawski has two

of the classic 'contacts' – a friendly detective and a reliable investigative journalist – she has other resources: women friends in business and financial circles who can access information, as well as her friend and mentor Dr Lotty Herschel who runs a medical centre. Warshawski, like others, is also constructed as having a distinctively gendered 'edge' when it comes to investigating – whether it be forms of 'sisterly solidarity' as a means of gaining information (from women secretaries, for example) or the fact that men consistently underestimate the woman detective.

A woman in a 'man's' world? Detective Inspector Tennyson (Helen Mirren) in ITV's Prime Suspect

The woman detective also has a more visible life alongside the job, which requires attention, compromises and negotiation. Such lives may involve sexual relationships and the problems that they present (Johnson, 1994); they may involve friendships and the tensions they bring with them; or they may involve families and the difficulties that they create. These ongoing 'real lives' are represented as interrupting the work rather than being marginal humanizing additions, and they are seen to require mundane maintenance if they are not to go wrong. Of course, some examples of male detectives now show the marks of feminism and provide representations of attempts to negotiate these issues and challenges. For example, Robert Parker's Spenser struggles to negotiate masculine codes in the face of female and feminist challenges (see *Looking for Rachel Wallace*, 1987, in particular; and the discussion of the shifting representations of cultural politics in Glover and Kaplan, 1992). Nevertheless, the 'realism' of the woman-centred detective story has tended to be achieved by reference to both a wider social order which is gendered and a more mundane conception of the detective's daily life being more than the job.

5.2 'Beyond the pale': detection, 'race' and ethnicity

Where the rise of the woman detective has turned the assumptions about gender in the social order of the detective story on their head – examining and exposing the assumptions of the male-centred detective story – the construction of the black detective poses rather different issues. There have been black detectives, but with the exception of Chester Himes's novels (for example, *The Heat's On*, 1992), such figures have tended to be peripheral rather than central: supporting faces in the cast of the police procedural. Even Arthur Brown, the black member of Ed McBain's 'melting pot' of a detective team in the *89th Precinct* series, somehow never quite gets the front-line roles allocated to the other characters.

In the last decades of the twentieth century, however, black detectives and investigators have been created, allowing authors to explore representations of a racialized social order as the context of crime and its resolution. In the USA, writers such as Walter Mosley and Gar Anthony Haywood developed the genre through the articulation of black points of view, while in the UK, black investigators in the work of Mike Phillips and D.G. Compton have provided the focal point for representations of crime, racism and the experience of inhabiting a racialized society. Such fictions both draw on and contribute to the social inventory of representations about crime and social order and their significance.

One might suggest that this is because the black detective threatens the generic representations of social order in a rather different way from the woman detective. In the conventional detective story, especially those set in the USA, we are aware of black people but stereotypically as a potentially dangerous or exotic 'other' – inhabiting an almost separate world and one which it is difficult or dangerous for the white detective to penetrate, even though it may need to be controlled or contained. In this conventional imaginary, black people exist to be policed rather than to do the policing. As a consequence, a detective story which starts from and has its point of view within that 'other' world makes the social order look very different.

So what happens when the point of view shifts to within that other world? What is represented in this 'view from the other side' is not separateness, but profoundly unequal interdependence. These worlds are seen to interlock, although almost always to the advantage, and on the terms of, white America. Viewed from the other side, black people are represented as providing a vital, though forgotten or invisible, sub-structure that makes possible the lives of white society. Dolores Komo's black woman investigator, Clio Browne, observes this social order from below, deliberately taking advantage of her 'racialized' invisibility by taking employment as a domestic servant:

> After flashing her Bi-State bus pass she seated herself near the front door, plunged her hand into the black recesses of her shoulder bag, and searched out a packet of business cards she'd collected over the years. Flipping through them, she selected one that read Maid-4-U domestics, a company that was now defunct. She'd used the ruse before and each time had been successful in gaining entrance to places that would have been off limits to anyone other than a dayworker… . It always amazed Clio how invisible the maid became as secrets were openly discussed or classified materials were left carelessly about.
>
> (Dolores Komo, *Clio Browne, Private Investigator*, 1988, p.9)

From this position as an invisible insider she is able to gain access to dimensions of the private or familial world which a conventional (white, male) detective would struggle to discover. Nevertheless, her racialized identity is simultaneously a source of social vulnerability in terms of how power is socially distributed. These experiences are shared by Walter Mosley's Easy Rawlins – a solver of problems within the black community of 1950s' Watts in Los Angeles, who is forced by circumstances to also solve crimes:

In my time I had done work for the numbers runners, churchgoers, businessmen, and even the police. Somewhere along the line I had slipped into the role of a confidential agent who represented people when the law broke down. And the law broke down often enough to keep me busy. It even broke down for the cops sometimes.

(Walter Mosley, *White Butterfly*, 1993, p.17)

Rawlins is a figure who stands uncomfortably on those borderlines where the worlds of black and white America intersect, who is used by the police as a potential informant in settings to which they cannot gain access. In the process, Rawlins has to juggle conflicting demands – of friendships, community loyalty, self-preservation and pressures from white officialdom. As Extract 2.3 from *White Butterfly* indicates, this milieu is ambiguous and contradictory, as both official and unofficial detectives work around and across the 'colour line' of 1950s' Watts. Rawlins both belongs to the black community and has to negotiate its interactions with white America. In *A Red Death* (1992), his investigations (forced on him by the threat of prosecution for his tax evasion) result in him being alienated from friends and sections of the community. Despite this, his identity – the basis from which he views the world – is represented as inextricably linked to his position in America's racialized social structure. Being pressured to take on working with the police again in *White Butterfly*, he responds to the demands of the (white) Captain Violette:

'What the hell are you trying to do, Rawlins?' Violette yelled.

'Man, I'm in my own house right? I ain't ask you over. Here you come crowdin' up my livin' room an' talkin' t'me like you got a blackjack in your pocket' – I was getting hot – 'an' then you cryin' 'bout some dead girl an' I know they's been three before this one but you didn't give one good goddam! Because they was black girls and this one was white!' If I had been on television every colored man and woman would have stood from their chairs and cheered.

Violette was up from his chair, but not to applaud. His face had turned bright red. That's when I remembered him. He was only a detective when he dragged Alvin Lewis out of his house on Sutter Place … I remembered how red his face got while he beat Alvin with a police stick. I remembered how cowardly I felt while three other white policemen stood around with their hands on their pistols and grim satisfaction on their faces. It wasn't the satisfaction that a bad man had paid for his crime; those men were tickled to have power like that.

(Walter Mosley, *White Butterfly*, 1993, p.50)

Like the generic PI, Rawlins is an 'outsider', not part of the power structures and relationships that dominate the social order. But he is not just an outsider – we see him as clearly located somewhere else, in another, but conventionally unacknowledged, part of society. And because he is based there, he has the advantage of seeing how these different elements of the social order interlock – and the problems of negotiating them.

The 'colour line' – or its equivalent forms of 'racialized' structuring – is a necessary feature of detective stories that feature detectives who are not part of the dominant ethnic group, whether the Native Americans in Tony Hillerman's Leaphorn and Chee series, or the interplay between Robert Parker's white investigator (Spenser) and his black associate (Hawk), or the positions of Kramer and Zondi in James McClure's South African-set novels. What they construct as imaginary social orders – and what is most explicit in Mosley's novels – are patterns of order which are not simple or uni-dimensional but complex, multiple and contradictory.

Extract 2.3 Mosley: 'Walking the line'

Quinten got his promotion because the cops thought that he had his thumb on the pulse of the black community. But all he really had was me. Me and a few other Negroes who didn't mind playing dice with their lives.

But I had stopped taking those kind of chances after I got married. I wasn't a stool for the cops anymore.

'I don't know nuthin' 'bout no dead girls, man. Don't you think I'd come tell ya if I did? Don't you think I'd wanna stop somebody killin' Negro women? Why, I got me a pretty young wife at home right now …'

'She's all right.'

'How do you know?' I felt the pulse in my temples.

'This man is killing good-time girls. He's not after a nurse.'

'Regina works. She comes home from the hospital, sometimes at night. He could be stalkin' her.'

'That's why I need your help, Easy.'

I shook my head. 'Uh-uh, man, I cain't help you. What could I do?'

My question threw Naylor. 'Help us,' he said feebly.

He was lost. He wanted me to tell him what to do because the police didn't know how to catch some murderer who didn't make sense to them. They knew what to do when a man killed his wife or when a loan shark took out a bad debt. They knew how to question witnesses, white witnesses. Even though Quinten Naylor was black he didn't have sympathy among the rough crowd in the Watts community; a crowd commonly called *the element*.

'What you got so far?' I asked, mostly because I felt sorry for him.

'Nothing. You know everything I know.'

'You got some special unit workin' it?'

'No. Just me.'

The cars passing on the distant streets buzzed in my ears like hungry mosquitoes.

'Three girls dead,' I said. 'An' you is all they could muster?'

'Hobbes is on it with me.'

I shook my head, wishing I could shake the ground under my feet.

'I cain't help you, man,' I said.

'Somebody's got to help. If they don't, who knows how many girls will die?'

'Maybe you' man'll just get tired, Quinten.'

'You've got to help us, Easy.'

'No I don't. You livin' in a fool's nightmare, Mr Policeman. I can't help you. If I knew this man's name or I knew somethin', anything. But it's the cops gotta gather up evidence. One man cain't do all that.'

I could see the rage gathering in his arms and shoulders. But instead of hitting me Quinten Naylor turned away and stalked off toward the car. I ambled on behind, not wanting to walk with him. Quinten had the weight of the whole community on his shoulders. The black people didn't like him because he talked like a white man and he had a white man's job. The other policemen kept at a distance too. Some maniac was killing Negro women and Quinten was all alone. Nobody wanted to help him and the women continued to die.

'You with us, Easy?' Roland Hobbes said. He put his hand on my shoulder as Naylor stepped on the gas.

I kept my silence and Hobbes took his friendly hand back. I was in a hurry to get to my house. I felt bad about turning down the policeman. I felt miserable that young women would die. But there was nothing I could do. I had my own life to attend to – didn't I?

(Walter Mosley, *White Butterfly*, 1993, pp.18–20)

5.3 'Off the straight and narrow': gay and lesbian detectives

The last disruption of the generic conventions of the detective story that we will look at here is associated with novels whose investigators do not conform to its heterosexual assumptions. Gay men and lesbians have not played major roles in the conventional detective story, except as 'bizarre' exceptions that demonstrate by their deviance the overwhelming 'normality' of everyone else. However, when they move to the centre of the detective story as investigators, this 'normality' comes to look rather different. For example, Joseph Hansen's Dave Brandsetter stories centre on a gay insurance investigator whose employment is protected by family wealth in the face of organizational prejudice. A rather more troubled existence is led by Milo Sturgis in Jonathan Kellerman's Alex Delaware novels. Delaware, the principal figure, is a child psychologist (and is actively heterosexual) and has formed a complex friendship with Sturgis, a Los Angeles Police Department detective. Sturgis, in other respects a classic 'good cop' of the genre, is given constant grief by the department for his homosexuality. In *Over the Edge*, his career is threatened by a new superior, Cyril Trapp:

> 'Used to be the biggest booze-hound, pillhead and whore freak in Ramparts Division. Then he found Jesus and become one of those scrotes who think everyone who doesn't agree with him deserves the gas chamber. He's opined in public that faggots are moral sinners, so needless to say, he adores me.' …

> 'It wouldn't be that bad if he were blatant about it – good old honest hostility. I could quietly put in for a transfer on the basis of personality conflict and maybe squeak through. I like working West LA, and it wouldn't do wonders for my personnel file, but I could handle it. But a transfer wouldn't satisfy Trapp. He wants me off the force, period. So he takes the subtle approach – psychological warfare. Puts on the polite act and uses the duty roster to make my life miserable.'

> 'Bad cases?'

Extract 2.4 Forrest: 'Challenging convention'

Kyle Jensen, his confession signed, had been officially arrested, and incident to that arrest had been booked, strip-searched and incarcerated, had had samples drawn of his blood and urine, as well as hair follicles taken from his head and crotch – all of this to his profane displeasure. On Monday he would be arraigned and assigned a public defender. And he would remain in jail, Kate was reasonably sure, until the disposition of his case; bail of any amount appeared beyond his resources.

She walked into the Detectives Squad Room, Taylor at her side, and dropped into her desk chair, feeling as if her bones had turned into quick-melting plastic.

Taylor propped a hip on the edge of her desk, crossed his arms, and gazed down at her. 'That's the best goddamn interrogation I've ever seen you do, maybe the best I've ever seen, period. Nobody else in the department could have pulled that confession out of him. We had diddley shit and you nailed him, trussed him up like a Thanksgiving turkey. Partner, you were great.'

Smiling her thanks, warmed by his appreciation, she felt – knew – that she had been like an athlete in peak performance, she had extended herself fully, used every ounce of her training, experience, instincts, knowledge, courage. She felt expended, spent.

'I figure a plea bargain, involuntary manslaughter,' Taylor said.

'You're not serious,' she said, gaping at him, realizi[ng] that she did have something left in her; astonishmen[t]

'I hope we *get* involuntary. He draws a public defen[der] that takes it to trial, he could even get off. Hey,' he said [as] she stared at him, 'figure it out for yourself. Teddie Crawf[ord] made a pass at another guy, backed up his cock wit[h a] knife. A jury's looking at this red-blooded normal guy, the[n] figure Jensen freaked out and just lost it, that's all.'

'*Just lost it?*' With effort she lowered her voice. 'Lo[ok] Ed, I know juries are capable of anything. But we thr[ow] in the towel and take manslaughter? This red-blood[ed] normal guy let himself get picked up by a gay man, [he] robbed him, he hacked and *mutilated* him to death.

'Hey, I'm on your side – sure the guy should do tim[e,]' Taylor said, spreading his hands. 'And maybe a jur[y's] gonna buy it. But I say Jensen's story hangs together j[ust] enough. I say a jury's gonna look at Kyle Jensen and s[ee] a regular guy who got freaked out by a cock-sucking fa[g.]'

'Let me ask you something, Ed.' She was amazed by t[he] calmness of her voice, the coherency of her words. 'W[hy] do men freak out over gay men? *Why is calling anot[her] man homosexual the ultimate insult? Why* are gay m[en] so completely disgusting to other men?'

He pinched the crease in his brown pants between [his] thumb and forefinger, pulled at it. 'Come on, Kate. T[he] shit they do to each other is so up-chucking putrid y[ou] can't even think about it.'

'*Faggot* cases!' He raised his big fist and put it down hard on the table. The Black couple looked over. I smiled and they returned to their headphones.

'For the last two months,' he went on in a low voice, starting to slur, 'I've had nothing but gay cuttings, gay shootings, gay stompings, gay rapes. Faggot DOA, call Sturgis, captain's orders. It didn't take long to see the pattern, and I protested right away. Trapp put down his Bible and said he understood how I felt but that my experience was too valuable to waste. That I was a specialist. End of discussion.'

(Jonathan Kellerman, *Over the Edge*, 1988, p.181)

This uncomfortable relationship between the gay or lesbian detective and the heterosexual culture of the police department is also a strong thread in the novels by Katherine V. Forrest, featuring detective Kate Delafield. In *Murder at the Nightwood Bar* (1987) and *Murder by Tradition* (1993), in particular, her own sexual identity is an integral element of the narrative. In the former, she is represented as caught in conflicting loyalties between the official culture in which she works and the lesbian community focused around the bar at which the murder of a young lesbian has taken place. Like Easy Rawlins, Delafield is located 'elsewhere' in the social order, increasingly identifying herself with the gay and lesbian community. She is both an insider and an outsider, able to use her social location to see the conventional norms of the official social order. As a consequence, her role as a detective is seen as being both informed, and made uncomfortable, by her lesbian identity. Extract 2.4 from *Murder by Tradition* represents a moment when these tensions come to a head in a case involving the killing of a gay man.

She could see his tension and discomfort. She pushed on. 'Why not? Please do your best to tell me, Ed,' she said. 'I really want to know.'

'Jesus, Kate.' He looked at a spot somewhere over her head. 'What's to tell? They aren't men. They're faggots.' He raised a hand, waved it limply. 'Mincy little faggoty fake-men.'

'That doesn't answer it. And not all of them are effeminate. Look at Rock Hudson,' she argued, wishing she could name other virile but closeted movie stars made known to her by gay friends Joe and Salvatore. 'Some of them are really masculine.'

'Rock Hudson was a pervert, not a faggot. All those masculine-type guys are perverts. They use the faggoty men like some guys use sheep or a piece of liver.'

She could hardly wait to pass on this piece of wisdom to Joe and Salvatore. 'Ed, so what if somebody's a mincy little fake-man? Some people grow to be over seven feet tall. Some people –'

'Some people are freakish, but they're still men or women. Faggots, they want to be fucked, so they turn themselves into women. If you're a real man, then you aren't a woman.'

She chose her words. 'Ed, what you just said – do you realize, do you have any idea how much it shows utter contempt for women?'

His face acquiring a florid cast, he got up from her desk. 'Hey, Kate. With all due respect – don't tell me how men feel about women. I'm a normal guy. I been married twenty-three years to a woman who's very happy about it. You don't understand. I don't expect you to. Just drop it.'

Here it was again, his unspoken judgment that being a lesbian rendered her invalid – an outsider, a misfit. 'Ed –'

'Do me a huge favor, Kate. Drop it. You're a great detective, a terrific partner. Let's not get into this other crap with each other, okay?'

Cold fury gathered within her. 'Then you do me a favor too, Ed. I intend to put together the best possible case for Kyle Jensen spending the rest of his unnatural life in the cage where he belongs. What he did was not manslaughter. It was murder.'

She watched in escalating rage as Taylor stood with his arms crossed and his legs spread, his face closed. 'Monday I'm in court so I need you at the autopsy.' She snapped off the words. 'The favor is, do only what you need to do on this case. Let me do the rest, and stay the hell out of my way.'

'It'll be a pleasure, not a favor.' He made a tiny, ironic bow, and turned his back on her. 'With your approval, I'll leave you to sweep up and I'll just take myself on home to Marie.'

(Katherine V. Forrest, *Murder By Tradition*, 1993, pp.66–8)

Although Delafield is an official investigator, other lesbian detectives have tended to be 'unofficials', tied to investigations by mischance or obligation (Sarah Dreher's trouble-prone Stoner MacTavish); through networks of solidarity (Barbara Wilson's Pam Nilsen); or by being in other investigatory trades such as journalism (Val McDermid's Lindsay Gordon). What these stories have in common is the representation of a complex social order which is hostile and oppressive but where there is an interlocking of 'straight' and 'alternative' worlds. There may be gay and lesbian 'sub-cultures', but, like the black America of Easy Rawlins, these are not treated as separate from or outside the social order – they are imagined as integral elements of it.

5.4   Absences and presences: the 'deviant' detective story

These new variations on the genre of the detective story create a more complex and conflictual sense of a social order composed of multiple social differences. Divisions based on 'races', ethnicity, gender and sexuality have become vital elements in the dynamics of the genre. Crime and its solution become intrinsically more problematic because they are seen as bound up in these social complexities and antagonisms. For these 'deviant' detectives to act – to bring about a resolution – not only must they solve the problem, but they must do so while negotiating the social minefield of divisions, inequalities and hostilities. Victims, villains, suspects, witnesses and the investigators are all placed in this complex of social relations. This complexity includes representations of how social, ethical and moral judgements are diverse, divided and contested. As the generic 'everyman' is displaced, the assumptions of a shared, consensual, popular morality are also called into question.

In the process, these innovations overturn the assumptions associated with the conventional nature of social order in the detective story. In the past, the imaginary social orders of the detective story have been predominantly concerned with class and status (the social distribution of power and wealth), and the allocation of other social roles, places and identities has been treated as unproblematic. They have 'naturalized' gendered, racialized and sexual identities. The rise of the 'deviant detective' makes these assumptions visible and renders them problematic. In the process, the nature of the imaginary social order changes, revealing different experiences, different structures of inequality and power and different sorts of crime – as well as placing familiar types of crime in new perspectives.

absences and presences

They do this by changing the characteristic structure of absences and presences in the detective story. In writing about the place of black people in the social sciences, Ann Phoenix (1990) has referred to the way in which they are defined by 'normalized absence' and 'pathologized presence'. When studying 'normal' patterns of social life in the UK and USA, social scientists tend to draw their evidence from the majority white population and identify its patterns as the 'norm'. In doing so, black people are invisible to such

deviant detective

research and theorizing – they exist only as a 'normalized absence'. Contexts in which they have been actively researched tend to be associated with 'deviant' behaviours, so that when they become visible they do so as a 'pathologized presence'. Although developed in relation to social science research, this framework also offers a way of understanding the changing social order of the detective story.

This is perhaps least obvious in the case of gender – in the English mystery, the PI story and the police procedural, women characters abound. But such women rarely escape a conventional repertoire of roles, ranging from the fragile flower to the *femme fatale*. They may well commit murders ('poison … a woman's weapon'), but they will do so from within a thoroughly conventional set of motives (greed, love, jealousy, revenge). In this sense, women have a 'conventionalized presence', in which the gendered differentiation of roles, character traits, motives and psychology are naturalized. The pattern of 'normalized absence' in the detective story tended to make detection a 'man's business' in which solving the problem of crime was a masculine prerogative, whether it was accomplished by rational thought or dynamic action.

Looking at racialized characterization in the detective story reveals more clearly the structure of normalized absence and pathologized presence. The world of the detective story is predominantly a white one – minority ethnic groups are not a feature of this world and do not provide central protagonists: they are a 'normalized absence'. Occasionally, they may appear peripherally in service roles, a 'conventionalized presence'. But if they do step out of the background, they are likely to do so as a 'pathologized presence': exotic, mysterious, suspicious and dangerous.

Similar observations can be made about the place of gay and lesbian characters. The interpersonal and sexual relationships of the conventional detective story are almost exclusively heterosexual ones – gay men and lesbians are a 'normalized absence'. Occasionally, they may gain a marginal appearance in stereotypical forms as an outrageously camp theatrical or hairdresser. If they move beyond this 'conventionalized presence', they represent the 'unnatural' and are suspect or dangerous because of it, a 'pathologized presence'.

It should be clear that the 'deviant' detective cannot be contained by these *naturalizing* assumptions. Indeed, the very presence of a woman, black or gay or lesbian detective at the centre of the story creates a different social order because we are viewing the world through what is, in the conventional story, an impossible perspective. We are seeing the world of conventional assumptions from outside rather than from inside and, as a result, we see different things. However, this metaphor of inside and outside is not really adequate or accurate – what we are seeing is the social order viewed from somewhere else within it. Such positions are usually 'looked at' rather than 'looking'. Seeing the social order from these 'elsewheres' changes the structure of normalized absences and pathologized presences – the 'deviant' becomes a normalized presence in a more complex social order.

In the process, some of the concerns of the conventional detective story take on different inflections. Like the traditional private eye, the deviant detective is a disenchanted observer of the social order and its corruption. For the woman detective, her disenchantment is not simply a state of mind but the product of her place and experiences – she will 'see' the patterns of power and wealth in both corporate crime and the gendered structure of relationships. Like the traditional solver of mysteries, she may be attentive to the 'familial' settings of crime, but her view of these settings will include an understanding of the gendered structuring and dynamics of power and its abuse. Like all the 'classic' detectives, she may understand the distinction between the Law and Justice, but she is likely to find it more complicated because neither individual justice nor social justice is easy to define. Perhaps most importantly, she must live with the problem that 'solving the problem' and restoring order at the end of the narrative is simultaneously restoring an order which is inequitable and oppressive.

Television's first lesbian detective? Detective Sergeant Maureen Connell (Siobhan Redmond) from BBC1's Between the Lines

Where analyses of the classic detective story have been able to assume that 'solving the problem' is equivalent to 'restoring order', in that it is crime which disrupts normality, no such easy assumption can be made in the context of the deviant detective story. *Crime is treated not as a disruption of a stable social order, rather as an expression of an order which is intrinsically unjust and dangerous.* In these representations, crime involves both 'crimes of the powerful' and the 'crimes of the powerless' – and is not separable from questions of power. Thus, there will always be a tension between 'solving the problem' and the wider context in which the conflict- and tension-ridden order continues. Even Warshawski's accomplishments in closing down a polluting chemical plant (Paretsky, 1990b), or stopping murderously corrupt corporate medicine (Paretsky, 1988), leave the structures which facilitate corporate crime untouched.

So what do these generic innovations add to the pleasures and satisfactions of the detective story? The most obvious is surely that they challenge the normalized assumptions and conventions of the detective story. While remaining within the genre, they disrupt or disturb our conventional expectations about crime and detection. In doing so, they increase the range of potential reading positions, and offer new points of identification to different types of reader. This may be as basic as saying that they create forms of detective fiction for new audiences, or at least audiences whose identities, experiences and points of view were previously excluded or marginalized. The 'new' detectives address and articulate (in fictional representations) experiences and identities of distinctive social constituencies. But it would be wrong to stop at this point, since the relationship between social position, or identity, and reading is rarely simple, one dimensional or exclusive. So these generic innovations also enable other readers to engage with the pleasures of differently imagined social orders and different points of view. Such novels offer readers different forms of 'cultural verisimilitude', presenting imagined worlds that draw on wider representations about gendered, racialized and sexualized social arrangements. Their 'realism' is constructed through a claim that 'we' know the world is like this, whether 'we' share the specific identity of the principal character or not. Gledhill has argued that popular genres are sites of engagement with other social and political representations of social arrangements and specifically of social change. Although she is writing about soap operas, her comments seem equally relevant to the detective story.

> ...multiple pressures towards innovation and renewal mean that popular genres not only engage with social change but become key sites for the emerging articulation of and contest over change. So the discourses and imagery of new social movements – for example, the women's, gay, or black liberation movements – which circulate into public consciousness through campaign groups, parliamentary and social policy debates, new and popular journalism, and other media representations, provide popular genres with material for new story lines and the pleasure of dramatic enactment.
>
> (Gledhill, 1997, p.362)

6   I have asked you all here ...

By now you must be wondering what the conclusion to all this is. Unfortunately, this is not a detective story in which all is revealed in the final section – no dramatic discovery of 'whodunit'. The reality is rather more dull. While there may be many reasons for enjoying detective stories, the concern here is with what is interesting about them in terms of a popular *imagery* of crime. We might simply note that they are not very 'realistic' in that they are predominantly concerned with the rarest of crimes – murder – rather than the commonplace. But that would be to miss the point that murder – perhaps more than anything else – is implicitly understood to be the most serious of crimes, the point at which the social relations of the social order are dramatically torn apart. Murder is so frequently the starting point or the focus for the detective story because it shows up the social relations of crime and order in stark relief. The extraordinary event, so to speak, casts a new light on the ordinary world, and is used to reveal things that might otherwise remain invisible. Detective stories, are, of course, 'only entertainment'. They do not claim to be factual analyses of crime and society or to offer profound theoretical investigations of crime and policing. Nevertheless, there are two ways in which paying these popular entertainments some attention is justified. The first of these concerns the conventional distinction between factual (or informational) reportage of crime and crime control and the fictional representation of these issues. Factual reportage – of crimes, policing, court cases and official statements about crime and criminality – aims to command our attention by telling us about something serious. In brief, such information tells us about the 'war against crime'. In such settings, 'crime' is the object of fear, anxiety and hostility on the part of society: it is something to be controlled and overcome. Popular entertainments such as the detective story do not fit this conventional assumption about the opposition between crime and society. Rather than crime being an object of 'repulsion', detective stories suggest that crime is simultaneously an object of fascination and attraction – an issue from which we can gain pleasure. Certainly, the detective story demonstrates this ambiguity. Its continuing popularity as a form of entertainment is a telling reminder about the seductions and attractions of crime. Our 'entertainments' are part of, not separate from, the social world that we inhabit. As such, the sources of pleasure that we choose and pursue may tell us something about that social world – and about how we live in it.

Poirot (Peter Ustinov) reveals all in Evil Under the Sun

Second, we need to think of the detective story as one of the strands contributing to our collective stock of images about crime and social order – such stories are one of the ways in which societies 'talk about crime'. Alongside official statements, reporting of criminal cases and documentary reconstructions, detective

social imagery stories both *draw on and contribute to* the social imagery of crime. They draw on social imagery in the ways in which they construct and present themselves as being realistic, plausible or even simply 'fun'. Like the classic mystery, they may lay claim to a nostalgically invented past of a stable aristocratic England, or, like the classic private eye stories, their 'realism' may be associated with everyday speech and the promise to reveal the 'seamy side' of life. But all of them have to make connections between their specific story and the wider stock of imagery about pasts, presents and futures of social order. Detective stories are one of the means through which representations of crime are circulated.

This raises a difficult point about the status or significance of such representations in social analysis. Detective stories do not present themselves as offering the 'truth' about crime and detection, even when they are celebrated for their 'gritty realism'. They are representations, and are fictional representations rather than non-fictional ones. As a result, we cannot discuss the genre, or variations in the genre, as simply 'reflecting' social reality or changes in it. As Richard Dyer has argued, 'what is re-presented in representations is not directly reality but other representations' (1993, p.2). In the case of detective novels, they selectively draw on, engage with or even challenge *both* generic conventions and the wider field of social representations – about crime, people, places, problems of order and disorder. This view of representation suggests that there is little value in trying to see either social order or social change having a direct impact on the detective story. But as the field of representations changes – for example around previously socially marginalized or subordinated groups – so the possibilities of 'realism' in detective stories change.

But if representations do not 'reflect' reality in a straightforward way, what relationship is there between reality and representation? One way of answering that question is to insist that representations are part of, not separate from, reality. Social reality in the contemporary world includes detective stories. They are material parts of life: consuming paper and print (or film stock or video tape) in their production. They occupy space and time. They are elements of commercial transactions, being bought and sold. They are sources of income and profit. But they are part of reality in ways that go beyond these material aspects. Reality includes our representations of it: how we define, construct and comprehend reality affects how we act in and on it. In this, detective fictions are an element in the repertoire of cultural resources on which we draw as social subjects (Dyer, 1993).

In the telling of their stories, though, detective fictions add to the collective imagery of crime and its social significance or meaning. They contribute to the ways in which we can understand and imagine the relationships between order and disorder. They provide other 'ways of seeing' crime – whether it be about tortuous family relationships, corporate corruption or how the social order looks when viewed from unfamiliar places. Like social science analyses, the detective story cannot escape making connections between crimes and their social settings, simply in order to be able to tell stories. In doing so, though, it may reinforce, reimagine or challenge conventional assumptions about both crime and the social order within which it takes place. The history of the detective story presents us not merely with changes in the sorts of crime that are the object of attention, and changes in who can be the detective, but also reveals shifting social perspectives on the societies in which crimes take place. In the course of this chapter, it has been possible to see the move away from a social order which was represented as stable and static (the mystery) to one which was flawed, disordered and corrupt (the PI). The rise of the 'deviant detective', however, has been accompanied by new representations of order as complex, unequal and *socially constructed*: no longer stable and 'natural' but tense and conflictual.

Review questions

- If you read or watch detective fictions, what do you think are the core pleasures of the genre?

- If you do not read or watch detective fictions, how would you go about explaining their widespread popularity?

- Why should social scientists give attention to things that are merely stories or only entertainment? Are such studies a diversion from more important business?

- Why might changes in who detects in crime fiction be significant?

- Is there just one 'problem of crime' in detective stories?

Further reading

The detective story has been subjected to very different types of analysis. Symon's *Bloody Murder* (1992) offers a literary history of the development of the detective novel, while Mandel's *Delightful Murder* (1984) presents a Marxist social history of the crime novel. Young's *Imagining Crime* (1996) explores different representations of crime, including detective stories, from a post-structuralist standpoint. Munt's *Murder By the Book* (1994) explores the relationships between gender, crime and detection in crime fiction, while Messent's *Criminal Proceedings: the contemporary American crime novel* (1997) explores the diversification of points of view in crime fiction. More generally, Dyer's studies of entertainment (*Only Entertainment*, 1992) and representation (*The Matter of Images*, 1993) address more general questions about fictional images.

Each of the novels which are the source of the extracts in this chapter bears reading. Of particular interest to those concerned with the intersection between crime fiction and theories of criminality is Philip Kerr's futuristic novel, *A Philosophical Investigation* (1992), which also raises issues about the relationships between gender, social order and policing.

References

Bailey, F.Y. and Hale, D.C. (1998) 'Popular culture, crime and justice', in Bailey, F.Y. and Hale, D.C. (eds) *Popular Culture, Crime and Justice*, Belmont, CA, West/Wadsworth Publishing Company.

Carr, J.D. (1964) *The Crooked Hinge*, New York, Collier Books. (First published in 1938.)

Chandler, R. (1988a) *The Big Sleep*, Harmondsworth, Penguin. (First published in 1939.)

Chandler, R. (1988b) *The Simple Art of Murder*, New York, Vintage Books. (First published in 1934.)

Christie, A. (1959) *Five Little Pigs*, Glasgow, Fontana Collins. (First published in 1943.)

Christie, A. (1968) *At Bertram's Hotel*, London, Fontana. (First published in 1965.)

Christie, A. (1993) *The ABC Murders*, London, HarperCollins. (First published in 1936.)

Clarke, J. (1990) 'Pessimism versus Populism: the problematic politics of popular culture', in Butsch, R. (ed.) *For Fun and Profit? The Transformation of Leisure into Consumption*, Philadelphia, Temple University Press.

Cody, L. (1982) *Dupe*, London, Pan.

Compton, D.G. (1997) *Back of Town Blues*, London, Verso.

Dyer, R. (1992) *Only Entertainment*, London, Routledge.

Dyer, R. (1993) *The Matter of Images: Essays on Representation*, London, Routledge.

Ellsworth, E. (1988) 'Illicit pleasures: feminist spectators and *Personal Best*', in Roman, L., Christian-Smith, L. and Ellsworth, E. (eds) *Becoming Feminine: the Politics of Popular Culture*, Brighton, The Falmer Press.

Ferrell, J. (1998) 'Criminalizing popular culture', in Bailey, F.Y. and Hale, D.C. (eds) *Popular Culture, Crime and Justice*, Belmont, CA, West/Wadsworth Publishing Company.

Forrest, K.V. (1987) *Murder at the Nightwood Bar*, London, Pandora.

Forrest, K.V. (1993) *Murder by Tradition*, London, Grafton. (First published in 1991.)

Gledhill, C. (1997) 'Genre and gender: the case of soap opera', in Hall, S. (ed.) *Representation: Cultural Representations and Signifying Practices*, London, Sage/Open University.

Glover, D. and Kaplan, C. (1992) 'Guns in the House of Culture? Crime fiction and the politics of the popular', in Grossberg, L., Nelson, C. and Treichler, P. (eds) *Cultural Studies*, New York, Routledge.

Goffman, E. (1959) *The Presentation of Self in Everyday Life*, New York, Doubleday Anchor.

Grella, G. (1980) 'The hard-boiled detective novel', in Winks, R.W. (ed.) *Detective Fiction*, New York, Prentice-Hall.

Hammett, D. (1975) *Red Harvest*, London, Pan. (First published in 1950.)

Hill, R. (1989) *Underworld*, London, Grafton.

Himes, C. (1992) *The Heat's On*, London, Allison and Busby. (First published in 1961.)

Johnson, P.E. (1994) 'Sex and betrayal in the detective fiction of Sue Grafton and Sara Paretsky', *Journal of Popular Culture*, vol.27, no.4, pp.97–106.

Kellerman, J. (1988) *Over the Edge*, London, Futura.

Kerr, P. (1992) *A Philosophical Investigation*, London, Arrow.

Komo, D. (1988) *Clio Browne, Private Investigator*, Freedom, CA, The Crossing Press.

Mandel, E. (1984) *Delightful Murder: A Social History of the Crime Novel*, London, Pluto.

Marcus, S. (1977) Introduction to Hammett, D. *The Continental Op*, London, Pan.

McLaughlin, E. (2001) 'From force to service: Issues in police, policing and police work', in McLaughlin, E. and Muncie, J. (eds) *Controlling Crime*, 2nd edn, London, Sage in association with The Open University.

Messent, P. (ed.) (1997) *Criminal Proceedings: The Contemporary American Crime Novel*, London, Pluto, 1997.

Mosley, W. (1992) *A Red Death*, London, Pan.

Mosley, W. (1993) *White Butterfly*, London, Serpent's Tail. (First published in 1992.)

Munt, S. (1994) *Murder by the Book: Crime Fiction and Feminism*, London, Routledge.

Palmer, J. (1991) *Potboilers: Methods, Concepts and Case Studies in Popular Fiction*, London, Routledge.

genre

105

Paretsky, S. (1988) *Bitter Medicine*, Harmondsworth, Penguin.

Paretsky, S. (1990a) *Burn Marks*, London, Chatto and Windus.

Paretsky, S. (1990b) *Toxic Shock*, Harmondsworth, Penguin.

Parker, R. (1987) *Looking for Rachel Wallace*, Harmondsworth, Penguin.

Phillips, M. (1995) *An Image to Die For*, London, Harper-Collins.

Phoenix, A. (1990) 'Theories of gender and black families', in Lovell, T. (ed.) *British Feminist Thought: A Reader*, Oxford, Blackwell.

Rosenberg, N.T. (1993) *Mitigating Circumstances*, London, Orion Books.

Sjöwall, M. and Wahlöö, P. (1978) *Cop Killer: The Story of a Crime*, New York, Vintage Books. (First published in Swedish in 1974, in English in 1975.)

Symons, J. (1992) *Bloody Murder: From the Detective Novel to the Crime Novel – A History*, 3rd edn, Harmondsworth, Penguin.

Watson, C. (1979) *Snobbery With Violence*, London, Eyre Methuen.

Weinkaupf, M.S. (1980) 'Miss Jane Marple and aging in literature', *Clues: A Journal of Detection*, vol.1, no.1, pp.32–40.

Wilson, B. (1986) *Sisters of the Road*, London, Virago.

Young, A. (1996) *Imagining Crime: Textual Outlaws and Criminal Conversations*, London, Sage.

CHAPTER 3

Crime, Order and Historical Change

by Jim Sharpe

Contents

1   Introduction

In this chapter we shall be examining a number of ways in which studying 'crime' as a historical phenomenon not only creates various points of contrast with current approaches to crime and criminals, but also suggests some long-term continuities. Although some reference will be made to earlier and later periods, our main concern will be with eighteenth-century England. (Regrettably, current levels of writing on crime and punishment in Scotland and Wales before the nineteenth century preclude these countries being treated with the same depth as England, while the study of crime in Ireland in the eighteenth and earlier centuries is impeded by the loss of records caused by fire in the Dublin Public Record Office in 1922.) It was the first two-thirds of the nineteenth century that were crucial in shaping 'modern' conventional thinking about crime and punishment (see also Chapter 4). For this reason, studying the very different law-enforcement system of the eighteenth century and the attitudes that underpinned it forces us to focus on a number of issues: definitional problems, including those arising from a conflation of sin and crime, from conflicting notions about property rights, and from the friction between customary practices and statute law; the peculiarities of a system of law enforcement dependent upon local, amateur officers; the peculiar logic of the ideology of punishment during this period; and the importance of the community in law enforcement. These and other factors combined to produce distinctive attitudes to crime and its control. Some of these seem very distant to the citizen of the modern, bureaucratized state.

This distance has not deterred intensive work on the history of crime over the last twenty-five years, and research on periods between the fourteenth and twentieth centuries has revealed a great deal about criminal behaviour in the past. There is no unified 'historical approach' to the study of crime in the past: historians, like criminologists, disagree about how best to gather, conceptualize and analyse their data. However, there is a substantial body of published work available which both presents research findings and discusses approaches to the subject (see Cockburn, 1977; Brewer and Styles, 1980; and Innes and Styles, 1986).

The need to have some historical background can be justified by two main lines of argument. The first is the frequency with which the current debate about crime and punishment all too easily slides into contrasting our present situation with some supposed earlier state, in which the problems we experience are presumed either to have been absent or to have been present in a much less serious form. Studying the history of crime and punishment does at least facilitate informed comment on this type of discussion. Second, and more relevant for the immediate purposes of this chapter, studying the history of crime (like studying the history of anything) forces us to forget the assumptions of our own culture and to confront those of another. In so doing, we have to accept the sometimes uncomfortable notion, equally present in anthropology, that other people act on other assumptions, and organize their ways of doing things differently from those in a declining post-industrial state at the beginning of the twenty-first century. Attempting to grasp these differences, to understand how they were rational in their own cultural context, can inform our understanding of the complexities we face. If nothing else, studying the history of crime and punishment reminds us that our current ways of thinking about and dealing with these problems are not the only ones that human beings have found appropriate.

2 Crime in eighteenth-century England: the problem of definition

Throughout this chapter we will be looking at how conceptions of crime have changed through time, and how this was often reflected in how crime was punished. This section discusses the problem of defining crime, and focuses on the eighteenth and early nineteenth centuries. Any attempt to range more widely would be confusing in the space available. However, it is important to grasp that by the beginning of the eighteenth century competing definitions of crime were already well established in two areas. The first was constituted by what could be described as competing notions of 'state' and 'community' perspectives on crime and law enforcement. The second was created by the problems which many contemporary observers had in distinguishing between 'crime' and 'sin'. To these might be added, at the risk of dipping too deeply into the complexities of legal history, a third complication: the distinction between civil and criminal law, which was not as clear in earlier periods as it is today. This could be especially relevant to the treatment of, and the formation of attitudes towards, certain types of property offences in a period that witnessed increasing commercialization and in which the law relating to property and to related matters of debt, credit and fraud was still developing (see Chapter 1, section 2.5).

As will be discussed later in this chapter, neither 'state' nor 'community' were unproblematic concepts in the eighteenth century. However, between the Middle Ages and the eighteenth century, in England as in much of western **state law** and central Europe, there was a general tendency for state law to impinge increasingly on the region or the community, and on the plural legal systems which these enjoyed. There are enormous problems in defining exactly what state law was, not least in a political system like eighteenth-century England where the state was at a curious stage of its development, showing both 'modern' and pre-modern tendencies. Broadly, state law could be regarded as the law being supported by central government, created, extended or redefined by parliamentary statute, and, arguably, representing either the values, ideas and interests of England's ruling elites or of sections of those elites or of interest groups within them. Thus, over the seventeenth and eighteenth centuries, the criminal law, constantly extended by parliamentary statute, was becoming increasingly important in the wider repertoire of social control.

The locus of law-making and legal thinking represented by parliament and central government contrasted with the situation in the localities. Although the common law, enforced in the monarch's courts, had long been, in theory at least, the decisive element in most legal matters, before the seventeenth century most villages and small towns were very much self-policing communities. Law-enforcement officers were local, and the law, although in England essentially the common law of the realm, was often modified by local custom, local laws, and local opinion on what might be the best way of dealing with specific offenders and offences. This situation was always at its most marked when petty offences were under consideration: the more serious offences, such as murder, theft, burglary, robbery and rape, were increasingly left to royal judges. But over the period 1500 to 1700 it is possible to trace a slow process by which petty offenders would be more likely to be tried before the local manorial courts in 1500, before the ecclesiastical (or church) courts (still in many respects locally based) in 1600, and before justices of the peace (local men, but essentially royal officials) at petty sessions in 1700. The law in eighteenth-century England was still not the preserve of a centralized sovereign state, but a transition towards something like this situation took place over the seventeenth and eighteenth centuries. This transition involved changing emphases on what was considered deviant.

The Bench, *an engraving by William Hogarth (1758)*

2.1 Sin and crime

Most local communities without doubt desired order, and the fact that the state legal system was able to make such an advance was largely due to a growing awareness in communities that this legal system offered an effective way of dealing with local troublemakers and settling local disputes. Sometimes the range of deviant behaviour reported by local law enforcement could be very wide, and might seem very odd to the modern observer. The archives of the ecclesiastical courts give a good indication of this. During the seventeenth century (and possibly later in some areas), the ecclesiastical courts were responsible for disciplining the clergy, maintaining the fabric of church buildings, and ensuring attendance at church and conformity to the rites of the Church of England, but they were also responsible for controlling sexual morality and matrimonial disputes. The occasional prosecution for working on the sabbath or for usury (the taking of interest on loans) involved the courts in economic regulation, while their role in testamentary business (the supervision of wills and the settling of disputes) rendered them important in property transactions. The function of the church courts in disciplining society demonstrates that studying the criminal law and its operation alone in the early modern period would lead us to miss a number of important points.

The importance of the ecclesiastical courts in maintaining social discipline is well illustrated from a contemporary document. The following presentment – the ecclesiastical courts' equivalent of a formal criminal charge – was made by the churchwardens of Banbury in Oxfordshire to the local archdeacon's court in 1610:

> wee present Anthony Hall upon a fame and suspition of incontinencie [sexual immorality] with Sarah Band. Wee present Wm Cooke for sicking in the church yeard the 1st of October. Wee present James West and John Greene for working on St Micaels Day. Wee present Thomas Tymber upon a suspition of incontinencie with Sarah Band. Wee present Sarah Band upon a fame of suspition of incontinencie with Anthony Hall & with Thomas Tymber. Wee present Humfray Devis for sicking in the church the 5 of November. Wee present Mary Smith for fornication. Wee present Robart, servant with the myller for fornication with a woman's daughter of Broughton. Wee present Epiphan Bird for unseemly speeches to Bartholomewe Naler Churchwarden. Wee present Henry Glover for making water in the church.
>
> (cited in Hair, 1972, p. 80)

This indicates the dimensions of control at which the authorities might aim in this period, and the range of behaviour that might be prosecuted once those dimensions were accepted. The presentment reminds us that in the seventeenth century, notions about the suppression of crime were very closely connected

sin

with ideas about the need to combat sin: indeed, before the eighteenth century it is very difficult to find much by way of discussion of 'crime' in the modern sense. It has been argued that over the eighteenth century a conventional wisdom about crime control that sprang from religion was replaced by one which saw the need to control crime as an important aspect of that most secular of concerns, the defence of property (Hay, 1975).

Despite the beginnings of a more secular attitude to crime, the religious input into thinking about crime in the eighteenth and early nineteenth centuries was considerable. The start of the eighteenth century witnessed a moral crusade against prostitutes, drunkards, the keepers of disorderly alehouses, swearers and sabbath-breakers in the form of the Societies for the Reformation of Manners, locally based and religiously driven organizations which sprang up in London and a number of provincial centres (Shoemaker, 1992). This development originated from a grassroots concern among respectable householders on what were then the fringes of London that these offences, many of them within the jurisdiction of the ecclesiastical courts, whose disciplinary work was probably fading in the metropolitan and other urban areas, were being allowed to flourish. The great drive towards prison reform in the later eighteenth century, symbolized by John Howard and Elizabeth Fry, similarly owed much to the religious values of its proponents. Throughout the century, the sermons preached at assizes, the accounts of the careers and executions of criminals written by the Ordinary of Newgate, and a continual output of moral tracts served to remind public opinion of the close connection between criminality and sinfulness.

2.2 Social crime

Despite these provisos, the eighteenth century and, perhaps less equivocally, the first half of the nineteenth century did witness the development of what we would consider to be 'modern' attitudes to crime and what ought to be done about it. Crime was increasingly seen as a phenomenon devoid of overtones of sin, which was best dealt with through legislation, trial before royal judges, and punishment in officially sanctioned methods by the state. Moreover, the eighteenth century, as we have hinted, was also the period which saw the emergence of crime or, perhaps more accurately, of law and order in general, as matters of public debate. By the middle of the century a number of writers, of whom the brothers John and Henry Fielding were the best known, were alerting the public to the menace posed by crime, and were suggesting methods of dealing with it (Rogers, 1992). At the same time, the respectable could read in their newspapers of sensational crimes, of the rewards that were being offered for stolen goods, or of the penalties awarded to run-of-the-mill offenders at the local county assizes. The media in earlier periods were just as likely as their modern counterparts to sensationalize the more newsworthy aspects of crime. Most important, perhaps, 'crime' was beginning to take on something like the modern layperson's definition: murder, rape, the more serious property offences like theft, robbery and burglary, and the host of lesser offences which served as precursors to them.

Yet, as historians have argued, even as the eighteenth-century elites were slipping into accepting this set of 'modern' attitudes towards crime, their social inferiors were holding alternative views. The key concept here is that of social crime. According to the classic definition of this concept, crime can be regarded as 'social' when it represents 'a conscious, almost a political challenge to the prevailing social and political order and its values'. It occurs when there exist conflicting sets of official and unofficial interpretations of the legal system, when acts of law-breaking manifest distinct elements of social protest, or when such acts are clearly connected to social or political unrest (Hobsbawm, 1975, pp.5–6). **social crime**

The concept is a somewhat slippery one. It was developed largely by a group of Marxist historians who were anxious to interpret certain forms of law-breaking as what might be termed 'pre-class, class conflict'. Therefore, a number of offences which could be portrayed as reflecting popular or community values, such as rioting, poaching, smuggling and wrecking, were singled out for special attention. The concept is of less use, as the group of historians in question accepted, in explaining the actions of 'those who commit crime without qualification: thieves, robbers, highwaymen, forgers, arsonists and murderers' (Hay *et al.*, 1975, p.14; for a revisiting of many relevant themes see Rule and Wells, 1997). It has, however, proved important in demonstrating how various forms of popular action and popular customs in this period, although criminalized by officialdom, were not regarded as blameworthy either by those committing them or by the communities from which they came. **popular custom**

Perhaps the clearest, and certainly best-documented, area where these differing attitudes can be seen in operation was constituted by rioting and other forms of popular disturbances (Stevenson, 1992). Close examination reveals that many eighteenth-century 'riots' were in fact what modern terminology would describe as demonstrations, and had rational ends rather than being the product of gin-sodden desperation. The historian E.P. Thompson has argued that those participating in riots often held legitimizing notions, 'legitimation' to Thompson meaning that 'the men and women in the crowd were defending traditional rights and customs; and, in general, that they were supported by the wider consensus of the community' (Thompson, 1975).

Other offences, less dramatic than the riot, allow us to reconstruct how the conflict between elite law and popular custom might work itself out in the local context. The game laws, which might have led to an agricultural labourer suffering severe legal penalties for stealing a rabbit or two for the pot, are an obvious example. Less well known, but equally important at the time, were disputes over 'gleaning' and the collection of firewood, which was redefined by landlords as a form of theft on many estates (Bushaway, 1982). Gleaning was the poor's customary right of picking over the fields for ears of loose corn at harvest time. As agriculture became more capitalist and more market oriented, landowners and farmers, increasingly anxious to maximize profits, became impatient of what they considered to be encroachment on their property.

Detailed study sometimes casts doubt on this 'custom into crime' paradigm. Gleaning provides an interesting example. The poor's notion that they had a right to glean was apparently quashed following a decision in a civil case, *Steel* v. *Houghton* (1788), in which the Court of Common Pleas decided that there was no right to glean under common law, and that persons gleaning fields without the permission of the landowner were trespassing. As might be imagined, this intensified confrontations between gleaners and farmers. It also prompted a minor social debate, in which a number of contributors argued in favour of gleaning on moral grounds (biblical texts could be found to justify it) and on the more pragmatic basis that denying the poor this access to gleaning would increase demands on the poor rates. The poor themselves pleaded that although they might have no common law right to glean, they had customary rights, and a number of legal decisions, sidestepping *Steel* v. *Houghton*, upheld this point of view. The upshot was that, despite the 1788 ruling, many of the rural poor in eastern England continued to feel that they had a traditional right to glean. As *The Farmer's Lawyer* of 1819 put it, the poor had no common law right to glean, but should be permitted to do so, subject to local practices, if there was 'an immemorial custom or usage in the parish' (King, 1989).

The definition of crime in rural areas was thus being complicated by popular ideas on custom, ideas which could hold such a consistent traditional view of social norms and obligations, and of the proper nature of economic relations between different social strata, as to constitute a moral economy. Meanwhile, the continuing economic development of the eighteenth and early nineteenth centuries was creating further complexities. Modern criminologists are now familiar with the concept of 'white-collar' crime – that is, crime committed by ostensibly 'respectable' people in the everyday course of their professional or business life. So far, historians have paid little attention to the historical antecedents of white-collar crime, yet it is obvious that something very like it was emerging with fraud and forgery cases in the eighteenth century. The subject awaits further investigation. It is clear, nevertheless, that forgery was regarded as a serious offence. In the middle of the eighteenth century, the celebrated

moral economy

legalist Sir William Blackstone claimed that the growth of statutory capital sanctions against forgery was the outcome of a perceived need to protect financial and banking interests which were seeking legal defences for paper credit and exchange in a period of rapid commercial growth. In the period 1804–15, 84 people were sentenced to death for forgery in London and Middlesex, and 47 executed. In the same period, and in the same area, 26 people were executed for murder, 18 for burglary, and 17 for highway robbery. Clearly the courts were treating forgery, essentially an offence created in the eighteenth century, with considerable severity (Emsley, 1996, p.258).

ACTIVITY 3.1

Historians studying early modern England have commented on the problems of distinguishing between sin, crime and social crime. To what extent can you sympathize with their comments? And how far, in a modern society, can thinking about crime be separated from wider concerns about morality? Make some notes of your own on why it might be difficult to reach an incontrovertible definition of crime.

When considering 'crime' in eighteenth- and nineteenth-century England, we are, as now, confronted by a wide range of behaviour and definitions. Then, again as now, 'crime' was essentially a blanket term that enfolded a number of acts, from murder to illicit wood-taking. Obviously people at the time had some notion of the relative seriousness of these acts, although different people might rank them differently, while, as we have seen, a number of different perspectives might add coherence to these rankings. Religious individuals, imbued with a strong sense of humankind's sinfulness, would have one set of ideas on crime. Rural labourers and their families performing acts which they thought were defended by custom but which were now declared illegal, and hence criminalized, might have another. Further complications lay in the right which many industrial and craft workers felt they had to the benefits of fiddles and of the right to 'waste' materials (a category which workers might interpret generously), generically known as 'perquisites', at the workplace. Men of property, whether country gentry concerned about the burglary of their houses or the theft of their horses, or merchants concerned over forgery, might have another. As a result, even a brief review of the problems of defining crime in just one historical period helps remind us of how definitions might shift and how, at any given point, there might not be an absolute, or indeed any, consensus as to what constituted a 'criminal' act.

3   The system of crime control

It is perhaps a little misleading to describe the apparatus for detecting, trying, punishing and deterring crime in eighteenth-century England as a 'system'. It was, rather, a complex of institutions, officers and practices which interacted, usually more or less in unison, to punish offenders. However, understanding at least something of this complex is a logical next step now that we have considered some of the definitional problems of crime. Unfortunately, the documentation of the period rarely provides us with more than scattered evidence of how those involved in enforcing the law felt about what they were doing. But, arguably, the attitudes of such people are crucial to our understanding of conceptions of crime. Similarly, a study of penal practices, not least of forms of punishment, gives us, if ony by inference, insights into how crime was regarded. Here, as elsewhere, the interplay between crime, law and control agencies is of importance because it tells us what crime meant, in practice. And, once again, consideration of these issues in a historical context provides us with a number of points of contrast and comparison with the current situation.

3.1   Capital punishment: the Bloody Code

The aspect of this complex that has perhaps attracted most attention from historians was the heavy dependence on capital punishment. Most contemporary European states exercised capital punishment, of course, while some regularly adopted aggravated forms of judicial killing, such as breaking on the wheel, which many English observers felt to be repugnant.

In eighteenth-century England, aggravated capital punishment was largely reserved for those convicted of treason: males thus convicted might be subjected to the barbarities of hanging, drawing and quartering, while women convicted of treason (which included wives murdering their husbands) might be burnt at the stake. For persons convicted of felony, the punishment was generally hanging. At the end of every county assize, and eight times a year at Tyburn, murderers, burglars, thieves, rapists, sodomites, highway robbers, forgers and infanticidal mothers were hanged, sometimes in large numbers (Linebaugh, 1991). The frequency with which different types of offenders were hanged, and fluctuations in the use of this punishment, will be discussed in section 3.1.1. The emphasis here is on the importance of the public execution of criminals as a symbolic expression of the majesty of the law.

As the eighteenth century progressed, the number of offences that could incur the death penalty increased steadily. Indeed, in 1688, the year of the Glorious Revolution, which the eighteenth-century English were to regard as the salvation of the English constitution and the English way of political life, about 50 offences already carried the death penalty. By 1800, this total had risen to about 200, all of the additions being imposed by parliamentary statutes, and most of these being concerned with the defence of property (see appendix to the report from the Select Committee on Criminal Laws, pp.118–19 below).

The statutes recommending capital punishment have commonly been referred to as the 'Bloody Code'. The reasons for this legislative process remain obscure, and research in progress suggests that they probably owed more to parliamentary processes and an extension of what were perceived as normal ways of dealing with crime than anything else. But established interpretation attributes the Bloody Code to an increased capitalist and commercial ethic among Britain's ruling class, who were therefore anxious to defend property through legislation. This has led a number of historians to consider the eighteenth-century Bloody Code as a straightforward example of the law as a form of class oppression, of the rule of the rich and propertied over the poor and propertyless (Hay, 1975; Linebaugh, 1991). The observations of some contemporaries lend support to such a view. For example, Adam Smith, the well-known proponent of capitalist economics, wrote:

> When … some have great wealth and others nothing, it is necessary that the arm of authority should be constantly stretched forth, and permanent laws or regulations made which may protect the property of the rich from the inroads of the poor … Laws and governments may be considered in this and in every case as a combination of the rich to oppress the poor, and preserve to themselves the inequality of the goods which would otherwise soon be destroyed by the attacks of the poor, who if not hindered by the government would soon reduce the others to an equality with themselves by open violence.
>
> (cited in Emsley, 1996, p.9)

Both what can be recreated of the formulation of statutes in parliament, and research into the actual workings of the courts, demonstrate that a simple model of 'class law' does not provide a complete explanation for the English situation in the eighteenth century. Even so, the heavy dependence of eighteenth-century English criminal law on capital punishment, and the frequent execution of property offenders in England, are remarkable phenomena.

3.1.1   Public execution

As many historians have noted, these frequent executions of property offenders and others were carried out in public. Again, there are considerable dangers of oversimplification: it is all too easy for the modern historian to write off the public execution as a sign of the barbarity of past periods. But the comments of some eighteenth-century observers lend weight to such a view:

> Tho' before setting out, the prisoners took care to swallow what they could, to be drunk, and stifle their fear; yet the courage that strong liquors can give, wears off, and the way they have to go being considerable, they are in danger of recovering, and without repeating the dose, sobriety would often overtake them: for this reason they must drink as they go; and the cart stops for that purpose three or four, and sometimes half a dozen times or more, before they come to their journey's end … At the very place of execution, the most remarkable scene is a vast multitude on foot, intermixed with many horsemen and hackney-coaches, all very dirty, or else cover'd with dust, that are either abusing one another, or else staring at the prisoners, among whom there is commonly very little devotion; and that, which is practis'd at dispatch'd there, of course, there is as little good sense as there is melody. It is possible that a man of extraordinary holiness, by anticipating the joys of heaven, might embrace death in such raptures, as would dispose him to the singing of psalms: but to require this exercise, or expect it promiscuously of every wretch that comes to be hang'd, is as wild and extravagant as the performance of it is commonly frightful and impertinent: besides this, there is always at that place, such a mixture of oddnesses and hurry, that from what passes, the best dispos'd spectator seldom can pick out any thing that is edifying or moving.
>
> (de Mandeville, 1725, pp.23, 24–5)

Yet this concentration on the bestial elements of public execution has tended to obscure a number of nuances. The public execution could be a complex cultural event (in fact, some have claimed that it marked a meeting point between elite and popular culture) in which a number of complex rituals might be observed.

The central performers (for the public execution was, on a number of levels, a piece of theatre) were the convicted felons. These were expected to 'die gamely'. Consequently, a highway robber, a category of offender which was

APPENDIX TO REPORT FROM

Appendix, No. 5—*continued*   -   -   -   -

A STATEMENT of the Number of Persons who were Capitally Convicted, and of

	YEARS:											
	1776.			**1777.**			**1778.**			**1779.**		
	Convicted of.	Committed for.	Executed.	Convict'd of.	Committed for.	Executed.	Convict'd of.	Committed for.	Executed	Convict'd of.	Committed for.	Executed
Arson - - - - -	—	—	—	—	—	—	—	—	—	—	—	—
Burglary - - - - -	19	13; Simple Larceny 5, Robbery, 1 } 9		19	13; Simple Larceny, 3 Highway Robbery, 3 } 12		29	28; Simple Larceny, 1 } 24		16	15; Highway Robbery, 1 } 7	
Cattle Stealing - - - -	—	—	—	1	1	—	—	—	—	—	—	—
Coin, counterfeit putting off at a lower rate, &c. having before been allowed the benefit of Clergy - - -	—	—	—	—	—	—	—	—	—	—	—	—
Customs, assembling with others, being armed, in order to rescue uncustomed Goods after seizure, and molesting the Officers in securing the Goods after seizure - - - - -	—	—	—	—	—	—	—	—	—	—	—	—
Dwelling-house, entering and destroying Silk in a loom - - - -	—	—	—	—	—	—	—	—	—	—	—	—
Forgery - - - - -	2	2	1	3	3	1	2	2	—	2	1; Stealing a Bill of Exchange, 1 } 2	
Horse, wilfully and maliciously wounding	—	—	—	—	—	—	—	—	—	—	—	—
Horse Stealing - - - - -	3	3	—	4	4	—	3	2; Robbery, 1 }	—	4	4	—
Housebreaking in the Day-time, and Larceny therein - - - -	—	—	—	4	Simple Larceny, 4 }	—	—	—	—	—	—	—
Larceny in a Dwelling-house to the value of 40 s. - - -	7	Robbery, 1 Privately Person, 1 Simple Larceny 4 Burglary, 1 } 3		8	2; Simple Larceny, 6 } 5		8	2; Simple Larceny, 6 } 2		10	2; Burglary, 1 Privately in a Shop, 1 Robbery, 1 Simple Larceny, 4 Larceny on Person, 1 } 4	
Larceny on a Navigable River, to the value of 40 s. - - -	—	—	—	—	—	—	—	—	—	—	—	—
Larceny privily from a Person, to the value of 1 s. - - - -	1	Simple Larceny, 1 }	—	—	—	—	—	—	—	—	—	—
Larceny privily in a Coach-house, to the value of 5 s. - - -	—	—	—	—	—	—	—	—	—	—	—	—

Appendix to the report from the Select Committee on Criminal Laws, 1819: a statement of the number of people who were capitally convicted and of those who were executed in London and Middlesex

APPENDIX TO REPORT FROM SELECT COMMITTEE ON CRIMINAL LAWS.

A STATEMENT of the Number of Persons who were Capitally Convicted,
those who were Executed in London and Middlesex, &c.

	YEARS:											
	1776.			1777.			1778.			1779.		
(continued.)	Con-vict⁴ of.	Committed for.	Exe-cuted.	Con-vict⁴ of.	Committed for.	Exe-cuted.	Con-vict⁴ of.	Committed for.	Exe-cuted.	Con-vict⁴ of.	Committed for.	Exe-cuted.
Larceny privily in a Shop, to the value of 5 s.	4	1; Simple Larceny, 3	–	1	1	–	1	Simple Larceny, 1	–	2	1; Simple Larceny, 1	–
Larceny privily in a Stable, to the value of 5 s.	–	–	–	–	–	–	1	1	1	–	–	–
Larceny privily in a Warehouse, to the value of 5 s.	–	–	–	–	–	–	–	–	–	–	–	–
Letter, Threatening	–	–	–	–	–	–	1	1	–	1	1	–
Letter, Secreting, containing valuable Securities, being employed in the Post Office	–	–	–	–	–	–	–	–	–	1	1	1
Mail, Stealing Bags and Letters from	–	–	–	–	–	–	–	–	–	–	–	–
Maiming a Person maliciously, and lying in wait	–	–	–	–	–	–	–	–	–	–	–	–
Murder	6	6	6	2	2	2	1	1	1	1	1	1
Naval Stores, Stealing, to the value of 20s.	–	–	–	–	–	–	–	–	–	–	–	–
Oath, False, to receive a Seaman's Wages	–	–	–	–	–	–	–	–	–	–	–	–
Personating another, and obtaining a Transfer of Bank Annuities	–	–	–	–	–	–	–	–	–	–	–	–
Personating another, to receive a Seaman's Wages	–	–	–	–	–	–	–	–	–	–	–	–
Rack and Tenters, Cutting and Stealing Cloth from	–	–	–	–	–	–	–	–	–	–	–	–
Rape	–	–	–	1	1	1	1	1	1	1	1	1
Riot, and demolishing Dwelling-houses, &c.	–	–	–	–	–	–	–	–	–	–	–	–
Robbery	23	27; Simple Larceny, 1	10	16	12; Maliciously Shooting, 1 Larceny in Dw. Ho. 1 Burglary, 1 Larceny on Person, 1	9	31	26; Simple Larceny, 3 Defraud, 2	6	13	11; Simple Larceny, 2	5
Sheep Stealing	1	1	–	–	–	–	–	–	–	1	1	–
Shooting at another maliciously	–	–	–	1	1	–	3	2; Transports at large, 1	3	–	–	–
Sodomy	2	2	2	–	–	–	–	–	–	–	–	–
Stamps, denoting the Payment of Duties, forging them	–	–	–	–	–	–	–	–	–	–	–	–
Transport at large, without lawful cause	3	2; Simple Larceny, 1	–	1	1	–	–	–	–	1	Robbery, 1	–
Treason, High, compassing the King's Death	–	–	–	–	–	–	–	–	–	–	–	–
Treason, High, relating to Coin	10	10	7	1	1	1	1	1	–	4	4	3
	86	–	38	62	–	31	82	–	38	57	–	24

already being mythologized as a popular hero, would be expected to die bravely, showing no signs of fear on the gallows. For other offenders, remorse might be seen as a more appropriate emotion; from the early seventeenth century onwards, convicted murderers in particular were expected to make a speech along more or less conventional lines, in which offenders would confess their crimes, express the hope that their fate would serve as a deterrent to others, and link their presence on the gallows to a gradual slide into sinfulness which usually began with disobedience to parents and went on to include idleness, drunkenness, and consorting with prostitutes. If the offender behaved appropriately, the crowd responded accordingly, cheering the game highwayman, perhaps weeping with the penitent murderer, booing and perhaps pelting the offender who behaved inappropriately or who was thought to have committed an especially heinous crime. The hangman was also expected to behave efficiently and with a proper regard for those suffering at his hands. Failure to do so on his part could lead to rioting by the crowd, who were also prone to attempt to rescue the bodies of hanged felons destined for dissection in anatomy classes (Linebaugh, 1975), or to save those 'half hanged' individuals who survived the initial attempt to strangle them at the rope's end. In the eighteenth century (indeed, down to 1868) executions of criminals were normally carried out in public. What do you think were the objectives and outcome of this practice?

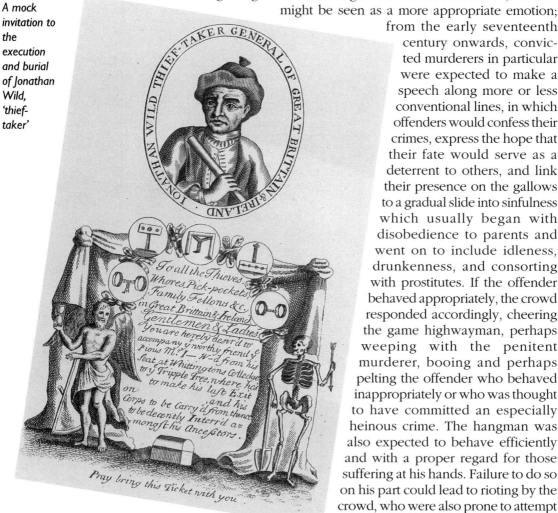

A mock invitation to the execution and burial of Jonathan Wild, 'thief-taker'

3.2   Courts and officers

This 'theatre of punishment' coexisted with a rather more mundane system of courts and law-enforcement officers (Sharpe, 1999). At the centre of the court system lay the assizes. Since the Middle Ages, the assize system had been a vital component of England's law-enforcement machine. The country, with the exception of London, Middlesex and a few provincial palatinate jurisdictions (that is, areas which, since the Middle Ages, had enjoyed a degree of autonomy within the English administrative system), was divided into six circuits, each comprising a number of counties. Twice every year, in January and around midsummer, teams of two judges would be sent out from Westminster to hear civil disputes in the provinces and to try criminal cases. Serious offenders would be held in the county gaols until the assize judges came, and would then be tried before them. The assizes thus constituted an effective, and by the eighteenth century, widely accepted means of bringing royal justice to the localities.

3.2.1 The criminal courts

The county assizes, like so much else in the eighteenth century, consisted of a curious mixture of the august and the ramshackle. As with public execution, the assizes were surrounded by ceremony. The judges were met at the borders of each of the counties they were to visit by the sheriff and a retinue of gentlemen. They were wined and dined in style, the proceedings of the court were attended with due ritual, and prefaced by a sermon in which a local clergyman would be allowed to display his rhetorical powers. Descriptions of trials (alas, all too rare for the earlier eighteenth century), however, reveal a rather less decorous situation. The accused and their accusers might indulge in unseemly wrangles. Idiosyncratic judges, then as now, might make the law an ass. The growing attractions of the assizes as an occasion for general socializing meant that there was usually a large crowd of spectators present in court. Indeed, by the eighteenth century, assize week was one of the main events in the social calendar for the county gentry and the elite of the town where the assize was held, the deliberations of the courts normally being accompanied by social gatherings, balls and horse races.

Although it was the assizes that most commonly dealt with serious crime, a number of other courts were still active. County quarter sessions, although by now concerned with local administration as much as crime control, still tried petty offences such as the less serious forms of larceny, assault and the breach of economic regulations. Many boroughs had the right to hold sessions, and tried a similar range of offenders. However, perhaps the most remarkable aspect of the English system was the use of petty sessions as a means of local regulation and crime control. The petty sessions, despite a number of earlier experiments, were essentially the result of an attempt to tighten local administration in 1631 after two years of economic crisis. One aspect of this push towards greater administrative efficiency was the practice of encouraging groups of local justices of the peace (in effect, normally three or four at a time) to meet every month to supervise various aspects of local government and law enforcement over a sub-unit of their counties known as a division. By the eighteenth century, these monthly meetings of justices were known as petty sessions, and were an established part of local government.

3.2.2 Justices of the peace

The operation of the petty sessions, and indeed the functioning of law enforcement in general, depended heavily on the justices of the peace. The office of justice had its origins in the fourteenth century, but perhaps experienced its most important formative period during the Tudor and Stuart periods, when the justices had an ever expanding burden of administration and law enforcement placed on them by statute. That the justices were willing to cooperate with this imposition is evidence of changes in the nature of local elites in England. Again, we confront a peculiarity of the English system. Most aspects of local law enforcement were dependent not on state-appointed salaried officials, but rather on unpaid amateur gentlemen administrators, many of them with little formal legal training. By the eighteenth century, it had long been established that becoming a justice of the peace was a sign that a gentleman had arrived socially and politically in his locality. The assize judges from Westminster might inject a professional judicial element into the trial of serious offenders, but the initial examination of those offenders and sending them to prison, as well as the punishment of petty offenders, was essentially the work of the justice of the peace.

Many justices kept notebooks in which they recorded their activities, and these can provide fascinating evidence into crime control in the period. Consider, for example, a series of entries from the notebook of William Hunt, a JP in Wiltshire:

> 11 May 1747. Granted a warrant at the complaint of Jane French of Earl Stoke against Mary Wise of the same parish, single woman, touching in particular the said Mary Wise's violent abusing of her the said Jane French so that she was actually in great fear of her life, as also her threatening to burn her house. She ran away so could not be apprehended whereby to be brought to justice.

> 13 May 1747. Granted by Thomas Phipps, esq, a warrant at the complaint of Mary the wife of Edward Tucker of Imber, carpenter, against Christopher Beaven of the same parish, thatcher, and Jane, his wife, for their violent assaulting and beating of the complainant in a barbarous manner and threatening to shoot her with a pistol. The parties agreed without a hearing.

> 15 May 1747. Granted a warrant at the complaint of Thomas Shipman or Sims of Allington, labourer, against Daniel Neat of the same parish, labourer, touching in particular the said Daniel Neat's unlawfully detaining and keeping in his custody divers household goods, the property of the said Thomas Shipman or Sims and for his refusing to deliver up the same on demand thereof. The parties agreed on hearing before me.

> 15 May 1747. Granted a warrant at the complaint of John Swain of the parish of Urchfont, labourer, against James Allexander of the parish of Tilshead, labourer, touching in particular the said James Allexander taking up a hat in the market place of Market Lavington and abusing it by pissing in it, the property of the said John Swain as he was about his lawful business as a sack-carrier. The defendant made the complainant satisfaction for the hat.

(Hunt, 1744–49, p.63)

One aspect of the justices' powers was that they enjoyed formidable powers of summary conviction. The country gentleman serving as justice of the peace (women JPs did not become a possibility until 1919) might expect to enjoy considerable informal paternalistic powers over his neighbourhood, and frequently used his influence to settle disputes between neighbours without invoking the law. William Hunt's notebook, as the brief passage cited above makes clear, contains numerous references to this practice. When the law needed to be invoked, the justice possessed considerable authority by statute. Thus, Gabriel Walters, a justice in Kent in the early eighteenth century, was involved in 304 cases between July 1708 and December 1710. Many of these involved purely formal action on the justice's part – signing 123 certificates that recently deceased persons had been buried in wool, for example (a practice required by late seventeenth-century statutes aimed at protecting the woollen industry). But 54 of these cases, heard in the parlour of his house, involved criminal matters (Landau, 1984, p.177). More generally, the justice was involved in such essential matters as binding over offenders, accusers or witnesses to appear at court, binding people over to keep the peace or to be of good behaviour, and taking pre-trial examinations of suspects in serious cases and committing them to prison. Whether one sees the justice of the peace as a benevolent paternalist or an agent of class oppression, it is clear that his role as a law enforcer was strengthened by his position in the local social hierarchy.

3.2.3   Parish constables

Considerable attention, much of it favourable, has been focused on the justice of the peace. Rather less has been devoted to the eighteenth-century parish constable. Most recent commentators have been content to accept the conventional wisdom that the parish constable was inefficient, lazy, and likely to employ a substitute. However, research into early seventeenth-century constables has created a rather different impression. The parish constable was, like the justice of the peace, an unpaid amateur, ideally a man of some wealth and ability chosen from his neighbours to serve his turn for a year. Work on the early Stuart periods has suggested that in some parishes at least, constables and other local officers worked reasonably efficiently within the limits of contemporary expectations about law enforcement. Like the county gentry from whom justices were recruited, the yeomen farmers, petty gentry and richer artisans and tradesman who served as constables now felt that they had a stake in upholding the status quo (Wrightson, 1980).

How far this situation obtained in the eighteenth century remains largely unexplored. What needs to be stressed is that most of our existing knowledge for that century comes from the London area, where, as might be imagined, a system originally designed for policing villages and parishes in small towns was being regarded as increasingly inadequate. Little is known for the eighteenth century about the situation outside the capital. Certainly, men chosen as rural constables in that century chose and paid deputies, and some of these deputies enjoyed sufficient length of service to constitute virtual 'professional' police officers. Conversely, the high constables, in charge of a subdivision of their counties, were men of social standing who occasionally involved themselves, as did some of the more active justices, in primitive detective work (Emsley, 1996, pp.216–20 and **Emsley, 2001**).

ACTIVITY 3.2

Make some notes on the defining characteristics of eighteenth-century law enforcement. One strand of thinking has stressed its paternalistic and localized nature. What did this amount to in practice? How did eighteenth-century criminal justice differ from its twentieth-century counterpart?

The eighteenth-century law-enforcement machine worked on assumptions that were in many ways different from those obtaining in a modern industrial state. There was little by way of crime detection or prevention, only the first glimmerings of a 'professional' police force, and a heavy dependence on the death penalty, publicly inflicted, as a method of punishing and deterring criminals. Yet the system had its own logic, and, in many respects 'worked', perhaps more certainly at the beginning than at the end of the eighteenth century. Without doubt, its functioning was partially dependent on the fear and deference which the lower orders felt towards their social superiors. Yet no system of authority can function without the cooperation, or at least acquiescence, of substantial sections of the ruled. The extent to which the eighteenth-century law-enforcement system worked was connected to the willingness of people to make it operate, for perhaps the main peculiarity of the system was its dependence on the participation of a large number of people: the county gentlemen who served as justices; the lesser gentlemen who served as chief constables or grand jurors; the farmers and artisans who still, in some areas, served as constables; the men who served as petty jurors; and the wide range of people who, in the last resort, made the system work through their willingness to take suspected criminals to court. Even the crowd at the public execution, cheering felons who died gamely, weeping with those felons with whom they sympathized, and booing incompetent hangmen, were participating in the suppression of crime. The catching, punishment and treatment of criminals was not yet the province of a professional specialist operating within the closed doors of police stations, local government offices or prisons.

4   Patterns of prosecution and punishment

4.1   Constructing criminal statistics

By the early nineteenth century, as now, arguments about crime were frequently couched in terms of whether levels of crime were rising or falling. Indeed, central government facilitated such arguments when in 1810 it published criminal statistics going back to 1805. Thereafter, statistics were published annually. By the 1830s and 1840s, discussing social problems on the basis of statistics, in England as in Europe as a whole, had become a standard method of social debate (see, for example, **Quetelet, 1842**). In 1834, as part of this general movement, the annual statistics in England, which thus far had appeared in elementary form, were published under six categories of offences, while from 1836 these figures were supplemented by an annual statistical digest of commitments to prison. This taste for collecting and publishing figures, totally appropriate to the period which saw the birth of social science in the modern sense, led to further developments in 1857 when, as a result of an appendage to the previous year's County and Borough Police Act, British criminal statistics were divided into three groupings: indictable offences reported to the police; commitments for trial, on both indictment and summary conviction; and the totals of those convicted and imprisonments (Emsley, 1996, p.23). Consequently, historians of crime in the nineteenth and twentieth centuries have easy access to quantified data in the form of statistics collected and published by central government.

Historians working on the periods before 1810 have a somewhat more difficult task in their attempts to quantify crime. As ever, the definitional problem arises. 'Crime', as we have argued, could include the felonies indicted at the assizes and the minor offences presented at the ecclesiastical courts or the local manorial leets, as well as those summary convictions before magistrates, records of which are largely missing before the late eighteenth century. Anybody attempting to amass global figures for prosecuted crime in the period before the publication of official criminal statistics needs to work systematically through the records of a multiplicity of courts. Records of all these courts survive very rarely for any given area, and hence it is difficult to construct 'crime rates' or to obtain an impression of the total dimensions of prosecuted crime.

For this reason, arguments about levels of crime over the eighteenth century have tended to concentrate on offences indicted before the assizes. Yet even here there are problems, since assize records have not survived for some areas (notably the Midlands), while for others they exist in only a broken series. Analysing assize records, even where they do survive in bulk, is a laborious business. Before the 1750s, indictments were kept in Latin, and a skilled eye and a patient frame of mind is needed to unlock their secrets. In addition to these particular problems, there are the more general ones inherent in attempting to interpret any set of criminal statistics. The early nineteenth-century positivists were convinced that social statistics, of which figures relating to crime were far from the least important, were facts which spoke for themselves. (Chapter 1 has already introduced some of the difficulties with this proposition, and they are equally marked for the period with which we are concerned.)

First, details of crime culled from eighteenth-century assize indictments, like those derived from nineteenth- or twentieth-century official criminal statistics, concern only a sample of crime: in the eighteenth century they relate to crimes that were formally prosecuted by indictment. The modern historian has no means of establishing what the relationship was between the total of crimes indicted and those actually committed. Nor is there any method by which it is possible to ascertain if the 'dark figure' of crimes which were committed but never brought to justice fluctuated. Second, levels of prosecuted crime can be affected by the intensity of official action. If twice as many offences of one type are prosecuted in one year than in the previous year, is this a reflection of rising levels of crime or simply of an increased propensity to prosecute? The modern mind is attuned to the idea of crime waves, but recent criminology has also alerted us to the effect on criminal statistics of control waves. This issue is probably more relevant to the regulatory offences tried so frequently in the seventeenth century, or to a state with a modern police force, than it is to an eighteenth-century assize. Clearly, however, it is one that must be considered.

crime waves and control waves

4.2 Patterns of indicted crime before the eighteenth century

The above problems notwithstanding, a number of historians have attempted to reconstruct the statistical pattern of crime in the eighteenth century. Our discussion here will focus on the most detailed published work on this subject, that arising from the researches of John Beattie on the records for Surrey and Sussex, supplemented by more recent work by Gwenda Morgan and Peter

Rushton on Co. Durham, Northumberland, and Newcastle-upon-Tyne in north-eastern England. However, let us first consider briefly the findings of historians who have worked on the earlier period. Their labours, dictated very much by record survival, have tended to concentrate on the south-eastern assizes (notably the county of Essex), and the palatinate of Cheshire, whose Court of Great Session (the local equivalent of the assizes) enjoys the best surviving run of records of criminal prosecutions in early modern England. Analysis of the records of these courts demonstrates a pattern which is rather surprising, and certainly challenges any notion of a simple development showing steadily increasing levels of crime (Sharpe, 1999, pp.76–90).

Briefly, indictments rose steadily from about 1580 onwards. This increase was the outcome partly of population growth, but it reached a peak (according to area) in either the 1590s or the 1620s, both of these decades being periods of severe economic and social disruption. In all areas, as in twentieth-century Britain, it was crimes against property (larceny, burglary and robbery) that formed the largest category of serious offence. As a result, between 1559 and 1625, 86 per cent of offences indicted at the Hertfordshire assizes were property offences, and 5 per cent homicide and infanticide. Levels of prosecution appeared to be dropping in the 1630s, while the disruptions of the 1640s, with the coming of the civil wars, meant that levels of indicted crime were low. Whatever the actual levels of lawlessness, courts were being held infrequently as the normal processes of law enforcement were disrupted. Levels of indicted crime stayed low both in the 1650s, when something like normal administrative processes were resumed, albeit without monarchical authority, and in the 1660s, when monarchical authority was restored.

4.3 Indicted crime over the 'long eighteenth century'

As a result, in 1660, the year at which Beattie commences his research on the assizes of the southern counties of Surrey and Sussex, crime of all sorts, and especially property offences, were running at a lower level than they had been fifty years previously. The later chronological pattern of offences reconstructed by Beattie, pared to its essentials, is straightforward. Turning first to property offences, we find that these tended to fluctuate seriously on an annual basis (we shall turn to the causes of these fluctuations shortly) but that there was little by way of a sustained rise in the areas of his study until the middle of the eighteenth century. There was a sharp rise around 1750, then a fall, but from 1760, levels of prosecution of property crimes rose, with a real and sustained take-off in the 1780s and 1790s. The situation was much the same in the north-east, with a predominance of prosecutions for property offences, and a marked rise in such prosecutions in the last two decades of the century. In 1800, prosecuted property offences in urbanized areas of Surrey (notably Southwark) were roughly three times what they were in 1700, an increase that could not wholly be explained by population growth (in the north-east, Newcastle also experienced disproportionate prosecutions). Throughout the period studied by Beattie, 1660–1800, property offences formed the greater part of indicted felony in Surrey and Sussex. On the sample of cases studied by Beattie, 7,061 persons were accused of property offences in Surrey over that period, as opposed to 334 accused as principals and 81 as accessories in homicide cases. Other felonies were much fewer: for example, only 42 men were tried at the Surrey assizes for rape, with a further 86 for attempted rape (Beattie, 1986; Morgan and Rushton, 1998).

Although indicted homicides in the sample of material studied by Beattie were running at a lower level than property offences, they too showed a clear pattern. Prior to 1660, rates of homicide in England had been high: most samples studied show an annual rate of more than 10 per 100,000 of population in the Elizabethan and early Stuart periods (Stone, 1983). In Beattie's analysis, this level had fallen to 2.5 per 100,000 of population by the post-Restoration period, 2.1 per 100,000 by the early eighteenth century, and less than 0.3 by the early nineteenth century (Beattie, 1986, p.112). Thus, the homicide rate in England, on these figures, experienced a massive decrease in the three centuries following the death of Queen Elizabeth I. Obviously, the strictures that apply to criminal statistics generally must operate here, but one major shift which historians of crime do seem to have established is that there was a major decline in felonious killing as England entered the modern world.

To these figures, however, must be added cases of infanticide – the killing of newborn children by their (usually unmarried) mothers. This offence was a fairly typical one in the early modern period, and one such killing was tried every eighteen months or so before the eighteenth-century Surrey assizes. Infanticide was unusual, of course, in being a predominantly female offence, and a number of studies (for example, Malcolmson, 1977; Jackson, 1996) have identified it as one of the characteristic female offences of the period, and one for which juries, in Scotland as well as England, became increasingly reluctant to convict as the eighteenth century progressed. Infanticide apart, most serious offenders tried before the courts were men, though to a lesser extent than now: only 24 per cent of those accused of property offences in Surrey between 1660 and 1800, and 13 per cent of those accused in the more rural county of Sussex, were women. In the north east, too, a high proportion, by modern standards, of serious property offenders were women. Combining quarter sessions and assize prosecutions, 32 per cent of those accused of theft in Co. Durham, 31.5 per cent of those accused in Northumberland, and exactly half of those accused in Newcastle, were women. These figures raise some interesting problems about the female experience of criminality in this period (Beattie, 1986, pp.239–40; Morgan and Rushton, 1998, pp.66–8).

4.4   Short-term fluctuations

It is possible, then, to trace long-term trends in the prosecution of serious crime in early modern England. It should also be appreciated that the level of indicted crime, and especially of property offences, might be subject to violent short-term fluctuations. Two main factors (leaving control waves aside) were present here (Hay, 1982). The first was economic. From the 1590s, a bad harvest was usually followed by an upsurge in property offences, while a depression in local industrial activity (notably textile production), although somewhat harder

Figure 3.1 The correlation between prices and indictments for crimes against property in Surrey and Sussex, 1762–69 (Source: Beattie, 1974)

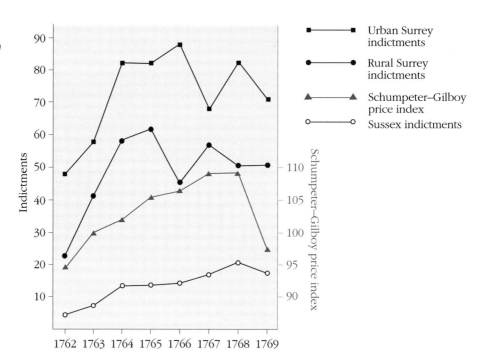

Figure 3.2 The correlation between prices and indictments for crimes against property in Surrey and Sussex, 1780–84 (Source: Beattie, 1974)

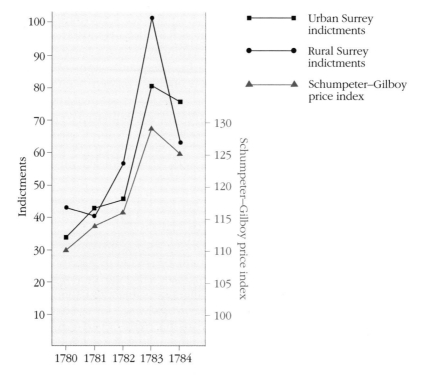

to measure, seems to have had the same effect. As Figures 3.1 and 3.2 demonstrate, this connection between short-term fluctuations in prices and property offences was still marked in local assizes in the late eighteenth century.

Perhaps less obviously, historians of eighteenth-century crime have also detected a tendency for levels of indicted crime, and for official fears of crime, to increase when any of the wars of the era ended. Isolated soldiers returning from foreign wars had caused law and order problems from the late Middle Ages, but the emergence of large standing armies and large navies in the eighteenth century meant that at the end of every conflict large numbers of young men from the labouring classes (the people most likely to be indicted for serious crime) were dumped on English society with little by way of means of support. It is therefore hardly surprising that in 1795 the *Leicester Journal* should note the paucity of criminals standing trial at the assizes in the eastern counties as one of the few benefits of the war against revolutionary France (Emsley, 1996, pp.33–4).

4.5   Patterns of capital punishment

As we have noted, the relationship between criminal statistics and crime actually committed is, in any period, a questionable one. Arguably, statistics concerning punishment are on a surer foundation, and it is certainly possible to trace real changes over the eighteenth and early nineteenth centuries. Once again, although we shall focus on these later periods, it is important to grasp that some major developments had taken place before 1660.

Despite the emphasis placed on public execution in the eighteenth century, levels of execution were much higher in the Elizabethan and early Stuart periods. As with criminal statistics, what we know about punishment in these earlier periods has to be pieced together from scattered and sometimes fragmentary materials. Even so, the pattern is plain. If we return to the excellent Cheshire records, we find that the Court of Great Sessions was passing death sentences at a very high rate in the 1590s and 1620s, with over 160 such sentences being found in the latter decade (Sharpe, 1999, p.64). Even if not all these sentences were inflicted, the rate of execution must have been far higher than the eighteenth century, in the first decade of which only about ten death sentences were passed in the county. In general, it seems that death sentences in England in the period 1580–1630 were running at roughly ten times the level of the early eighteenth century. These death sentences were passed overwhelmingly for property offences rather than murder. At the Chester Court of Great Sessions between 1580 and 1619, some 337 death sentences were passed, 294 (87%) for property offences, 35 (10.5%) for homicide, and 8 (2.5%) for other felonies (see Figure 3.3 overleaf). Compared to this, the eighteenth-century penal regime, so often characterized as harsh, seems positively humane (Sharpe, 1990, p.31).

Sufficient materials survive to allow us to chart the progress of capital punishment over the eighteenth century, although it should be emphasized that most analyses carried out so far have concentrated on London or the south east. Beattie's work on Surrey shows that an average of seven persons a year were being hanged by that county's assizes in the 1660s, a figure which rose to a peak of 13 or so in the 1720s, but which fell back to its 1660s' levels, despite a tripling of the level of crime and a doubling of the county's population, by 1880 (Beattie, 1986, p.589). Even at that later date, most of those suffering execution

Figure 3.3 Capital convictions for felony, Court of Great Sessions, Chester, 1580–1709 (Source: Sharpe, 1999)

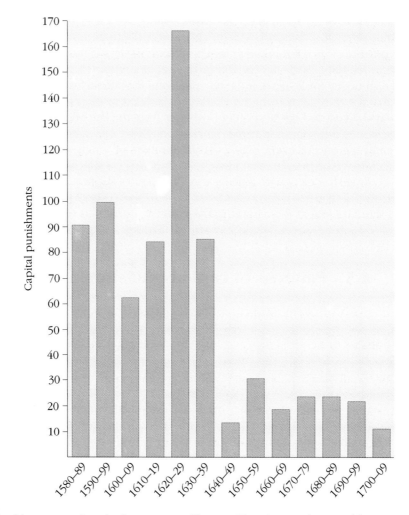

had been convicted of property offences. Turning to the neighbouring courts of London and Middlesex, between 1795 and 1804, 23 persons were hanged for burglary, 22 for highway robbery, 40 for forgery, and only 18 for murder. In the rural Western Assizes Circuit over the same ten years, 34 persons were executed for burglary, 11 for forgery, 25 for highway robbery and 25 for murder. The idea that the death penalty should only be inflicted for killing another human being was clearly not yet established in the early years of the nineteenth century (Emsley, 1996, pp.256–8).

4.6   The logic of reprieve and execution

These figures for execution in the eighteenth century lead us into one of the great peculiarities of eighteenth-century capital punishment, a peculiarity which in turn helps us to understand the rationale of the system. Let us consider those sentenced to death in London and Middlesex between 1795 and 1804. True, 23 people were hanged for burglary, but this was from a total of 168 capitally convicted for the offence, while the 22 hanged highway robbers were drawn from 127 who had been capitally convicted. Although the practice of pardoning was not unknown in the seventeenth century, it seems that in the eighteenth century pardoning a high proportion of those capitally convicted was common, and, a few exceptional years notwithstanding, became more so as the century progressed.

pardoning

What detailed research *has* revealed is that the eighteenth-century Bloody Code, for all its theoretical ferocity, masked a system of penal practices in which those actually executed, especially for property offences, were only a small sample of those who might have been so treated. If law enforcement in the eighteenth century depended on terror, it was a selective terror. From the mid-eighteenth century, of course, criticisms of high levels of execution, and of public execution more generally, were being raised. The motives which lay behind these criticisms, however, are currently a source of contention among historians. As recent research has emphasized, there was no unified body of opinion pushing for reform, while such pressure for curtailing the use of the death penalty as there was cannot be simply regarded as a symptom of a growth of civilized, humanitarian values (Gatrell, 1994). Certainly, when reformers began to criticize the system in the later eighteenth century, its defenders could argue that its whole point was that it provided the capacity to bring stern retribution upon a minority of offenders: typically, those with a bad record or reputation, those who had committed unusually heinous offences, or those who were unfortunate enough to commit capital offences in a crisis period when it was thought necessary to make examples. Most of those capitally convicted of property offences would, under normal circumstances, be pardoned and escape the noose. In the eighteenth century, as in modern Britain, the courts operated a sentencing policy in which punishments were adjusted as far as possible to meet a variety of factors felt by the court to be relevant. But in the eighteenth century, it has been argued, clemency in sentencing strengthened the ideological authority of the law by demonstrating that it could be merciful as well as harsh. Moreover, given that most of those pardoned escaped through the intercession of their social superiors, anxious to extend and demonstrate the extent of their patronage or win the good opinion of their locality by helping a member of the poor to escape the noose, it helped strengthen the hegemony of the existing social hierarchy (Hay, 1975).

ACTIVITY 3.3

Read Extracts 3.1 and 3.2 below, which both reflect on the broader significance of the law in eighteenth-century England. The first, by the Canadian social historian Douglas Hay, is written from a Marxist viewpoint and comes at the end of an essay arguing that the criminal law's ability to mix terror and mercy made it a more effective agent for maintaining ruling-class hegemony. The second, by the United States legal historian John Langbein, is part of a critique of that essay. The two views suggest different ways of interpreting the criminal law in the eighteenth century. Which do you find the more convincing? Are they incompatible? Reflect on whether they have any bearing on current law-and-order problems.

4.7 Secondary punishments

Pardoning criminals so that they escaped execution made it necessary to find some other means of dealing with them, and one of the more interesting areas of recent research into eighteenth-century law enforcement has been the unearthing of changing patterns in secondary punishments. Clearly, by the early eighteenth century, escape through the old legal fiction of benefit of clergy was no longer felt to be appropriate. The first major innovation came in 1718 when, in the face of a crime wave created by demobilized servicemen at the end of the War of Spanish Succession, an Act was passed making it possible to transport convicted criminals as indentured servants (in effect, temporary slaves) to the American colonies. This practice was ended with the outbreak of the American War of Independence in 1776, by which time some 30,000 convicted criminals from England, 13,000 from Ireland and a few hundred from Scotland had crossed the Atlantic (Ekirch, 1987).

The other major innovation, apparently enmeshed in the practice of the courts rather than established by one sweeping statute, was the use of brief periods of imprisonment. Although the use of imprisonment, in the modern sense the standard punishment for serious crime, was essentially a nineteenth-century innovation, it is evident that from the 1730s onwards, English assize judges and justices of the peace at quarter sessions were becoming increasingly used to sentencing offenders to a few months in prison, perhaps also with a whipping or hard labour added (Beattie, 1986, pp.520–618; Morgan and Rushton, 1998, pp.68–76). Thus, the eighteenth century, so often portrayed as the great era of the death penalty, in fact saw an increasing use of other punishments.

What can be learnt about the 'problem of crime' from studying patterns of crime and punishment in the eighteenth century? Studying patterns of serious crime and its punishment in the eighteenth century allows us to move a step

Extract 3.1 Hay: 'Property, authority and the criminal law'

Opposing repeal [of capital punishment for housebreaking] in a major debate in 1811, Lord Eldon declared 'that the property of an industrious cottager should be protected, who is often obliged to leave his cottage, and his little hoard of perhaps not more than 40s deposited in a tin-box in a corner of a room'.

It is difficult to assess the weight such arguments had with the mass of Englishmen. Eldon's argument was jejune: few cottagers had savings of £2, the wages of a month or more, in the harsh year 1811. Equally few cottagers could afford to go to law to recover stolen goods. Ideologies do not rest on realities, however, but on appearances, and there were enough prosecutions on behalf of poor men to give colour to the Lord Chancellor's claims.

Many historians, confronted with the hegemony of the eighteenth-century ruling class, have described it in terms of absolute control and paternal benevolence … It seems more likely that the relative insecurity of England's governors, their crucial dependence on the deference of the governed, compelled them to moderate [ruling-class] ferocity … Benevolence, in short, was not a simple positive act: it contained within it the

ever-present threat of malice. In economic relations a landlord keeping his rents low was benevolent because he could, with impunity, raise them. A justice giving charity to a wandering beggar was benevolent because he could whip him instead. Benevolence, all patronage, was given meaning by contingency. It was the obverse of coercion, terror's conspiracy of silence. When patronage failed, force could be invoked; but when coercion inflamed men's minds, at the crucial moment mercy could calm them.

A ruling class organizes power in the state. The sanction of the state is force, but it is force that is legitimized, however imperfectly, and therefore the state deals also in ideologies. Loyalties do not grow simply in complex societies: they are twisted, invoked and often consciously created. It was a society with a bloody penal code, an astute ruling class who manipulated it to their advantage, and a people schooled in the lessons of Justice, Terror and Mercy. The benevolence of rich men to poor, and all the ramifications of patronage, were upheld by the sanction of the gallows and the rhetoric of the death sentence.

(Hay, 1975, pp.36, 61, 62–3)

Extract 3.2 Langbein: 'Albion's fatal flaws'

If the criminals were often poor, their victims (whom we see serving as private prosecutors in the Old Bailey trials) were not much better off – a point that is played down in Hay's essay.... The victim is usually more propertied than the person who victimised him, though often only slightly. I have not hit upon a way of quantifying this, in part because information about the social status of the victim is so haphazard in the Old Bailey sources, but I think that anyone who studies a volume of the Old Bailey Sessions papers will conclude that the victims seldom come from the propertied elite. They are typically small shopkeepers, artisans, lodging-house keepers, innkeepers and so forth. Included in the list of victim-prosecutors for the first dozen cases for the 1754 sessions, for example, are a loom maker, a brass founder, a wire merchant, and a pewterer, each prosecuting pilfering employees; a baker's servant and a journeyman tailor prosecuting thieving prostitutes; a lodging-house keeper and a former room-mate prosecuting for the theft of furniture and domestic goods from lodgings; and a calico printer who had been mugged on the street.

The criminal law is simply the wrong place to look for the active hand of the ruling classes. From the standpoint of the rulers, I would suggest, the criminal justice system occupies a place not much more central than the garbage collection system. True, if the garbage is not collected then society cannot operate and ruling-class goals will be frustrated, but that does not turn garbage collection into a ruling-class conspiracy. The Hay thesis, in a similar fashion, confuses necessary and sufficient conditions ...

I have been maintaining two themes about the administration of the criminal law in the eighteenth century. First, most of the discretion was exercised by people not fairly to be described as the ruling class, especially the prosecutors and the jurors. Secondly, the discretion that characterized this system was not arbitrary and self-interested, but rather turned on the good-faith consideration of factors with which ethical decision-makers ought to have been concerned. The historian does not need a conspiracy theory to explain the discretion, and the discretion does not fit the theory. I concede fully that when men of the social elite came into contact with the criminal justice system in any capacity, they were treated with special courtesy and regard, just as they were elsewhere in this stratified society. To seize upon that as a *raison d'être* of the criminal justice system is, however, to mistake the barnacles for the boat.

(Langbein, 1983, pp.101, 119–20)

further from the impressionistic perceptions of contemporaries and the folklore constructed about crime and punishment in the past by later generations. We are able to trace trends in serious crime, to see how they fluctuated over the long term and also how they reacted to other social phenomena in the short term. The pattern leads us back to the notion that 'crime' is a term which covers a wide variety of behaviour: even if we restrict ourselves to the two most obvious categories of serious offence, we see two completely different patterns. Property offences fluctuated violently in the short term in response to economic and social stimuli, and began a pronounced and sustained upward movement at the end of the eighteenth century. Homicide, conversely, seems to have occurred at a decreasing rate over the period 1660–1800. With punishment, too, we see a system which at first sight, with its apparent dependence on the large-scale use of the death penalty for property offences, might seem very alien, but which was in fact regarded by contemporaries as flexible and one into which new elements could be incorporated.

5   Crime and the community

5.1   Defining 'community'

community

Whether used in the context of the debate over current law-and-order issues or in discussion of crime as a historical phenomenon, the term community is not an unproblematic one. Contrary to popular myth, the inhabitants of England before the Industrial Revolution did not live in idyllic village settlements. The early modern small town or village was as likely to be riven by problems, albeit of a different nature, as any modern city. Legal records, criminal and civil alike, contain ample evidence of social tensions and interpersonal malice. Indeed, by the eighteenth century, most English villages, although capable of showing community spirit on occasion, were often so socially stratified as to make it possible to speak of a number of 'communities' within their boundaries. The most significant divergence was between the poorer inhabitants of the parish and a stratum of richer villagers: farmers, tradesmen and petty gentry who were doing well economically, whose education and literacy put them in contact with the cultural mainstream, who were regular churchgoers, and from whose ranks constables, churchwardens and parish Poor Law officials were drawn, and who formed the stable and respectable element in their communities.

At the other end of the local social system resided a stratum of agricultural labourers and rural industrial workers. Many of these were doubtless honest and respectable, but they all suffered from considerable economic hardship. Most of them might expect to be in receipt of poor relief at some point in their lives, while it was from the less respectable elements in this group that unmarried mothers, many of the fathers of their children, drunkards, swearers, petty thieves and potential vagrants were drawn. The notion of 'community' looks very shaky in a period when one section of the local population was involved in policing the other (Wrightson, 1980).

If 'the community' therefore is something which currently figures prominently in discussions of crime, law and order, it was also of vital importance to these subjects in the past. If nothing else, the community was a medium through which a large number of criminal accusations were filtered. In the absence of a professional police force, most criminal accusations were brought by private individuals, and hence community values might be involved when the decision to prosecute a specific offender was taken. As we have seen, in many villages and small towns such policing as existed was essentially carried out by local men (women were generally barred from holding office at any level) serving temporarily as law-enforcement officers. Once again, therefore, we return to community values, with decisions about the practicalities of law enforcement often being taken in the context of an awareness of local needs and conditions. Even the justice of the peace, although a member of the gentry, might well be a man of a paternalistic cast of mind, who would pride himself on his knowledge of his locality and the people living within it.

5.2   The mechanisms of local law enforcement

Policing the local community might take many forms, and one of the lessons to be derived from law enforcement at this level is that communities, however defined, had methods of combating crime other than formal prosecution before a court. For evidence on this point, let us turn to Richard Gough, who in 1700 wrote what was more or less a recent history of his parish, Myddle in Shropshire. Gough's work consists in large measure of reminiscences about his co-parishioners, among whom were the Wenlockes, one of the 'problem families' of the parish.

Two brothers, Reece and John Wenlocke, were descended from a man described by Gough as 'a bad husband, and a pilfering, thievish person'. The two sons were as bad as the father, typical rural petty criminals, who never stole any substantial goods, but 'stole hay when out of meadows, and corn when it was cut in the fields, and any small things that persons by carelessnesses had left out of doors'. Reece in particular had a reputation for wood theft, and the neighbourhood feared depredations on its hedges and fences when news spread that he had built a new oven and was planning to fire it. Richard Mercer, 'a very waggish fellow' and the servant to one of the parishioners, decided on a stratagem. As he walked by Reece's house, he saw a large dry stick which he took home, hollowed out, filled with gunpowder, and replaced in the hedge. Reece found the stick, and used it when he fired his oven, with the result that the oven was blown up and the end of his house set on fire. One suspects that this informal action gave the community as much satisfaction as having Reece Wenlocke prosecuted for theft would have done (Gough, 1700, p.46).

Such stories place us directly in the context of local law enforcement, a context where much depended on reputation, where a degree of petty crime was tolerated, if only because it was too much trouble to take to court, and where a range of informal sanctions might be mobilized against the wrongdoer. The nature of these sanctions might very much depend on the nature of the offence or offences in question, and the status, reputation or sex of the offender. Thus at one end of the scale there were such common practices as the dismissal of pregnant servant girls or thieving manservants, while at the other might come ritualized statements of communal disapproval.

informal sanctions

A good example of an informal community sanction occurred at the Gloucestershire village of Westonbirt in 1716. When an unpopular estate bailiff had allegedly committed a homosexual act with another man, the villagers turned out to perform a 'groaning', in the course of which what was perceived as an unnatural sexual act was parodied, and a mock birth acted out (Rollinson, 1981). The more familiar aspects of 'police' action were therefore at one end of the spectrum whose other pole might include folkloric popular actions (Sharpe, 1980). Given the range of informal sanctions available, it seems that formal prosecution was often most readily employed against habitual local offenders who were thought to have gone too far, or against outsiders, especially vagrants who committed theft as they passed through the parish.

5.3   Local knowledge and the offender in court

These 'community' aspects of law enforcement – the adjustment to knowledge of local circumstances – also affected the legal process proper. As we have seen, the large number of pardons that followed capital conviction at the assizes were in large measure the result of offenders being reprieved in the light of their personal circumstances, or the result of a gentleman or some other notable interceding on their behalf. For the most part, assize judges and jurors seemed happy enough to go along with the perception of local circumstances and to adapt the law to the individual. John Aston, another deviant inhabitant of Myddle recorded by Richard Gough, provides a good example of how the courts might react. Aston, 'a sort of silly [simple] fellow much given to stealing of poultry and small things', was frequently 'caught in the act' and, as was probably typical of many such local delinquents, was 'sometimes well cajoled by those that would trouble themselves no further with him'. At length, however, 'he grew unsufferable', and was indicted at Shrewsbury assizes for stealing cocks and hens. The judge, 'seeing him a silly man', advised the jury that they had no alternative but to find him guilty, but dropped them a broad hint to undervalue the stolen goods, a common way of saving criminals from a charge of grand larceny. The jury followed this advice, 'at which the judge laughed heartily and said he was glad to hear that cocks and hens were so cheap in this country' (Gough, 1700, p.78). In the seventeenth century, then, we were still some way from the standards of a modern, bureaucratized law-enforcement system.

5.4   Towards new forms of policing

As the eighteenth century progressed, it became evident that the old world of informal sanctions and adjustment to local perceptions of the individual offender was passing, even in many rural parishes. The professional police, as established in 1829, was still some way off, but attempts were made to inject a more businesslike element into the parish constable system, and a number of other expedients were tried. Perhaps the most significant of these were the Associations for the Prosecution of Felons which sprang up from about 1760. The dependence on the victim of crime to bring criminal charges had always begged the question of the victim's ability to find and apprehend the relevant offenders, and bear the cost of prosecuting them. Such costs could stretch to well over £10 by the later eighteenth century. The Associations for the Prosecution of Felons, numerous by the 1780s, were essentially private institutions which were usually composed of and formed by local property owners to organize and provide funding for the prosecution of offenders against their members or their property. The associations flourished in a period when concern about crime was increasing, and when the deficiencies of England's 'police' system and plans for reforming it were being eagerly debated. Some associations organized their own police, although many were content to work in conjunction with the established system of parish constables. What the associations demonstrate, for our immediate purposes, is how far the concept of community was fractured by the end of the eighteenth century, and how far it was felt on a local level that the traditional methods of dealing with crime were no longer operable.

Arguably, such a perception had long since informed ideas about crime and law enforcement in London. By 1750, the London area's population was probably about 675,000, which made it the largest city in Europe and, by a very wide margin, the biggest urban centre in England. By that date, crime in the metropolitan area was becoming a regular source of comment and debate. The size of the capital, the anonymity it was felt to offer the law-breakers, and the concentration of wealth which offered such a tempting target for thieves were all held to contribute to the capital's unique crime problem. It is hardly surprising therefore that the novelist and justice of the peace Henry Fielding should begin his *Enquiry into the Causes of the Late Increase of Robbers* of 1751 with the claim that 'the streets of this town, with the roads leading to it, will shortly be impassable without the utmost hazard; nor are we threatened with seeing less dangerous gangs of rogues among us, than those which the Italians call the Banditti' (Fielding, 1751, p.292).

Fielding, like so many of those who participated in the burgeoning law and order debate which commenced about the middle of the eighteenth century (and, indeed, like many subsequent commentators on law and order), was arguing a case, and we must be careful in treating as fact a rhetorical flourish from even so well informed an observer. More research needs to be done on the social life of the capital before the picture of social breakdown and a high crime rate can be accepted. There were certainly bad areas, some of them recognized from the Elizabethan period as places where criminals were likely to reside. Conversely, other London parishes were still run fairly effectively along traditional local government lines, and in these something like community values operated. Certainly, the occasional practice of mob action against thieves, which might include their being violently doused under the parish pump, would suggest this. Overall, however, the traditional notions of control, both formal and informal, seemed redundant in the London area. From the late seventeenth century onwards, it is apparent that petty crime in the metropolitan area was being dealt with by a flexible yet official system, with the authorities making considerable use of binding over and short spells of incarceration in houses of correction (a penalty favoured for prostitutes) as alternatives to indictment, a sign, perhaps, of the development of a distinctively urban method of combating the small-scale criminal. It also seems that the paternalistic rule of justices aspired to in some rural areas was waning around London. By the eighteenth century, gentlemen on the fringes of the capital were refusing to become justices because of the workload involved, while, in any case, the gap between the lives of the rich and poor in the capital ended even that partial understanding by the rich of the life of the poor upon which the old system to some extent depended. Fielding, describing conditions in cheap lodging houses around the capital in a tone which was to become common in Victorian social reportage, pointed out that 'this picture, which is taken from the life, will appear strange to many; for the evil here described is, I am confident, very little known, especially to those of the better sort' (Fielding, 1751, p.387). Given such a growing social gulf, it is little wonder that the 'better sort' should look to more efficient policing as the way of protecting their interests. (This theme is explored more fully by **Emsley, 2001**).

5.5   Law and the sense of 'national community'

common law

If crime and law enforcement were important issues on a local level, it is important to understand that a respect for the law was part of a national consciousness. The English common law had long been held up as a matter of national pride by legal writers, but it was the constitutional conflicts of the seventeenth century, and above all the Glorious Revolution of 1688–89, that placed the common law squarely in the consciousness of the 'free-born Englishman'. After the revolution, men of property were able to look back at the supposedly tyrannous actions of the Stuarts, or look across the Channel at the reportedly oppressive conditions suffered by the subjects of the French and other European monarchs, and count their blessings. The common law was held to be a fundamental of English political culture: the terms constitutional

Gin Lane, *Hogarth's famous portrayal of the degradation resulting from drinking gin (1754). On an immediate level, Hogarth's message is obvious. It has been suggested, however, that he is intending not just to show the degradation of the lower orders, but also to expose the lack of responsibility on the part of the lay and secular authorities which allowed such conditions to flourish. The year after this print appeared, effective licensing legislation was introduced which curbed the worst excesses of the gin trade. Before this legislation, it was reported that in some parts of the capital one house in five was a gin-shop*

and unconstitutional were more or less equated with legal and illegal. This increased weight on the constitutional and ideological significance of the English common law coincided with, and was part of, that process by which what could be characterized (if a little simplistically) as 'central' or 'state' law was reaching a decisive stage in eroding the importance of other legal systems and custom. Hence even the informal aspects of justice and crime control were regarded as operating within a known constitutional framework, while other concepts of legality, notably those of the church and of customary law, while still present and occasionally important, were gradually losing their significance.

Surprisingly, it was not just men of great property, the men whose interests might be thought to have benefited most obviously from the provisions of the Bloody Code, who held this view. Even men of little or no property (the opinions of women on the matter are not much recorded) to a greater or lesser degree accepted the law as part of the constitution they lived under. The poor knew they lived in a land which manifested massive variations in wealth and status, but, in so far as they had internalized ruling-class ideology, they also 'knew' that they lived under the same law as the rich. Consequently, they believed that their country was not an arbitrary tyranny, but rather a land that was governed by a known and rational constitution. The law was one of the ideological cements which held society together.

The concentration on crime and punishment tends to obscure the degree to which the law was part of early modern culture. The two centuries before 1700 had seen an explosion of civil litigation in both the local courts and the central courts at Westminster. Indeed, it could be argued that litigation was one of the main social phenomena of the early modern period. By that date, the great age of expansion in litigation had finished, but even in the eighteenth century, people were much more used to settling disputes by going to the law than is currently the case. One consequence of this was a continuing dislike of lawyers.

An anti-lawyer satire of 1790: inverting the image contrasts the happy lawyer with a distressed client

Another consequence was the tendency for people to interpret disputes in legal terms, which might involve a clash between an older, customary law, and law as it was being interpreted in the interests of eighteenth-century men of property. Until well into the nineteenth century, it is possible to interpret clashes between the people and landlords in rural areas in terms of differing notions of common right usages, law and property rights. But what is obvious is that these clashes were conducted, to a sometimes surprising extent, in terms of legal rights. The point is perhaps most clearly made in E.P. Thompson's discussion of the rule of law in eighteenth-century England.

ACTIVITY 3.4

Read Extract 3.3, and then answer the following questions: How does Thompson explain the relationship between law and class power? Was the law used against or to protect local community interests?

Extract 3.3 Thompson: 'The rule of law'

The law when considered as institution (the courts, with their class theatre and class procedures) or as personnel (the judges, lawyers, the Justices of the Peace) may very easily be assimilated to those of the ruling class. But all that is entailed in 'the law' is not subsumed in these institutions ...

What was often at issue was not property, supported by law, against no-property; it was alternative definitions of property: for the landowner, enclosure; for the cottager, common rights; for the forest officialdom, 'preserved grounds' for the deer; for the foresters, the right to take turfs. For as long as it remained possible, the ruled – if they could find a purse and a lawyer – would actually fight for their rights by means of law ...

Turn where you will, the rhetoric of eighteenth-century England is saturated with the notion of law. Royal absolutism was placed behind a high hedge of law; landed estates were tied together with entails and marriage settlements made up of elaborate tissues of law; authority and property punctuated their power by regular 'examples' made upon the public gallows. More than this, immense efforts were made ... to project the image of a ruling class which was itself subject to the rule of law, and whose legitimacy rested upon the equity and universality of those legal forms. And the rulers were, in serious senses, whether willingly or unwillingly, the prisoners of their own rhetoric; they played the games of power according to rules which suited them, but they could not break those rules or the whole game would be thrown away. And, finally, so far from

the ruled shrugging off this rhetoric as a hypocrisy, some part of it at least was taken over as part of the rhetoric of the plebeian crowd, of the 'free-born Englishman' with his inviolable privacy, his habeas corpus, his equality before the law ...

What had been devised by men of property as a defence against arbitrary power could be turned into service as an apologia for property in the face of the propertyless. And the apologia was serviceable up to a point: for these 'propertyless' ... comprised multitudes of men and women who themselves enjoyed, in fact, petty property rights or agrarian use-rights whose definition was inconceivable without the forms of law. Hence the ideology of the great struck root in a soil, however shallow, of actuality, and the courts gave substance to the ideology by the scrupulous care with which, on occasion, they adjudged petty rights, and, on all occasions, preserved proprieties and forms.

We reach, then, not a simple conclusion (law = class power) but a complex and contradictory one. On the one hand, it is true that the law did mediate existent class relations to the advantage of the rulers; not only is this so, but as the century advanced the law became a superb instrument by which these rulers were able to impose new definitions of property to their even greater advantage, as in the extinction by law of indefinite agrarian use-rights and in the furtherance of enclosure. On the other hand, the law mediated these class relations through legal forms, which imposed, again and again, inhibitions upon the actions of the rulers.

(Thompson, 1975, pp.260–4)

Thompson's comments serve to remind us of the degree to which an acquaintance with law had penetrated into local English society, and arguably this penetration was of some consequence for local law enforcement. However, the use of the law as a mediator may be more applicable to what modern terminology would regard as civil disputes than the criminal law.

Discussing the law and the community introduces a complex set of problems. On one level, the law operated as one of the great constitutional glories of post-1688 England, and respect for the law was one of the great rhetorical commonplaces of political discourse. Conversely, its actual implementation against criminals often involved a pragmatic flexibility and, on a local level, considerable informality. What needs to be stressed is that the criminal law, like the civil law, was something that people *used*. One interpretation is that the law was obviously something which people of property (but not only large property) used to protect that property. Peers in the House of Lords and rich gentry in the Commons passed the law, country gentry administered it in the shires, and substantial farmers acting as parish constables administered it in their communities. But throughout the system the criminal law was subject to adjustments, to choices made by people administering or using it, and to the pressures of local knowledge and local circumstance. In most ways the law was created from above, but its actual implementation involved a spectrum of 'decision makers', frequently ordinary people, who were pulled into the legal process (King, 1984).

The statutes creating the Bloody Code are part of the history of crime in early modern England. So, too, are Reece Wenlocke's exploding oven in Myddle or the assize judge at Shrewsbury joking as the jury found John Aston guilty of a non-capital charge. Beneath such anecdotes, there rest the recurring themes of shifting definitions, of choice, flexibility and the distinctiveness of a system of law enforcement which depended on a wide measure of public participation. Modern law-enforcement and crime-control systems depend, to a far greater degree than is apparent on initial analysis, on the actions of decision-makers. Historical materials help illuminate this point, and suggest how it was equally true in very different contexts.

6 Towards modern thinking on crime

6.1 The nineteenth-century context

As has been stressed throughout the preceding sections, the eighteenth-century law-enforcement system was not static or unchanging. Nevertheless, it is true that the system developed very rapidly over the first two-thirds of the nineteenth century, and, as was suggested at the beginning of this chapter, it was in this period that many of the main characteristics of 'modern' thinking on crime were established.

Crucial to this development was the context provided by the broader changes in government of the period. As ever, it is easy to caricature the situation before the nineteenth century. 'Government' in the broad sense of the word was developing, both in terms of the national state and in terms of local, and especially urban, government. Yet the period between the outbreak of the wars against revolutionary France in the late eighteenth century and the Great Exhibition of 1851 saw the emergence of a state in something like the modern sense. The exact forces behind this development are difficult to unravel: certainly, interpretations that attribute all such developments to the influence of Jeremy Bentham and utilitarianism are over-simplified. A broader set of elite objectives, a religious input, and the emergence of the state almost as an independent historical actor all had a bearing on what happened. The problems of socialization and conceptualizations of order on a more general level are also relevant. As we have suggested, early modern England was a society characterized by a plurality of legal orders. The nineteenth-century changes did not entirely alter this situation, and it is still possible to see differing attitudes to crime and punishment depending on class, religious sympathies, or political persuasions. Yet a marked relative shift occurred, whereby the state achieved at least a near monopoly over that arena where competing moral orders met: the criminal justice system. As important elements in this process there emerged professional police forces, a national prison system, and a clear notion of a 'criminal' or 'dangerous' class.

6.2   Industrial society and a rise in crime

These developments took place against a rising concern over crime. Those given to examining the newly available crime statistics found little that was encouraging. The peace of 1815 was followed by a massive increase in the number of people committed for trial in England and Wales, from 5,000 annually in the first decade of the nineteenth century to nearly 15,000 in 1820. After a brief decline, the upward trend continued in 1825. People who discussed the issue of crime and punishment, whether in parliament or at the middle-class dinner table, now thought they had hard evidence to go on (Emsley, 1996, p.35).

class relations

Such discussion, especially among the middle classes, would be heightened by a conflation of crime and revolution. In early nineteenth-century England older models of social hierarchy, based on notions of deference and paternalism, were replaced by a conceptualization of society based on class relations. To elite observers, the industrialization and urbanization of the period meant the end of the old social ties, and they felt threatened by a two-pronged attack. The new industrial workforce could easily be characterized as disorderly and potentially criminal, impervious to the traditional controls. But this workforce was also seen as potentially revolutionary. To traumatic memories of the French Revolution were added the concerns generated by a number of domestic phenomena: the Luddites – craft workers who broke the new industrial machines in the Midlands and the north; the Swing Riots, those outbreaks of desperation among the depressed agricultural workers of the south; Chartism, that national political movement of artisans and industrial workers who saw gaining the vote and entry into parliament as the way forward; and early trade unionism. Here are the comments of Harriet Martineau, the daughter of a Norwich manufacturer, made in a year when revolution was about to recur on the continent and agitation over parliamentary reform seemed to be making it an issue in Britain:

The year 1830 opened gloomily. Those who believed that revolution was at hand, feared to wish one another a happy new year, the anxiety about revolution was by no means confined to anti-reformers. Society was already in a discontented and tumultuous state; its most ignorant portion being acted upon at once by hardship at home and example from abroad; and there was every reason to expect a deadly struggle before Parliamentary Reform could be carried. The ignorant and misled among the peasantry and artisans looked upon the French and other revolutions as showing that men had only to take affairs into their own hands.

(Martineau, 1850, p.24)

What Martineau would doubtless have described as the least ignorant portion of society could read in their newspapers during 1830 that getting on for 20,000 committals for criminal offences had been made in England and Wales that year. Among them were two men, John Morgan and James Lilburne, accused of theft at Dunstable, who claimed that they were in such distress that they stole in the hope of being 'taken up': prison was seen as preferable to starvation (Emsley,1996, pp.36–9).

6.3   Victorian crime and the rhetoric of 'social problems'

How was the 'problem of crime' constituted in the early nineteenth century? Was it simply a concern about crime, or was it broader concerns about economic hardship, foreign revolution and social protest that fired the Victorian imagination?

Whatever the reality of the threat of revolution or social breakdown, the mid-nineteenth-century willingness to conceptualize crime in terms of the activities of a 'criminal' or 'dangerous' class is symptomatic of wider developments. The origins and progress of these developments are complex issues (Wiener, 1990). Historians are now wary of linking them to any simplistic notion of the influence of an emergent middle class impacting on policy-making, although it is clear that changing class structures and class relationships were involved. Equally, few historians would now accept an interpretation of nineteenth-century penal developments in terms of a simple model of reform, or of nineteenth-century thinking about crime in terms of a simple model of progress, although these models were clearly favoured ones in the rhetoric of the period. In many areas, government was expected to be more interventionist, to be a broader provider of services, and in the realms of law and order, this expectation, by the mid-Victorian period, was symbolized in the existence of a national prison system and of professional police forces. As well as such institutional innovations, how people thought about crime and punishment was changing. The language of social debate, encouraged by early positivist social investigation, now increasingly led to identifying 'problems' which government could, preferably with the aid of relevant interest groups, 'solve'. For non-specialist observers, thinking about crime and punishment could be packaged, and people could deal conceptually with crime in terms of stereotypes and conventional wisdom. At the very least, thinking about crime now interacted

'dangerous' classes

with concerns over other issues (see Extract 3.4 and Chapter 4). Both the early modern criminal justice system of the seventeenth and eighteenth centuries, and the discourses and preconceptions which surrounded that system, were replaced by methods of dealing with crime and ways of thinking about crime that were essentially similar to those which are familiar in modern Britain.

To take one example, it is significant that the concept of the 'juvenile delinquent' was essentially an invention of the period 1820–50 (Magarey, 1978; Shore, 1999). There had, of course, been earlier schemes aimed at saving the young criminal, for instance the Marine Society of 1756, founded on the perhaps unlikely premise that criminally inclined youths might be reformed by serving in the Royal Navy, and Robert Young's Philanthropic Society of 1788. But it was the first half of the nineteenth century, when the tendency in contemporary social science towards a more detailed categorization of social phenomena coincided with concern over social reform, that a category of young offenders was created, and a body of institutions aimed at reforming them set up (see **Muncie, 2001**).

Another aspect of crime that appears frequently in current social debate – domestic violence – was also widely commented on in the Victorian period (see Chapter 5 and Doggett, 1992). As so often, it is unclear whether the problem was new or merely talked about more: work on earlier periods suggests the latter (Beattie, 1986, pp.105–6). Certainly, legal theory, at least until the eighteenth century, held that a husband's rights over his wife included that of moderate physical chastisement. This practice was upheld in 1782 when Judge Buller summed up the legal position by declaring that a man was entitled to beat his wife with a stick, so long as it was no thicker than his thumb.

Extract 3.4 Gatrell: 'Crime as a social problem'

Victorian observers would have been struck by their forefathers' relative indifference to crime as a 'problem', and by their relative satisfaction with the apparently arbitrary and capricious mechanisms which contained it. This was not because crime was infrequent then: it is not at all clear that there was less thieving and violence *per capita* in eighteenth-century cities than in nineteenth. But crime did not as yet appear to threaten hierarchy, and the terms in which crime might be debated as a 'problem' were not yet formed. Historians of early modern crime must realize not only that 'their subject was not known then by that name' but that as a subject it did not exist. The word 'crime' when used at all before the 1780s, usually referred to a personal depravity. It lacked the problematic and aggregative resonance it was soon to acquire. Despite occasional panics about the ubiquity of thieving, crime in aggregate was not yet thought to be increasing as a necessary and potentially uncontrollable effect of social change. Similarly, the 'criminal' was not yet discerned as a social archetype, symbolic of the nation's collective ill-health …

By the time Peel took up the challenge of penal, police and law reform in the 1820s, the political and cultural climate was quite transformed. Crime was fast becoming 'important'. In the post-war world, and on into the 1840s, the subject came to be cemented into an ideology about the Condition of England. Crime was becoming a vehicle for articulating mounting anxieties about issues which really had nothing to do with crime at all; social change and the stability of social hierarchy. These issues invested crime with new meanings, justified vastly accelerated action against it, and have determined attitudes to it ever since.

(Gatrell, 1990, pp.248–9)

It is impossible to calculate how frequently wife-beating took place in the past, not least because the factors that inhibit the reporting of domestic violence today were even more prevalent in the eighteenth or nineteenth centuries. Indeed, given that divorce was not an option for most people, reporting a violent husband to the law would probably have been regarded as inherently counter-productive. But if the incidence of domestic assault cannot be traced accurately, changes in attitudes can. Legal commentators and social reformers alike became increasingly unhappy with the traditional right of chastisement. These feelings led, in 1853, to the passing of an Act for the Better Prevention and Punishment of Aggravated Assaults upon Women and Children. How effective the Act was in saving wives and children from the consequences of domestic violence remains uncertain, although its provision that complaints could be brought by third parties at least lessened the chances of a husband complained against taking revenge on his wife. It did, however, represent an important change in legal thinking.

6.4   The media and a moral panic: garrotting

By the 1850s, then, thinking about crime was changing, and was moving towards a set of attitudes with which we are currently familiar. To conclude, and perhaps confirm this point, it is instructive to look at one of the great moral panics of the nineteenth century, the 'garrotting panic' of 1862.

The background to this panic lay in a widespread, but not altogether justified, fear that crime was increasing and that respectable society was threatened by the core elements of the criminal class. Transportation to Australia had fallen off rapidly over the 1850s, so that what were categorized as 'habitual criminals' were discharged out of prison into England rather than being sent to the other side of the world. In theory, such criminals were still under police supervision, but this proved difficult to enforce. Moreover, faith in the reformatory notions that had influenced early nineteenth-century thinking about dealing with criminals was fading. The occasion for the panic came on 17 July 1862 when the MP Hugh Pilkington was attacked and robbed on Pall Mall as he was walking from the Houses of Parliament to the Reform Club. Pilkington was attacked from behind and 'garrotted' – that is, temporarily incapacitated by choking. The robbery, and a few others of a similar nature, provoked a full-scale press campaign in which facts were rapidly left behind and opinions allowed to flourish unhindered. A comparison could be made with similar modern episodes, notably the concern prompted by 'mugging' in the 1970s (see Chapter 1). At the very least, it is noteworthy that the arguments put forward about the punishment of criminals are still familiar:

> Under the influence of our humanity-mongers, we have nursed and fostered a race of hardened villains … well the public is now learning, in rather a startling fashion, what is the natural result of making pets of thieves and garrotters.
>
> (*Manchester Guardian*, 2 November 1862)

> Money should be spent on the real punishment of criminals, instead of squandering the hard earnings of honest mechanics and working men and making them objects of interest to idle spinsters and gaol chaplains of the maudlin class.
>
> (*The Observer*, 30 November 1862)

The immediate result of the garrotting panic was the passing of the Security from Violence Act, which, among other things, reversed the previous trend away from the use of corporal punishment for adult offenders (Davis, 1980). The harsher mood against criminals was reinforced by the passing of a severe Penal Servitude Act in 1865, and by the appointment in 1869 of Edmund du Cane, a hardliner, as Chairman of the Directors of Convict Prisons (see **Muncie, 2001**).

Nevertheless, the significance of the garrotting panic is deeper than the harder line against criminals that it encouraged, this line itself being reversed by a swing to more liberal policies by the end of the nineteenth century. It serves to symbolize the emergence of modern ideas on crime and its treatment. With the panic we find ourselves firmly in the world of professional police forces, of national prison systems, of the widespread acceptance of criminal stereotypes, and of crime and punishment as issues that were debated by newspapers, usually in terms of straightforward appeals to the instinctive reactions of potential readers.

7 Conclusion

The first half of the nineteenth century thus constitutes a distinct watershed between current 'conventional thinking' about crime and punishment and those earlier attitudes and practices that we have examined in this chapter. It is to be hoped that discussing these earlier phenomena, through their very 'otherness', will help to understand and challenge both everyday and criminological debate about the criminal universe which we currently experience. Definitions of crime change, as do the agencies that are designed to control and eliminate it, and the means by which it is punished. Yet in all periods there is a natural tendency to regard the criminal justice and penal systems that are familiar to us as the only ones that are appropriate. The fact that these systems have changed in the past, sometimes radically, might encourage reflection on how our current thinking about and methods of dealing with crime might be subjected to constructive criticism. Studying the history of crime also serves to cast doubt on the cosy assumptions that there have never been crime waves or fears of social disintegration in the past. Crime has been a recurrent theme in social complaint, social debate, and social fears for a long time, even if those complaints, debates and fears have usually expressed themselves in rhetorics different from those currently in vogue. This knowledge is of some use, and possibly of some reassurance, as we attempt to understand, and defend ourselves against, crime as we know it today.

Review questions

- In what ways did eighteenth-century conceptions of 'crime' differ from those of the present?
- How much were the machinery of justice and the class structure of eighteenth-century society related?
- Can the shift in crime control from the eighteenth to nineteenth century be adequately conceived as one from custom to law?
- Was the criminal law an instrument of class power?
- Why did 'crime' become a key concern for social reformers in the mid-nineteenth century?

Further reading

Newcomers to the history of eighteenth-century crime should begin with three collections of essays: Hay *et al.* (1975), Cockburn (1977) and Brewer and Styles (1980). Innes and Styles (1986) summarize the first wave of writing on the subject and suggest directions for future research. Sharpe (1999) is an initial introduction to the subject, while Beattie (1986) is the most advanced and technically accomplished regional study. Morgan and Rushton (1998) raise some important points of similarity and divergence with Beattie's work from a different regional perspective. Shoemaker (1991) is a superb study of petty crime in the metropolitan area, especially valuable in demonstrating how the law-enforcement system was being remodelled to deal with ever-increasing problems. Gatrell (1994) is an immensely thought-provoking study which challenges any simplistic explanations of the curtailment of capital punishment and the end of public executions in England.

References

Beattie, J.M. (1974) 'The pattern of crime in England, 1660–1800', *Past and Present*, no.62, pp.42–95.

Beattie, J.M. (1986) *Crime and the Courts in England 1660–1800*, Oxford, Clarendon Press.

Brewer, J. and Styles, J. (eds) (1980) *An Ungovernable People*, London, Hutchinson.

Bushaway, B. (1982) *By Rite: Custom, Ceremony and Community in England 1700–1880*, London, Junction Books.

Cockburn, J.S. (ed.) (1977) *Crime in England 1550–1800*, London, Methuen.

Davis, J. (1980) 'The London garrotting panic of 1862: a moral panic and the creation of a criminal class in mid-Victorian London', in Gatrell *et al.* (1980).

de Mandeville, B. (1725) *An Enquiry into the Causes of the Frequent Executions at Tyburn*, London, J. Roberts.

Doggett, H.E. (1992) *Marriage, Wife-Beating and the Law in Victorian England*, London, Weidenfeld and Nicolson.

Ekirch, A.R. (1987) *Bound for America: The Transportation of British Convicts to the Colonies, 1718–1775*, Oxford, Oxford University Press.

Emsley, C. (1996) *Crime and Society in England 1750–1900*, 2nd edn, London, Longman.

Emsley, C. (2001) 'The origins and development of the police', in McLaughlin and Muncie (2001).

Fielding, H. (1751) *An Enquiry into the Causes of the Late Increase of Robbers*, London, publisher unknown.

Gatrell, V.A.C. (1990) 'Crime, authority and the policeman state', in Thompson, F.M.L. (ed.) *The Cambridge Social History of Britain 1750–1950*, vol. 3, Cambridge, Cambridge University Press. (Extract reprinted in Muncie *et al.*, 1996.)

Gatrell, V.A.C. (1994) *The Hanging Tree: Execution and the English People 1770–1868*, Oxford, Clarendon Press.

Gatrell, V.A.C., Lenman, B. and Parker, G. (eds) (1980) *Crime and the Law: The Social History of Crime in Western Europe since 1500*, London, Europa.

Gough, R. (1700) *The History of Myddle*, reprinted 1979, London, Caliban Books.

Hair, P. (1972) *Before the Bawdy Court*, London, Elek.

Hay, D. (1975) 'Property, authority, and the criminal law', in Hay *et al.* (1975).

Hay, D. (1982) 'War, dearth and theft in the eighteenth century: the record of the English courts', *Past and Present*, no.95, pp.117–60.

Hay, D., Linebaugh, P., Rule, J.G., Thompson, E.P. and Winslow, C. (eds) (1975) *Albion's Fatal Tree: Crime and Society in Eighteenth-Century England*, London, Allen Lane.

Hobsbawm, E. (1975) 'Distinctions between socio-political and other forms of crime', *Society for the Study of Labour History Bulletin*, no.25.

Hunt, W. (1744–49) *The Justicing Notebook of William Hunt 1744–1749*, ed. E. Crittall, Devizes, Wiltshire Record Society, 1982.

Innes, J. and Styles, J. (1986) 'The crime wave: recent writing on crime and criminal justice in eighteenth-century England', *Journal of British Studies*, vol.25, no.4, pp.380–435.

Jackson, M. (1996) *New-Born Child Murder: Women, Illegitimacy and the Courts in Eighteenth-century England*, Manchester, Manchester University Press.

King, P. (1984) 'Decision-makers and decision-making in the English criminal law, 1750–1800', *The Historical Journal*, vol.27, no.1, pp.25–58.

King, P. (1989) 'Gleaners, farmers and the failure of legal sanctions in England 1750–1850', *Past and Present*, no.125, pp.116–50.

Landau, N. (1984) *The Justices of the Peace, 1679–1760*, Los Angeles and London, University of California Press.

Langbein, J. (1983) 'Albion's fatal flaws', *Past and Present*, no.98, pp.96–120.

Linebaugh, P. (1975) 'The Tyburn riots against the surgeons', in Hay *et al.* (1975).

Linebaugh, P. (1991) *The London Hanged: Crime and Civil Society in the Eighteenth Century*, London, Allen Lane.

Malcolmson, R.W. (1977) 'Infanticide in the eighteenth century', in Cockburn (1977).

Magarey, S. (1978) 'The invention of juvenile delinquency in early nineteenth-century England', *Labour History*, no.34, pp.11–25.

Martineau, H. (1850) *History of England during the Thirty Years Peace*, London, publisher unknown.

McLaughlin, E. and Muncie, J. (eds) (2001) *Controlling Crime*, 2nd edn, London, Sage in association with The Open University.

Morgan, G. and Rushton, P. (1998) *Rogues, Thieves and the Rule of Law: the Problem of Law Enforcement in north-east England, 1718–1800*, London, University College London Press.

Muncie, J. (2001) 'Prison histories: reform, repression and rehabilitation', in McLaughlin and Muncie (2001).

Muncie, J., McLaughlin, E. and Langan, M. (eds) (1996) *Criminological Perspectives: A Reader*, London, Sage in association with The Open University.

Quetelet, M.A. (1842) *A Treatise on Man*, Edinburgh, Chambers. (Extract reprinted as 'Of the development of the propensity to crime', in Muncie *et al.,* 1996.)

Rogers, N. (1992) 'Confronting the crime wave: the debate on social reform and regulation, 1749–1753', in Davison, L., Hitchcock, T., Keirn, T. and Shoemaker, R.B. (eds) *Stilling the Grumbling Hive: the Response to Social and Economic Problems in England, 1689–1750*, London, Allen Sutton.

Rollinson, D. (1981) 'Property, ideology, and popular culture in a Gloucestershire village 1660–1740', *Past and Present,* no.93, pp.70–97.

Rule, J. and Wells, R. (eds) (1997) *Crime, Protest and Popular Politics in southern England, 1740–1850*, London, Hambeldon Press.

Sharpe, J.A. (1980) 'Enforcing the law in the seventeenth-century English village', in Gatrell *et al.* (1980).

Sharpe, J.A. (1990) *Judicial Punishment in England*, London, Faber and Faber.

Sharpe, J.A. (1999) *Crime in Early Modern England 1550–1750*, 2nd edn, London, Longman.

Shoemaker, R.B. (1991) *Prosecution and Punishment: Petty Crime and the Law in London and Rural Middlesex, c.1660–1725*, Cambridge, Cambridge University Press.

Shoemaker, R.B. (1992) 'Reforming the City: the reformation of Manners Campaign in London, 1690–1738', in Davison, L., Hitchcock, T., Keirn, T. and Shoemaker, R.B. (eds) *Stilling the Grumbling Hive: the Response to Social and Economic Problems in England, 1689–1750*, London, Allen Sutton.

Shore, H. (1999) 'Cross Coves, Buzzers, and general sorts of Prigs: Juvenile crime and the criminal "Underworld" in the early nineteenth century', *British Journal of Criminology,* no.39, pp.10–24.

Stevenson, J. (1992) *Popular Disturbances in England 1700–1832*, 2nd edn, London, Longman.

Stone, L. (1983) 'Interpersonal violence in English society 1300–1980', *Past and Present,* no.100, pp.22–33.

Thompson, E.P. (1975) *Whigs and Hunters: The Origins of the Black Act*, London, Allen Lane.

Wiener, M. (1990) *Reconstructing the Criminal: Culture, Law and Policy in England, 1830–1914*, Cambridge, Cambridge University Press.

Wrightson, K. (1980) 'Two concepts of order: justices, constables and jurymen in seventeenth-century England', in Brewer and Styles (1980).

CHAPTER 4

Dangerous Places: Crime and the City

by Peggotty Graham and John Clarke

Contents

1   Introduction

In Chapter 3, Jim Sharpe discussed the emergence of specifically 'modern' conceptions of crime in the early nineteenth century (see also **Gatrell, 1990**). These modern conceptions are closely linked to the rise of the city and to processes of urbanization. During the nineteenth century, they became linked to ideas of the city as a 'dangerous place': a place where people become criminals and victims. The city is always the subject of a tension between two representations. On the one hand, it is seen as the embodiment of progress – the basis for the development of the 'good society' – and is constantly being reconstructed in search of that objective. On the other hand, the city is also seen as a place of danger that is constantly at risk from crime and disorderliness. This chapter focuses on the dynamics of these representations. It is not an attempt to tell the history of the city or the history of crime (for a different approach to this relationship see Taylor, 1999, Chapter 4).

In reading this chapter, it will be useful to keep in mind a few key themes and concepts. A central theme is that there has been a continuing association between notions of 'the city' and 'dangerousness'. Changing definitions of dangerousness have interacted with ideas of the city and crime. Although dangerousness and crime are related, it is important to remember that they are not the same (recall the discussion of differing definitions of crime in Chapter 1 of this volume). A second theme is that dangerousness (however defined) has become associated in the popular imagination with the concept of a 'class apart' or 'other'. The chapter examines the ways in which this notion of 'other' has at different times provided a metaphor for the city as a crime-ridden and dangerous place. It appears in different guises. The 'dangerous classes', the 'casual poor', the 'social residuum' and the 'underclass' are all terms that have been used to denote this idea of a class apart. Dangerousness evokes ideas of both 'dangerous classes' and 'dangerous places'.

It is important to remember that any consideration of crime and the city brings certain kinds of crime to the fore and minimizes others. The focus tends to be on crimes of the street and the alleyway, such as mugging, assault, car theft and crime against personal property. Different types of urban crime, for instance financial fraud and other white-collar crimes, tend to go unremarked and are rarely associated with processes of urbanization (this will be explored more fully in Chapter 6). Similarly, domestic violence is a feature of city life but until recently was not designated a crime and was rendered invisible (see Chapter 5 for a more in-depth discussion of this). In short, the connections between crime and the city tend to refer to crime that is 'visible' and 'on the street'.

In this chapter, our main focus is on changing representations of order and disorder in the city and the place of crime in these representations. We begin, in section 2, with the period in which this 'modern' conception of crime and the city was formed – the second half of the nineteenth century. The basic elements established then have continued, in changing combinations, to dominate our understanding of how the city is a dangerous place. Section 3 provides a brief account of some of the practical attempts that were made between 1900 and **social order** 1970 to remake the social order of city life. This, we suggest, was a period of optimism, though we also find evidence for our contention that the city is constantly caught in a tension between the two representations of progress and danger. Section 4 focuses on the 1980s and 1990s and argues that these two decades saw the emergence of a new set of concerns about dangerousness which gave rise to renewed fears about crime and threats to social order. Woven throughout the chapter is the idea of struggle – struggle about the city as an arrangement of space and as a configuration of public and private places, and struggle over who has rights and over what. Our argument is that in the processes of urban reform, renewal and reconstruction that have gone on since the mid nineteenth century there have been struggles over the organization of urban space in which issues of crime, criminality and criminalization have always appeared central rather than peripheral. This is because each attempt to change the social and spatial organization of the city poses the question of social order – in particular, *what sort of social order* is being sought in the reorganization of the city. Finally, therefore, in section 5 we look to the future and ask what sorts of urban order we might expect in the twenty-first century. Will it be a future of progress, based on urban renewal, inclusion and community involvement, or one of perpetual crisis, in which privatized 'fortress mentalities' create new forms of exclusion and multiply fears about the 'other'?

2 Nineteenth-century nightmares: the city and the dangerous classes

The city became firmly connected in the popular imagination with notions of dangerousness and crime during the nineteenth century. The city evoked powerful and disturbing images. In the city were to be found the 'teeming hordes' living in an unimaginable squalor. The city was the engine of national economic and social progress, but it was also a turbulent and troubling nightmare of disorder. 'Here was a Dickensian city-scape of dirty, crowded and disorganized clusters of urban villages … where the "Great Unwashed" lived in chaotic alleys, courts and hovels just off the grand thoroughfares' (Walkowitz, 1992, p.19). London especially 'was regarded as the Mecca of the dissolute, the lazy, the mendicant, "the rough" and the spendthrift' (Stedman Jones, 1971, p.12).

The intimacy of order and disorder – the proximity of the 'great unwashed' to the 'great and the good' – was understood in terms of dangerousness. The threat was from the dangerous classes, the paupers and the criminals who made up the so-called 'casual poor', whose existence at the heart of the city represented a multiple threat to safety and order. The idea of the 'great unwashed' gives a clue to some of the ways in which this dangerousness was perceived.

dangerous classes

First, there was a perceived threat to public health posed by insanitary and overcrowded living conditions and the constant threat of contagion to those leading more ordered lives. Second, there was the perceived threat to public order posed by these groups as an 'unruly mob' – a different sort of contagion involving the risk of the labouring classes becoming infected by the mob with dangerous political ideas and enthusiasms such as Chartism, socialism and the like. Third, by their difference and diversity, the casual poor were seen as a threat to moral order – a contagion arising from ways of life not founded on the

153

principles of thrift, sobriety and self-discipline that were being articulated as the essential Victorian values. Fourth, there was the threat to the legal order from those leading half-lives involving marginal patterns of employment, begging and outright criminality. Finally, there was the threat that all of these would undermine the very force of progress itself, as Britain developed in the twin dynamic of industry and empire (Pearson, 1975).

These multiple threats were wrapped together in an overarching perception of a dangerousness which lay in the heart of the city. Mayhew's description of the 'nomad' sums up some of the themes:

> The nomad ... is distinguished from the civilized man by his repugnance to regular and continuous labour – by his want of providence in laying up a store for the future – by his inability to perceive consequences ever so slightly removed from immediate apprehension – by his passion for stupefying herbs and roots ... and for intoxicating fermented liquors ... by an immoderate love of gaming ... by his love of libidinous dances ... by his delight in warfare and all perilous sports – by his desire for vengeance – by the looseness of his notions as to property – by the absence of chastity among his women, and his disregard for female honour.
>
> (Mayhew, 1851–62, vol.1, p.6)

These notions of dangerousness were fed by stories, supplied by those who went into the poverty-stricken areas of the city, of a strange and worrying underworld: a social residuum who were quite different from the respectable working class. The fevered imaginations of educated readers were fed with literary constructs of the metropolis as a 'dark, powerful and seductive labyrinth' (Walkowitz, 1992, p.17). There remained the nagging anxiety that all the progress and accomplishments of the Victorian era were vulnerable to the disorders of the street. The nightmare was that 'progress might be swamped by the corrupting features of urban life' and that, unless checked or reformed, the residuum would overrun the Victorians' 'newly built citadel of moral virtue and economic rationality' (Stedman Jones, 1971, p.16). These feelings of danger and fear can be illustrated by examining three features of the nineteenth century which indicate some of the ways in which the inner city became a symbolic place of danger and associated fear.

social residuum

2.1 Dangerous places

The urban poor became seen as dangerous through the differences in the customs and habits of the poverty-stricken that set them apart from the emerging middle-class norms of respectability and propriety (Hall, 1998). The very degree of the difference – the 'strangeness' of working-class life – created for the middle-class Victorians a sense of an 'alien people' in their midst. It was perhaps no coincidence that at the same time as missionaries and explorers were venturing into Africa, the same language of danger and adventure was adopted by the new breed of urban explorers who were venturing into the 'unknown' at home. 'Urban explorers never seemed to walk or ride into the slums but to "penetrate" inaccessible places where the poor lived in dark and noisy courts, thieves' "dens", foul smelling "swamps" and the black "abyss" ' (Keating, 1973). Pearson argues that the description of these places combines their physical condition with the moral condition of their inhabitants:

Sewage and drains were guiding metaphors for those who depicted the deviants of this time. 'Foul wretches' and 'moral filth' lay heaped in 'stagnant pools' about the streets. When they moved they were seen to 'ooze' in a great 'tide'. The population was 'slime' which gathered in ghettos which were described as 'poisoned wells', 'canker-worms', 'sinks of iniquity' and 'plague-spots'. Their houses were described as 'cess-pits'; and their way of life was a 'moral miasma', for it was essentially a moral condition which was captured in these lurid images. The city 'reeked' of vice; the 'scum' and the 'dregs' of society was a 'moral debris' and 'residuum': the words 'pustule', 'fever', and 'wart' came readily to hand when describing the moral condition of the labouring and dangerous classes.

(Pearson, 1975, p.161)

Such language reflected the tendency of moral reformers to see the urban poor as a 'race apart' from the national community. Jennifer Davis comments that the missionaries and reformers constructed the residuum as a group which had been 'left behind by the mid-Victorian march of moral and material progress' (Davis, 1989, p.11). Furthermore, the values and behaviour attributed to this residuum – violence, licentiousness, thriftlessness, criminality and political volatility – 'were those which many believed had now been spurned by the respectable majority of the English nation' (Davis, 1989, p.11).

Moss Street, Bankside, London, 1896. The inhabitants of the houses on Moss Street were classified as 'Lowest class. Vicious; semi-criminal' and 'Very poor, casual. Chronic want' by Charles Booth in his social survey, Life and Labour of the People in London (1889–1902)

2.2   Dangerous people

The language of exploration and the imagery of anthropological reportage were products of, and deeply embedded within, the processes and ideologies of contemporary imperialism. It was the domestic usage of this imperial framework that was in part responsible for the transformation of the unexplored territory of the inner-city poor into an 'alien place', since it provided both ways of thinking about, and the language to describe, the 'other'. The context of imperial Victorian Britain therefore imparted a racialized overtone to the concept of an 'alien place'. Victorian missionaries and reformers articulated a strong sense of the superiority of the (white) British race which emanated from Britain's role as a colonial power. Imperial Britain abroad was still engaged in 'taming the savage', and images of the 'uncivilized' (black) savage fused with the excitement of the exotic to provide a heady cocktail of 'racialized danger' in the colonial imagination.

eugenics

The notion of white supremacy received additional impetus from the emergence in the 1880s of the new science of eugenics. Based on the theories of Social Darwinism, eugenics was the study of ways in which the mental and physical abilities of a people could be shaped and developed through breeding. White peoples – and the British in particular – were understood as representing the highest point of human evolution. Looked at from the imperial vantage point of the time, the evidence from the missionaries, explorers and administrators abroad of the lack of civilization of 'the African' simply confirmed the theories back home. Its domestic significance was manifested in fears about the 'degradation' of the British race being brought about by the overbreeding of the 'unfit' parts of society.

spatial and social segregation

Victorian Britain witnessed spatial and social segregation between the prosperous and impoverished, between respectable and unrespectable people, and between secure and insecure places (Stedman Jones, 1971). This took on a particularly sharp focus in London, though it applied in differing degrees to all the major industrializing towns and cities of Britain. The segregation was arguably far more complete *symbolically* than it ever was in reality, though the stark difference in the living conditions of the prosperous middle classes and the poor was real enough. But it is the symbolic division that interests us here. Representations of East and West London in the mid nineteenth century suggested two distinct cities. For example, commentators of the time 'juxtaposed a West End of glittering leisure and consumption and national spectacle to an East End of obscure density, indigence, sinister foreign aliens and potential crime' (Dore and Jerold, 1872, cited in Walkowitz, 1992, p.20).

This was a contrast based on differences in both visible and imagined lifestyle. It is significant for its notion of a semi-submerged danger and the association of that danger with 'sinister foreign aliens'. Walkowitz (1992), in her study of late Victorian London, argues that by the end of the century the opposition of East and West London had taken on imperial as well as racial dimensions. She contrasts a West End in Queen Victoria's Golden Jubilee year (1887), with its national monuments, government and colonial offices, with an East End which by then had become an international entrepot and was receiving succeeding waves of migrants: 'Gravitating to the central districts, the declining inner industrial rim, the "foreign element" had to compete with the indigenous labouring poor for housing and resources' (Walkowitz, 1992, p.26).

The significance of these influxes of 'the foreign element' comes into particular focus in the match girls' strike of 1888. It was a time of crisis – a severe economic depression as a result of poor trade; the structural decline of some of the older industries; a chronic shortage of working-class housing; and an emerging socialism and collectivism challenging traditional liberal ideology (Stedman Jones, 1971). This was the context in which the poor Jewish immigrants fleeing the pogroms of Eastern Europe in 1886–87 found themselves competing for jobs in the clothing and footwear industries and disturbing the precarious relations of East London trades by making visible the conditions of work in the sweat shops of the East End. This led to widespread publicity over wages and conditions, and there were large-scale strikes by match girls and by East End dockers. According to Walkowitz (1992, p.28), 'Both strikes involved unskilled and impoverished labourers and were heavily dependent on public sympathy and financial support'. The match girls' strike in particular was a demonstration of mass solidarity and the power of unionization. More ominously for many members of the propertied class, 'The demonstrations confirmed their worst fears of Outcast London as a vast, unsupervised underclass that could be readily mobilized into the revolutionary ranks of the new socialist movement' (Walkowitz, 1992, p.29). Such fearful responses had been prefigured in reactions to an earlier demonstration and subsequent riot in February 1886, when a political rally of mainly unemployed dock and building workers traversed the fashionable streets of the West End attacking property and all signs of wealth and privilege. One significant aspect of this riot was 'the strength of the middle-class reaction to it and the extent of the fear of the casual residuum that it revealed' (Stedman Jones, 1971, p.292). Not only were middle-class fears of class conflict and social disintegration confirmed as the 'menacing presence of "King Mob" in their part of town threatened the imaginative boundaries erected to mark off and contain the poor' (Walkowitz, 1992, p.29), but both riot and strikes seemed to confirm much more general anxieties about urban pathology and the potential for an uprising of the casual poor (see Chapter 3).

2.3   Dangerous sexualities

Such fears of the mob were accompanied by other anxieties about the state of the nation as manifested in the urban centres: anxieties which focused on the Victorian obsession with sexuality. This obsession had three dimensions which are particularly significant here: unregulated sexuality and the future of the 'race'; the public visibility of sexuality in the guise of prostitution, and the discovery of 'unnatural' sexuality in the form of homosexuality.

unregulated sexuality

We have already touched on the first of these in terms of the eugenics movement and its arguments about the threat of racial decline. Such perspectives draw a sharp contrast between the increasingly planned and regulated family life of the middle classes (including a decline in middle-class family size) and the unregulated sexuality and breeding habits of the poor. According to the eugenicists, this discrepancy was likely to weaken the genetic stock of the British race as the weak and feckless overproduced while the sensible and provident middle classes underproduced.

In the deepening anxiety about sexuality and marriage, prostitution represented a distinct, though related, source of concern. Prostitutes, almost more than any other single group, became an overarching metaphor for the threat to social order. Walkowitz (1980, p.32) reports: 'An object of fascination and disgust, the prostitute was ingrained in public consciousness as a highly visible symbol of the social dislocation attendant upon the new industrial era. By the 1850s prostitution had become "the Great Social Evil" '. Some of what Walkowitz calls 'fascination and disgust' in Victorian views of prostitution are visible in Henry Mayhew's descriptions of the classes of prostitutes in London (see Extract 4.1 below).

contagion   The Victorian prostitute became constructed as a potent source of contagion. The prostitute represented what Mort (1987, p.47) has called the encounter between 'working class female sexuality and professional masculinity'. As the

---

Extract 4.1 Mayhew: 'London's underworld'

The second class of prostitutes, who walk the Haymarket – the third class in our classification – generally come from the lower orders of society. They consist of domestic servants of a plainer order, the daughters of labouring people, and some of a still lower class. Some of these girls are of a very tender age – from thirteen years and upwards. You see them wandering along Leicester Square, and about the Haymarket, Tichbourne Street, and Regent Street. Many of them are dressed in a light cotton or merino gown, and ill-suited crinoline, with light grey, or brown cloak, or mantle. Some with pork-pie hat, and waving feather – white, blue, or red; others with a slouched straw-hat. Some of them walk with a timid look, others with effrontery. Some have a look of artless innocence and ingenuousness, others very pert, callous, and artful. Some have good features and fine figures, others are coarse-looking and dumpy, their features and accent indicating that they are Irish cockneys. They prostitute themselves for a lower price, and haunt those disreputable coffee-shops in the neighbourhood of the Haymarket and Leicester Square, where you may see the blinds drawn down, and the lights burning dimly within, with notices over the door that 'beds are to be had within'.

Many of those young girls – some of them good-looking – cohabit with young pickpockets about Drury Lane, St Giles's, Gray's Inn Lane, Holborn, and other localities – young lads from fourteen to eighteen, groups of whom may be seen loitering about the Haymarket, and often speaking to them. Numbers of these girls are artful and adroit thieves. They follow persons into the dark by-streets of these localities, and are apt to pick his pockets, or they rifle his person when in the

bedroom with him in low coffee-houses and brothels. Some of these girls come even from Pimlico, Waterloo Road, and distant parts of the metropolis, to share in the spoils of fast life in the Haymarket. They occasionally take watches, purses, pins, and handkerchiefs from their silly dupes who go with them into those disreputable places, and frequently are not easily traced, as many of them are migratory in their character.

The third and lowest class of prostitutes in the Haymarket – the fourth in our classification – are worn-out prostitutes or other degraded women, some of them married, yet equally degraded in character.

These faded and miserable wretches skulk about the Haymarket, Regent Street, Leicester Square, Coventry Street, Panton Street and Piccadilly, cadging from the fashionable people in the street and from the prostitutes passing along, and sometimes retire for prostitution into dirty low courts near St James Street, Coventry Court, Long's Court, Earl's Court, and Cranbourne Passage, with shop boys, errand lads, petty thieves, and labouring men, for a few paltry coppers. Most of them steal when they get an opportunity. Occasionally a base coloured woman of this class may be seen in the Haymarket and its vicinity, cadging from the gay girls and gentlemen in the streets. Many of the poor girls are glad to pay her a sixpence occasionally to get rid of her company, as gentlemen are often scared away from them by the intrusion of this shameless hag, with her thick lips, sable black skin, leering countenance and obscene disgusting tongue, resembling a lewd spirit of darkness from the nether world.

(Mayhew, 1851–62, vol.4, pp.358–9)

streetwalkers ventured into the fashionable thoroughfares, tempting middle-class sons (or so it seemed to the evangelical upholders of the patriarchal family), they appeared both literally and figuratively to be the conduit for all the immorality, pestilence, pollution and infection that emanated from the 'great unwashed': 'Like the slums from which she emanated, she carried with her … "the heavy scents of the masses" with their "disturbing messages of intimate life". She evoked a sensory memory of all the "resigned female bodies" who serviced the physical needs of upper-class men in respectable quarters' (Walkowitz, 1980, p.22).

This imagery of the prostitute belied the reality of most prostitutes' lives and backgrounds. The majority were members of the casualized labouring poor, rural migrants forced to leave the countryside for economic reasons, or city 'natives' pushed into prostitution in response to local conditions in the labour market. In both cases poverty was the underlying cause for the move to prostitution, giving lie to the stereotypical vision of girls seduced, pregnant and abandoned and turning to prostitution. The majority of prostitutes catered for a working-class clientele, again refuting the claim that prostitutes were in the business of seducing middle-class men (Walkowitz, 1980).

If the reality was so far from the image, how is it that the prostitute and prostitution became so potent a symbol of danger? The real threat was arguably to patriarchal social relations and social order. Sexuality in the nineteenth century became the site for other struggles, especially around gender and class. Prostitutes challenged the gender norms of Victorian patriarchal society. They were women who had broken out of the stranglehold of 'normal' female socialization and the confinement of women to the private sphere of domesticity. Many prostitutes ran their own lives, organizing their trade, and often living together as part of an all-female sub-group. Prostitutes were still subject to many forms of male domination, but they had wrested some control over their lives. Here were women who contradicted the prevalent ideological imagery of women in passive domesticity. Furthermore, when dressed up in fine clothes, patrolling the elegant shopping streets at the smart end of town, they were frequently indistinguishable from their 'respectable' sisters. For an ideology of womanhood which depended on clearly visible and identifiable differences between 'the fallen' and 'the virtuous', and of class divisions which depended on the working class being kept clearly segregated, such confusions were a potent signal that everything was far from in its rightful place and, worse, was getting out of control.

In the 1860s, attempts were made to address this issue of control, and prostitution was officially labelled a dangerous form of sexuality through the Contagious Diseases Acts of 1864, 1866 and 1869, introduced primarily to address the 'problem' of prostitution in garrison towns. This is not the place to examine the details of the Acts nor the subsequent successful campaign for their repeal, but it should be noted that the Acts inadvertently created a fulcrum around which new challenges to the existing social order could coalesce: 'The double standard of sexual morality, the participation of women in political activity, the control of women by male doctors, and the role of the state in enforcing sexual and social discipline among the poor were all subjected to public scrutiny' (Walkowitz, 1990, p.3). To the degree that the Acts aimed to control sexuality and via such control to reinforce class and gender domination, they failed. However, in this failure, the imagery of the subversive power of the prostitute (and the threat she posed to the social order) was confirmed.

The Victorian enterprise of scientific classification was leading to the delineation of 'normal' and 'abnormal' sexualities. While the idea of 'unnatural passion' in the form of homosexuality was unadmitted within the average Victorian household, it was nonetheless an area of scientific enquiry, moral anxiety and criminalization. A series of legal changes, beginning with the Labonchère Amendment to the Criminal Law Amendment Act of 1885, defined and proscribed 'Acts of gross indecency' between men. The Vagrancy Act of 1898 refined the law relating to importuning for 'immoral purposes' in relation to homosexual men (Weeks, 1981, p.103). Weeks suggests that the public and political discourses about – and against – homosexuality intersected with other central social anxieties: the purity of the race, the fears of imperial decline, and the prospect of unregulated or undisciplined 'male lust' (see also Mort, 1987).

> It is striking that the social-purity campaigners of the latter part of the 1880s saw both prostitution and male homosexuality as products of undifferentiated male desire … In the debates before the 1885 Criminal Law Amendment Act was rushed through Parliament, male homosexual behaviour was quite clearly linked with the activities of those who corrupted young girls. What was at stake was on the one hand the uncontrolled lusts of certain types of men, and on the other the necessary sanctity of the sexual bond within marriage.
>
> (Weeks, 1981, p.106)

In these ways sex, like 'race', became a metaphor of danger. Unregulated sexualities threatened the reproductive capacity and moral order of the nation. This 'threat' combined with visions of illicit, extra-marital and unrepressed sexuality in the slums and ghettos of the working poor to raise the spectre of a multiplication of the 'great unwashed'. The eugenicists' concern with the purity of the race not only received validation from abroad, but it was deeply rooted also in fears at home. For the safety of the nation (the white, middle-class and *male* nation) homosexual men had to be imprisoned and prostitutes had to be labelled as deviant and dangerous, and treated as criminals.

2.4   Order and danger: the dynamics of the city and crime

The dangers represented by the 'dangerous classes' in the nineteenth century define the problem of social and political order in ways which have carried forward into perceptions of the modern city. The dangerous classes are both the 'other' and inextricably linked with the development of the city as a way of life. Their dangerousness is only partly a matter of crime. Their criminal deeds are invariably represented as the visible tip of an iceberg and hint at the multiple dangers below. Their symbolic existence at the heart of the city has provided an essential underpinning to the ways in which ideas about the city have subsequently developed and coalesced into a vision of urban areas as criminal places.

reform   The dangers embodied in the dangerous classes formed the targets of multiple attempts at reform, rescue, regulation, reconstruction and institution building. From sanitary improvements to the emergence of modern forms of policing, these attempts can be best understood through the language of social disorder and disorganization. In the twentieth century we tend to speak of social problems in the plural – referring to poverty, criminality, juvenile delinquency, mental illness, or deviant sexualities as more or less separate phenomena, each requiring particular types of analysis and intervention. In the mid nineteenth century, and notwithstanding the new forms of classification that were coming into vogue, many observers still tended to view 'the social problem' in the singular. For these, the obsession remained with the notion of the dangerous classes – in whom were condensed the multiple dangers and threats of the disordered lower classes.

These responses to 'danger' also helped to shape the modern city. The city became the focus of efforts to incorporate and domesticate the working classes (Stedman Jones, 1983, see also Trachtenberg, 1982, on the process of 'incorporation' in the US). A multi-faceted array of interventions was developed in order to reform and regulate the lower orders. It is beyond the scope of this chapter to go into detail, but they included the following:

- The physical destruction and reconstruction of areas of the city – combined with sanitary reform and other public health initiatives – opened up the 'dangerous places', establishing new forms of residential segregation which 'rescued' the respectable from too great a proximity to the dangerous and created places which could be more systematically subjected to surveillance, regulation and policing.

- 'Street life' – in the form of casual trades, begging, prostitution, petty crime or mere 'hanging about' – was subjected to greater legal control and policing, following on from the creation of 'professional' police forces.

- The provision of 'rational' forms of recreation and temperance movements offered a more 'ordered' use of free time among the poor, paralleled by greater legal and social restrictions on 'irrational' leisure pursuits (gambling, drinking, and so on).

ACTIVITY 4.1

What were the general aims of these interventions? What different kinds of 'dangerousness' were associated with mid-nineteenth-century fears of the inner city? Make a few notes and then consider in what ways any of these might be seen as continuing themes in fears about the city today.

The aim of these and other interventions was to impose a physical, social and cultural order on the city in the image of respectability by repressing the city's dangerousness and making it a place where the law-abiding could 'go about their normal business' in safety and comfort. In doing so, the interventions sowed the seeds for many of the responses to the 'problem' of the inner city which followed in the twentieth century. The use of planning laws to determine areas of development (or decline), slum clearance schemes which rehoused the poor in tower blocks or on the city periphery, public housing allocatory mechanisms which created 'respectable' or 'sink' estates, the routines of inner-city policing – all had their origins in this period.

3   Progress and the urban problem: twentieth-century dreams

From the beginning of the century through to the 1970s, crime was almost exclusively understood and responded to as an urban phenomenon. Rural crime, like the countryside itself, was seen as a 'backwater', an innocent hangover from old ways, by contrast with both the dynamism and the danger of city.

3.1   Grounds for optimism: mobility

The starting point for any discussion of this period must be the sheer scale of urbanization during the twentieth century – towns and cities became the dominant places of the British landscape. Between the start of the century and the late 1970s, there was an unchecked population flow towards urban centres. In the process, the city grew, condensing work, leisure and home in a compressed and organized space. The city simultaneously expanded and became denser.

spatial and social mobility

The theme of growth is inseparable from the theme of mobility – both spatial and social. In spatial terms, people moved to the city – they gravitated there in search of work, in pursuit of leisure, in the quest for excitement. As the city expanded, it also became a more complex space for people to move within. It developed its own spatial dynamics. Some of these dynamics involved the increasing separation of home and paid employment. Others arose from the unceasing quest for better places to live within the city. For much of the twentieth century, the search for these better

---

Extract 4.2 Park *et al.*: 'The growth of the city'

In Europe and America the tendency of the great city to expand has been recognized in the term 'the metropolitan area of the city', which far overruns its political limits, and in the case of New York and Chicago, even state lines. The metropolitan area may be taken to include urban territory that is physically contiguous, but it is coming to be defined by that facility of transportation that enables a business man to live in a suburb of Chicago and to work in the loop, and his wife to shop at Marshall Field's and attend grand opera in the Auditorium …

No study of expansion as a process has yet been made, although the materials for such a study and intimations of different aspects of the process are contained in city planning, zoning, and regional surveys. The typical processes of the expansion of the city can best be illustrated, perhaps, by a series of concentric circles, which may be numbered to designate both the successive zones of urban extension and the types of areas differentiated in the process of expansion.

This chart [see Figure 4.1] represents an ideal construction of the tendencies of any town or city to expand radically from its central business district – on the map 'The Loop' (I). Encircling the downtown area there is normally an area in transition, which is being invaded by business and light

manufacture (II). A third area (III) is inhabited by th workers in industries who have escaped from the area c deterioration (II) but who desire to live within easy acces of their work. Beyond this zone is the 'residential are (IV) of high-class apartment buildings or of exclusiv 'restricted' districts of single family dwellings. Still farthe out beyond the city limits, is the commuters' zone suburban areas, or satellite cities – within a thirty- to sixt minute ride of the central business district.

This chart brings out clearly the main fact of expansio namely, the tendency of each inner zone to extend its are by the invasion of the next outer zone. This aspect c expansion may be called *succession*, a process which ha been studied in detail in plant ecology. If this chart is applie to Chicago, all four of these zones were in its early histor included in the circumference of the inner zone, the presen business district. The present boundaries of the area c deterioration were not many years ago those of the zon now inhabited by independent wage-earners, and withi the memories of thousands of Chicagoans contained th residences of the 'best families'. It hardly needs to be adde that neither Chicago nor any other city fits perfectly int this ideal scheme. Complications are introduced by the lak front, the Chicago River, railroad lines, historical factors i

---

places pushed back the boundaries of the city, as social mobility, linked with spatial mobility and the imperatives of the economy, caused an upward and outward movement to the city's edge – a process described by Rex (1973, p.84) as the 'great urban game of leapfrog'. The spatial outcome of this economic and social mobility was suburbanization in the shape of new developments on the city edge. Suburbanization – the confluence of spatial and social mobility – represented progress towards a better life away from the hustle, dirt and 'messiness' of city life. In the direction of that progress, looking outwards not inwards, the older grand homes and respectable housing of the nineteenth-century city rim were left behind to run down and decay, to move 'downmarket' and become the resting place of those unable to afford access to the newer and better places at the edge of the expanding city.

3.2 Zones of transition: the Chicago School

This combination of expansion and mobility underpins what remains the most famous approach to urban sociology of this century, the work of the Chicago School, most notably that of Robert E. Park and Ernest W. Burgess (Park *et al.*, 1925). In this context, the most significant element is Burgess's zonal theory of city development and its relation to both the dynamics of urban change and the problems of crime and social disorder. The theory is based on the idea that, as the city expands, so, outside the central business district, residential zones develop as a series of concentric rings of increasing affluence moving from centre to periphery (see Extract 4.2 below and Figure 4.1 overleaf).

he location of industry, the relative degree of the resistance of communities to invasion, etc. …

In the expansion of the city a process of distribution takes place which sifts and sorts and relocates individuals and groups by residence and occupation. The resulting differentiation of the cosmopolitan American city into areas typically all from one pattern, with only interesting minor modifications. Within the central business district or on an adjoining street is the 'main stem' of 'hobohemia', the teeming Rialto of the homeless migratory man of the Middle West. In the zone of deterioration encircling the central business section are always to be found the so-called 'slums' and 'bad lands', with their submerged regions of poverty, degradation, and disease, and their underworlds of crime and vice. Within a deteriorating area are rooming-house districts, the purgatory of 'lost souls'. Nearby is the Latin Quarter, where creative and rebellious spirits resort. The slums are also crowded to overflowing with immigrant colonies – the Ghetto, Little Sicily, Greektown, Chinatown fascinatingly combining old world heritages and American adaptations. Wedging out from here is the Black Belt, with its free and disorderly life. The area of deterioration, while essentially one of decay, of stationary or declining population, is also one of regeneration, as witness the mission, the settlement, the artists' colony, radical centres – all obsessed with the vision of a new and better world.

The next zone is also inhabited predominatingly by factory and shop workers, but skilled and thrifty. This is an area of second immigrant settlement, generally of the second generation. It is the region of escape from the slum, the *Deutschland* of the aspiring Ghetto family. For *Deutschland* (literally 'Germany') is the name given, half in envy, half in derision, to that region beyond the Ghetto where successful neighbours appear to be imitating German Jewish standards of living. But the inhabitant of this area in turn looks to the 'Promised Land' beyond, to its residential hotels, its apartment-house region, its 'satellite loops', and its 'bright light' areas.

This differentiation into natural economic and cultural groupings gives form and character to the city. For segregation offers the group, and thereby the individuals who compose the group, a place and a role in the total organization of city life. Segregation limits development in certain directions, but releases it in others. These areas tend to accentuate certain traits, to attract and develop their kind of individuals, and so to become further differentiated.

(Park *et al.*, 1925, pp.49–52, 54–6)

Figure 4.1   The growth of the city

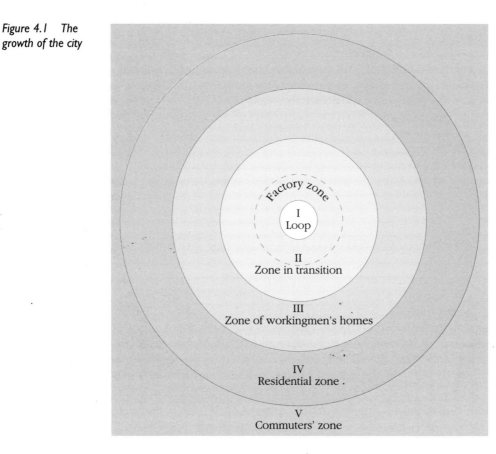

Factory zone

I
Loop

II
Zone in transition

III
Zone of workingmen's homes

IV
Residential zone

V
Commuters' zone

zone of transition

It was the zone of transition in Burgess's model – an area characterized by older, low-cost housing intermingling with factories and close to the centre of the city – that was identified with successive waves of migrants. In the context of the USA (and Chicago in particular), these were Irish, Italian and Eastern European, together with black families from the South who all sought the American Dream in the urban-industrial centres of the northern states. The point about the zone of transition in the model is precisely that it is *transitional*. New migrants would move into it because of its cheap housing and proximity to factories, but as they became economically established they would migrate onwards. These were people who were on their way to somewhere, moving outwards into more permanent and stable accommodation in the outer rings as they became assimilated to the 'American way of life' (Clarke, 1991, Chapter 3). It was thus a continuous process: as each successive generation of migrants became 'Americanized', each progressed and moved on. Mobility – social, spatial and cultural – underpinned the essential optimism of this model.

Within the zone of transition, life was hard and it was disorderly. It lacked the social, spatial and cultural stability of the outer rings. Instead, it was characterized by transitions, transience and turbulence and as such was both a zone of disorder and potential criminality – widely referred to by the Chicago School as an area of **social disorganization**. Indications of this potential were identified by another classic Chicago study – that of Shaw and McKay (1942). Basing their approach on Burgess's zonal theory, Shaw and McKay mapped where juvenile delinquents in

Chicago (and other American cities) lived according to zone of residence. Their finding that juvenile delinquency was highest in the innermost ring and declined steadily outwards, *and* that this pattern appeared to remain stable over time, appeared to support the view that crime could be equated with the socio-spatial disorderliness of the zone of transition (Shaw and McKay discussed in Bottoms, 1994, p.590 and also in **Bottoms and Wiles, 1992**). In trying to explain this finding, Shaw and McKay focused mainly on the constant population movement of the zone of transition. But they also noted its cultural heterogeneity, and equated this with an absence of cultural integration. They contrasted this heterogeneity with an assumed high level of cultural integration in the outer residential areas. They saw the zone as a place that was conducive to the development of a criminal subculture and to the cultural transmission of delinquent values (Bottoms, 1994, p.50). Both social disorganization and the idea of 'criminal sub-culture' have been important strands in subsequent explanations of crime. However, what is relevant here is the way in which cultural differences were represented as deviations from the norm and as a lack of culture, both 'creating' social disorganization. In this view, crimes of violence and crimes against property were the effect of the 'ecology' of the inner area – its inability to provide integrative mechanisms that could link inhabitants to the wider social order. Here was the downside of the optimism about urban growth and mobility.

The other feature which helped to dramatize the zone of transition as different and deviant was that it was transitional in another sense. It was regularly traversed or passed through by those making their way from work to home, from the outer residential areas to the central business district. What such commuters perceived was *difference* – neither the orderly commercial world of the business district nor the planned residential order of the outer suburbs. Instead, they confronted a microcosm of disorder – decaying properties, marginal businesses, a diverse population and a visibility of 'life on the streets'. The zone of transition almost necessarily involved forms of what Whyte (1959) called 'street corner society' because of the particular distribution of private and public space. Since the accommodation in the zone was dominated by forms of multi-occupancy – lodging houses, sub-divided properties, small-scale rented accommodation – the access to private space taken for granted in the suburbs was much less available. As a result, life in these areas of the city spilled out into the public spaces of the street. In the process it fed a spectre of disorder identified with inner-city life.

There have been arguments about both the validity of this ecological model and its applicability to non-US settings. For example, Taylor (1999, pp.92–104) contrasts the Chicago model with the trajectories of 'market' and 'industrial' cities in Europe. In the context of this chapter, though, the Chicago School model is significant because it captures two central themes. One is the predominant optimism of mid-twentieth-century views about the city, grounded in the ideas of mobility and transitions. The pattern of urban processes demonstrated an apparently infinite capacity of the city to absorb, assimilate and civilize its newest inhabitants, as most of its succeeding waves of migrants moved upwards and outwards on the escalator towards suburbia. Second, the model embodies the growing conception of a changing relationship between crime and the city in which crime and dangerousness become associated with specific places. The Chicago School's concept of a zone of transition prefigures what comes, in the 1960s and 1970s, to be defined as the 'inner city' – a disorderly place which breeds disorderly behaviour.

3.3   Grounds for optimism: urban reconstruction

The growth of the city and the forms of mobility associated with that were not just the result of the workings of the market in land and housing, but also involved self-conscious attempts to plan the future through systematic urban reconstruction. The New Towns movement in Britain in the 1950s was one such example. Another was urban reform in the shape of slum clearance and rehousing programmes intended to reclaim the declining areas of the city. These were either on the fringes of the zone of transition (replacing older working-class/artisanal housing built in the mid to late nineteenth century) or on peripheral public housing estates developed by town and city councils. In these latter developments, working-class families found themselves made part of the 'great urban game of leapfrog' and rehoused beyond the old suburbia on the

Typical middle-class, low-density suburb laid out in gentle curving roads and cul-de-sacs. Note also the presence of gardens and trees, giving the whole a very different look to the stark bareness of the working-class suburb

Typical working-class suburb of a planned type with its virtually identical houses, laid out in straight lines with the occasional cul-de-sac. The wide straight roads and lack of trees, together with the sameness of the houses, gives the area a bare, uniform appearance (Thorns, 1972)

city's rim. Such shifts were rarely in the same direction as the new suburbia, creating different 'corridors' of housing type and social class radiating outwards from the city (Thorns, 1972).

Urban reform was a testament to the power of municipal politics and to the underlying belief in the transformative power of the built environment. Moving people from the slums to rational, well-planned and modern forms of housing was equated with changing them from the habits of 'slum culture' to being 'modern citizens'. The idea of housing as a way of promoting assimilation to the social order had underpinned urban reform from the beginning. The slum clearance programmes added to the earlier private/market escalator of suburbanization a municipal or public escalator to a better life in new council estates. Each testified to the city's capacity to absorb and assimilate as part of a continual programme of modernization and progress (see also Taylor, 1999, pp.104–12). As the photographs on the facing page show, spatial and the social characters of private and public development differed markedly.

3.4 Lingering pessimism

The reform of the city in the late nineteenth and early twentieth centuries destroyed the 'wens and rookeries' that had seemed to be the natural habitat of the dangerous classes. The dangerous places had been levelled or opened up to public regulation and policing. The rehousing of the poor had promised both the spatial separation of the respectable and labouring classes from their dangerous neighbours and, at the same time, attacked the environment that bred dangerousness. In the process, the great fear of the 'social problem' had been dispersed, and the dangerous classes disappeared along with their dangerous places. For the most part, then, it seemed that order had triumphed over disorder. But worries remained.

These residual problems were associated with residual areas – the unreconstructed slums, the 'transitional' areas and, subsequently, the 'rough estates'. Each was identified – and identifiable – as different from the rest of the social order of the city. Each had its reputation – 'tough', 'rough', 'unrespectable', 'disreputable', the 'red light district' (see, for example, White, 1980). Overlaid on these spatial distinctions were patterns of class, gender and, particularly, age difference. Crime and disorder were seen as a problem of the 'lower orders', the 'rough' sections of the working class. They were perceived as an almost exclusively male phenomenon – in part because crime and disorder were associated with public places and spaces that were masculine processes (see Massey, 1994, pp.178–9). Finally, by the end of the nineteenth century, concerns about crime and disorder had come to focus primarily on juvenile delinquency. Adolescence has been constructed as a distinct and separate life phase, involving biological and psychological disturbance that necessitated adult surveillance and intervention (Muncie, 1999, Chapter 2). Youth and crime became inextricably intertwined in the popular imagination and in political and professional discourses about the crime problem (see, for example, Burt, 1925). Despite the belief in adolescence as a universal stage of life, official attention was primarily directed at male working-class youth and their ways of being in public space (Clarke, 1984). For the most part, crime and disorder were to be explained by reference to 'slum culture', or the 'culture of poverty' or 'lower-class values' – explanations which marked a suitable distance between such problems and the respectable majority – or by reference to the 'transitional phase' of adolescence and explanations which emphasized the temporary and correctable nature of the disturbance. Disorder persisted, although in apparently more mundane and manageable forms. Crime and disorderliness, rather than outright dangerousness, characterized the city in the first half of the twentieth century. These were certainly 'problems', but they were concentrated in some places rather than others – in the haunts of the 'habitual criminal'. They disturbed the peace rather than threatened the breakdown of social order. They became simply matters of policing. There were only isolated fragments of the old social problem: here a few juvenile delinquents, there a few prostitutes; here the odd 'criminal family', there a few maladjusted 'problem families'. Crime and disorder became the province of the expert rather than the focus of popular attention. The connection between the city and crime became 'routinized' – something to be left in the hands of professionals who were best able to secure progress and reform.

3.5 Emerging new concerns

This view of the *residual* nature of crime in the context of urban modernization and progress was undercut by a multiplicity of different processes in the 1960s and 1970s. At the risk of oversimplifying, we have identified three clusters of processes which were particularly significant in changing the perceived relationship between the city, crime and danger:

1 a crisis of 'progress' in the city;

2 the emergence of new spatial struggles over the social order of the city; and

3 new patterns and perceptions in the zones of transition.

In addition, from the mid 1970s, cities faced financial crises. Global recession together with changing central government priorities acted to produce a fiscal crisis at local and municipal government level (Cochrane, 1993). There is not the space here to examine this in detail. The point to note for our purposes is that just as doubts about whether all the problems had been resolved were appearing, so the ability of urban governments to finance new initiatives aimed at their resolution came under threat.

We have argued that the promise of progress underpinned the view that disorderly behaviour in the twentieth-century city was simply a 'residual' matter, and that this promise rested on the idea that there were 'escalators' (new housing markets and urban reform) which moved people upwards and outwards. By the 1960s and 1970s, there were growing doubts about the effectiveness of these 'escalators', as those left behind began to look more like structural features of the urban social order than groups who were merely waiting their turn. Two key factors seemed to be significant in solidifying the inner areas of the city. The first was age. The social composition of the inner areas was structured around the extremes of age – they contained young and old rather than working-age adults and families. The young were generally too poor to enter housing markets or public housing and, whether in education or early working careers, were looking for cheap rented accommodation. The elderly were simply too poor to move on and often too attached to old neighbourhoods to want to do so.

The second factor was the structuring effect of racialized divisions which resulted in a heavy concentration of black and other minority ethnic groups in the older, inner areas of the city – as individuals and as families. Barred from both the housing market and public housing by discrimination, accommodation in the zone of transition and the older areas of workingmen's housing became the focal points for minority ethnic groups. Although the density of these racialized divisions of British cities never approached that of the USA, the imagery of the ghetto did cross the Atlantic, as did the 'blaming the victim' ideologies of 'ghetto culture' and the 'culture of poverty' which sought to explain the immobility of such groups in terms of their own cultural patterns and choices.

The effect of these two changes was to create specific cultural patterns and tensions around life on the streets in the inner areas. These streets, more than anywhere else in the city, displayed the symbolic forms of a multi-ethnic society and the tensions associated with the non-integration of old white and new minority ethnic communities. The potential for disorder and danger was demonstrated by the riots of Nottingham and London's Notting Hill area in the 1950s. Equally significant for the state of the inner areas was the population bifurcation between young and old and the lack of visible family life in the inner-city areas. Life on the streets increasingly became the province of the young – particularly in the male-dominated youth cultures of the 1960s and the 'bohemian' or counter-cultural patterns of the late 1960s and early 1970s. The effect was an increasingly disconcerting vision of the inner areas as socially and ethnically diverse, mixing complex cultural forms in highly public ways and making public places look and sound highly disorderly and potentially criminal. Parties, loud music, groups of young people, drug use and street crime emerged as the dominant imagery of the inner areas. In the early 1970s, these concerns came to focus on 'mugging' as an index of both the increasing fear about public safety in the city and the presence of black youth on the city's streets (Hall *et al.*, 1978 and Chapter 1).

The third element of the 'crisis of progress' related to what happened at the other end of one of the escalators – the new public housing estates. This crisis became focused most explicitly on the patterns of high-rise developments ('cities in the sky'). Disaffection among their populations about the physical and social environments was eventually reflected in professional and political disenchantment with these approaches to urban renewal. A particular focus was on their apparent lack of 'community' and the implied decline in informal social controls. Subsequently, the project designs themselves came under criticism for not building in a 'defensible space' against crime (Newman, 1973), and the question of a relationship between building design and crime more generally was considered (Coleman, 1990). Similarly, the role of city planners in deciding land use and thereby creating (or eliminating) the potential for 'dangerous space' became the focus of some attempts to explain the apparent association of crime with particular areas of the city (Herbert, 1982).

The second cluster of processes marks the beginnings of attempts to reshape the spatial and social orders of the city. Historically, mobility had meant movement outwards – the trend of suburbanization. However, the 1970s saw a reverse trend, involving pressures to 'reclaim' the inner areas of the city. An expanding middle class, particularly those sections based in state welfare professions, began to identify older housing as an economic and cultural alternative to moving out to suburban estates, and embarked on the process known as 'gentrification' – the rescue of 'nice houses' in unrespectable areas. As a result the inner areas became the focus for new spatial and social struggles. As gentrification proceeded and more and more areas became identified as potentially desirable, the members of the economically and racially marginalized social residuum found themselves further displaced, with their housing rehabilitated and sold off or rented at prices far beyond their reach (Goldberg, 1993).

Following such changes in the housing market were wider cultural attempts to 'clean up' the area, architecturally, socially and culturally. Central to these were efforts to control and, if possible, remove the disorderliness of street life – disorderliness which was recognizable in the forms of prostitution, of young people 'hanging about', and of the homeless and transients (who became known pejoratively as 'street people'). These struggles exposed the complex cultures of the inner areas as 'problems' of public order.

Finally, all of these processes underpinned the changing imagery of the inner areas in the 1960s and 1970s. This is best captured in the language used to describe these areas: they become either 'ghettos' or the 'inner city'. Both terms identify these places as solidified spaces (clearly identifiable and distinguishable from the rest of the city) and as problem areas. These terms are different from the Chicago School's concept of a zone of transition. They identify the inner areas as no longer transitional. Rather they have become blocks to progress. They are sullen and resistant to change. They have become dangerous places once again, not safe for respectable people.

ACTIVITY 4.2

Before reading on, make a few notes on how you perceive the key characteristics of dangerousness in the city implied by the changes from the beginning of the twentieth century up to the 1970s.

As in the nineteenth century, the revival of dangerousness of the inner city was multi-dimensional. It was spatial, in that specific parts of the city were identified as dangerous, and the physical characteristics of these parts were linked to the social problems within them (decaying properties and disorganized households). It was also spatial in the way that attention was focused on the dangerousness of public places – the street in particular – as posing problems about the maintenance of both public order and the social order. It was also sexual: there were recurrent concerns with prostitution; with the sexual misdemeanours of the young; with the growing visibility of gay sexualities; and with the apparent fecundity of black and other minority ethnic families. It was potentially political, as the traditional right began to see municipal socialism as 'the enemy within'. It was profoundly racialized, with the black 'other' seen as a social, cultural and criminal threat to a naturalized English social order or way of life. Above all, it was criminal: it was about crime, and crimes of the street in particular, but crime which exceeds the capacity of society to contain or manage it. It was crime seen as the basis of a crisis of law and order (see **Hall, 1980**).

4 Fin-de-siècle nightmares

By the early 1980s the optimism outlined in section 3 appeared to be over. Recorded crime had been rising since the 1960s, and in the ten years, 1975–85, there was an apparently startling increase of 63 per cent (Smith, 1989, p.270). Public concerns again turned to the city, and in the 1980s the inner cities came to stand for and represent the 'crime problem' just as they symbolized equally powerfully economic and social decay and the challenge of 'urban regeneration' (Deakin and Edwards, 1993; Robson, 1988).

4.1 Urban decline

One of the ways in which these concerns about the city were manifest was in a sharpening sense of urban decline. Cities up and down the country saw their remaining factories closing, manufacturing being replaced by service industries, and already run-down areas appearing ever more derelict. It seemed as if the old industrial-urban centres of Britain were in a terminal condition, and popular anxieties about this were given impetus by visions of an urban landscape of extreme decay in which the remaining public areas were covered in graffiti and vandalized. A more general feeling of street lawlessness crept into the public consciousness. Such feelings were further fuelled by an association of the city's 'twilight districts' and estates with a 'tangle of pathologies' (Robins, 1992, p.1). Truancy, crime, family and community breakdown were among the issues which made up this 'tangle' and which, along with the degradation of the physical environment, made people ever more fearful that the city and city life were disintegrating.

The complexity of the meanings embedded in the ideas of 'urban decline' means that any assessment of how far such fears are objectively justified is fraught with difficulties. However, what is relevant here is not the issue of whether decline (whatever that might mean) was occurring (however that might be measured) but the idea that there is a symbolic link between people's views about the health of the city and their feelings about security and *civilization* and, ultimately, the state of the nation. 'Urban decline' in the late twentieth century resonated with many of the same perceptions of threat that fear of 'the mob' had engendered a century earlier (Katz, 1995). The effect of the rhetoric about urban decline was to tap into a much wider set of feelings of social malaise at the heart of the city – including fears about crime – than simply worries about a declining urban landscape. As Beauregard (1993, p.192) puts it, 'Urban commentators cannot refer to urban decline without setting in motion subtle harmonics that cause many listeners and readers to reflect on the precariousness of their way of life'.

4.2 The enemy within?

These 'subtle harmonics' set the context for the re-emergence of other fears. The riots that took place in the inner cities of England in the early 1980s were regarded by many as 'without equal in this century' (Waddington *et al.*, 1989, p.142), and they revived long-standing fears relating to notions of an 'enemy within'. It seemed as if the sites of rioting could be pinpointed on a map simply by identifying those areas where there were concentrations of black or Asian people (Young, 1992). The spectre of the 'race riot' appeared to be once again reaching across the Atlantic to become resident in Britain.

To read these uprisings of black communities as race riots, however, is to misunderstand their background and also to misread the history of policing in working-class areas. The riots were the product of long-standing relations of conflict between the police and local black communities in the areas in which they occurred. These were places 'resonant with contested meanings' (Keith, 1993a, p.154). They were the symbolic 'front lines' in which the place of black people in Britain was being played out and redefined on a daily basis. The relationship with the police was the central element of these processes. This had 'deteriorated steadily for more than 30 years through the combined influences of racism, marginalization, labelling and criminalization' (Keith, 1993a, p.159). The 'front lines' marked the points of resistance to police oppression, where challenges to police authority had become a part of the daily routine. It is this notion of *routine* that is the key to understanding the riots. It was not that police/black relations were worse in the riot areas; rather, the riots were in locales where resentment of power relations had been transformed into routine resistance (see **Keith, 1993b**). The riots occurred when some 'trigger' event tipped this routine of daily resistance into collective disorder.

Although the disorders of the 1980s were not race riots, they were of symbolic significance in that they appeared to forge a new link between 'race' and inner-city disorder. There was a new 'enemy within' and it was black (Gilroy, 1987). In this sense the 1980s riots marked a turning point in the public perception of the 'urban other' and a re-emergence of nineteenth-century fears about the 'alien'. The significant result of the racial dimension of the riots was that 'blackness' was coming to play 'a cautionary role similar to … that once occupied by nineteenth-century fears of the crowd' (Cross and Keith, 1993, p.10).

routine resistance

4.3 Law and order

More specific fears also flourished concerning issues of law and order. At the same time as recorded crime was rising, it seemed that the capacity of society and the police to cope with crime was diminishing. The clear-up rate for crimes *reported* to the police had fallen steadily from 45 per cent in 1970 to 31 per cent in 1986. Unreported crime was on the increase. The streets were increasingly perceived as risky and unsafe. Low-level harassment, not in itself criminal, could nonetheless be at one end of a spectrum of activity at whose other end were criminal acts (for example, from sexual harassment to rape). All these factors fuelled fears about urban crime such that, by the middle of the decade, 60 per cent of the public said they were worried that 'they or members of their household might become victims of crime'. The conditions were set for the politicization of law and order, and it was notable that by the late 1980s, 25 per cent of those surveyed said they regarded law and order as 'today's most important political issue' (Smith, 1989, p.272; see also Chapter 1).

Meanwhile, the police were also under pressure. In addition to the pressure from the public concern about escalating lawlessness, there was a chorus of criticism about the routine policing practices employed in the so-called 'notorious' inner-city areas. Historically, policing the working-class areas of the city had always been a politics of choice between enforcing law *or* maintaining order (Cohen, 1981). One result was that the police had come increasingly to rely on the use of discretionary powers, with all that implied, for undermining 'the official posture of the force as neutral arbiters of justice' (Cohen, 1981, p.126). As a result there was a strong likelihood that the targets of police action would feel unjustly treated.

Such feelings of injustice were given affirmation through the implementation of the 'sus' law (which permitted police to stop and search any individual on the grounds only that their behaviour was 'suspicious'). As applied by police in the inner city – overwhelmingly to black and Asian young men – it was highly discriminatory and conflicted with the citizenship rights of the black population as a whole. The effects of 'sus' were of wider significance, too, in that its use against *some* members of black and ethnic minority groups was read as 'providing validation of hostility towards *all* members of ethnic minorities as potential criminals' (Waddington *et al.*, 1989, p.146). In the context of a government committed to tougher measures, such validation of hostility aided the politicization of law and order by drawing more rigid boundaries between criminals and victims. The 'support for the fight against crime is best mobilized where there are clear symbolic distinctions between the deviant few and the law abiding majority' (Smith, 1989, p.274). The labelling of black inner-city residents as 'criminal' in the public mind thus served the purposes of those who wanted to push law and order up the political agenda.

4.4 Discovering young men

The themes of decline and dangerousness in the city were intensified in the 1990s. As the recession of 1990 persisted, there was an outburst of rage as gangs of youths (white and black) rioted and laid siege to some of the most depressed housing estates in the country. From Ely on the edge of Cardiff and Blackbird Leys just outside Oxford to the Meadowell, Elswick and Scotswood estates on Tyneside, riots became 'routine' as 'incendiary young bucks confronted the Boys in Blue' (Campbell, 1993, p.2). The triggers were diverse, but arguably the underlying causes were the same. What appeared to unite those taking part in the 1990s' riots was a common (class and gender) experience of economic *extremis*.

The riots were only the tip of the iceberg. The estates on which they occurred were in many respects 'doomed': they were mostly in areas evacuated by business and industry, so there was little hope of employment for their poverty-stricken inhabitants. As a result, a large cohort of young men and women found themselves not only 'on the edge of politics but exiled from the social world' (Campbell, 1993, p.94). 'Exiled' from access to the social institutions and roles which might provide legitimate meaning to their lives, they turned violently on their own communities. What characterized the estate crime of the 1990s was that it took place 'at home' against friends and neighbours and even family. Young men (very few women) 'took over the streets', illegally riding motor-cross bikes across the estates' vacant grass, racing up and down in stolen cars, and terrorizing their communities with a criminal tidal wave of personal harassment, vandalism, burglary, car theft, drug-dealing and riotous behaviour. The problem for the estates was not just crime against the individual, dangerous though the streets might feel; it was also the feeling of total impotence against the power of 'youths on the rampage'.

The riots marked a new phase in working-class relations with the police. As already noted, policing the city had never been an entirely neutral affair, especially in the relations between different classes. Moreover, since the emergence of the modern police force, policing has had an ideological as well as a repressive role in targeting those who were seen to be disturbing the social order (Cohen, 1981). Inevitably, given middle-class perceptions of the street culture of the working class, this involved targeting working-class youth. Such targeting established a pattern of antagonism between police and working-class youth, the result of which, along with contradictions within the police force itself, narrowed 'the scenario of law and order down to a battle between two rival gangs, both composed of young, single, working-class males, each seeking territorial control over the class habitat' (Cohen, 1981, p.131). This was the battle that, in part, was played out in the streets of the run-down estates in the 1990s.

These riots were significant because they indicated in dramatic form a new spatial patterning of dangerous places:

> The 'symbolic locations' shifted from the *frisson* of chaos and cosmopolitanism in the inner city – *the interior* of the celebrated metropolis – to the edge of the city, archipelago, out there, anywhere. These were places that were part of a mass landscape in Britain, estates were everywhere. But in the Nineties estates came to mean crime.
>
> (Campbell, 1993, p.317)

Rioting youth thus became constructed as part of the new dangerous classes, and the estates where they lived finally lost their status as the proud emblems of urban reform. Instead, they became symbolic of a new 'disordered' class – home to the single mothers and 'disorganized families' who had failed to instil in their young men a proper respect for authority. By the century's end, such estates were the targets of increased policing, and a range of initiatives aimed at promoting 'renewal', 'regeneration' and 'social inclusion' (e.g. Social Exclusion Unit, 1999).

4.5   The old in the new: discovering the underclass

underclass

This 'disordered class' – the 'disorganized' families, the 'single parents', and the 'unruly' and 'criminal' youth of popular representation – has become understood as an underclass. A twentieth-century incarnation of the dangerous classes of a century earlier, the underclass is a concept whose origins are American, although it has been exported from there to Britain. It overshadows contemporary discussions of 'urban problems' and 'social problems' (see **Murray, 1990**). It points to decay, disorganization, disorder and demoralization at the heart of the contemporary city. One of the earliest attempts to research and define the nature of this underclass was provided by Auletta, who saw it as composed of a range of threatening groups:

I learned that for most of the 25 to 29 million Americans officially classified as poor, poverty is not a permanent condition. Like earlier immigrant groups, most of these people overcome poverty after a generation or two. There are no precise numbers for this but an estimated 9 million Americans do not assimilate. They are the underclass. Generally speaking, they can be grouped into four distinct categories: (a) the *passive poor*, usually long-term welfare recipients; (b) the *hostile* street criminals who terrorize most cities and who are often school drop outs and drug addicts; (c) the *hustlers* who, like street criminals, may not be poor and who earn their livelihood in an underground economy, but rarely commit violent crimes; (d) the *traumatized* drunks, drifters, homeless shopping-bag ladies and released mental patients who frequently roam or collapse on city streets.

(Auletta, 1983, p.xvi)

This description and others like it evoke the 'otherness' of the underclass as a disorderly and unassimilated presence in the city. They are, as one American magazine made clear, to be feared: 'Behind [the ghetto's] crumbling walls lives a group of people who are more intractable, more socially alien and more hostile than almost anyone had imagined. They are the unreachables: the American underclass' (*Time*, 19 August 1977).

The underclass has come to carry exactly the mixture of 'horrible fascination' that characterized nineteenth-century investigations into, and reportage of, the dangerous classes. They are in, but not of, the city, representing an exotic and unregulated other way of life. As in the nineteenth century, the underclass plays across our concerns and fears about class, 'race' and gender (Gans, 1995; Katz, 1995). The very idea of the under*class*, especially in supposedly 'classless' societies, solidifies the identity attributed to this group. It confirms their difference from the majority and deflects attention from differences between the groups who make up this supposed class. For example, the groups identified above by Auletta would seem to have little in common except their undesirability. Just as the idea of the dangerous classes in the nineteenth century condensed a variety of groups and behaviours into one entity that could be distinguished from the respectable, so the underclass condenses a variety of 'dangers' in order to separate 'us' from 'them' (Morris, 1993). Partly because of its American origins, the idea of the underclass comes loaded with racialized meanings. In the USA, poverty, welfare dependence, street crime, disorganized families and inner-city ghettos are all understood to refer to the experience of black people. Despite the fact that there are more white Americans living in poverty than black, the underclass is presumed to be mainly black (Clarke, 1991, Chapter 6).

The concern with the family and moral order brings us to the role of gender in the underclass. The underclass story has drawn on, and revitalized, nineteenth-century conceptions of male–female differences, treating women as 'home-makers' and the guardians of culture, morality and respectability. In contrast, men are viewed as self-interested and irresponsible beings, in need of taming or civilizing influences (Gordon, 1996). Above all, the underclass is both marked by, and seen as, the product of households headed by lone mothers. It is claimed that liberal welfare provisions for child support have made it possible for lone mothers to live without their children's fathers. Although some moral outrage has been directed at the 'absent father', this has been much less significant than the condemnation of the lone mother, who is viewed as being encouraged by social policies to make bad choices. In the process, such women have become identified as 'failures'. They 'fail' to keep their men in stable and monogamous family relationships. As a result, they fail to 'civilize' men, allowing them instead to break free of the ties of responsibility to maintain and provide for their family. Women are viewed as essentially oriented to domestication and civilization and thus have a responsibility to rein in undisciplined masculinity. This is one reason why prostitution was seen in the past as such a potent threat to the social order. The final failure of the underclass mother is in respect of the next generation. Denied by their mother's failure, these children grow up without access to male role models and paternal discipline, thus producing the next generation of the underclass – feckless mothers-to-be and uncontrolled males. Just like their nineteenth-century predecessors, they are seen to breed too much.

The underclass has been the subject of extensive debate. There have been arguments about whether such a group exists or whether it is an ideological fiction which lumps together different groups and different behaviours in an unwarranted way. There are also arguments about the causes of poverty, marginalization and disorganization (see for example Katz, 1989, and Morris, 1993). For the purposes of this chapter, however, the significance of the underclass lies in the way that the idea has revived older themes about dangerousness and the city. Fears about the underclass bear a remarkable similarity to the nineteenth-century anxieties about the dangerous classes that we discussed earlier. Once again it is claimed that the city contains a virulent threat to the social order, and one that is a volatile cocktail of immorality, criminality and political instability.

4.6   Fears confirmed?

In the 1980s, feelings of anxiety took on a specific form as victimization research – particularly those localized left-realist versions – appeared to show that people's fears about the risks of crime and the dangers of the city were founded in the day-to-day reality of many city residents. It should be noted that there are a number of problems with 'victim surveys' and the measurement of fear. For example, it is not clear what *exactly* such surveys are measuring (fears and worries are influenced by much broader factors than just crime, as we indicated earlier). There are also problems with the process of *labelling* people as victims (since labelling involves a statement of values and different people give different meanings to being victimized). Furthermore, surveys that depend upon legal definitions of crime are intrinsically flawed. A focus on crime in the inner city simply tends to confirm a political point: the urban *is* dangerous and therefore 'something must be done' (see Chapter 1 for a discussion of the shortcomings of victim surveys).

In the light of these problems, the results of both local and national surveys must be treated with caution. Nevertheless, the reports in the popular press of the findings of the British Crime Surveys succeeded in turning into a 'moral panic' the mix of fears about crime, danger and the inner city that had been brought to the fore by the apparent collapse of law and order. In other words, by establishing that recorded crime statistics represented just the tip of an iceberg, the surveys appeared to confirm everybody's worst fears. Further research (some of it based on secondary analysis of the survey data) also appeared to ground some of the fears in firm evidence. The city could be a dangerous place, for some people (but not always those who were most fearful) at some times of the day. Certain 'routine practices of an urban lifestyle' did seem to increase the likelihood of becoming the subject of criminal action (Smith, 1989). In addition, evidence from the USA suggested the existence of 'hot spots' of crime where people going about their daily business were especially vulnerable (Sherman *et al.*, 1989). It became clear that it was not just the inner city that was suffering high rates of victimization. Many of the poorest council estates on the city rim were experiencing high and increasing rates of victimization and crime. The deprived were becoming the multiply victimized as evidence indicated that 'areas with the highest rates of criminal victimization also had the highest rates of multiple victimization' (Bottoms, 1994, p.616). The spatial dispersion of crime was undermining the assumed connection between the inner city and dangerousness.

However, in contradiction to what had been supposed, it was the young, not elderly people, who were more at risk from personal and property crimes. Furthermore, with the important exceptions of rape and domestic violence, it was men who were more at risk than women from violent attack on the street (Smith, 1989). In addition, the vision of black and Asian ethnic communities as perpetrators of crime was counterbalanced by evidence of a higher risk of (racial) attack among those groups as compared with whites. These findings need qualification and illustrate the shortcomings of the surveys. Women walking city streets face a range of 'non-criminal' offensive behaviour (often directed at their sexuality) which profoundly shapes their experience of danger in a way that is very different from that of men (Painter, 1992). Similarly, low-level racial harassment often does not get counted in the crime statistics (since it remains largely unreported) but together with the experience of 'multiple stop and search' creates a very different street reality for blacks than for whites. In other words, by focusing on *legal* definitions of crime, the crime surveys glossed over key differences in how the 'dangers' and disorders of urban street life are experienced.

4.7   The problem of the crime problem

Although the 'crime problem' is the constant subject of public and political attention, the evidence suggests that there is no such thing as the 'crime problem'. Rather, there exists a variety of different and occasionally overlapping crime *problems* which rarely focus on the same issues and concerns (see Chapter 1). These crime problems will tend to move into or out of focus partly in response to media interest, partly in response to what and who the police choose to target. So when rioting youth in the 1990s drew police attention to the outer-city estates, these became the new 'criminal places', just as the 'ghettos' of the inner city had been labelled in the 1980s. What is striking in this process of crime definition and the connections between crime and the city is that it never includes white-collar or corporate crime. The 'City', with its crimes of fraud, corruption, illegal trading and misuse of funds (such as pension funds) is never included as a 'criminal place', even though the personal consequences of its crimes can be devastating and are intimately bound with urbanism as a way of life (see Chapter 6).

the 'problem of crime'

To the extent that there is overlap between the different crime problems, it is that they relate to 'traditional' or 'conventional' concerns about crimes against the person and property. Within this frame of reference there are different interests and priorities about types of crime: sexual harassment and abuse, racial violence, burglary, street theft, vandalism, and so on. Around each focal concern clusters a range of fears and anxieties which are only partly about crime in its legal sense. We have noted the kinds of questions raised by women in relation to the gamut of potentially threatening but non-criminal behaviour that they face. Anti-racist groups have demanded that racially motivated violence be made a distinct and specific criminal offence (Iganski, 1999). They, too, have pointed to a range of behaviour which runs from direct assaults to harassment and intimidation. People living in the inner city or on council estates have long complained about vandalism, but this covers a wide range of environmental defacement and destruction only some of which is perpetrated by 'yobs'; other aspects may result from neglectful councils or landlords. All, however, contribute to a perception of a decaying or disorderly environment. Car-driving commuters may identify the crime problem as one of personal safety or car theft, but may themselves be perceived as a problem by parents concerned about the vulnerability of children to the dangers of drivers passing through at excessive speeds, or kerb-crawling on their way home to suburban respectability.

There are, then, different crime problems. The divergences reflect the different experiences, locations and concerns of social groups within a heterogeneous society (Cooper, 1998a). These bear particularly on how public spaces are experienced, used and traversed (Cooper, 1998b). Suppressing these differences in the name of a singular, supposedly consensual, 'crime problem' draws attention away from the complex social dynamics and inequalities of urban life. But the issue is made still more complex because controlling crime (or perceived dangers and disorders) has also involved criminalizing particular social groups – targeting them as 'suspicious persons'. Young people – and young black people especially – face the presumption that they are 'suspect', with all the resulting surveillance, intrusion and harassment that this entails. Young women in public spaces (especially after dark) have the prospect of being viewed as likely prostitutes – both by the police and by would-be clients – as a result of the assumption that 'respectable' women are not out on the streets alone. Youngsters roaming unsupervised and 'street people' loitering in shopping centre precincts are moved on in order to keep the place safe and clean for the 'real' customers. In such ways, the control of public space has increasingly come to involve a binary distinction between the 'respectable' and the 'suspicious'.

5   Contested cities: constructing social orders

Throughout this chapter, we have tried to draw attention to the dynamics of urban change and the ways in which the question of crime is linked to changing social orders in the city. In this final section, we want to concentrate on new trends in the remaking of the social order of the city that became visible in the 1990s and their connections to issues of crime and disorder.

ACTIVITY 4.3

In looking to the future, the question implicitly posed is: can the city be a safe place to live, and if so for whom? We suggest you take a little time before reading on to consider and make notes on your own views about this question.

5.1   New urban spaces

The 1980s and 1990s saw a multiplication of urban spaces. In Britain, attempts at city centre redevelopment, inner-city regeneration and new developments on the outer edges of the city reshaped the urban environment. Inner areas were 'rejuvenated' both individually, as 'gentrification', heralded by the ubiquitous 'skip', reclaimed previously run-down inner-city streets, and collectively, through the attempt to reconstruct whole city centres in order to 'rescue' the city from its decline and make it attractive to inward investment and population movement. Competing with the attempt to rejuvenate the centre was the development of out-of-town hypermarkets and new superstores – 'monuments to consumption' built to cater for the car-owning residents of the private housing estates on the city rim. In many areas the shopping mall has taken over from the high street as the place to go for consumer goods.

Across the Atlantic new developments can also be found, some of which hint at possible futures. 'Edge city' is the term that has been used to describe a new genre of urban area which contains all the functions of a city but in a spread-out form tied together by 'jetways, freeways, and rooftop satellite dishes' (Garreau, 1991, p.4). Its hallmarks are jogging trails, single-family detached dwellings and glass atria 'reaching for the sun and shielding trees perpetually in leaf at the cores of corporate headquarters, fitness centres, and shopping plazas' (Garreau, 1991, p.4). 'Edge city', it is claimed, is the logical next step from suburbanization and the growth of the out-of-town mall, developing when the strains of commuting and disillusion with the old inner city mean that the jobs begin to locate where most people now live and shop.

Spatially and socially, the result in both Britain and the USA is a growing 'disconnection' between the environment and its geographical location (Harvey, 1989) and between the concept of 'urbanism as a way of life' and the places where the routine activities that make up that way of life take place. There is so little sense of grounding in a specific place or locale or culture in many of the new developments that they could 'almost be anywhere in the world' (Savage and Warde, 1993, p.140). The shopping mall epitomizes this new trend – a self-contained and enclosed environment of exotic greenery, international muzak, marbled floors and subtle lighting. Once inside, 'The visitor is wrenched … away from the culture of the specific city in which it is located, into a new imaginary realm' (Savage and Warde, 1993, p.141).

The dynamics of decline and regeneration affect cities unevenly, creating new inequalities between cities and within cities (Sassen, 1998). For example, industrial decline has systematically improved some British cities whose development was founded on heavy industry, while other cities have flourished through their association with new technology or service sector investment.

But within cities, too, there are deepening divisions between rich and poor areas (Taylor, 1999, pp.126–9). These dynamics are also accompanied by new methods of controlling – or attempting to control – crime and disorder. In particular, strategies of segregation and surveillance have been significant (McLaughlin and Muncie, 1999). Segregation involves the closure of urban places and spaces to the undesirable: the creation of closed communities, walled cities, and zones to which access is carefully controlled. Segregation leaves the 'unwanted' in the spaces between these controlled places. Surveillance by public or private police forces has been increasingly supplemented by technological means (such as CCTV) in public or semi-public spaces: city centres, shopping malls and so on. Such scrutiny aims to deter as much as detect forms of 'disorderly conduct'. Both segregation and surveillance reflect the concern with, and the conflicts over, forms of social order.

5.1.1   Exclusion and the 'model' citizen

social exclusion

The development of these new urban spaces has been accompanied by forms of social exclusion: processes through which people are systematically disadvantaged, marginalized and subordinated. These processes combine economic, spatial, cultural and political divisions, producing deepening structures of social inequality. Many of the new housing developments are unaffordable to the previous inhabitants of the regenerated areas. Waterfront schemes (popular in both Britain and North America as mechanisms of cultural and urban regeneration) typify the case. An illustration is the London Docklands, where it was middle-class 'yuppies' from the City who moved into the converted river-front warehouses and bijou terraces of the in-filled docks. 'Edge city' has been hailed as the next step in the search for the American Dream, but past history suggests that it will not be available to all Americans. Some will get left behind, just as many of the poor, black and dispossessed were unable to get on the escalator and out of the zone of transition.

In Britain, other forms of exclusion have arisen as a result of cash-strapped municipal authorities going into partnership with private developers. All too frequently in the process of negotiation, public amenities such as a library, or a community centre, or shops selling basic foodstuffs lose out to the commercial pressure to achieve a 'profitable' rate of return. Shareholders gain but the town centre as a civic or collective amenity is devalued. Here is an example of another trend – that of an increasing demarcation between public and private space. The case of the shopping malls illustrates the point. When built by local authorities, malls were designed to be thoroughfares and public spaces in addition to providing shops, restaurants, community areas, and so on. But across Britain they have been sold off in a process which has been described as 'the privatization of the public realm' (John Punter, professor of planning at University of Strathclyde, on BBC Radio 4's *File on 4*, 1 March 1994). Once privatized, they become subject to new exclusions ranging from the closing of the centre after shopping hours because it is 'too expensive' in terms of security to keep open, to controlling anything and everything that is seen as a potential threat to the task of maximizing returns. That this can take some curious forms was illustrated in the same *File on 4* programme, which documented the banning of preaching by the Salvation Army (too 'political'), the advertising by a Women's Institute of home-made jam (a threat to established businesses), and primary school children with clipboards (too intrusive). Even sitting was discouraged by making the seats less comfortable, and in one case was justified by reference to market research which purported to demonstrate that the general public was 'particularly distressed' by the sight of old people sitting down. The underpinning purpose was that nothing should hinder people's willingness to part with their money. As one centre manager put it, he didn't want people disturbed by contentious issues, so 'we don't allow people to come in in an uncontrolled manner'.

Such dynamics of change and processes of exclusion have at their heart an imagery of the 'model' citizen whose needs the new urban spaces and places are intended to serve. These model citizens wish to live somewhere 'interesting' (whether in privatized family spaces at the edge of the city or in renovated places within the city). They expect, and are expected, to be 'consumers', exercising 'lifestyle choices' in the boutiques and malls. They are 'affluent', possessing the financial basis for exercising consumer choice. Perhaps most important, they are mobile, having the means to move between spatially distributed sites of home, work, shopping and entertainment. The dynamics of urban development in the 1990s reflect this model of what it means to live in the city. Such 'model citizens' have their opposites: those who cannot be affluent consumers. Bauman (1998, p.38) calls such groups 'the new poor': lacking the means to create lifestyles, to be mobile, to participate as consumers – becoming 'internal exiles' in a land of visible riches. Bauman (pp.74–80) also suggests that a consumerist society will tend to demonize, criminalize and exclude those who are 'failed consumers'.

5.2 Crime control or criminalization? The regulation of public and private space

The new urban geography impinges on crime in a number of ways, some of which can be seen if we examine how crime control, as well as urban space, is being remapped. Alongside the process of privatization, there has been the development of a new set of relationships between the individual and private action against crime, and the role of the police.

Throughout the 1980s and 1990s individuals and communities have been exhorted to take more responsibility for their own crime protection, which at times has engendered a fortress mentality. This ranges from taking care to lock doors and windows, installing household security systems or fitting anti-car theft devices, to community schemes like Neighbourhood Watch or the emergence of privately financed 'street patrol' officers and other forms of 'community force'. Some of these are funded by local councils who see the 'real' police as being overworked and understaffed and 'are prepared to operate their own streetwise forces' despite their 'strictly limited legal powers' (*The Guardian*, 16 April 1994), but others are run by private security firms called in to police affluent suburban neighbourhoods. By the mid 1990s, it has been estimated that in Britain there were already more people employed in *private* security firms than in the *public* police force. Meanwhile, government policy

fortress mentality

was to seek a new 'partnership between police and community', including a force of 'special constables' (unpaid part-timers, under police control).

What effect this will all have against crime is hard to assess. More surveillance (whether Neighbourhood Watch or CCTV) may result in crime displacement to other areas (see also **Walklate, 2001**). The issue of where crimes take place is complex and involves not only 'suitable targets in the absence of direct social control' but also the 'cognitive spatial awareness of offenders' (Bottoms, 1994, p.621); that is, not only opportunity but perception of that opportunity are needed for the crime to occur. More significant, perhaps, suspicious neighbours and community patrols may create less tolerance of 'unusual' behaviour. The tougher line on trespass embodied in the 1994 Criminal Justice and Public Order Act was felt most keenly by those on the margins of society – protesters, squatters, gypsies and travellers. Securing the city by enlisting respectable citizens to 'clean it up' may result in anything that seems exciting, 'exotic', 'dangerous', or that is simply different, being seen as a threat to that cleansing operation.

Private policing and the more elaborate neighbourhood security strategies are in their infancy in the UK, although it is clear that this is a direction in which the government wishes to go. Some indication of their possible implications for the future can again be gleaned from the USA. Davis has termed Los Angeles 'Fortress LA', and he describes how new luxury developments just outside the city limits are becoming like mini fortress cities, 'complete with encompassing walls, restricted entry points with guard posts, overlapping private and public police services, and even privatized roadways' (Davis, 1990, p.294; see also McLaughlin and Muncie, 1999). He also documents an increasing privatization of public space, observing that traditional 'luxury enclaves', like Beverley Hills or San Marino, are restricting access to *public* facilities to 'residents only' by using municipal regulations to 'build invisible walls' in the form of preferential parking arrangements, residential requirements for access to parks, or restricted opening times. Davis (1990, p.246) concludes from his observations that 'residential areas with enough clout are thus able to privatize local public space, partitioning themselves from the rest of the metropolis, even imposing a variant of neighbourhood "passport control" on outsiders'. Davis has provided an ironic re-working of the Chicago school's social map of the city to represent these new trends (see Figure 4.2 opposite).

Such trends highlight the dichotomy within views of city life. It is a place of excitement but it is also a place of danger. It is a place to get 'out and about' and to take advantage of all that it offers, but it is being outside on the streets that feels threatening and that leaves property unguarded. It is a place to be young, free and mobile, but it is 'the young who riot'. This dichotomy is played out in the new spatial arrangements. The shopping mall is the exemplar of the general trend as today's urban spaces are increasingly cordoned off by high-level security cameras, foot patrols and locked gates after hours. The built environment has become less and less *accessible* as traditional 'transitional' areas between public and private space such as street-level shops have been replaced by blank walls, dark glass frontages and curtained offices. Remaining public spaces contain 'ingenious design deterrents' against 'undesirables'. In England seats in some public spaces have been made uncomfortable, but in

THE ECOLOGY OF FEAR

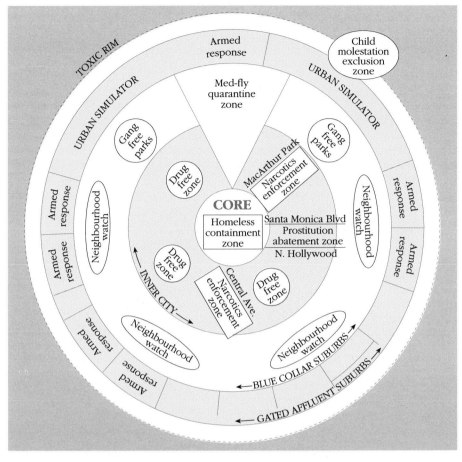

Figure 4.2 The ecology of fear (Source: Davis, 1994)

Los Angeles the barrel-shaped bus bench has been specially designed to make sleeping impossible, and outdoor sprinklers are randomly deployed at night as an extra deterrent to would-be park sleepers.

5.2.1 The enemy without

Against whom is it that such deterrent measures are being deployed? The new enemies, who this time will be prevented from becoming 'within', are the poor, the homeless, the vagrants, street people and all the other 'unsuitables' who are unable to measure up to the consumerist demands of the twentieth century and so who are not wanted in the new citadels of consumerism. According to Davis, in the USA there has been a 'conscious "hardening" of the city surface against the poor' (Davis, 1990, p.232). He puts this down to two interlocking trends. First, in a market-oriented economy, market provision of 'security' will inevitably generate its own demand – there is in short a consumerist 'imperative' for more security. Second, in the absence of first-hand knowledge of actual conditions in the inner city, the 'white middle-class imagination will magnify the perceived threat through a demonological lens' (Davis, 1990, p.224). Between these two,

Extract 4.3 Davis: 'The destruction of public space'

The universal and ineluctable consequence of this crusade to secure the city is the destruction of accessible public space. The contemporary opprobrium attached to the term 'street person' is in itself a harrowing index of the devaluation of public spaces. To reduce contact with untouchables, urban redevelopment has converted once vital pedestrian streets into traffic sewers and transformed public parks into temporary receptacles for the homeless and wretched. The American city, as many critics have recognized, is being systematically turned inside out – or, rather, outside in. The valorized spaces of the new megastructures and super-malls are concentrated in the centre, street frontage is denuded, public activity is sorted into strictly functional compartments, and circulation is internalized in corridors under the gaze of private police.

The privatization of the architectural public realm, moreover, is shadowed by parallel restructuring of electronic space, as heavily policed, pay-access 'information orders', elite data-bases and subscription cable services appropriate parts of the invisible agora. Both processes, of course, mirror the deregulation of the

economy and the recession of non-market entitlemen The decline of urban liberalism has been accompani by the death of what might be called the 'Olmstedi vision' of public space. Frederick Law Olmsted, it w be recalled, was North America's Haussmann, as well the Father of Central Park. In the wake of Manhattan 'Commune' of 1863, the great Draft Riot, he conceiv public landscapes and parks as social safety-valve *mixing* classes and ethnicities in common (bourgeoi recreations and enjoyments. As Manfredo Tafuri h shown in his well-known study of Rockefeller Centi the same principle animated the construction of th canonical urban spaces of the La Guardia–Roosevelt ei

This reformist vision of public space – as the emollie of class struggle, if not the bedrock of the American po – is now as obsolete as Keynesian nostrums of fu employment. In regard to the 'mixing' of classe contemporary urban America is more like Victori England than Walt Whitman's or La Guardia's New Yor In Los Angeles, once-upon-a-time a demi-paradise of fr beaches, luxurious parks, and 'cruising strips', genuine democratic space is all but extinct. The Oz-lil

the conditions are set for justifying the creation of a segregated 'defensible space' against the 'contagion' of disreputable and disorderly elements. It is a 'creation' which *necessarily requires* the destruction of accessible public space and a cordoning-off of the private and 'safe' areas (see Extract 4.3). But, as Caldeira argues, such changes are bound up with processes of crime and disorder – and not just responses to them:

> Contemporary urban segregation is complementary to the issue of urban violence. On the one hand, the fear of crime is used to legitimate increasing measures of security and surveillance. On the other, the proliferation of everyday talk about crime becomes the context in which residents generate stereotypes as they label different social groups as dangerous and therefore as people to be feared and avoided. … In this sense, they contribute to a construction of inflexible separations in a way analogous to city walls. Both enforce unforgiving boundaries. In sum, one of the consequences of living in cities segregated by enclaves is that while heterogeneous contacts diminish, social differences are more rigidly perceived and proximity with people from different groups considered as dangerous, thus emphasizing inequality and distance.
>
> (Caldeira, 1996, p.352)

The other side of these changes is the relative abandonment of poor housing areas and estates – those not attractive enough to be thought worth redeveloping, whose inhabitants are unable to afford household security measures, whose local authorities have run out of cash for crime prevention measures, and where the police no longer go. Such areas form the 'spaces between the places' in the new urban map. They are passed through or by-passed by the 'respectable' citizen. They do not attract inward investment – indeed, they are more likely to

chipelago of Westside pleasure domes – a continuum
tony malls, arts centres and gourmet strips – is
ciprocally dependent upon the social imprisonment of
e third-world service proletariat who live in increasingly
pressive ghettos and barrios. In a city of several million
arning immigrants, public amenities are radically
rinking, parks are becoming derelict and beaches more
gregated, libraries and playgrounds are closing, youth
ngregations of ordinary kinds are banned, and the
eets are becoming more desolate and dangerous.

nsurprisingly, as in other American cities, municipal
licy has taken its lead from the security offensive and
e middle-class demand for increased spatial and social
sulation. De facto disinvestment in traditional public
ace and recreation has supported the shift of fiscal
sources to corporate-defined redevelopment priorities.
pliant city government – in this case ironically
ofessing to represent a bi-racial coalition of liberal
hites and blacks – has collaborated in the massive
ivatization of public space and the subsidization of
w, racist enclaves (benignly described as 'urban
llages'). Yet most current, giddy discussions of the

'postmodern' scene in Los Angeles neglect entirely these
overbearing aspects of counter-urbanization and
counter-insurgency. A triumphal gloss – 'urban
renaissance', 'city of the future', and so on – is laid over
the brutalization of inner-city neighbourhoods and the
increasing South Africanization of its spatial relations.
Even as the walls have come down in Eastern Europe,
they are being erected all over Los Angeles.

The observations that follow take as their thesis the
existence of this new class war (sometimes a continuation
of the race war of the 1960s) at the level of the built
environment. Although this is not a comprehensive
account, which would require a thorough analysis of
economic and political dynamics, these images and
instances are meant to convince the reader that urban
form is indeed following a repressive function in the
political furrows of the Reagan–Bush era. Los Angeles,
in its usual prefigurative mode, offers an especially
disquieting catalogue of the emergent liaisons between
architecture and the American police state.

(Davis, 1990, pp.226–8)

be marked by the loss of public and commercial facilities, as reduced public
spending or low profit margins impact upon them. Their inhabitants fail to
measure up to the new model citizen: they are too poor to attract commercial
services or exercise much by way of consumer choice, they are predominantly
dependent on public income support rather than a wage or salary, and they are
too immobile to take advantage of the city's new possibilities. Where they are
mobile – where they venture into the new places – they look 'out of place' and
are likely to be treated as such. Dress codes at entertainment venues, the policing
of shopping areas against the 'disreputable', the 'hardening' of the city's
architecture, the suburban suspicion of 'outsiders' – all aim to exclude those
who 'have no business being here'.

5.3   Dreams and nightmares: urban futures

Speculations about the possible future of the city emphasize the dynamic tensions
between order and disorder and between progress and crisis that have been
centrally connected to the development of the modern city. The tendencies
towards a new urban order, based on greater privatization, policing and
exclusion, represent a new version of 'progress'. But they also create new
problems: the costs of security, the erosion of public space, and the question of
how to manage or control the 'excluded populations'. In the process, they create
new tensions between those who belong to this new order and those who are
excluded – they multiply fears about the 'other'.

Not all 'progress' is being sought in this direction. Alternative approaches to urban renewal recognize that deprivation and crime remain glaringly obvious on the streets of London or Los Angeles, but stress that cities, at least 'successful' ones, offer more of an opportunity than a threat. Such approaches range from the pursuit of 'zero tolerance' (as in New York) designed to repress and drive out crime and 'incivilities' to produce a more congenial city-scape, to efforts to rebuild communities, through valuing public space and stressing the importance of community participation in planning and development schemes. Such strategies stress the need to 'empower' communities against the wider economic and political tendencies of globalization that threaten to overtake the city and create 'unimaginable mega-monsters' by the early twenty-first century (Davis, 1994).

This revived emphasis on the importance of community has to confront the problem of the unstable meaning of 'community' in contemporary society. The idea of community evokes images of a more stable world in which people and place were intimately connected. These images have been undermined by social and spatial mobility but also by the more diverse senses of attachment that people now have. Communities of place coexist uneasily with communities of identity (as in references to black or minority ethnic communities, for example) which may not live in the same place (Hughes and Mooney, 1998). Creating communities in the face of social mobility and social diversity is a daunting task, but the problems involved need to be compared with the problems that the other vision of a new urban order might create (Cooper, 1998b, explores new possibilities for constructing heterogeneous public spaces).

In this chapter we have talked about 'the city' in general, looking at broad themes and processes rather than trying to trace the history and patterns of development in a particular city. We have worked at this level of generality in order to be able to focus on the themes and imagery of urban order, disorder and danger. Any particular town or city will both share in these general themes and have its own particular history in which the themes are played out (see the discussions in Massey, 1994, and Taylor, 1999). These particular histories will combine wider processes (of economic, political and social development) with local conditions, choices and struggles in the making of urban order. But none of them will have escaped the recurring questions of 'what sort of urban order' and 'what sort of dangers' are at stake in the city.

Review questions

- In what ways have cities been perceived as dangerous?
- How have the connections between cities and danger changed?
- To what extent are crime, disorder and danger synonymous?
- What sorts of social order are being pursued in contemporary urban settings?
- For whom, and against whom, are new urban spaces designated?

Further reading

Jones (1971) and Walkowitz (1992) both provide significant historical studies of 'dangerousness' and problems of social order in nineteenth-century London, while Cohen (1981) presents important arguments about strategies of social control in the city. The Chicago School's approach to crime and the city is well exemplified in Shaw and McKay (1942) and is critically discussed in **Bottoms and Wiles (1992)** and Bottoms (1994). The relation between the city and crime is examined by Taylor (1999) in relation to the dynamics of socio-spatial struggles.

Contemporary debates about the city, disorder and the underclass have been heavily influenced by the work of **Murray (**1984 and **1990)**, while the idea of the underclass has been subjected to critical analysis by Morris (1993). More widely, Katz (1989) provides a valuable discussion of ideas of urban poverty and social disorder.

Finally, Davis's (1990) study of Los Angeles provides a bleak but gripping account of one city's historical development and the sorts of future social order that might be at stake in the contemporary remaking of the city.

References

Auletta, K. (1983) *The Underclass,* New York, Vintage Books.

Bauman, Z. (1998) *Work, Consumerism and the New Poor,* Buckingham, Open University Press.

Beauregard, R.A. (1993) 'Representing urban decline: postwar cities as narrative objects', *Urban Affairs Quarterly,* vol. 9, no.2, pp.187–202.

Booth, C. (ed.) (1889–1902) *Life and Labour of the People in London,* 17 vols, London, Macmillan.

Bottoms, A.E. (1994) 'Environmental criminology', in Maguire, M., Morgan, R. and Reiner, R. (eds) *The Oxford Handbook of Criminology,* Oxford, Oxford University Press.

Bottoms, A.E. and Wiles, P. (1992) 'Explanations of crime and place', in Evans, D.J. *et al.* **(eds)** *Crime, Policing and Place***, London, Routledge. (Reprinted in Muncie** *et al.***, 1996.)**

Burt, C. (1925) *The Young Delinquent,* London, University of London Press.

Caldeira, T. (1996) 'Fortified enclaves: the new urban segregation', *Public Culture,* vol.8 (2), pp.329–54.

Campbell, B. (1993) *Goliath,* London, Methuen.

Clarke, J. (1984) 'Managing the delinquent: the children's branch of the Home Office', in M. Langan and B. Schwarz (eds), *Crisis of the British State 1880–1930,* London, Hutchinson.

Clarke, J. (1991) *New Times and Old Enemies,* London, HarperCollins.

Cochrane, A. (1993) *Whatever Happened to Local Government?,* Buckingham, Open University Press.

Cohen, P. (1981) 'Policing the working-class city', in Fitzgerald, M., McLennan, G. and Pawson, J. (eds) *Crime and Society: Readings in History and Theory*, London, Routledge and Kegan Paul.

Coleman, A. (1990) *Utopia on Trial: Vision and Reality in Planned Housing*, Eynsham, Shipman.

Cooper, D. (1998a) *Governing Out of Order*, London, Rivers Oran Press

Cooper, D. (1998b) 'Regard between strangers: Diversion, equality and the reconstruction of public space', *Critical Social Policy*, vol.18, no.1, pp.465–92.

Cross, M. and Keith, M. (eds) (1993) *Racism, the City and the State*, London, Routledge and Kegan Paul.

Davis, J. (1989) 'Jennings Buildings and the Royal Borough: the construction of the underclass in mid-Victorian Britain', in Feldman, D. and Jones, G.S. (eds) *Metropolis London: Histories and Representations Since 1800*, London, Routledge and Kegan Paul.

Davis, M. (1990) *City of Quartz*, London, Verso.

Davis, M. (1994) 'Beyond Blade Runner: Urban control: the ecology of fear', Westfield, New Jersey, Open Magazine Pamphlet Series.

Deakin, N. and Edwards, J. (1993) *The Enterprise Culture and the Inner City*, London, Routledge and Kegan Paul.

Dorn, N., Murji, K. and South, N. (1992) *Traffickers*, London, Routledge and Kegan Paul.

Gans, H.J. (1995) *The War Against The Poor*, New York, Basic Books.

Garreau, J. (1991) *Edge City: Life on the New Frontier*, New York, Doubleday.

Gatrell, V.A.C. (1990) 'Crime, authority and the policeman state', in Thompson, F.M.L. (ed.) *Cambridge Social History of Britain*, 1750–1950, vol. 3, Cambridge, Cambridge University Press. (Reprinted in Muncie *et al.*, 1996.)

Gilroy, P. (1987) 'The myth of black criminality', in Scraton, P. (ed.) *Law, Order and the Authoritarian State*, Buckingham, Open University Press.

Goldberg, D.T. (1993) 'Polluting the body politic: racist discourse and urban location', in Cross and Keith (eds).

Gordon, L. (1996) *Pitied but not Entitled*, Cambridge MA, Harvard University Press.

Hagan, J. (1994) *Crime and Disrepute*, California, Pine Force Press.

Hall, C. (1998) 'A family for nation and empire', in G. Lewis (ed.), *Forming Nation, Framing Welfare*, London, Routledge/Open University.

Hall, S. (1980) *Drifting into a Law and Order Society*, London, Cobden Trust. (Extract reprinted in Muncie *et al.*, 1996.)

Hall, S., Critcher, C., Jefferson, T., Clarke, J. and Roberts, B. (1978) *Policing the Crisis*, London, Macmillan.

Harvey, D. (1989) *The Condition of Post Modernity*, Oxford, Blackwell.

Herbert, D. (1982) *The Geography of Urban Crime*, London, Longman.

Hughes, G. and Mooney, G. (1998) 'Community', in G. Hughes (ed.) *Imagining Welfare Futures*, London, Routledge/Open University.

Iganski, P. (1999) 'Legislating against hate: outlawing racism and anti semitism in Britain', *Critical Social Policy*, vol.19, no.1, pp.129–41.

Jones, G.S. (1971) *Outcast London*, Oxford, Oxford University Press.

Katz, M. (1989) *The Undeserving Poor*, New York, Pantheon.

Katz, M. (1995) *Improving Poor People*, Princeton, Princeton University Press.

Keating, P. (1973) 'Fact and fiction in the East End', in Dyos, H.J. and Wolff, M. (eds) *The Victorian City*, 2 vols, London, Routledge and Kegan Paul.

Keith, M. (1993a) 'From punishment to discipline? Racism, racialization and the policing of social control', in Cross and Keith (eds).

Keith, M. (1993b) *Race, Riots and Policing*, **London, UCL Press. (Extract reprinted as 'Criminalization and racialization' in Muncie** *et al.*, **1996.)**

Lee, M. (1995) 'London: community damage limitation and the future of drug enforcement', in Dorn, N., Jepsen, Y. and Savona, E. (eds) *European Drug Policies and Enforcement*, London, Macmillan.

Massey, D. (1994) *Space, Place and Gender,* Cambridge, Polity Press.

McLaughlin, J.E. and Muncie, J.P. (1999) 'Walled cities: surveillance, regulation and segregation', in Pile, S., Brook, C. and Mooney, G. (eds) *Unruly Cities*, London, Routledge/Open University.

Mayhew, H. (1851–62) *London Labour and the London Poor*, 4 vols, reprinted 1967, London, Cass.

Morris, L. (1993) *Dangerous Classes*, London, Routledge and Kegan Paul.

Mort, F. (1987) *Dangerous Sexualities: Medico-Moral Politics in England since 1830*, London, Routledge and Kegan Paul.

Muncie, J. (1999) *Youth and Crime: A Critical Introduction*, London, Sage.

Muncie, J., McLaughlin, E. and Langan, M. (eds) (1996) *Criminological Perspectives: A Reader*, **London, Sage in association with The Open University.**

Murray, C. (1984) *Losing Ground: A Critical Introduction,* London, Sage.

Murray, C. (1990) *The Emerging Underclass*, **London, Institute of Economic Affairs. (Extract reprinted as 'The underclass' in Muncie** *et al.,* **1996.)**

Murray, C. (2000) 'Baby beware', *Sunday Times,* 13 February 2000, pp.1–2.

Newman, O. (1973) *Defensible Space,* London, Architectural Press.

Painter, K. (1992) 'Different worlds: the spatial, temporal and social dimensions of female victimization', in Evans, D., Fyfe, N. and Herbert, D. (eds) *Crime, Policing and Place*, London, Routledge and Kegan Paul.

Park, R.E., Burgess, E.W. and MacKenzie, R.D. (1925) *The City*, Chicago, University of Chicago Press.

Pearson, G. (1975) *The Deviant Imagination*, London, Macmillan.

Rex, J. (1973) 'The sociology of a zone of transition', in Raynor, J. and Harden, J. (eds) *Cities, Communities and the Young*, London, Routledge and Kegan Paul.

Robins, D. (1992) *Tarnished Visions – Crime and Conflict in the Inner City*, Oxford, Oxford University Press.

Robson, B. (1988) *Those Inner Cities*, London, Routledge and Kegan Paul.

Sassen, S. (1998) *Globalization and its Discontents*, New York, The New Press.

Savage, M. and Warde, A. (1993) *Urban Sociology, Capitalism and Modernity*, London, Macmillan.

Shaw, C.R. and McKay H.D. (1942) *Juvenile Delinquency and Urban Areas*, Chicago, University of Chicago Press.

Sherman, L.W., Gartin, P.R. and Burger, M.E. (1989) 'Hot spots of predatory crime: routine activities and the criminology of place', *Criminology*, no.27, pp.27–55.

Smith, S. (1989) 'The challenge of urban crime', in Herbert, D. and Smith, D. (eds) *Social Problems and the City*, Oxford, Oxford University Press.

Social Exclusion Unit (1999) *Opportunity for All: Tackling Poverty and Social Exclusion* (First Annual Report), CM.4445, London, The Stationery Office.

Stedman Jones, G. (1971) *Outcast London*, Oxford, Oxford University Press.

Stedman Jones, G. (1983) *Languages of Class,* Cambridge, Cambridge University Press.

Taylor, I. (1999) *Crime in Context,* Cambridge, Polity Press.

Thorns, D.C. (1972) *Suburbia*, London, MacGibbon and Kee.

Trachtenberg, A. (1982) *The Incorporation of America*, New York, Hill and Wang.

Walklate, S. (2001) 'Community and crime prevention', in McLaughlin, E. and Muncie, J. (eds) *Controlling Crime* (2nd edn), London, Sage in association with The Open University.

Walkowitz, J. (1980) *Prostitution and Victorian Society: Women, Class and the State*, New York, Cambridge University Press.

Walkowitz, J. (1992) *City of Dreadful Delight: Narratives of Sexual Danger in Late Victorian London*, London, Virago Press.

Weeks, J. (1981) *Sex, Politics and Society: the regulation of sexuality since 1800*, London, Longmans.

White, J. (1980) *The Worst Street in North London, Campbell Park: Islington between the Wars*, London, Routledge and Kegan Paul.

Whyte, W.F. (1959) *Street Corner Society*, Chicago, University of Chicago Press.

Young, J. (1992) 'Riotous rage of the have-nots', *Independent on Sunday,* 19 July.

CHAPTER 5

Dangerous Places:
The Family as a Site of Crime

by Esther Saraga

Contents

1   Introduction

In the previous chapter we saw how the problem of crime has come to be understood as mainly an urban phenomenon, with the city being linked in the popular imagination with dangerousness and crime. In contrast to this dangerous outside world, 'the family' is widely assumed to be a place of privacy and safety. The contrast between these two worlds has been highlighted at times when there has been a spate of murders or attacks on women and children. Certain neighbourhoods or areas of the city can suddenly become 'no-go areas' for women. For example, for five years from 1975 to 1980, before Peter Sutcliffe the 'Yorkshire Ripper' was caught, women in West Yorkshire were advised to stay at home or to not go out alone. In emphasizing the dangers of the public world, implicitly it is assumed that 'home' is the place which is 'safe' (Hamner *et al.*, 1989).

This chapter is concerned with critically examining this idea of the safe private world of the family, and with exploring ways in which the intimate world of personal relationships, home, domestic life and families might also be thought of as a dangerous place or even a site of crime. We shall focus in particular on events most commonly described as 'domestic violence' and 'child abuse', and explore the contested and contradictory ways in which they have, both historically and in the contemporary world, been understood and responded to. We shall consider whether one of the consequences of the way in which 'crime' is placed in the public sphere is that events occurring within the private sphere of the family are rendered invisible, or if seen they are less likely to be considered serious and, as a consequence, less likely to be called 'crime'. Domestic violence and child abuse are, for example, rarely discussed as part of political and public concerns about 'rising crime' or a 'crisis of law and order'. In exploring these issues we shall be further involved in the process of deconstructing the concept of crime as described in Chapter 1.

'Family violence', understood primarily in terms of cruelty to children, but also involving what was described as 'conjugal violence', was first identified as a serious social problem in the late nineteenth century. But public concern at the time was short-lived, and did not re-emerge until the second half of the twentieth century. Since the 1960s there has been a gradual and ongoing 'rediscovery' and redefinition of the different forms of violence and abuse that take place between family members. In this chapter we shall:

1   Explore factors which contributed to such events being visible in the nineteenth century and to their 'rediscovery' in the second half of the twentieth century.

2   Analyse the nature of the visibility – whether and by whom these events are viewed as serious, understood as 'crimes', and, if so, what kinds of crimes.

3   Consider why these issues have not traditionally been constructed as 'crimes', but more commonly as 'social problems' requiring welfare interventions.

4   Examine differences in the ways in which violence between adults within domestic relationships and violence by adults as parents against children have been constructed, so that by the end of the twentieth century domestic violence was very visible and commonly described as a crime, when, by contrast, child abuse within the family has remained predominantly a welfare issue.

5   Consider whether domestic violence has been constructed as a specific kind of crime, different from those of major public concern.

The chapter is not intended to provide a comprehensive account of theory and research on domestic violence and child abuse. Rather, through an examination of these events within families, it aims to explore further some of the arguments presented in the conclusion to Chapter 1 of this book. In particular, it will address:

■   the fact that crime is not as simple a concept as at first presumed, that it has numerous contexts and consequences and remains a site of legal, political and moral contestation;

■   the nature of the social order which remains selective and partial in delineating which social harms are to be deemed 'criminal' and which are not.

We shall see in the process that, as Chapter 1 emphasizes, there are no easy answers, but rather a variety of perspectives for understanding these issues.

2   Mapping the relationship between the family and crime

2.1   Public and private

Conventionally, the social world is understood as divided into separate public and private spheres, with 'the family' situated firmly within the private domain. There is, of course, no one kind of family, but a great diversity of household arrangements in which people live; family forms vary historically, socially and culturally (Muncie *et al.*, 1995). Despite this diversity, the ideology of the 'normal family' is so powerful that we routinely speak of, and seem to understand, what

The 1950s family embodied the ideals of safety, security and a sense of identity

is meant by 'the family'. There is an 'image that the vision of the British family conjures up; an image of a settled, harmonious, wholesome and orderly unit, instilling the correct social values into its children, and capable of prudent housekeeping without needing the interference of the state and its army of functionaries to prop it up' (Blagg and Smith, 1989, p.23).

the 'ideal' family

This ideal-type family is also usually seen as a place of close intimate personal relationships, of loyalty and harmony, and as a haven from the rigours of the public world (social activities such as work, politics and, indeed, crime). 'Family' is also strongly associated with relationships of dependency and of care. In this popular discourse, women, children, disabled and older people are seen as vulnerable, dependent and in need of care; and it is expected that such care will be provided predominantly within families, primarily by women. Though adult women are responsible for the care of other family members, this discourse of the traditional family also constructs them as in need of protection by a male head of the family. Men it seems do not need this kind of protection, but, in return for being the protector, are in receipt of care, domestic services and sexual intimacy. Families are also widely assumed to regulate themselves and remain largely, if not entirely, independent of state support.

public and private

Implicit in this representation of the ideal family is a clear distinction between its 'safe intimate private world' and the dangerous public world of crime. While family members might be on the receiving end of crimes such as burglary, car theft, or street attacks, the danger in all these cases is seen to come from 'outside'. But events that outside the family might be identified as criminal may, except in so-called 'extreme' cases, be seen as normal if they occur within the context of family relationships. For example, if one adult assaults another in the street, it is likely to be considered a criminal act; but if a man hits his wife at home this may be seen as a domestic argument. Similarly, if a parent hits a child, this may be seen as normal discipline, an understandable reaction to a difficult child, an overreaction to stress, or at worst 'cruelty'; yet infant murders are more common than in any other age group: 44 deaths per million, in comparison with the national average of 12 deaths per million (Home Office, 1997; see also Maguire, 1997).

It is within this context of the ideology of the traditional family that we have to consider the increasing awareness, since the 1960s, of violence and abuse within families. Over four successive decades, different forms of family violence have come to be identified and publicly visible: physical abuse and neglect of children in the 1960s, followed in the 1970s by domestic violence, in the 1980s by child sexual abuse, and in the 1990s by 'elder abuse'. Taking account of these events can lead to a very different image of the family:

> War and riots aside, physical aggression occurs more often among family members than among any others. Moreover the family is the predominant setting for every form of physical violence from slaps to torture to murder. In fact some form of physical violence in the life cycle of family members is so likely that it can be said to be almost universal … If this is indeed the case, then violence is as typical of family relationships as is love.
>
> (Hotaling and Straus, 1980, p.4)

2.2 'Strong' and 'fragile' families

These normative views on families have been accompanied by the idea, across the party political spectrum, of the importance of 'the family' as the cornerstone of society, its natural building block. Strong families are seen as essential for the maintenance of social order: 'Despite attempts to subvert it, our laws and systems must acknowledge the family as the basic building-block of the nation' (Gerald Howarth, Conservative MP, 1991); 'Family life is the foundation on which our communities, our society and our country are built' (Jack Straw, Labour Home Secretary, in Home Office, 1998, p.2). Acknowledging violence and abuse within the family has the potential to open up the private world of the family to external scrutiny, and therefore to challenge the image of the ideal strong family.

One way of preserving the image intact is to see the violence as exceptional and located within a few deviant or 'dysfunctional' families. Such families are generally those that do not conform to the traditional structure; they are said to have 'broken down' and to be characterized by abuse, neglect and lack of parental authority and discipline, leading 'inevitably' to delinquency and crime. It is claimed, for example by 'mainstream' criminologists and psychologists, that the most important predictors of juvenile conduct problems are 'poor parental supervision or monitoring, erratic or harsh parental discipline, parental disharmony, parental rejection of the child and low parental involvement with the child …' (Farrington, 1997, p.387). **the 'dysfunctional' family**

These ideas reflect the more common way in which 'family' and 'crime' are linked within both popular and political policy discourses, which construct the family also as fragile, at risk of breakdown, and through this as contributing to an increase in crime. In this context, the sequence of *family breakdown → lack of parental discipline/authority → juvenile delinquency → criminality → moral malaise → threat to social/moral order* is readily applied. It follows that 'strengthening' the family can also be seen as the cure for crime. Restoration of traditional family values will, it is assumed, decrease crime and ensure and restore moral/social order.

Concerns about the traditional family and family breakdown have surfaced at various times in history. The end of the twentieth century saw increasing anxiety across the political spectrum about a crisis in the family, linking a decline in 'family values' to concerns about moral, social and economic order: 'All the major political parties denigrate what they see as contemporary trends towards "selfish individualism" and offer in their place a return to "family values"' (Jagger and Wright, 1999, p.1). Traditionally, family relationships were expected to be self-regulatory with the need for state intervention being widely seen as a sign of failure. However, in a consulatation paper *Supporting Families*, New Labour discourse on the family recognized that 'All families face pressures in their everyday life and all families want some measure of support' (Home Office, 1998, p.40). More 'serious' family problems 'such as youth offending, teenage pregnancy, domestic violence and problems with children's education' were understood as occurring only within 'a minority of families' (*ibid.*, p.40).

Many of the changes in family life, in particular the diversity of family forms that had taken place in the latter half of the twentieth century, were acknowledged by the Labour government. Nevertheless, in his first conference speech after winning the general election in 1997, the Prime Minister Tony Blair emphasized the importance of family life:

> We cannot say we want a strong and secure society when we ignore its very foundations: family life. It is not about preaching to individuals about their private lives. It is addressing a huge social problem ... Nearly 10,000 teenage pregnancies every year; elderly parents with whom families cannot cope; children growing up without role models they can respect and learn from; more and deeper poverty; more crime; more truancy; more neglect of educational opportunities, and above all more unhappiness.
>
> (*The Guardian*, 1 October 1997; quoted in Silva and Smart, 1999, p.3)

Indeed, the idea that strong families are vital for ensuring social stability and reducing crime has continued into the twenty-first century. Serious social problems and crime continue to be associated with family breakdown. Although the label of 'dysfunctional families' is used less frequently, the distinction between two types of family has been preserved.

2.3   Challenges to 'the family'

These ideas on traditional families, family values and family breakdown have of course long been challenged. For example, second-wave feminists in the 1970s and 1980s (e.g. see Barrett and McIntosh, 1982) argued:

- against the naturalness of the family and of the public/private distinction;

- that the 'personal is political', and hence that the inner world of the family should be open to public scrutiny;

- for 'disaggregation' of the family; that is, instead of discussing it as a homogeneous unit, seeing it in terms of its component parts, thus making visible inequalities and power relationships within families.

Thus, Gordon (1989, p.296) maintained that: '[U]sually "the family" becomes the representation of the interests of the family head, if it is a man, carrying the assumption that all family members share his interests.' As a result, she claimed, divisions of age and gender and the associated relationships of power and dependency within families were rendered invisible or natural. The power of the ideology of the normal family meant that it was so taken for granted that the lack of information about what constitutes 'normal' family life was not even noticed, and acts of violence and abuse occurring within families were rendered invisible.

Feminists argued that, whilst acts of violence by strangers are events in the public domain that fit in well with everyday notions of crime, there was a reluctance to extend the idea of crime to the private domain of the family, even though it was here that women, children and elderly people were more likely to be attacked. As we shall see later, feminist campaigning contributed in a major way to putting issues of violence in the family once more on to the public agenda in the late twentieth century. From then, new discourses of domestic violence and child abuse have been developed, although these remain framed in ways that rarely challenge dominant ideas about 'family'.

We saw in Chapter 1 some of the difficulties that there are in obtaining reliable estimates of the incidence of particular kinds of crimes. The private nature of the family, and the fact that abusers are often people in close intimate relationships to their victims, have made it particularly difficult to find out how commonly domestic violence and child abuse occur. Moreover, it is difficult to know what is meant by the 'extent' or 'frequency' of violence in the family. Unlike a crime such as burglary, child abuse and domestic violence are rarely experienced as discrete incidents. Nevertheless, by the end of the twentieth century domestic violence and child abuse were clearly visible again. Taking its figures from the British Crime Surveys in 1996 and 1998, and from homicide statistics in 1998, the Labour government described the extent of the domestic violence problem in the following terms:

- one woman in four experiences domestic violence at some stage in her life and it is estimated that between one in eight and one in ten has experienced domestic violence in the past year;
- every week two women are killed by their current or former partners;
- every day thousands of children witness cruelty and violence behind closed doors. More than a third of children of domestic violence survivors are aware of what is going on and this rises to a half if the woman has suffered repeat violence;
- domestic violence accounts for one quarter of all violent crime.

(Home Office and Cabinet Office Women's Unit, 1999, Chapter 1, p.2)

In contrast, child abuse does not appear in victim surveys; official estimates of child abuse are commonly taken from the numbers of children whose names have been placed on child protection registers, or from criminal statistics of convictions for child abuse offences. In April 1999, the National Society for the Prevention of Cruelty to Children stated: 'At the end of last year more than 35,000 children were on child protection registers in England, Wales and Northern Ireland. There are at least 110,000 men living in England and Wales who have been convicted of a sexual abuse offence against a child' (Noyes, 1999, p.14).

By the end of the twentieth century there was general agreement that domestic violence and child abuse existed and that they should be taken seriously. However, there was little agreement on how they should be viewed or understood.

ACTIVITY 5.1

Pause for a moment and think about the different ways in which domestic violence and child abuse within families have been understood.

Domestic violence and child abuse are constructed within a range of competing discourses, including:

- **discourses of the normal family** which see a certain amount of violence between spouses as natural, 'ordinary' or an inevitable part of family life; moderate physical discipline of children is either legitimate, or regrettable but understandable. (Sexual abuse of children is not included within this discourse.)
- **welfare discourses** which either see the perpetrators of violence in terms of a medical model of individual pathology, or see the families in which it occurs as dysfunctional. When different forms of violence are discussed together as related issues, it is generally as social problems and hence in the context of welfare policies and practices rather than criminal justice. These discourses are often identifiable by their use of the label 'abuse' rather than 'violence'.

- **feminist** discourses which describe these kinds of violence as abuses of power and as crimes; they link domestic violence and child abuse to ways in which masculinities are constructed.
- **human rights discourses** which emphasize that all individuals, including children, have the right to be free from acts of violence or abuse. However, issues of 'parental rights' and 'children's rights' are often seen as in conflict with each other.

It will be helpful to keep these competing discourses in mind while reading the rest of the chapter.

3 Changing definitions and conceptions of child abuse

child abuse

'Throughout history children have been subjected to the kind of treatment we now call abuse and neglect' (Parton, 1985, p.21). However, when child abuse re-emerged on to the public agenda (in the 1960s as physical abuse, and in the 1980s as sexual abuse), it was presented as if it was an entirely new problem, or at least a problem that had been permanently hidden and was being discovered for the first time. Finding out what goes on within the intimate world of the family, while always difficult, is even harder when seeking historical evidence. In addition, 'the intermittent nature of public concern is the most striking historical feature of the problem and is reflected in the paucity of historical research into this aspect of family relationships' (May, 1978, p.135). Whilst recognizing these difficulties, an examination of the history of recognition of child abuse is nevertheless valuable in demonstrating struggles between competing discourses, and ways in which dominant discourses have changed historically. The following discussion will focus on some 'key moments' during which child abuse became more or less publicly visible. (For more detailed discussions, see Gordon, 1989; Pinchbeck and Hewitt, 1973; May, 1978; Parton, 1985.)

ACTIVITY 5.2

Whilst reading the rest of Section 3, make notes for yourself on some of the following key themes:
- The context in which child abuse became visible or invisible.
- Dominant and competing discourses of child abuse, and how these have changed historically.
- Links between dominant discourses and policies and practices of intervention.
- Constructions of children on the receiving end of abuse – for example, as victims, delinquents, or as wasted national resources.

3.1   The emergence of 'cruelty to children' as a social problem

During the late eighteenth and early nineteenth centuries in Britain there was a universal belief in the sanctity of parental rights, including the use of 'reasonable chastisement' (May, 1978). Physical punishment was probably a normal part of childhood. The low status of children was reflected in sentences for killing children, which were both lenient and which varied with the age of the victim. The death of a baby less than 48 hours old was not considered very serious: 'You cannot estimate the loss to the child itself, you know nothing about it at all. It creates no alarm to the public' (St James Fitzjames giving evidence to the Capital Punishment Commission 1866; quoted in Conley, 1991, p.110).

However, as we saw in Chapters 3 and 4 of this volume, during the nineteenth century there were growing concerns about the general level of violence in society. By the end of the century a particular problem of working-class *family violence* had been identified, and defined mainly in terms of cruelty to children. On the one hand, the response of the upper-class charity workers involved with the voluntary societies was one of saving or 'rescuing' these children. On the other hand, the authorities did not wish to challenge the 'unshakeable faith in the sacred bonds between parent and child' (Conley, 1991, p.105), nor the common law rights of parents, nor to be seen to be intervening in personal or familial matters: 'The evils you state are enormous and indisputable, but they are so private, internal and domestic a character as to be beyond the reach of legislation, and the subject indeed, would not, I think, be entertained in either House of Parliament' (Lord Shaftesbury, 1871; quoted in Pinchbeck and Hewitt, 1973, p.622). It seems that the law was only to be used when there was a clear threat to the public interest.

It was during this time that a new response to family violence developed, with the establishment of Societies for the Protection of Children (SPCCs). The first SPCC was set up in New York in 1871 following publicity about the case of Mary Ellen Wilson who had been treated very cruelly by her adoptive parents: 'She was only rescued after a judge interpreted the word "animal", under laws against cruelty to animals, to include "children"' (Morgan and Zedner, 1992, p.8). Events in England were influenced by what had happened in the USA. The first SPCC (in Liverpool) grew out of an appeal for a dog's home, extended to include the protection of children at a meeting of the Society for the Prevention of Cruelty to Animals. The National Society for the Prevention of Cruelty to Children (NSPCC) was founded in 1889 and gained its Royal Charter in 1895, 20 years after the equivalent society for animals. As Conley comments: '[A]uthorities were very slow to act against child abuse. In Harold Perkin's memorable phrase, the English in the nineteenth century "diminished cruelty to animals, criminals, lunatics and children (in that order)"' (Conley, 1991, p.105).

The campaigns of the SPCCs and other voluntary organizations resulted in legal changes – in particular, in 1889, the Prevention of Cruelty to, and Better Protection of Children Act. Cruelty and neglect of children became, for the first time, criminal offences, though punishment was 'confined to acts of wilful cruelty, that is to acts of criminal intention, and not to cases of neglect due to ignorance, poverty or any of the other prevailing evils of the time' (Pinchbeck and Hewitt, 1973, p.623). It was a 'criminal' rather than a social welfare approach (Parton, 1985). Since parental cruelty was assumed to result in delinquency, concern about children was part of the wider anxiety about disorderly working-class life.

child sexual abuse

Other organizations focused on the sexual abuse of children, particularly on the sale of young girls into prostitution. The social purity movements expressed a desire 'to protect girls from the sexual attentions of their adult male relatives, particularly in the overcrowded slums of urban areas' (Morgan and Zedner, 1992, p.10). We can see that, again, abuse was associated with the 'dangerous classes'. The 1885 Criminal Law Amendment Act raised the age of consent for sexual intercourse from 13 years to 16 years. The stated aim was to deter men from abusing mainly working-class girls, but it also led to greater surveillance of these girls, who could be legally defined as in moral danger and incarcerated 'for their own good'. However, this legislation was seen as inadequate for protecting girls within their own families, and 'incest was particularly heinous because of the bonds of kinship that it violated and that therefore it required a unique form of sanction' (Smart, 1989, p.53). Nevertheless, it was not until the 1908 The Punishment of Incest Act that, for the first time, sexual acts between people within families were criminalized. However, its definitions of incest included only 'sexual intercourse' between people in particular blood relationships (parent and child, grandfather and granddaughter, brother and sister). Thus, for example, step-daughters were excluded from protection, suggesting that the main concern was with 'the "unnaturalness" of the offence rather than the question of an abuse of authority or the exploitation of a minor' (Smart, 1989, p.54). As with many of the other laws passed at this time, it was rarely used. These two Acts, which were consolidated into the 1956 Sexual Offences Act, have remained the basis for criminal prosecutions into the twenty-first century.

3.2   Relative invisibility

In 1908 the first Children Act brought together existing legislation on the treatment of children. Although it included abuse of children in the family by violence and neglect, this aspect of the law was rarely enforced. The main concern instead was with the employment of children, their involvement in 'dangerous performances' and being sold intoxicating liquor: 'Most of the offences created concerned the public. They were observable, as they took place in public places and places of employment and not in the family' (Hall and Martin, 1992, p.2).

The early part of the twentieth century was characterized by concerns about 'national efficiency' and the regulation and supervision of working-class 'family life' through the development of a series of welfare reforms. Periodic concerns about children were primarily expressed within discourses that constructed abused children as a 'wastage' of natural resources. Similarly, eugenic concerns about the quality of the 'race' lay behind much of the alarm about incest (Williams, 1989; May, 1978). Attention shifted from cruelty to neglect and from criminal to welfare interventions. The professionalization of different types of social work, especially in child care and probation, gave these experts the authority to define the nature and consequences of 'normal' family life. Local authorities now had

welfare discourses

responsibility for intervention; their role was explicitly preventative, with coercion held in readiness for those who would not conform to the moral standards of family life.

A change took place with the 1933 Children and Young Persons Act. It established for the first time the 'welfare principle' (i.e. that in making decisions, courts must have regard for the welfare of the child), and made it a criminal offence wilfully to assault a child. However, crucially, it retained the rights of parents, teachers and other adults in charge of children to administer punishments. It also gave statutory recognition to the common law defence, established in 1860, of 'reasonable chastisement', but there was no guidance on what constituted 'moderate' or 'reasonable' punishment.

reasonable chastisement

Parton (1985) suggests that two central themes from the nineteenth century continued up until the Second World War: the goal of intervention was as much to prevent delinquency as to protect children, and the primary way of acting in the interests of the child's welfare was to remove the child from his or her home. Cruelty and neglect were subsumed into more general concerns about delinquency, which was thought to arise from abuse or other family or environmental circumstances. Children, as victims or offenders, 'deprived' or 'depraved', were to be treated the same. It was often difficult to distinguish between these two categories. The emphasis on removing children, though a welfare strategy, can be seen as a legal version of the nineteenth-century strategy of 'rescue'.

Concern about incest also declined from the 1920s in the context of two shifts of emphasis: sexual assaults were associated with 'perverted strangers', rather than family members, and female victims were frequently constructed as both sexually delinquent and criminal. Protection of children by care orders was clearly gendered; girls were likely to be seen as in moral danger, whereas boys were more likely to be seen as criminal or potentially criminal.

Experiences during the Second World War had a significant impact on views of the family. The major concern shifted to children in public care, leading eventually to the 1948 Children Act, described as the last in a series of post-war statutes that together 'represented a "family charter", which strengthened and supported the family as never before' (Pinchbeck and Hewitt, 1973, p.651). Evacuations had produced evidence of wide scale neglect and deprivation of children, and the emphasis in post-war policies was to maintain the stability of the family. Motherhood was idealized, and young children were seen to need full-time mothering; mothers who went out to work (predominantly working-class and black mothers) were 'bad mothers' whose children were said to suffer from 'maternal deprivation'. The aim of welfare policy was not to punish parents but to maintain children whenever possible within their own family. The primary concern continued to be with delinquency, resulting in the Children and Young Person's Act 1969: '[I]ts philosophy assumed that delinquent children and abused children needed the same kind of protection and treatment. This had the effect of confusing the police function. Was it detecting crime or protecting children?' (Hall and Martin, 1992, p.3). Parton argues that: 'any reference to children as victims was lost. It is almost as if it was assumed that a conflict of interests between child, parents and the state had disappeared and the nineteenth-century problems of cruelty and neglect had been virtually abolished' (Parton, 1985, p.45). Sexual abuse within the family was almost entirely invisible.

3.3   The 'rediscovery' of child abuse

The public invisibility of child abuse does not mean that it does not occur. From time to time in the mid-twentieth century, publicity was given to particular cases, especially when children were killed by parents or step-parents. But these were seen as one-off events, not as part of a significant social problem. Both the general public and doctors had difficulty in accepting the possibility that adults maltreated or sexually abused children. When presented with physical injuries in children, doctors rarely connected them to child abuse; either it did not occur to them or they were not prepared to believe that adults, particularly parents, could do this. However, in the 1960s abuse of children was 'discovered' by the medical profession, specifically by paediatricians, initially in the USA, who described a pattern of injuries they had observed as the phenomenon of 'battered babies'. This discovery and naming also gave doctors the power to define it within medical discourses as a disease arising from family breakdown. The initial discovery was followed, over the next three decades, by a series of scandals concerning children who died at the hands of a parent or step-parent or while in the care of the local authority. Attention was also drawn to 'less dramatic' forms of abuse, described as 'failure to thrive' due to maternal emotional deprivation, and chronic neglect (Kempe and Kempe, 1984).

There were two important contexts within which sexual abuse was 'rediscovered' as an issue of social concern. Firstly, professionals were much slower to identify sexual abuse. They have suggested that the 'life-and-death decisions involved in serious physical abuse' (Kempe and Kempe, 1984, p.3) explain why this form of abuse had taken priority. However, they also acknowledged that the legacy of Freudian ideas that women's reports of incest were fantasies meant that sexual abuse was perhaps even harder to acknowledge than physical abuse; it was described as the 'last taboo'. So it was not until the 1980s that professionals regularly identified the occurrence of sexual abuse. In line with the medical discourses of 'battered babies', professional discourses on child sexual abuse spoke of the 'diagnosis' of a disorder from symptoms (MacLeod and Saraga, 1991). For all kinds of abuse, parental abusers were constructed in terms of individual psychopathology: as 'immature', or having poorly controlled aggression, resulting from emotionally deprived or abusive childhoods. This idea of the 'cycle of violence' was widely accepted as a 'truth'. 'Lack of control' was particularly cited in relation to sexual violence by men; perpetrators of child sexual abuse having been described as having an 'addiction', comparable to being an alcoholic (Fawcett, 1989).

The failure of such models to distinguish abusers from non-abusers led many professionals to turn instead to the growing field of family systems theory for explanations of violence, and to family therapy for forms of intervention. In one of the most influential forms of this approach, violence is seen as a 'symptom' of something wrong in the family as a whole. According to this approach, there are no victims or abusers. Moreover, even when the violence was perpetrated by the child's father, the mother was seen as at least sharing the responsibility. Professionals adopting a family systems approach used terms like 'the battering couple', 'violent families' and 'sexually abusing families', which construct the couple or family, rather then the abuser, as abusive (e.g. see Bentovim *et al.*, 1988).

The second important context for the 'rediscovery' of sexual abuse was second-wave feminism. As we shall see in the next section, the women's movement of the 1970s was particularly influential in bringing to public attention violence and abuse perpetrated by men, in particular rape and domestic violence. A key feature of feminist interventions was to allow women to tell their own story. Many spoke not only of abuse experienced as an adult, but also of sexual abuse as a child by their father, or other close adult male. Not suprisingly, throughout the 1980s there was contestation between dominant professional discourses, that constructed sexual abuse (like physical abuse) as a product of dysfunctional families, and feminist discourses that emphasized gender, seeing sexual abuse as an abuse of male power and a crime of violence.

Prior to 1988 the only data available on the incidence of child abuse came from the child protection registers administered by the NSPCC in some parts of the country. The growing awareness among professionals of sexual abuse led to a dramatic increase in such cases. Over the five years 1983–1987, 'the physical injury rate increased from 0.63 per thousand children under 17 in 1983 to 0.82 per thousand in 1987, whilst *the sexual abuse rate increased from 0.08 to 0.65 per thousand children over the same period*' (Creighton and Noyes, 1989, p.5).

The importance of adult testimony for making sexual abuse visible also influenced the development of new ways of obtaining evidence – that is, the use of retrospective surveys in which adults reported on childhood experiences (this approach was not adopted for physical abuse). Such studies produced higher estimates of the prevalence of sexual abuse, though no agreement on actual figures which ranged from 12 per cent to 62 per cent for women, and from 4 per cent to 31 per cent for men (Kelly *et al.*, 1991).

The 'rediscovery' of child abuse was accompanied by the development of child-abuse specialists amongst welfare and criminal justice professionals. Although the adult perpetrators were sometimes prosecuted within the criminal justice system, the main responsibility for intervening remained with social workers, and all forms of child abuse continued to be seen as primarily welfare and civil law issues. The dominant view was that the criminal law was not appropriate for dealing with 'family matters', and particularly not with parent-child relationships. Similarly, increased public awareness of child abuse did not raise questions about 'family life'. Rather, the prime focus of concern was on what were seen as 'failures of intervention'. The 1980s were characterized by a series of scandals in which social workers in particular were blamed either for failing to prevent children's deaths, or for removing children unnecessarily from their families following sexual abuse allegations. Each scandal resulted in a public inquiry leading to a tightening up of welfare policies and practices (Parton, 1985, 1991; Frost and Stein, 1989).

These scandals led to greater police involvement, as part of multi-agency teams, in child abuse cases, now described as 'child protection investigations'. This change in terminology within official discourse from 'child abuse' to 'child **child** protection' has been described as a shift from a medico-social to a socio-legal **protection** construction (Parton, 1991). The goal of welfare intervention had been to 'diagnose the disease' and to offer therapeutic help to the child and family. By contrast, the primary concern of child protection investigations was to obtain 'evidence' in a way that would determine whether or not a crime had been committed, and to secure a conviction in court (Parton *et al.*, 1997).

Of particular significance in these developments were the events in Cleveland in 1987 where a large number of children were removed from their homes on suspicion of having been sexually abused. The subsequent Inquiry Report (HMSO, 1988) was not concerned with whether or not the children had been abused, but great criticism was levelled at (predominantly female) doctors who had 'diagnosed' the abuse, and at the social workers who had removed the children. Although, as stated in the Report, only one of the 121 allegations of abuse was against a woman, this was not part of the public discussion of Cleveland. On the contrary, increasingly a discourse of 'parents' rather than mothers and fathers was adopted. Cleveland also made it harder to locate abuse within 'dysfunctional' families as many of the families involved were normatively middle class (see MacLeod and Saraga, 1991).

The scandals of the 1980s and the subsequent inquiry reports had a major influence on the 1989 Children Act for England and Wales (followed in 1995 by The Children (Scotland) Act and The Children (Northern Ireland) Order). These Acts have been described as attempting to strike a new balance between the contradictory needs, on the one hand to protect children from danger, even from their own parents, and on the other hand to protect the family from unwarrantable intrusion into its privacy. Subsequent research in the 1990s (DOH, 1995) reinforced the idea that professionals were acting too coercively in relation to families, arguing for a shift in the balance back to 'family support' (Pinkney, 1998).

Since the 1990s, child protection has remained an important part of the work of health and social services professionals and of the police. We shall consider in Section 6.1 whether, in the context of this move towards supporting families, there was once again a shift away from the public and political recognition of the family as a major site of child abuse.

4   Changing definitions and conceptions of domestic violence

domestic violence

Domestic violence has been an issue of public concern since the 1970s. However, as with child abuse, it is argued that it has always occurred: 'From earliest record, many, if not most, societies gave the patriarch of a family the right to use force against women and children under his control ... The basis for such power often was a deeply held religious belief and concerns over societal maintenance of order' (Buzawa and Buzawa, 1996, p.26). A husband's right to control his wife was reinforced by many religions; for example, passages in the Bible have been interpreted to justify man's primacy over women and right to exercise authority. Crucially, marriage has been seen as a sacred institution. Buzawa and Buzawa argue that as a result, even if violence occurs, the attacker and victim are on the same moral plane. Abuse, if visible at all as violence, did not justify leaving a marriage. They suggest that although there have been attempts by many denominations to change, their influence remains in deeply held attitudes.

ACTIVITY 5.3

Before reading this section, on the history of visibility and invisibility of domestic violence, look back at Activity 5.2. Make notes for yourself on:

■ the equivalent key themes in relation to domestic violence; and

■ any similarities and differences you can see between domestic violence and child abuse, in relation to these themes.

4.1   The emergence of 'conjugal violence' as a social problem

As we saw in Chapter 3, by the middle of the nineteenth century in Britain there was considerable public concern about violence against wives in the context primarily of concerns about social order. What was described as conjugal **conjugal** violence 'was depicted as one facet of the general "savagery" of the uncivilized **violence** masses, reflected in their brutal sports and pastimes, and the frequency of street brawls in which women often participated' (May, 1978, p.142). Two groups campaigned around this issue: law enforcement agencies concerned about the general level of violent crime, since 'a man who assaulted his wife might easily attack others or transfer his aggression to the streets' (*ibid.*, p.143); and feminists agitating for the emancipation of women. No specific laws were enacted to criminalize violence against wives, though such assaults could be included in the 1861 Offences Against the Person Act. Under English common law, married women had a different status from single women. Through marriage a woman came under the control of her husband who had the right to chastise her if she failed to fulfil her obligations as a wife:

> The husband also, by the old law, might give his wife moderate correction. For, as he is to answer for her misbehaviour, the law thought it reasonable to intrust him with this power of restraining her, by domestic chastisement, in the same moderation that a man is allowed to correct his apprentices or children, for whom the master or parent is also liable in some cases to answer. But this power of correction was confined within reasonable bounds, and the husband was prohibited from using any violence to his wife [except in so far as he may lawfully and reasonably do so in order to correct and chastise his wife – *translation from Latin*].
>
> (Sir William Blackstone, 1763; quoted in Hecker, 1911, p.125)

'In practice, however, few, if any, restraints were imposed on the husband's ability to chastise his wife' (Buzawa and Buzawa, 1996, p.28). This reluctance of judges reflected the belief that men had usually been provoked, as well as concerns about disruption to the marriage bond. These views were challenged by women's groups, resulting in the first changes in the law. In 1878 the first of the Matrimonial Causes Acts offered a civil remedy to women. They could obtain a separation order if their husband was convicted of *aggravated* assault and if they were considered in *grave* danger. Witnesses to a parliamentary committee in 1874, hearing evidence on violence against children and wives, 'expressed some concern for brutally assaulted wives but voiced little concern for women experiencing "ordinary assaults"' (Dobash and Dobash, 1992, p.157).

IN 1877, A MAN COULD BEAT HIS WIFE WITH A STICK - IF IT WAS NO THICKER THAN HIS THUMB

SO WHAT'S CHANGED?

WOMEN'S AID FEDERATION (ENGLAND) LTD
PO BOX 391, BRISTOL, BS99 7WS
TEL: 0272 428368 (helpline) 0272 420611 (admin)

Thus, whilst domestic violence was to some extent recognized, it was also treated with ambivalence. Women were frequently seen as provoking the attack, or as taking advantage of the new laws to bring malicious complaints or disgrace to their husbands, since the disgrace seemed to stem from public knowledge of the event rather than from the violence itself. The abuse continued to be seen as 'legitimate chastisement' by the husband, perhaps most strikingly illustrated by the 'rule of thumb', which is supposed to have derived from the ancient right of a husband to beat his wife with a stick no thicker than his thumb. It seems that maintenance of family order was more important than ending violence.

Most judges believed that 'a good man had the right to beat a bad woman' (Conley, 1991, p.80). 'Bad' women included those who were 'immoral' or 'irritating', and a woman who did not fulfil her expected role might expect to be chastised. Thus, adultery, failure to do the cooking and cleaning, working outside the home, being verbally abusive or drunk were all seen as an extenuation for the violence.

The right to protection was based on the assumption that women were weaker, softer and generally very different from the strong men who protected them. Therefore, protection was often reserved for middle-class women. While it was possible for a working-class woman to be respectable, some of the more delicate aspects of the feminine ideal were clearly beyond her (Conley, 1991, p.71). The men who were not of good character were those from the 'dangerous classes' or immigrants. Even feminist social reformers such as Frances Power Cobbe, who campaigned vigorously on this issue, saw men who assaulted their wives as 'predominantly Irish immigrants who were distinct from the civilized English males who were the "natural" inhabitants of Britain' (Dobash and Dobash, 1992, p.235).

We can see that, as with the nineteenth-century concerns about cruelty to children, discussion of violence against wives occurred within moral discourses of the social movements that drew attention to the problem. They 'shared the feminist emphasis on illegitimate male power, the moralism characteristic of the social purity (anti-drinking, anti-prostitution) campaigns, and the socially elite assumptions of both' (Gordon, 1989, p.20). Culprits were constructed in terms not only of gender, but also class and 'race', as primarily the 'disorderly working class' and the 'immigrant poor'. To a large extent, and within limits, men were seen as having the right to chastise their wives as well as their children, so that domestic violence and child abuse were seen as normal parts of family life.

4.2 Domestic violence marginalized

At the beginning of the twentieth century, as we saw in Section 3, the primary focus of concern was with the standards of family life. Little or no attention was paid to wife beating as a legally sanctioned crime. Although the suffragette movement did address domestic violence, it was seen as marginal in relation to the central issue of securing the vote for women. The dominant public view was that the problem of violence against wives no longer existed. Previous feminist concerns were rejected in favour of the scientific judgements of the new experts, particularly psychologists and social workers. The idea of a male crime of wife beating was replaced by the idea of mutual violence between husband and wife induced by stressful conditions.

In the context of post-Second World War policies and the idealization of motherhood and marriage, 'wife beating', where visible, was seen as part of a general picture of problem families. The solution was not prosecution but rehabilitation, in particular of the women who were portrayed as 'bad mothers, bad managers, slatternly and probably nagging or vituperative wives' (Wilson, 1983, p.87). Professional discourses constructed their behaviour as pathological: they were seen as either responsible for provoking the violence or even for seeking it out, and frequently as being in need of treatment themselves. Within this context there are different ideas about why domestic violence was rendered invisible. Wilson suggests that 'wife beating was easily seen as merely an extreme form, though rather an unfortunate one, of *appropriate masculine* behaviour' (Wilson, 1983, p.87). Alternatively, Hague and Wilson (1996) argue that the social climate in Britain had made wife beating less acceptable than in previous historical eras, but this may have made it become more hidden, because it violated the idea of the ideal marriage: 'People did not talk openly about it. Those who can remember the 1940s and 1950s will probably recall the moral censure, the embarrassment, the shame and the cultural "disguising" which often accompanied the issue' (Hague and Wilson, 1996, p.7).

4.3 The 'rediscovery' of domestic violence

Domestic violence re-emerged as an issue of social concern in the 1970s, primarily in the context of second-wave feminism. The women's movement focused on violence and abuse associated with men, so they campaigned equally around rape and domestic violence. This new visibility has been associated more widely with the development of various radical social movements (civil rights, student and women's movements), all of which, in different ways, challenged the sanctity of family privacy (e.g. see Gordon, 1989). Feminists campaigned simultaneously on four fronts:

■ demanding that the state take domestic violence seriously as a crime;

- establishing a network of self-help support for women including women's refuges through Women's Aid (a voluntary, feminist organization);
- challenging the expertise of professionals, and demanding that women be allowed to define their own experiences;
- researching into the prevalence of domestic violence.

In 1975 a report by a House of Commons Select Committee on Violence in Marriage established the abuse of women within their homes as a social problem, but recommended that it was not to be treated as a crime. This was based on the idea that the causes of domestic violence were psychological. The major form of intervention advocated was that offered by Women's Aid backed up by welfare services. The only legal remedies proposed were, within the civil law, injunctions to keep the man away from the woman. The criminal justice system was not seen to be relevant. Hamner (1989) argues that the attitudes of the police and their evidence to the Select Committee were important influences on this approach. She quotes the Association of Chief Police Officers of England, Wales and Northern Ireland:

> Whilst such problems take up considerable police time during say, 12 months, in the majority of cases the role of the police is a negative one. We are, after all, dealing with persons 'bound in marriage', and it is important for a host of reasons, to maintain the unity of the spouses. Precipitate action by the police could aggravate the position to such an extent as to create a worse situation than the one they were summoned to deal with. The lesser of two evils principle is often a good guideline in these situations.
>
> (Select Committee, 1975, p.366; quoted in Hamner, 1989, p.91)

Generally, domestic violence was seen as trivial compared to 'more serious matters such as traffic offences and theft'. The police believed that in most cases the prime responsibility for dealing with this problem should lie with social services and counselling agencies, with their own role being to take 'positive action at the time, to give advice, to keep the peace, and most of all to prevent injury' (Select Committee, 1975; quoted in Dobash and Dobash, 1992, p.150). The Lord Advocate of Scotland argued: 'Sentences of imprisonment could well have an adverse effect upon a family by removing of the "breadwinner", and imposing heavy fines will likewise reduce the "purchasing power" of the family and place the burden of subsidizing such families on the taxpayer' (*ibid.*, p.151). The police seemed to maintain the nineteenth-century distinction between 'normal' and 'exceptional' violence, arguing that in cases of extreme violence they did intervene, and that existing legislation was adequate for these purposes. They were reluctant to attach powers of arrest to injunctions, arguing that that this could be seen as offering women preferential treatment. Others too said that the criminal justice system must also offer men protection from false accusations from women.

In the 1970s, the Women's Aid movement used the term 'battered woman' deliberately as a powerful emotive phrase that emphasized women's experiences of severe and persistent violence. It was seen as preferable to gender-neutral terms such as 'domestic violence'. However, in the context of the dominant welfare approach, medical discourses constructed domestic violence as a disease. In 1979 two new categories, 'battered spouse' and 'battered woman', were added to the International Classification of Diseases: Clinical Modification Scheme, compiled in the USA (Dobash and Dobash, 1992). The associated term 'battered woman syndrome' was coined to describe the long-term psychological effects of battering on the woman. Therapeutic discourses were particularly dominant in the USA, but they have also been quite powerful in the UK, and this official recognition was the starting point for the development of appropriate therapeutic responses.

The consequences of such discourses are, firstly, to construct the abuse or violence as an individual problem to be 'treated' therapeutically by the medical or psychiatric professions. They also transform 'complex social, cultural and political issues' into 'psychological syndromes' (Dobash and Dobash, 1992, p.215). Secondly, such discourses shift attention away from the male perpetrator of the violence on to the female victim. Despite the fact that no research was able to find psychological characteristics associated with women on the receiving end of violence, battered women continued to be constructed as victims in terms of their own psychopathology. They were variously described as 'violence-prone', 'addicted to violence' (through experiences in childhood, or even in the womb), 'masochistic', or suffering from 'learned helplessness'. In the nineteenth century, women were seen as provoking or deserving the violence if they were 'bad wives'; in the twentieth century, provocation was more commonly described in terms of 'nagging'.

These victim-blaming discourses were challenged by feminists, and this helped to shift the focus on to the violent men. However, within professional welfare discourses violent men too were largely constructed as suffering from individual psychopathology, with alcohol as a prime cause. Violence has been seen variously as a clinical condition (resulting, for example, from an abnormal blood glucose level), as a psychological disorder, or as arising from bad childhood experiences – the 'cycle of violence'. In all cases men were seen as not being in control of their actions.

4.4 A 'knowledge explosion' on domestic violence

Kelly (1988) has used the term 'knowledge explosion' to describe the outpouring of research activity on domestic violence in the 1970s and 1980s in both the UK and the USA. Feminist research and campaigning were concerned with making domestic violence visible and taken seriously as a crime; with providing resources for women; with obtaining information about the extent and nature of domestic violence; with changing public attitudes; with an analysis of the failure of statutory services, particularly the police, to act to protect women; and with attempts to educate the policy makers. They described the many different forms that domestic violence can take, including physical and sexual assaults, emotional abuse and threats of violence. They also emphasized the ways in which women were controlled by fear of violence as well as by actual assaults.

Feminist researchers criticized much of the existing research on domestic violence. In particular, they argued that criminal statistics were likely to represent a very small proportion of violent events as very few were ever reported to the police, and even when they were, this resulted in few prosecutions and even fewer convictions. Although the British Crime Survey did include crimes against adults living in private households, this was only for physical assaults. Other forms of abuse or violence were seen as too difficult to measure, and/or they did not conform to the legal criteria of crime: 'The main crime counting component ... has tended to define domestic violence as woundings and common assaults committed by any household member or relative' (Mirrlees-Black, 1999, p.3).

Feminists argued that these surveys would still be likely to give low estimates of domestic violence, not only because of the restricted definitions, but also because of the reluctance of many women to answer questions about such incidents. Moreover, the surveys could not provide any qualitative information about the nature of domestic violence, nor about the context in which it occurred. The highest estimates of domestic violence came from (usually small-scale) surveys carried out by feminist researchers who designed their studies in a way that facilitated women talking about personal painful information of this kind. For example, Hamner and Saunders (1984) interviewed 129 women in a small community in Yorkshire. 59 of them had experienced incidents of 'threats, violence or sexual harassment' during the past year, and 21 per cent of these incidents had occurred in their own homes. The disadvantage of such studies was they did not provide estimates of the prevalence of domestic violence at a national level, nor could they give information about trends over time.

Feminists also campaigned around rape, and demanded that rape within marriage be criminalized. In a survey of 1,007 women, Painter (1991) found that, contrary to dominant constructions of rape as an assault by a stranger, marital rape was the commonest form of rape. 14 per cent of the women had been raped by their husbands, and in most of these cases violence had been used or threatened. 80 per cent of these women said the rape occurred frequently; 84 per cent were living with their husbands when the rape took place. At that time in England and Wales such acts were not legally defined as crimes. (The crime of rape has been applied to cases involving cohabiting men and women since 1989 in Scotland, and since 1991 in England and Wales.) Perhaps not surprisingly, therefore, only three out of 140 victims had reported the rape to the police. The much higher reported incidence in Scotland may well have been because rape within marriage was by then legally recognized.

The failure of the criminal justice system, especially the reluctance of the police to take action in what they called 'domestics', was one of the main targets of feminist campaigns of the 1970s: 'Police did not usually arrest men for assaulting their wives or cohabitees, rarely offered assistance to women and sometimes denigrated them for seeking protection within the law. Judges, prosecutors and other criminal justice personnel also failed to deal with the violence in a meaningful manner' (Dobash and Dobash, 1992, p.146). A decision on whether to act, or how to act, depended upon the discretion of the individual police officer or officers present at the time. Factors found to increase the likelihood of an arrest by the police included the presence of children or older people, visible signs of injury, threats or violence against the police, court injunctions with powers of arrest, a woman not seen to 'deserve' violence, the legal status of the partnership, and the man already being known to the police or wanted for another crime (Hamner, 1989).

More generally, as in the nineteenth century, powerful discourses of 'real and legitimate or false and illegitimate victims' (Edwards, 1989, p.92) operated:

Police may be less willing to protect poorer women and black women, whom they may perceive as less deserving … Police officers generally come to regard domestic assault as a 'normal' occurrence in run-down inner-city neighbourhoods, where victims because of their powerlessness may be seen to forfeit their right to protection. For example, domestic violence assault committed against Asian women by Asian men is often seen as a 'family matter'.

(Edwards, 1989, p.92)

These police responses were further reinforced by the responses of the Crown Prosecution Service, magistrates and judges (Smith, 1989). The effect of these class and 'race' stereotypes was to locate domestic violence in disorderly working-class and/or black families, thus simultaneously ignoring violence by middle-class men, and justifying non-intervention for black and working-class women.

Women's expectations of the likely response they would get almost certainly discouraged them from reporting violent incidents. In research carried out during the 1970s and 1980s, estimates of the proportion of domestic violence reported to the police varied from 2 per cent in the research by Dobash and Dobash (1980) to 71 per cent in research by Pahl (1985). But women in the latter study were already living in refuges, so the police may have been their last resort.

A study of domestic violence in London's black communities found that 'police may be particularly insensitive, and on occasion brutal, towards black women' (Mama, 1989, p.182). Reluctance by these women to call the police, even when they had been badly beaten and had no-one else to turn to, was influenced by: (a) the men concerned having been harassed or brutalized previously by the police; (b) the women's own experiences of racist attitudes and treatment from the police; and (c) experience of the police carrying out other agendas such as surveillance of a particular household. In some cases domestic violence incidents were turned into immigration matters, resulting in the victim being deported.

ACTIVITY 5.4

Look back over Sections 3 and 4 and your notes on the previous activities. What similarities and differences are there between child abuse and domestic violence in relation to the key themes indicated in Activity 5.2? What can we learn from this examination of historical developments about contemporary debates on child abuse and domestic violence?

■ Since the late nineteenth century there have been competing discourses of both child abuse and domestic violence, with different discourses being dominant at different times. We have seen, for example, that there has been a long tradition of a patriarchal family discourse that sees the male head of household as having the right to control both his wife and children, using 'moderate' or 'reasonable' chastisement, and a certain amount of physical violence has thus been seen as legitimate and part of 'normal family life'.

■ Both child abuse and domestic violence emerged as social problems in the late nineteenth century in the context of wider social concerns about the 'dangerous classes' and delinquency. Distinctions were made between 'ordinary' and 'extreme' forms of violence, and the latter were criminalized for the first time.

- By the twentieth century, a man did not often claim the right to punish a wife; more often he claimed that he had lost control, particularly through drink, or that she had provoked him. Nevertheless, research demonstrates the legacy of such discourses: 'Men who believe that wife beating is legitimate are more likely to become perpetrators' (Walby and Myhill, 2000, p.2).

- By the end of the twentieth century, ideas about the right of the male head of household to chastise his wife were no longer seen as acceptable. By contrast, parental rights to chastise children using physical punishments were still largely seen as legitimate, although this had become an issue of considerable controversy.

- The emergence of welfare discourses in the context of concerns about family life and the growth of particular kinds of professional expertise have played an important role in constructing all forms of violence within the family as 'social problems', rather than as 'crimes'. There has been an ongoing tension within welfare policies and practices between the desire to maintain and support family privacy, and the recognition that, for children, 'family' could be a dangerous place. By the end of the twentieth century, domestic violence was commonly described as a crime, but welfare discourses remained dominant in relation to child abuse.

- Feminist discourses have been very significant in challenging ideas of family privacy, in making violence in the family visible, and in establishing domestic violence as a 'crime'. The 1980s in particular saw a struggle between feminist and welfare discourses, with important consequences for definitions of abuse and violence and for policy and practice.

5   Feminist discourses on child abuse and domestic violence

feminism has been particularly significant in this area in several different ways: as a political campaigning movement; in providing services and establishing resources, particularly for adult women; as an ideology and in producing new kinds of knowledge. It is appropriate therefore to consider its contributions in detail.

Feminist discourses

Since the 1970s when feminists began campaigning, first around rape and domestic violence, and later also around child sexual abuse, they criticized welfare discourses for promoting violence and abuse as 'family problems' and hence for ignoring power relations of gender and age within families. Responsibility tended to be shifted away from the perpetrator and on to the victim. Far from being pathological, '[domestic] violence is seen as intentional behaviour chosen by men as a tactic or resource associated with attempts to control and dominate women' (Dobash and Dobash, 1992, p.248). Similarly, far from being out of control, child sexual abusers are seen as planning the abuse carefully, often 'entrapping' children over a period of time (Conte *et al.*, 1989). Crucially, feminist analyses defined domestic violence and child sexual abuse as related phenomena, as social problems and as 'crimes'. They rejected the idea that an assault taking place within the family or in the context of a current

A feminist demonstration in the 1980s against violence against women

or previous close relationship was less serious than an attack from a stranger. They argued that the voices of the women and child victims were silenced by the voices of 'experts' who spoke for them and constructed them as a homogenous group, all suffering from the same psychological disorder.

Feminist approaches to violence in the family have taken multiple directions. Typically, feminist ideas of the 1970s and 1980s were derived from the testimony of adult women survivors of rape, domestic violence and child sexual abuse. They focused in particular on violence perpetrated by men, analysing it in terms of the construction of masculinity, and of the power relations between men, women and children: 'The basis of wife beating is male dominance – not superior physical strength or violent temperament ... but social economic, political and psychological power ... ' (Gordon, 1989, p.251). Similarly, child sexual abuse was seen as 'one part of a spectrum of male violence against women and children' (MacLeod and Saraga, 1988, p.40).

masculinity

The major concerns of feminists to draw attention to the gendered nature of both domestic violence and child sexual abuse, and to challenge the gender-blind and mother-blaming discourses of the professionals, also meant that consequently feminists themselves tended to ignore abuse (mainly physical or emotional abuse of children) perpetrated by women. They were even more reluctant to acknowledge the small incidence of sexual abuse by women (e.g. see Turton, 2000). They were more successful in establishing a wide consensus on the gendered nature of domestic violence than child sexual abuse amongst police, professionals and the government. However, feminists have also differed in their views of male violence; for some it was part of a continuum of 'normal' masculine behaviour associated with all men; others believed that, on the contrary, it was vital to recognize and to examine differences *between* men, in order to understand and prevent violence.

213

Extract 5.1 by Segal summarizes these two positions. The second set of ideas has been developed in later research, by both women and men, which has attempted to theorize masculinity, posing the idea that there are multiple masculinities, though one form is dominant and taken for granted: 'The connection between hegemonic masculinity and violence is an important theme in the critical literature on masculinity' (Connell, 1995, p.255; see also Jefferson, 1997).

Extract 5.1 Segal: 'Continuities and discontinuities in men's use of sexual violence'

There is a ... development in feminist thinking on sexual assault which ... directs us towards seeing all men as perpetrators of violence, and all women as its victims. This is the feminist extension of the definition of 'male violence', whereby it is seen as not only general and pervasive, but occurring along a 'continuum of sexual violence'. The continuum ranges from the everyday abuse of women in pornographic images, sexist jokes, sexual harassment and women's engagement in compliant but unwanted marital sex, through to the 'non-routine' episodes of rape, incest, battery and sex murder. Elizabeth Stanko, for example, groups together a wide selection of such behaviour from men towards women as threatening or violent, arguing that they all serve to remind women of their vulnerability to men: 'Try as they might women are unable to predict when a threatening or intimidating form of male behaviour will escalate to violence' [Stanko, 1985, p.1]. In her recent, clear and comprehensive overview of work on male sexual violence, Liz Kelly adopts a similar position. She makes three key points which she presents as the background to her own research: most women have experienced sexual violence; the different forms of violence are connected along a continuum of abuse; sexual violence occurs in the context of men's power and women's resistance [Kelly, 1988, p.1]. This means, she argues, that rape is but one of the ways men maintain power through sexual violence. It is men's 'taken for granted' use of aggression – for example, in sexual harassment in workplaces – which enables men's gender power to override other power relations like that between teacher and pupil [Kelly, 1988, p.27]. And it is the limited definitions of sexual violence, she adds, which have enabled men individually and collectively to benefit from distinctions between a so-called 'deviant' minority of men and the 'normal' majority [Kelly, 1988].

Such feminist extensions of notions of sexual violence have real advantages. There is no doubt that men's intrusive staring, touching, sexist joking and worse is not only often extremely discomforting for women, but also consolidates sexual hierarchy, affirming in men a shared sense of themselves as the dominant, assertive, active sex. Similarly, the so-called 'harmless' acts of flashing, grabbing of breasts or obscene phone calls are not only frightening in their sudden violation of women's immediate personal space, but can induce a more chronic sense of fear in women – turning public places into hostile environments. Furthermore, there is truth in the feminist reflection that what gross and petty acts of sexual intrusion have in common is the sexist myths to which they give rise, and which seek either to render them harmless or, when regarded as more serious, to blame women for not preventing their occurrence.

Nevertheless, there are problems both with the idea that the high incidence of unreported rape suggests all men are guilty, and with the notion of a continuum of men's sexual violence, from heterosexual acts initiated by them (rather than women) through to acts of rape and sex murder. At least, there are problems if we are seeking to understand the causes, and prevent the occurrence, of men's use of violence. Although absent from most feminist writing on men's violence, there is evidence that there are significant differences not only between men who commit sexual assault on women and other men, but between different types of violent men – and between different types of violent acts – and their meanings. Rather than ignoring these differences, the endeavour to understand them seems to me crucial to tackling the problems of violence and to finding the appropriate variety of solutions to prevent men from resorting to them.

References

Kelly, E. (1988) *Surviving Sexual Violence*, Cambridge, Polity.

Stanko, E. (1985) *Intimate Intrusions: Women's Experience of Male Violence*, London, Routledge and Kegan Paul.

(Segal, 1990, pp.243–5)

Some feminists also analysed violence within the family in the context of wider challenges to the ideology of the family as a place of privacy and intimacy. Gordon (1989) challenged the idea that state intervention was always an intrusion into family privacy and a violation of civil liberties, asking 'whose privacy?' and 'whose liberties?' are being violated. Outrage over state intervention, she suggested, 'was frequently an outrage over a territorial violation, a challenge to male authority; or expressed differently, an outrage at the exposure of intra-family conflict and of the family head's lack of control' (Gordon, 1989, p.296).

The ideology of the harmonious private family made it particularly difficult for victims of violence or abuse to be able to name their experiences, let alone disclose them to anyone else.

The testimony of those on the receiving end of domestic violence and child sexual abuse offered explanations for why they frequently did not tell anyone: they did not think that they would be believed; they were frightened of retaliation from the aggressor; they felt embarrassed or ashamed and responsible themselves for provoking the violence; they often feared the consequences of telling – for themselves, for the aggressor or for their whole family or community. Accepting that it had happened, let alone telling someone else, was particularly difficult if the abuser was someone they also loved, and/or on whom they were emotionally, physically or financially dependent. There was frequently a reluctance to see what had happened to them as a crime:

> Concepts which are now commonplace simply did not exist before the present wave of feminist activism, for example, domestic violence, sexual harassment, child sexual abuse. While these behaviours undoubtedly existed – they were revealingly described by first wave feminists as 'unspeakable outrages' ... what women lacked were social definitions. Names provide social definitions, make visible what is invisible, define as unacceptable what was accepted; make sayable what was unspeakable ... .

> (Kelly and Radford, 1990, p.40)

Recognition of these issues influenced the development of feminist methodologies for research which aimed to facilitate disclosure of such personal and painful information. Examples included small-scale qualitative surveys and/or questions that avoided terms like 'abuse'. In a study of child sexual abuse, Kelly *et al.* (1991) avoided some of these difficulties by asking adults not about abuse but about 'unwanted sexual experiences' during childhood. They demonstrated clearly how the definition employed can have a dramatic effect on estimates of prevalence. Figures varied from 5 per cent to 50 per cent for women, and from 2 per cent to 27 per cent for men, depending upon which of these 'unwanted experiences' the researchers chose to define as 'sexual abuse'.

Feminist discourses also challenged the construction of those on the receiving end of violence as 'victims', describing them instead as 'survivors'. **victims/survivors** They emphasized the way that women are rarely passive, despite enormous physical and emotional suffering (Dobash and Dobash, 1992). Women on the receiving end of severe violence had frequently sought help for themselves and their children from state agencies, even if it meant risking losing their children (Gordon, 1989). This rejection of victimization was extended to a focus on listening to children, and to recognizing the ways in which they too could be seen as active agents, resisting, even in limited ways, abuse from which they were physically unable to defend themselves (Kelly, 1988).

By the late twentieth century there had been challenges from within feminism to the idea of a universal womanhood. Instead, feminist writings recognized the diverse experiences of women, and the importance of analysing the specific context in which they lived. This was demonstrated by research conducted in particular by Irish and black feminists. For example, McWilliams and McKiernan (1993) considered whether there is a specific Northern Ireland dimension to domestic violence:

> Public attention emphasizing the violence resulting from 'The Troubles' makes it more difficult to attract the necessary resources and public concern for the problems associated with other forms of violence.
>
> ...
>
> For example, when a woman is the target of a sectarian murder in Northern Ireland, invariably there is a great sense of outrage. This outrage exposes the gendered nature of public morality in its opposition to the murder of women in political conflict. However, when a woman has been murdered in a 'domestic' assault in the 'sanctuary' of her own home, there is less of a sense of violation. In Northern Ireland, as elsewhere, there is a kind of continuum that ranges from the least- to the most-acceptable type of murders, which is perhaps best symbolized in the way in which murders not related to the political situation have been euphemistically referred to by police officers as 'ordinary decent murders'.
>
> (McWilliams and McKiernan, 1993, p.130)

Between 1990 and 1994, at least 25 per cent of these 'ordinary murders' were related to domestic violence, more than half the number who had died as a result of political violence, yet they received minimal public attention. McWilliams and McKiernan also point out that this was a higher rate than in either the Republic of Ireland or in other regions of Great Britain. This was partly because of a greater use of legally held firearms. When guns were used, the majority of the victims were married to members of the security forces.

Similarly, several research studies have explored the experiences of many black women in the UK (e.g. see Mama, 1989; Choudry, 1996; Uddin in Home Office, 2000). The findings are illustrated in Extract 5.2, taken from a magazine published by the Radio 2 Social Action Team to accompany a 1994 radio broadcast, *When Home Is Where the Hurt Is*.

It seems that by the late 1990s feminist discourses had had an enormous influence on political and public concerns about domestic violence. The gendered nature of such violence was largely accepted within both popular and political discourses. It was also commonly described as a crime, though not as one of the 'ordinary' crimes that featured in the law and order debates. In relation to child abuse, feminist discourses had also had some success in challenging 'mother-blaming' and in the development of legal ways to remove abusers from the family home. However, 'family systems' approaches remained popular with medical professionals (e.g. see Jones and Ramachandani, 1999), and the shift to socio-legal discourses of 'child protection' in the context of multi-agency interventions, described in Section 3.3, rendered feminist concerns much less visible.

Extract 5.2 Byrne 'The problems facing black, Asian and ethnic minority women'

Women from Asian, Afro-Caribbean and ethnic minority communities face additional problems when it comes to violent marriages. The cultural tradition of keeping the family together at all costs may well put enormous pressure on you to stick with your husband, whatever his behaviour. In addition, society's institutions may make assumptions about women from ethnic minorities. For instance, Southall Black Sisters, who are based in an area of London with a majority Asian population, say that there is often an assumption that Asian women have 'higher tolerance levels' of domestic violence. They say that Asian women sometimes feel that the police may be unwilling to intervene in domestic disputes within ethnic minority families because they think that the community is 'self-policing'. And not all police stations, GP's surgeries, hospitals or social services have adequate interpreting facilities for women whose first language is not English. The possibility of facing questions about their immigration status, often deters women from reporting incidents of violence.

Immigration laws mean that you often have to rely on your husband if you want to stay in Britain. The main immigration dilemma for a woman born outside this country is the One Year Rule laid down by the Home Office. It requires you to stay married for at least a year before you are granted 'Given Leave to Stay Indefinitely' status. If your husband is violent, you are faced with an impossible choice. If you stay in the marriage, you might put your safety and that of your children at risk. If you leave, your husband can report you are no longer happily married and you could be deported. Back in your country of origin it is possible you will be ostracised by your family and your whole community, and may even face violence from them. This is especially so in some cultures, where the concept of family honour will have been violated by the wife leaving her husband.

Without this immigration status, you can't claim Social Security. You won't be entitled to claim Housing Benefit (which refuges rely on to keep going), although you should still be accepted into a women's refuge. Other minority communities have their own cultural expectations, for instance, women in the Jewish community face the problem of having to keep up the myth that there is never any friction in Jewish families. This has meant an enormous reluctance by women to report violence to the police. In Orthodox families, the great emphasis on having lots of children means a women is more financially dependent on her husband, and less likely to leave while her children are growing up.

(Byrne, 1994, pp.16–17)

6   Taking family violence seriously?

By the 1990s, both child abuse and domestic violence were matters of public and political/policy concern. The focus in both cases was on developing appropriate multi-agency responses. This section will explore the contradictory and contested ways in which family violence has been taken seriously, in the context of a series of other social/political and moral agendas, including:

- strengthening of family values;
- crime reduction and law and order;
- developing discourses of human rights within international and European frameworks.

6.1 Child protection and family support

We have seen in this chapter so far that child abuse has provided the focus for competing discourses about family privacy and state intervention to protect children, and this contestation has continued into the twenty-first century. By 2000, it seemed as though 'family support' was the dominant approach. Thus, there had been a blurring of distinctions between different kinds of child abuse; to a large extent, the term 'child abuse' had come to be synonymous with 'sexual abuse', so that other forms of abuse and violence against children were ignored or downplayed. Public and media concerns in the 1990s and early twenty-first century were focused more on the issue of 'sex offenders', paedophile rings and on a series of scandals about abuse in children's homes (e.g. see DOH, 1991; Waterhouse, 2000), sometimes years after the events and involving testimony from adults who had not been believed when they were children. This contributed to the development of more detailed vetting procedures for adults who work with children. This concern with the quality of public care for children and with excluding unsuitable adults from working with children helped to shift attention away from discussions of abuse within the family setting at the hands of parents and adult carers, even though many of the children in residential care had previously experienced abuse at home.

family support

Child abuse within the family, when referred to explicitly, was most likely to be seen as one of many problems that required family support. For example, in March 1999 the NSPCC launched, with strong endorsement from the Prime Minister, Tony Blair, the Full Stop Campaign to end cruelty to children within a generation. The Campaign was planned to last for a year, with its aim being to 'greatly increase public awareness of the issues surrounding child abuse' (NSPCC, 1999, p.1). In an article about the campaign, the NSPCC's Director of Public Policy described the five 'Vision Programmes' of the Campaign: Child Protection; Quality Parenting and Family Support; Education; Child Friendly Communities; and Cultural Change (Noyes, 1999, p.14). The emphasis, in line with government welfare policy, was on support for families. There were no specific references to parents as abusers, though there were mentions of 'paedophile rings' and '*organized* child abuse'. One of the stated goals was 'to provide ... [s]pecialist support services to vulnerable parents and families, especially where there are concerns around sexual abuse, domestic violence, mental health and substance abuse' (Noyes, 1999, p.15).

Similarly, the Labour government programme for 'modernizing social services' saw child abuse as a risk resulting from other 'family problems':

> Most families who become caught up in the child protection system are at high risk of social exclusion ... many have multiple problems – poverty, family breakdown, mental health problems, domestic violence, alcohol, and drug misuse – which need careful assessment and targeted intervention by local authorities to ensure that children are not put at risk.
>
> (DOH, 1998a, Chapter 3, para.3.9)

Parton *et al.* suggest that the shift of focus from 'child abuse' to 'child protection' was very significant for accounting for the dominance of family support discourses: '... the notion of protection subsumes within it not only the protection of the child but also the protection of parents and family privacy from unwarrantable state interventions' (1997, p.41). They propose that this can be understood in terms of the impact of the 'rediscovery' of sexual abuse in the 1980s:

> The issue of sexual abuse touches a range of sensitivities which were rarely evident in earlier concerns about physical abuse and neglect: it reaches into the most intimate, hidden and private elements of family life and adult–child relations; it represents a major set of debates round patriarchy and male power and thereby opens up a range of political arguments never evident previously; and for the first time the issues threatened not just men but middle class and professional households in ways which had never happened previously. No longer could child abuse be seen to be associated only with the marginalized and disreputable, it seemed to permeate 'normal' families.
>
> (Parton *et al.*, 1997, p.219)

On the other hand, the tension between this support for families and the need to protect children was still apparent. In 1998, in the context of the Human Rights Act 1998, the government set up a review of the law on sexual offences in England and Wales, the first such review since the 1956 Sexual Offences Act. The review was triggered by concerns about the effectiveness of the criminal law (both to protect victims and to punish offenders), and also by the government's desire to be seen to take child sexual abuse within the family seriously. This review discussed the idea of new offences for sexual abuse within families as part of the aims of providing 'coherent and clear sex offences which protect individuals, especially children and the more vulnerable, from abuse and exploitation; to enable abusers to be appropriately punished; and to be fair and non-discriminatory in accordance with the ECHR [European Convention of Human Rights] and Human Rights Act' (Home Office, 2000, p.12, para.85).

6.2   Children's rights discourses

The last two decades of the twentieth century can be characterized as a time of fiercely contested ideas about children, their needs and their rights. 1979 was the International Year of the Child, leading to the development of a United Nations (UN) Convention on the Rights of the Child (adopted in 1989 and ratified by the UK in 1991). In this context, as well as the concerns about child abuse that were highlighted in the 1980s, a number of Children's Rights Organizations were founded, and new kinds of services for children such as ChildLine developed. By the late 1990s the power of children's rights discourses to frame political rhetoric became apparent. (See, for example, the House of Lords Debate on the question of a Children's Rights' Commissioner: *Hansard*, 23 February 1999, col.949).

children's rights

Young people on the march against smacking

parental discipline

It was in this context of children's rights that the issue of parental discipline came to public attention again in the 1990s. In particular, smacking as a form of discipline, which is widespread in the UK (Newson and Newson, 1970, 1989), became an issue of public controversy and debate. In 1998, a young boy who had been regularly beaten by his stepfather between the ages of 5 and 8 took his case to the European Court of Human Rights. The stepfather had been acquitted of assault by the UK court on the grounds that his behaviour constituted 'reasonable chastisement', but the European Court ruled that the law in the UK breached the European Convention of Human Rights. In response, the government issued in early 2000 a consultation document for England on the physical punishment of children: *Protecting Children, Supporting Parents* (DOH, 2000). Note how even the title of this document reflects the tension between protection and support that has been discussed. Similar documents were also planned for Wales, in collaboration with the Welsh Assembly, for Northern Ireland, and by the Scottish Executive for Scotland.

Many children's organizations pressed for the defence of reasonable chastisement to be removed, placing children in roughly the same position as adults in relation to assault. They invoked the UN Convention on the Rights of a Child which was ratified by the UK in 1991, and which stressed that 'corporal punishment of children is incompatible with the Convention' (United Nations Committee on the Rights of the Child, 1994, Annex IV, 63; quoted in Freeman, 1999, p.135).

They also elicited children's own views on their treatment by parents. A study of 76 children aged between 5 and 8 found that over 90 per cent of the children thought smacking was wrong and they rejected the distinction between a gentle tap and a hard hit (Hyder and Willow, 1999).

However, the government explicitly ruled out abolishing the 'reasonable chastisement' defence, as well as the possibility of introducing a new offence outlawing all physical punishment of children. Instead, they proposed to clarify the criteria for identifying whether physical punishment constituted 'reasonable chastisement' in terms of: (a) the factors to be taken into account, such as the nature, context and duration of the punishment and its physical and mental effects; and (b) the people who are able to claim such a defence (whether just parents or also those in a parental role). Critics of the government argued that support for 'children's rights', though present in political rhetoric, is not extended to children's rights in relation to their parents.

6.3   Child abuse as 'crime'

We have seen that, historically as well as contemporaneously, child abuse has been regulated predominantly via the use of civil legal proceedings and welfare policy and practices, rather than by the use of the criminal justice system. Only in severe cases was there police and criminal justice intervention.

The use of criminal proceedings in relation to child abuse has remained controversial. It is important to recognize that there is no single criminal offence of abusing a child. Depending upon the harm that is caused, an abuser could be charged with 'assault or battery, aggravated assault or, in extreme cases, murder or manslaughter' (Cobley, 1995, p.5), but these offences apply equally to adult victims. The law distinguishes between adults and children by granting parents, and those in *loco parentis,* the right to discipline and punish children, so long as it is in a 'moderate and reasonable' manner. We saw that, in the 2000 consultation paper, the Labour government was not willing even to discuss the abolition of the defence of 'reasonable chastisement', only to restrict its use.

Criminal law has been much more specific about the behaviour that is prohibited in relation to sexual abuse. However, again there has been no single offence of sexually abusing a child, and all sexual offences have related to children in the same way in which they relate to adults: 'The criminal law of England and Wales includes several hundred different sexual offences, the majority of which date from the reign of Queen Victoria or later' (Cobley, 1995, p.6).

Specific offences in relation to children have been constructed mainly through the setting up of a statutory age of consent, below which sexual activity with a child is always a criminal offence. However, this criminalizes not only sexual activity between adults and children, but also that between, for example, two 15-year-olds, an event not commonly understood as sexual abuse. As we saw in Section 3.1, intra-familial sexual abuse has been regulated through the law of incest, though this is defined in terms of sexual intercourse. Incest is not only restricted to a limited set of blood relationships, but it also does not include sexual abuse by women. Adult women cannot commit incest against a child. If a woman commits the offence of incest, it is because she has consented to having sex with a man with whom she is in one of the prohibited relationships. Specific offences against children of taking indecent photographs were introduced during the 1980s and 1990s, but there is disagreement about whether these should be included as child abuse (Cobley, 1995). We saw earlier that, in 2000, the government was reviewing the law on sexual offences.

The separation of civil and criminal processes has several consequences: 'Firstly, on the one hand, parents must be worked with in "partnership" in accordance with the principles that they retain parental responsibility, and that children are best cared for by their parents. On the other is the prosecution and punishment of (very often) that very same person' (Wattam, 1997, p.98). Morgan and Zedner suggest that this separation 'may well obscure the fact that a criminal offence has often been committed. The tendency to marginalize children as victims of crime is reinforced by use of the term "abuse" rather than "assault"' (1992, p.20).

Secondly, in many cases of child abuse, particularly those involving sexual abuse, criminal prosecutions are hard to mount, as there is unlikely to be any visible evidence of harm. This means that prosecutions have to rely on children's evidence, which is deemed to be unreliable as children are assumed to be highly suggestible, to fantasize and exaggerate, and not to understand the duty to tell the truth. Children have been denied therapeutic help whilst waiting for the trial, in case it 'contaminates' the evidence. As a result of these concerns, attempts were made in the 1980s and 1990s to change the procedures for child witnesses in order to ease the experience of children in court. However, their introduction proved very controversial. On the one hand, the amended procedures did not appear to reduce the trauma for the children, and on the other hand they raised fears about reductions in civil liberties for the accused which could be disguised as an increase in rights for children (Woodcraft, 1988). Nevertheless, at the end of the twentieth century there were continued attempts by children's ɔ get these changes fully implemented, and in its *Response to the* *eguards Review* in 1998 the government stated that it 'attaches ᴄe' to improving the position for abused children in court (DOH,

uestions have been raised about whether the criminalization of ꜱ in children's best interests. Wattam (1997, p.98) suggests that ᴉes for children are sacrificed in the interests of these wider political claims' to punish offenders against children. Others, such as 996), have argued that preserving 'normal' family relationships, in ᴉntact with an absent father, has been seen as more important than hildren from intra-familial abuse. She points to civil child custody cases where there has been domestic violence in the adult relationꜱᴉᴘ. Despite the increasing evidence both of links between child abuse and domestic violence, and of the detrimental effects on children of witnessing domestic violence against their mothers, in most cases access to fathers is granted. It seems that the maintenance of an ongoing relationship with their father is seen as more important for the child than protection from abuse: 'So strong is the emphasis on actual physical contact with fathers that it continues under supervision even with men who have killed the children's mother, sometimes with the children watching ... , and with fathers who have abused the children' (Mullender, 1996, p.197). In many instances this also puts the woman at risk of further violence if her address is given to her former husband/partner.

Prime responsibility for child abuse has continued to rest with social services. Where children are mentioned in the context of crime prevention and crime reduction programmes, the references are not to reducing child abuse but to tackling social exclusion and anti-social behaviour among children and young people.

6.4   Domestic violence as a police priority

In contrast to child abuse, domestic violence has increasingly, since the late 1980s, been constructed as a crime, at least within political rhetoric. Partly in response to feminist campaigning, crucial changes took place in the late 1980s, in particular in police policy and practice. The Metropolitan Police introduced a 'force order' in 1987 which advised officers to make use of their powers of arrest since 'an assault which occurs within the home is as much a criminal act as one that which may occur in the street' (Home Office circular 10/1990; quoted in Mullender, 1996, p.4). This was followed by best practice guidelines in 1990, and advice by the Home Office and Scottish Office for similar improvements for the whole of Britain. Mullender suggests that most local police forces (now police services) responded to these developments, and that the numbers of women calling the police, and the numbers of assaults recorded as crimes did increase. The police also got involved in inter-agency work around domestic violence and set up specialist 'Domestic Violence Units' (DVUs) or units combining their response to domestic violence and to child sexual abuse.

Some feminist critics remained sceptical about both the political agendas being served by some of the apparently progressive developments, and about their effectiveness in protecting women. They argued, for example, that working with the police gave the latter legitimation whilst producing little change. Others recognized, as in the research of Gordon (1989), that women had always made use of state institutions to try to protect themselves against male violence, and therefore they continued to campaign for more effective policing (e.g. see Edwards, 1989).

Despite the changes in police practices, some research suggested that little had changed, particularly for specific groups of women. For example, a local community group in London, Southhall Black Sisters, found that both racial attacks and domestic violence were 'under-policed'; that is, they were downplayed or turned into 'non-crimes' (Lewis and Shah, 1993, unpublished). This was in contrast to the over-policing in the same area of black young men in relation to 'gangs' supposedly involved in drug and immigration offences. The 'under-policing' of domestic violence was combined with the kind of attitudes described earlier which claimed that police intervention in cases of domestic violence would cause conflict with community leaders because of the importance of the patriarchal structure in Asian communities.

Later action research by Kelly (1999) continued to find that the actions of police and prosecutors were often informed by assumptions about women, in particular that they would withdraw their accusations; as a result this often became a self-fulfilling prophecy. She concluded that 'factors influencing whether or not police arrest are frequently not matters of law but value judgements about "victim worthiness" and on the spot assessments about likelihood of withdrawal, that the incident is a "one off", and previous calls to the same address' (Kelly, 1999, p.ix).

However, Hoyle (1998) analysed inadequate police responses in a different way. She emphasized the importance of asking the women what they wanted, and found that 'women used the word protection more than any other word in discussing both what they wanted and what they got from the police' (Hoyle, 1998, p.194). In many cases women were reluctant to break up their relationship, they also feared retaliation if they pursued a prosecution, or felt that the likely sentence a man would receive would in any case be derisory. In some cases the women ended up paying the man's fine as well, because he was unemployed. In one-third of cases they wanted immediate protection (i.e. the man removed); in one-third they wanted him arrested; and in the final third they wanted advice and information and for the man to restore the peace.

6.5   Domestic violence established as a crime

In addition to campaigning for the criminal law to be enforced, some feminists have also campaigned around legal discourses on violence against women and children, since the law is seen to play an important symbolic role: '... a society which presses for changes without at the same time codifying these sentiments within its legislative framework cannot effect any real change' (Edwards, 1990, p.148); 'The law plays the central role in constructing "what counts" as crime, and in the case of sexual violence (unlike, for example, public order offences) it focuses almost entirely on extremes, thereby discounting many women's experiences' (Kelly and Radford, 1990, p.41). As a result, it is argued, only a proportion of women's complaints are seen as legitimate. The success of the campaigns to criminalize rape within marriage were similarly seen as important symbolically, despite the recognition that in practice it would not lead to many prosecutions.

Poster campaigns of the 1990s against child abuse and domestic violence, produced by
(a) the Edinburgh Zero Tolerance Campaign;
(b) the Association of London authorities' Zero Tolerance Campaign; and
(c) the Home Office

However, the use of the law was also recognized as problematic and limited as a mechanism for change as it 'tends to frame issues in terms of individual pathology and, consequently, to offer individual remedies', and because 'the law has traditionally encompassed *men's* accounts of events because it is men who legislate and then interpret the law' (Gelsthorpe and Morris, 1990, pp.143, 144).

Mullender (1996) suggests that 1992 was a pivotal year for the greater recognition of domestic violence as a crime. Firstly, there was a lot of media publicity given, as a result of feminist campaigning, to three particular cases of women in prison for killing violent partners, resulting in them being released by the Court of Appeal. Secondly, this year also saw the beginning of inter-ministerial cooperation administered by the Home Office, resulting in a Home Affairs Committee inquiry looking at policing and civil remedies. Despite some hesitation shown by the Home Office, '... before the end of 1992, the issue had become unstoppable' (*ibid.*, p.5). Popular and media interest were also fuelled by the soap opera *Brookside* in 1995, with its focus on a woman who received a life sentence for killing her abusive husband.

In 1995, the case of Emma Humphreys drew further attention to the way in which assumptions within the law are gendered. Emma Humphreys was released from prison when a 10-year sentence for murder was replaced by one of manslaughter. Her original defence claim of 'provocation' had been rejected because the law on provocation required the defendant to have killed as a result of 'a sudden and temporary loss of control'. It meant that for women who had experienced violence for years, the cumulative effect of the violence was irrelevant; only the 'final straw' could count. However, it was successfully argued that this represented a typical 'male' behaviour pattern, and in this case the idea of provocation was extended to anger that was not sudden, but that built up over a period of time.

Despite such successes, some feminists have argued that the law is so saturated with patriarchal beliefs and structures that it cannot embody discourses and practices which represent women's experiences of violence (Smart, 1989). Others have seen the law as a legitimate site of struggle, even though '[T]he law not only reflects but also constructs a very limited definition of sexual violence, and thereby plays a significant role in denying or trivializing women's experience of male sexual violence' (Kelly and Radford, 1990, p.39).

Similarly, feminists have argued that that the criminal justice system is based on notions of crime relevant to men, that are not helpful to dealing with male violence against women:

> Women's experiences of violence – overwhelmingly (though not exclusively) at the hands of known men – brought a muddiness to the justice fact finding process ... The criminal justice system geared its inquiry to the damage that strangers did to each other ... This was still predominantly the kind of violence men perpetrated on each other.
>
> (Stanko, in Home Office, 2000, para.13)

Reporting of domestic violence as crime had greatly increased, but many women who had been physically assaulted still did not feel that they had been victims of crime (Moxon, in Home Office, 2000, paras 59 and 61). The Home Office Minister Paul Boateng recognized the need for the criminal justice system to continue to adapt to the requirements of dealing with 'intimate offences' (see

Home Office, 2000, para.34). In addition, the contrasts between the civil and criminal justice systems, in terms of both their aims and effectiveness, became increasingly apparent:

> ... in the civil sphere the victim was an equal partner, not on the sidelines. Women felt they could participate in the civil courts, but were simply a witness in the criminal justice system. The criminal justice process dealt with incidents, not patterns of behaviour, and concentrated on convicting the offender rather than protecting the victim which was the priority of the civil courts. But civil injunctions could be weak compared to the powers available to a criminal court ....
>
> (Marriage, in Home Office, 2000, para.328)

The 1990s saw a wide range of significant developments: Home Office-sponsored research, pilot projects specific to domestic violence, and a series of government initiatives in relation to law and policy. Home Office-sponsored research included the British Crime Survey. Its measures had been criticized for counting incidents of violence, which did not reflect women's experiences of it as ongoing, often for many years. The 1992, BCS therefore attempted to measure women's 'lifetime' experiences of domestic violence in a separate set of questions: 'Women who had lived with a partner at some time were asked which of five options best applied to their relationships, ranging from "there have never been any arguments" to "treatment for physical violence from a doctor or nurse has frequently been required"' (Mirrlees-Black, 1999, p.3). However, the question explicitly excluded psychological, and implicitly also sexual, violence; it offered no definition of physical violence.

In an attempt to gain more reliable estimates in a large-scale survey, the 1996 BCS included a new computer assisted self-interviewing (CASI) questionnaire on domestic violence. This was given to both men and women aged 16–59: 'The interviewers pass the laptop computer over to the respondent who reads the questions on the screen and inputs responses directly into the computer ... CASI improves data quality (questions cannot be left unanswered) and respondents also seem to perceive a greater degree of confidentiality' (Mirrlees-Black and Byron, 1999, p.1). The assumption made by the researchers was that, because of the greater confidentiality, the results would be more accurate. However, this method also rules out any possibilities of clarifying or developing responses. The researchers acknowledge that 'because responses must be pre-coded, the detail required to classify incidents into offence categories cannot be collected' (*ibid.*).

The findings of this survey (Mirrlees-Black, 1999) were typically reported in the press in 1999 as suggesting that men and women were *equally likely* to be victims of domestic violence: 'Men are increasingly the victims of domestic violence, and are just as likely as women to be assaulted by a partner, according to Home Office research published yesterday. The men most likely to be attacked are in their early 30s and unmarried, but living with a woman' (*The Guardian*, 22 January 1999, p.12). However, by this time there was a generally accepted consensus that women were the majority of victims. An analysis of this same study in a briefing note for the Home Office by Walby and Myhill (2000) supported the gendered nature of domestic violence and reinforced the importance of collecting data that go beyond a simple counting of incidents:

- Over their lifetime, 22.7 per cent of women and 14.9 per cent of men reported being a victim of domestic assault.

■ Women were significantly more severely affected than men:

they were twice as likely to have been injured in attacks;

they were much more likely to have been subject to frightening threats;

they were more likely to have suffered multiple assaults; and

they were much more likely to have been upset and frightened at the time of the incident.

(Walby and Myhill, 2000, p.1)

A later version of the BCS, in 1998, demonstrated the importance of defining 'domestic' broadly, and in terms of an intimate relationship rather than as a description of current living circumstances, or even a physical place. The highest incidence of domestic violence was experienced by women who were 'separated', followed by those who were divorced, although it was acknowledged that these might still be underestimates as 'victims of domestic violence may not define their experiences as crimes' (Mirrlees-Black *et al.*, 1998, p.6).

Pilot projects in relation to domestic violence included the establishment, in 1999, of a special magistrates court in Leeds for dealing only with domestic violence cases.

ACTIVITY 5.5

Read the article about this new initiative reproduced from *The Guardian*, 3 June 1999. What discourses of domestic violence discussed in this chapter can you identify?

Domestic violence on trial in new court

Martin Wainwright

EIGHT alleged cases of a crime once dismissed as a waste of police time will make headlines next week with the opening of the first magistrates court dealing solely with domestic violence. The weekly sitting in Leeds, west Yorkshire, was welcomed yesterday by the home secretary, Jack Straw, as the probable forerunner of a national system, aimed at encouraging more victims to break their silence.

'Like racial harassment, domestic violence is one of those rare fields where we want to see an increase in recorded crime,' said Mr Straw, who inspected final preparations in the city with police, probation officers and family support agencies.

'We have left the dark days when people were told to stop bothering the police over "mere domestics", but it isn't acceptable that on average it takes 35 alleged assaults before a case comes to court.'

The domestic violence court, which hears the first eight cases on Monday, will use mainstream magistrates' procedures but with greatly enhanced specialist back-up.

The bench will be able to call on staff from the National Society for the Prevention of Cruelty to Children and a national lottery-funded pilot project, Stop (Stop Terrorising and Oppressing Partners), for background on both victim and perpetrator, as well as referral to support programmes for both. The move follows the launch of the first drugs court by magistrates in neighbouring Wakefield this year, but is not seen as a trend towards more specialised JPs.

Adrian Smith of the Magistrates' Clerks Society said: 'We are not looking for particular magistrates to concentrate on this work. Everyone on the bench is familiar with domestic violence cases, and the extra training will go to all JPs whose rota includes court on Monday afternoons.' The pilot scheme hopes to speed up hearings by concentrating probation and support agencies on one weekly session, but will not hold out soft option treatment to convicted offenders.

Brian Walker, leader of Leeds city council, which has helped the partnership arrangements behind the experiment, said: 'The court is designed to bring offenders to book, with extra measures going to support and protect the victims.'

Domestic issues are responsible for the overwhelming majority of violent crimes, with west Yorkshire's statistics of 80% annually – including 30 homicides – reflected in most of the rest of Britain. Chief Inspector Tim Grove said his force recognised this and considered domestic violence to be a priority, but one where working with other, specialised agencies was essential.

Ian Lankshear, assistant chief probation officer for west Yorkshire, said the issue was overwhelmingly one of women suffering violence from men. 'We are well aware that a small number of cases involve men as victims, but we refer to victims as "she" because that is almost always the case,' he said. 'We hope this court will help to make sure that they feel confident enough to report violence, which ruins lives and families, in the knowledge that they will be protected and that the perpetrator will be held to account.'

(*The Guardian*, 3 June, 1999, p.9)

In line with feminist discourses, domestic violence is recognized as a matter of social concern and a crime rather than as a private family matter. The gendered nature of such violence is also accepted. However, it would seem from this article to be viewed as a very specific kind of crime:

■ The Home Secretary's statement links domestic violence and racial harassment as rare fields in which he wishes to see an increase in recorded crime. There is no indication of any wish to understand why such crimes occur; the only solution it seems is to prosecute offenders.

■ The involvement of specialist back up services to provide background information on both victim and perpetrator reflect the continued influence of welfare discourses.

Table 5.1 outlines the most significant of the law and policy changes of the 1990s and 2000, a period during which both Conservative and Labour governments developed a multi-agency strategy for domestic violence. However, unlike child protection, where the lead was taken by Social Services within the Department of Health, strategy on domestic violence was led by the Home Office.

It is clear that, by the end of the 1990s, domestic violence was firmly on the domestic political agenda of the UK. In *Living Without Fear* (Home Office and Cabinet Office Women's Unit, 1999), the government set out their strategy framework together with examples of good practice from around the country. The foreword, written jointly by Margaret Jay, Minister for Women, and Jack Straw, Home Secretary states: 'Violence against women is a serious crime which this Government is committed to tackling with vigour' (*ibid.*, p.3).

All these developments would seem to reflect an acceptance of domestic violence as a crime. This development was welcomed by feminists. Indeed, many of those who had campaigned most actively in the 1970s and 1980s were, by the twenty-first century, engaged in projects financed by the Home Office. At the same time the government was criticized for not providing the resources of refuges, policing and other services needed to protect women. Moreover, we have seen that the recognition of domestic violence as a crime has not necessarily meant that women report such crimes, nor that the criminal law is enforced.

Perhaps most significantly, strategies to reduce domestic violence have been presented primarily as part of crime reduction and crime prevention programmes, rather than in terms of an analysis of gender relations or of the nature of families. Exceptions to this have occurred within European and international contexts, and within developing human rights discourses. Thus, in the 1990s, domestic violence also became established internationally as an issue of human rights. In 1995, The United Nations Fourth World Conference on Women held in Bejing agreed a Global Platform for Action including as one of its strategic objectives 'Integrated measures to prevent and eliminate violence against women' (Women's National Commission, 1996). This goal was incorporated into a National Agenda for Action in the UK in 1996 by the Women's National Commission and the Equal Opportunities Commissions for Great Britain and Northern Ireland. They argued that 'there is a widespread misconception of domestic violence as a personal or relationship problem rather than a social and institutional one rooted in gender equality' (*ibid.*). In 2000, the European

Table 5.1 Chronology of law and policy developments on domestic violence through the 1990s and in 2000

1990	Guidance issued to the police in England and Wales and Scotland (1991 in Northern Ireland) for dealing with incidents of domestic violence
1993	A Report on Domestic Violence by the Home Affairs Select Committee (HASC)
1994	An official Interdepartmental Working Party on Domestic Violence to promote a coordinated response at national and local level to the HASC report; Home Office awareness campaign – 'Domestic Violence is a Crime Don't Stand For It' (leaflets, posters and a cinema commercial)
1995	A strategy document 'Tackling Domestic Violence: A Policy for Northern Ireland' published jointly by the Department of Health and Social Services (Northern Ireland) and the Northern Ireland Office, accompanied by publicity campaigns, including television advertising, posters and information leaflets together with a 24-hour telephone helpline
1996	Changes to the civil law via the Family Law Act which:
	- Introduced a non-molestation injunction, and an occupation order specifying criteria for deciding who could stay and who must leave the family home
	- Recognized the impact of domestic violence on children
	- An amendment to the 1989 Children Act enabled abusers to be removed from the home
1997	The appointment of two Ministers for Women, supported by a Women's Unit
	A Department of Health circular outlining ways of supporting the NHS and Social Services to work in partnership to tackle domestic violence
	The Protection from Harassment Act
1998	A Scottish strategy for consultation and the establishment of a Scottish Partnership on Domestic Violence to bring together all the main service providers concerned with domestic violence
	In December a publicity campaign *Domestic Abuse – There's No Excuse* launched via television, radio and posters
	Provisions in the Criminal Justice Act allowing for prosecutions to proceed without witnesses having to go to court
1999	In January, *Break the Chain*, a domestic violence publicity campaign for England and Wales
	In June, a document *Living Without Fear: An Integrated Approach to Tackling Violence Against Women* –aimed at service providers in local government and the voluntary sector as well as at women themselves
	The 'Reducing Violence Against Women' initiative as part of the Government's Crime Reduction Programme
2000	In March, a 'Ten Point Plan for Tackling Domestic Violence' as part of the Home Office's new Multi-Agency Guidance

Note: The information in the above table comes from the Home Office website pages on domestic violence. These pages are regularly updated.

Commission launched a 'Campaign against Domestic Violence' to 'curb this sad phenomenon, and to coax it out of the closed family environment' (European Commission, 2000).

European Commission Campaign against Domestic Violence: campaign posters

7   Conclusion

This chapter has explored the extent to which the family can be seen as a dangerous place, in particular for women and children, by looking at changing and competing conceptions of child abuse and domestic violence. Such an analysis challenges traditional views not only of what constitutes 'crime' but also of what constitutes 'family'.

In relation to 'crime', we have seen how the public visibility of violence in the family has varied historically, and that at all times definitions have been contested. By the beginning of the twenty-first century, both child abuse and domestic violence were recognized and taken seriously, but even when constructed as 'crimes' they remained outside the mainstream law and order debate about the 'problem of crime'. This reluctance to accept them as 'ordinary crime' means that they have retained many of the qualities of 'hidden crimes'.

In relation to 'family', the chapter has demonstrated that as each form of violence was 'rediscovered' in the twentieth century, it was seen as a new problem, and described as 'the last taboo', or one of the 'last myths of family life to be exposed'. It is interesting to note that this process continued into the last decade of the twentieth century, with the emergence of new discourses around 'elder abuse'. Like other forms of violence in the family, it had been known before – the phenomenon of 'granny battering' had been described in the 1960s – but it was not recognized as a social problem until the 1990s when campaigns, helplines and official recognition of 'elder abuse' developed (e.g. see Biggs *et al.*, 1995).

Ever since the first public awareness and concern about violence in the family in the nineteenth century there has been an ongoing tension between preservation of the ideology of the 'normal family' and the recognition that violence occurs and should be taken seriously. Sometimes the dilemma has been resolved by constructing two types of family, normal harmonious families, and dysfunctional or problem families. It is only in the latter that abuse and violence are thought to occur. At other times, violence has become invisible again, been marginalized, or constructed in terms of non-family discourses. At the beginning of the twenty-first century, domestic violence has been recognized as a crime linked to gender, but the dominant discourses of domestic violence do not raise serious questions about gender relationships, nor about families.

This tension, and the constantly shifting balance between support for family privacy on the one hand, and the public recognition of abuse on the other, is particularly striking in relation to child abuse. On several occasions new legislation, such as the Children Act 1989, was described as striking a new balance. The government initiatives of the turn of the twenty-first century on domestic violence did include concern for children, and there was increasing recognition of links between domestic violence and child abuse. For example, we saw (in Section 2.2) that these concerns appeared in the policy initiative *Supporting Families* in 1998. But at the same time intra-familial child abuse was absent from that document. It was viewed primarily as a consequence of other multiple family problems, to be dealt with as far as possible through family support. On the other hand, the increasing power of human rights discourses, including those of children's rights, contributed in 2000 to ideas of changing the law in a way that would suggest taking sexual abuse within the family more seriously within the criminal justice system.

Physical abuse of children is both publicly visible, and responded to as crime in extreme cases when children die or are very badly treated. However the link between physical abuse and discipline has remained an area of great controversy and contestation. When the issue of parental discipline re-emerged on to the public agenda at the end of the twentieth century, with a defence of the parental right to 'reasonable chastisement', it demonstrated again the tension between preservation of traditional family forms, and the protection of children. In particular, fears that children's rights might undermine parental authority, which is seen as key to avoiding crime, might explain the reluctance to make links between punishments and child abuse.

Finally, in analysing the social construction of violence within families, this chapter has demonstrated the roles played by the victims themselves in putting such violence on to the public agenda, in constructing definitions and influencing forms of intervention. Recognition of this reminds us that a discussion of this kind can never be purely academic: 'to call family violence political is not to deny that each subjective experience of it is wholly personal and unique' (Gordon, 1989, p.292).

Review questions

- In what ways are domestic violence and child abuse taken seriously as 'crimes'?

- In what ways does discussion of violence in the family contribute to the discussion of crime as a contested concept?

- In what ways are child abuse and domestic violence understood differently in relation to crime? Why might this be?

- To what extent does treating violence in the family as crime challenge discourses of the normal family?

- Why is there no clear consensus on how violence in families should be understood?

Further reading

Relatively few texts discuss child abuse and domestic violence in the context of crime. It is always interesting to use the index of criminology textbooks such as Maguire *et al.* (1997) to see how and in what contexts domestic violence and child abuse are discussed (e.g. under headings such as 'victims'), and also where they are absent. Historical accounts of family violence can be found in Gordon (1989), which focuses on the USA, and in Dobash and Dobash (1980), Pinchbeck and Hewitt (1973), May (1978), and Parton (1985). The development of feminist debates can be found in a volume of *Feminist Review* (1988, no.28), Edwards (1989, 1990), Smart (1989), Gelsthorpe and Morris (1990), and Dobash and Dobash (1998). Political and policy developments in relation to children can be followed in journals such as *ChildRight* and *Children and Society*. For both child abuse and domestic violence, the best information is obtained from the websites of government departments or voluntary organizations. The most useful one for domestic violence is the Home Office website. For child abuse, look at the Department of Health website, or the websites of organizations such as Save the Children, NSPCC, ChildLine.

References

Barrett, M. and McIntosh, M. (1982) *The Anti Social Family,* London, Verso.

Bentovim, A., Elton, A., Hildebrand, J., Tranter, M. and Vizard , E. (eds) (1988) *Child Sexual Abuse Within the Family,* London, Wright.

Blagg, H. and Smith, D. (1989) *Crime, Penal Policy and Social Work,* Harlow, Longman.

Biggs, S., Phillipson, C. and Kingston, P. (1995) *Elder Abuse in Perspective,* Buckingham, Open University Press.

Buzawa, E.S. and Buzawa,C.G. (1996) *Domestic Violence: The Criminal Justice Response* (2nd edn), London, Sage.

Byrne, J. (1994) *When Home Is Where the Hurt Is: BBC Radio 2's Guide to Dealing with Domestic Violence,* London, BBC Radio Two Social Action Team and the Women's Aid Federations.

Choudry, S. (1996) *Pakistani Women's Experience of Domestic Violence in Great Britain,* London, Home Office Research Findings, no.43.

Cobley, C. (1995) *Child Abuse and the Law,* London, Cavendish Publications Ltd.

Conley, C.A. (1991) *The Unwritten Law: Criminal Justice in Victorian Kent,* Oxford, Oxford University Press.

Connell, R.W. (1995) *Masculinities,* Cambridge, Polity Press.

Conte, J.R., Wolf, S. and Smith, T. (1989) 'What sexual offenders tell us about prevention strategies', *Child Abuse and Neglect,* vol.13, pp.293–301.

Creighton, S.J. and Noyes, P. (1989) *Child Abuse Trends in England and Wales, 1983–1987,* London, National Society for the Prevention of Cruelty to Children.

Dobash, R.E. and Dobash, R.P. (1980) *Violence Against Wives: A Case Against Patriarchy,* Shepton Mallett, Open Books.

Dobash, R.E. and Dobash, R.P. (1992) *Women, Violence and Social Change,* London, Routledge.

Dobash, R.E. and Dobash, R.P. (eds) (1998) *Rethinking Violence Against Women,* London, Sage.

DOH (1991) *Children in the Public Care,* A review of residential care carried out by Sir William Utting, HMSO, London.

DOH (1995) *Child Protection: Messages From Research,* London, HMSO.

DOH (1998a) *Modernising Social Services: Promoting Independence, Improving Protection, Raising Standards,* Cm.4169, HMSO.

DOH (1998b) *The Government's Response to the Children's Safeguards Review,* Cm.4105, London, HMSO.

DOH (2000) *Protecting Children, Supporting Parents: A Consultation Document on the Physical Punishment of Children* [on line] http://www.doh.gov.uk/scg/pcspcon.htm [accessed 12 July 2000]

Edwards, S. (1989) *Policing 'Domestic Violence': Women, the Law and the State*, London, Sage.

Edwards, S. (1990) 'Violence against women'; feminism and the law' in Gelsthorpe, L. and Morris, A. (1990).

European Commission (2000) 'European Campaign against Domestic Violence: Rationale' [on line] http://www.europa.eu.int/comm/dg10/women/violence/index3_en.html [accessed 29 June 2000]

Farrington, D.P. (1997) 'Human development and criminal careers', in Maguire *et al.* (1997).

Fawcett, J. (1989) 'Breaking the habit: the need for a comprehensive long term treatment for sexually abusing families', in NSPCC *The Treatment of Child Sexual Abuse,* London, National Society for the Prevention of Cruelty to Children.

Freeman, M. (1999) 'Children are unbeatable', *Children and Society*, vol.13, pp.130–141.

Frost, N. and Stein, M. (1989) *The Politics of Child Welfare*, London, Harvester Wheatsheaf.

Gelsthorpe, L. and Morris, A. (eds) (1990) *Feminist Perspectives in Criminology,* Buckingham, Open University Press.

Gordon, L. (1989) *Heroes of Their Own Lives: The Politics and History of Family Violence 1880–1960,* London, Virago.

Hague, G. and Wilson, C. (1996) *The Silenced Pain: Domestic Violence 1945-1970,* Bristol, Press.

Hall, J.G. and Martin, D.F. (1992) *Crimes Against Children*, Chichester, Barry Rose Law Publishers Limited.

Hamner, J. (1989) 'Women and policing in Britain', in Hamner *et al.* (1989).

Hamner, J., Radford, J. and Stanko, E.A. (1989) *Women, Policing and Male Violence: International Perspectives*, London, Routledge.

Hamner, J. and Saunders, S. (1984) *Well-Founded Fear*, London, Hutchinson.

Hecker, E.A. (1911) *A Short History of Women's Rights*, New York, The Knickerbocker Press.

HMSO (1988) *Report of the Inquiry into Child Abuse in Cleveland, 1987*, Cm.412, London, HMSO.

Home Office (1997) *Criminal Statistics for England and Wales 1996*, Cm.3764, London, HMSO.

Home Office (1998) *Supporting Families: A Consultation Document*, London, HMSO.

Home Office (2000) *Criminal Justice Conference: Violence Against Women*, Conference Report, London, Home Office.

Home Office and Cabinet Office Women's Unit (1999) *Living Without Fear: An Integrated Approach to Tackling Violence Against Women* [on line] http://www.cabinet-office.gov.uk/womens-unit/1999/fear [accessed 27 June 2000]

Hoyle, C. (1998) *Police, Criminal Justice and Victims,* Oxford, Clarendon Press.

Hotaling, G.T. and Straus, M.A. (1980) 'Culture, social organization and irony in the study of family violence', in Hotaling, G.T. and Straus, M.A. (eds) *The Social Causes of Husband-Wife Violence,* Minneapolis, MN, Minnesota University Press.

Hyder, T. and Willow, C. (1999) *Children Talking About Smacking,* London, National Children's Bureau in association with Save the Children.

Jagger, G. and Wright, C. (eds) (1999) *Changing Family Values,* London, Routledge.

Jefferson, T. (1997) 'Masculinities and crimes', in Maguire *et al.* (1997).

Jones, D.P.H. and Ramachandani, P. (1999) *Child Sexual Abuse: Informing Practice from Research,* Oxford, Radcliffe Medical Press.

Kelly, L. (1988) *Surviving Sexual Violence,* Cambridge, Polity.

Kelly, L. Regan, L. and Burton, S. (1991) *An Exploratory study of the Prevalence of Sexual Abuse in a Sample of 16–21 Year Olds,* London, Child and Woman Abuse Studies Unit, University of North London.

Kelly, L. (1999) *Domestic Violence Matters: An Evaluation of a Development Project,* Home Office Research Study no.193, London, Home Office.

Kelly, L. and Radford, J. (1990) 'Nothing really happened: the invalidation of women's experience of sexual violence', *Critical Social Policy,* issue 30, vol.10, no.3, pp.39–53.

Kempe, R.S. and Kempe, C.H. (1984) *The Common Secret,* New York, W.H. Freeman and Company.

MacLeod, M. and Saraga, E. (1988) 'Challenging the orthodoxy: towards a feminist theory and practice', *Feminist Review,* no.28, pp.16–55.

MacLeod, M. and Saraga, E. (1991) 'Clearing a path through the undergrowth: a feminist reading of recent literature on child sexual abuse', in Carter, P., Jeffs, T. and Smith, M. (eds) *Social Work and Social Welfare Yearbook 3,* Buckingham, Open University Press.

Maguire, M. (1997) 'Crime statistics, patterns, and trends: changing perceptions and their implications', in Maguire *et al.* (1997).

Maguire, M., Morgan, R. and Reiner, R. (eds) (1997) *The Oxford Handbook of Criminology* (2nd edn), Oxford, Clarendon Press.

Mama, A. (1989) *The Hidden Struggle: Statutory and Voluntary Sector Responses to Violence Against Black Women in the Home,* London, Race and Housing Research Unit.

May, M. (1978) 'Violence in the family: an historical perspective', in Martin, J.P. (ed.) *Violence and the Family,* Chichester, Wiley.

McWilliams, M. and McKiernan, J. (1993) *Bringing It Out in the Open: Domestic Violence in Northern Ireland,* Belfast, HMSO.

Mirrlees-Black, C. (1999) *Domestic Violence: Findings from a New British Crime Survey Self-Completion Questionnaire,* Home Office Research Study No. 191, London, Home Office.

Mirrlees-Black, C., Budd, T. Partridge, S. and Mayhew, P. (1998) *The 1998 British Crime Survey (England and Wales),* Home Office Statistical Bulletin Issue 21/98.

Mirrlees-Black, C. and Byron, C. (1999) *Domestic Violence: Findings from the BCS Self-Completion Questionnaire*, Research Findings No.86, London, Home Office Research, Development and Statistics Directorate.

Morgan, J. and Zedner, L. (1992) *Child Victims*, Oxford, Clarendon.

Mullender, A. (1996) *Rethinking Domestic Violence: The Social Work and Probation Response,* London, Routledge.

Muncie, J. McLaughlin, E. and Langan, M. (eds) (1996) *Criminological Perspectives: A Reader*, London, Sage in association with The Open University.

Muncie, J., Wetherell, M., Dallos, R. and Cochrane, A. (eds) (1995) *Understanding the Family*, London, Sage.

Newson, J. and Newson, E. (1970) *Four Years Old in an Urban Community,* Harmondsworth, Penguin.

Newson, J., and Newson, E (1989) *The Extent of Parental Physical Punishment in the UK,* London, Association for the Protection of All Children Ltd.

Noyes, P. (1999) 'A fullstop to child abuse', *childRight,* no.155, pp.14–15.

NSPCC (1999) *The NSPCC Full Stop Campaign* [on line] http://www.nspcc.org.uk/fullstop [accessed 28 June 2000]

Pahl, J. (ed.) (1985) *Private Violence and Public Policy*, London, Routledge and Kegan Paul.

Painter, K. (1991) *Wife Rape, Marriage and the Law: Survey Report: Key Findings,* University of Manchester, Department of Social Policy and Social Work.

Parton, N. (1985) *The Politics of Child Abuse*, Basingstoke, Macmillan.

Parton, N. (1991) *Governing the Family: Child Care, Child Protection and the State*, Basingstoke, Macmillan.

Parton, N., Thorpe, D. and Wattam, C (1997) *Child Protection, Risk and the Moral Order*, London, Macmillan.

Pinchbeck, I. and Hewitt, M. (1973) *Children in English Society Volume II: From the Eighteenth Century to the Children Act 1948,* London, Routledge and Kegan Paul.

Pinkney, S. (1998) 'The reshaping of social work and social care', in Hughes, G. and Lewis, G. (eds) *Unsettling Welfare*, London, Routledge.

Segal. L. (1990) *Slow Motion: Changing Masculinities, Changing Men,* London, Virago. (Extract reprinted as 'Explaining male violence' in Muncie *et al.*, 1996.)

Silva, E.B. and Smart, C. (1999) *The New Family*, London, Sage.

Smart, C. (1989) *Feminism and the Power of Law*, London, Routledge.

Smith, L.J.F. (1989) *Domestic Violence: An Overview of the Literature*, London, HMSO.

Turton, J. (2000) 'Maternal sexual abuse and its victims', *childRight*, no.165, pp.17–18.

United Nations Committee on the Rights of the Child (1994) *Report of the Seventh Session*, UN Doc CRC/C/34, Geneva, United Nations.

Walby, S. and Myhill, A. (2000) *Reducing Domestic Violence ... What Works?*

Assessing and Managing the Risk of Domestic Violence, Crime Reduction Research series, Briefing Note, London, Home Office Policing and Reducing Crime Unit.

Waterhouse, Sir R. (2000) *Lost in Care – The Report of the Tribunal of Inquiry into the Abuse of Children in Care in the Former County Council Areas of Gwynedd and Clwyd Since 1974* [on line] http://www.doh.gov.uk/lostincare/20102.htm [accessed 28 June 2000]

Wattam, C. (1997) 'Is the criminalisation of child harm and injury in the interests of the child?', *Children and Society,* vol.11, pp.97–107.

Wilson, E. (1983) *What Is To Be Done About Violence Against Women?,* Harmondsworth, Penguin.

Williams, F. (1989) *Social Policy: A Critical Introduction,* Cambridge, Policy.

Womens National Commission (1996) *National Agenda for Action Policy Paper 6: Violence Against Women,* London Central Office of Information for the Women's National Commission.

Woodcraft, E. (1988) 'Child sexual abuse and the law', *Feminist Review,* no.28, pp.122–30.

CHAPTER 6

Good or Bad Business?: Exploring Corporate and Organized Crime

by Gordon Hughes with Mary Langan

Contents

1   Introduction

Alongside the familiar images of 'ordinary' crime presented in media representations and 'law and order' discourses, namely that of localized violence against people and street crimes against property, we are hearing increasingly vocal concerns raised about seemingly new, 'global' and 'organized' trends in crime and economic illegalities. Such trends appear to transcend national boundaries and threaten traditional forms of social control and prohibition. Witness the sensationalized tales of new Mafia-style gangs in the deregulated, post-communist countries of Eastern Europe, the international trade in drugs, and the massive frauds among transnational big business and financial corporations which have now entered into the popular imagination about the 'problem of crime'.

Of course tales of, and myths about, the organized criminality of criminal gangs and mobsters are nothing new in popular representations of crime and law and order. Such tales have been a key element in the often lurid culture of fear and fascination with 'all things criminal' throughout the twentieth century. Indeed, where would the Hollywood film industry and the book trade be without its gangsters and hoodlums often operating on the margins of the law? What is perhaps most important to note, however, at the beginning of the twenty-first century, is the connection now being drawn between the activities of organized crime across the increasingly 'globalized' world and the control of new trading flows and economies in both 'faraway' places like South-East Asia and in the heartlands of the previously 'safe' homelands of nation states like the UK. To say that organized crime is becoming increasingly globalized is not the same as saying that crime occurs throughout the world (which is certainly true). It is also to highlight ways in which crime is becoming organized *across* national and continental borders. Examples of cross-border, global organized crime flows include:

- trade in humans (e.g. illegal immigration and the supply of children for childless couples) and human parts (e.g. transplant organs);
- trade in animals;
- drug trafficking (e.g. cocaine, heroin and cannabis);
- sex trade and sex tourism (e.g. prostitution);
- cyber crime (e.g. pornography on the Internet);
- money laundering (that is, turning illegally gained profits into legitimate bank-deposited money).

Such developments also pose new threats and uncertainties for the traditional public authorities based on local and national policing strategies, and have generated increasingly sophisticated transnational policing initiatives (see **McLaughlin, 2001**).

This chapter will explore the realities of contemporary organized crime, arguing that much of the popular understanding and expert commentary on this complex phenomenon has been characterized by a shared reliance on certain myths and stereotypes of the criminal 'underworld' and its classic 'outsider' villains. The dominant imagery of at once exotic, alien and pathological organized criminal cultures fails to capture the close connections between organized crime ('crime as work': Ruggiero, 1996) and the routine business of other economic activities, not least legitimate enterprises.

If organized crime has always attracted public attention and academic concern, the crimes of legitimate business and public institutions – corporate or white-collar crime – have had a much lower public profile. When we discuss 'ordinary' crime we may feel that it is something familiar from our day-to-day experience or at least as experienced through the media's representation of the crime problem. It appears to be easily recognizable, clear-cut and straight-forward (see Chapter 1). By contrast, offences and harms committed by financiers and businessmen, by corporations or even by small firms, by employees, entrepreneurs or professionals, often appear remote, difficult to perceive, complex and obscure. There is then great ambivalence surrounding the nature of white-collar and corporate crime (Nelken, 1997). Not only does the state sometimes deal differently with white-collar offenders and 'ordinary' criminals, but there is also a marked difference in public attitudes towards them. Whereas murderers and burglars provoke hostility and condemnation, public opinion on fraudsters, embezzlers and tax evaders is more ambivalent. And as Levi (1999, p.11) notes, 'Fraud is not a coherent signifier of images of disorder, pain and bodily invasions'.

Though 'crimes of the street', and organized crime to a lesser extent, remain at the forefront of public attention, what have become known as 'crimes of the suites' have also led to official investigations and sanctions, as well as attracting wider media and academic recognition. In the UK this was largely the result of a series of major frauds and financial scandals that emerged in the City of London and increasingly global money markets from the late 1980s onwards.

Robert Maxwell: a charismatic, flamboyant and successful entrepreneur, but he defrauded thousands of their pensions

The following were some of the most notorious and exceptional cases of corporate crimes which were publicly exposed:

- the collapse of the investment company Barlow Clowes in 1988 left 17,000 small, mainly elderly, investors short of a total of £200 million, and managing director Peter Clowes was subsequently imprisoned for fraud;

241

- the Guinness-Distillers affair, which culminated in criminal convictions for three senior Guinness executives for insider dealing and other offences in September 1990;

- the closure of the Bank of Credit and Commerce International (BCCI) in July 1991 after the misappropriation of around £10 billion was exposed;

- following the mysterious death of publishing tycoon Robert Maxwell in November 1991, it was revealed that around £500 million had disappeared from his employees' pension funds;

- in May 1993, Asil Nadir jumped bail and fled to Northern Cyprus to escape criminal charges arising from the collapse of his Polly Peck International empire and the disappearance of some £450 million;

- in 1995, Nick Leeson's illegal activities in the world's commodities trading markets led to the closure of the prestigious Barings Bank.

Violations of civil and even criminal codes by apparently respectable persons are not confined to the world of business and high finance, and nor are the consequences only to be recorded in sums of money. In the UK in the 1980s and 1990s, there was a spate of disasters leading to major loss of life and serious injuries, in which criminal neglect of safety standards and regulations by public authorities and private companies was commonly alleged and occasionally proved. These included:

- the King's Cross tube station fire in 1987 (31 deaths);

- the sinking of the *Herald of Free Enterprise* passenger ferry at Zeebrugge in 1987 (192 deaths);

- the Piper Alpha North Sea oil rig fire in 1988 (168 deaths);

- the capsize of the *Marchioness* pleasure boat in the Thames in 1989 (51 deaths).

- the Hillsborough football disaster in 1990 (96 deaths);

- the Southall and Paddington railway crashes in 1997 and 1999 (7 and 30 deaths respectively).

In this chapter we move beyond the sorts of offences that commonly engage the attention of the police and the courts – not to mention journalists, politicians and the public – to consider a range of offences which have rarely been the major concern of criminologists. This exploration of crimes which infrequently enter into the official statistics on recorded crime will also necessitate us moving beyond the confines of established criminological concerns and into the realms of politics and economics.

Corporate and organized crime in most criminological studies have been analysed separately and in a compartmentalized manner. This separation of the two types of crime events has meant that the possibly close connections between the two types of organized enterprises have been obscured. According to Ruggiero, to speak of corporate crime *and* organized crime may be a tautology, since both are forms of organized criminal activities (Ruggiero, 1996). In accord with this view, our discussion of illegal enterprises – both corporate and organized crime – is structured as follows. Section 2 considers the distinctive characteristics of corporate crime as well as the diversity of offences that may be considered to fall within this category. In particular, we focus on the issues of diversity and ambiguity around this complex phenomenon. In Section 3, we examine the myths surrounding organized crime and then move on to explore this realm of criminal activity in terms of its changing institutional forms and character as illegal but rational enterprise. Section 4 examines some of the issues raised by the study of organized and corporate crime that have wider relevance to the debate about crime, social order and power. In particular, we explore how patterns of crime are related to the economic and political structures of society. Developing this theme further, Section 5 looks at the increasingly blurred boundaries and interconnections between licit and illicit enterprises in their pursuit of profit, power and control, while in Section 6 we focus on a specific case study of the rise of a criminal economy in post-communist Russia in the context of rapid social transformation, political destabilization and the forces of globalization. Finally, in Section 7, we examine the main issues raised by the foregoing discussion for both criminology and law and order debates.

2 Corporate crime: questions of ambiguity and power

2.1 Defining corporate and white-collar crime

One of the principal difficulties in conceptualizing the field of corporate crime lies in problems of basic terminology. The phenomenon has been variously referred to in academic literature as business, commercial, white-collar, occupational crime, crimes of the powerful as well as corporate crime. These conceptual problems are probably insoluble. What we need to note is that such activities all take place within an occupational or business environment. However, these crimes, whilst commonplace, are frequently complex, ambiguous and diverse. They are not 'self-evident' as in standard criminal offences. According to some commentators, this in turn means that the methods of control tend to express 'our' ambivalence and are hence themselves ambivalent and diverse (Clarke, 1990a). Throughout the discussion which follows, the question of whether corporate misdemeanours are 'real' crimes or not cannot be answered in any unequivocal manner. Our discussion will instead raise questions about the complex and contested nature of 'corporate crime' and the harms associated with it.

> corporate crime

Corporate or white-collar crime therefore remains a profoundly contested concept. In Nelken's view (1997), it is surrounded by ambiguities over how it may be defined, what causes it, how it should be responded to and whether it may be seen as 'real' crime. The variety of actors associated with the terms corporate and white-collar crime is certainly enormous. Actors involved may range from the owner of a corner shop, a small business to whole multinational corporations, as well as from individual salespersons to senior executives.

The vast scope of forms of crime associated with the term white-collar and corporate crime is captured succinctly in Extract 6.1 by the American sociologist Edwin Sutherland, written in 1949. Sutherland's work represents the earliest attempt to define what white-collar crime is.

white-collar crime

Extract 6.1 Sutherland: 'The problem of white-collar crime'

[My] thesis … , stated positively, is that persons of the upper socio-economic class engage in much criminal behaviour; that this criminal behaviour differs from the criminal behaviour of the lower socio-economic class principally in the administrative procedures which are used in dealing with the offenders; and that variations in administrative procedures are not significant from the point of view of causation of crime …

These violations of law by persons in the upper socio-economic class are, for convenience, called 'white-collar crimes'. This concept is not intended to be definitive, but merely to call attention to crimes which are not ordinarily included within the scope of criminology. White-collar crime may be defined approximately as a crime committed by a person of respectability and high social status in the course of his occupation …

The significant thing about white-collar crime is that it is not associated with poverty or with social and personal pathologies which accompany poverty. If it can be shown that white-collar crimes are frequent, a general theory that crime is due to poverty and its related pathologies is shown to be invalid. Furthermore, the study of white-collar crime may assist in locating those factors which, being common to the crimes of the rich and the poor, are most significant for a general theory of criminal behaviour …

The financial cost of white-collar crime is probably several times as great as the financial cost of all the crimes which are customarily regarded as 'the crime problem' …

This financial loss from white-collar crime, great as it is, is less important than the damage to social relations. White-collar crimes violate trust and therefore create distrust; this lowers social morale and produces social disorganization. Many of the white-collar crimes attack the fundamental principles of the American institutions. Ordinary crimes, on the other hand, produce little effect on social institutions or social organization.

(Sutherland, 1949/1967, pp.9–10, 12–13)

ACTIVITY 6.1

Having read the extract from Sutherland, now try to answer the following questions:

1   According to Sutherland, what type of person commits white-collar crime?

2   How does Sutherland's account challenge conventional aetiologies of criminality?

3   Why is white-collar crime viewed by Sutherland as a serious social problem?

Table 6.1 Forms of white collar and corporate crime

Occupational crime

- Employee theft which may include money, goods or intangibles such as 'computer time'.
- Frauds on consumers, including abstracting money from accounts, overcharging or charging for work which has not been done.
- 'Fiddling' expenses.
- Tax evasion, which includes 'moonlighting' (working outside formal employment but not declaring this to tax authorities), failing to disclose all earnings, evading VAT.
- Frauds on the NHS, including prescriptions frauds.
- Sales frauds including those perpetrated through telecommunications networks.

Computer crime

Includes many of the above activities in which computers are used and also includes crimes specific to computers such as computer hacking, stealing competitors' mailing lists and the many sales frauds now perpetrated via the Internet.

Corporate/organizational crime

Crimes against consumers include

- 'Food frauds' – adulterating or falsely describing the contents of food.
- Manufacturing or selling food 'unfit for human consumption', which includes food poisoning.
- Selling goods with short weight, which includes food, alcohol and other goods.
- Offences under the Trade Descriptions Act, which includes car 'clocking' (turning back the odometers of cars), counterfeiting and otherwise misdescribing the quality or contents of goods.
- Manufacturing or selling dangerous goods, including toys (this may also involve some counterfeit goods).

Health and safety offences include

- Failure to comply with health and safety regulations covering all industrial or commercial premises and also transport. These include considerations of:
  - passenger safety
  - the safety of workers
  - the safety of consumers
  - the safety of the general public – for example, in leisure centres, adventure centres, fairs and playgrounds, football matches and as residents.

Environmental offences include breaking regulations to prevent pollution such as those involving:

- the safety of water for consumers;
- rivers and coastal waters;
- the control of toxic emissions and toxic waste.

Financial frauds, including those involving:

- The sale of financial services such as pensions or savings plans.
- Insurance frauds, including those where companies 'torch' or set fire to premises to claim insurance where the business is failing.

Source: adapted from Croall, 1998, p.274

Sutherland's definition was important in helping criminology to reconstruct the problem of crime so as to include those high status, respectable members of society rarely portrayed in popular stereotypes of the criminal in the mid-twentieth century. It also alerts us to the rational, non-pathological character of such actors. And finally it points out that the economic and social costs of white collar or corporate crime are significant (see Chapter 1).

However, critics have noted that Sutherland's definition also suffers from a lack of clarity. Nelken questions whether it is possible to have one overarching definition for the vast range of misbehaviour covered by white-collar and corporate crime: 'What, if anything, is there in common between the marketing of unsafe pharmaceuticals, the practice of insider dealing, "long-firm" (bankruptcy) fraud, computer crime, bank embezzlement, and fiddling at work?' (1997, p.869). Furthermore, corporate misdemeanours may be both intentional and unintentional. Ambiguities surround the phenomenon – as with crime in general – and will remain the key to the exploration of the topic.

In this section we restrict ourselves to a very broad definition of corporate crime, namely *illegal or harmful activities – both acts of commission and omission – engaged in by business organizations or members of such organizations in pursuit of their goal of maximizing power and profit in relatively unpredictable social, political and economic environments.* Such activities may be in the interests of the organization or in the interests of the specific individual or group. In this section we also restrict ourselves to the most significant form of white-collar crime, namely that associated with large corporations. This covers the offences and harms committed (sometimes by omission) and violations of civil or criminal law which may affect a wide range of victims, including employees, consumers, the wider public, the environment, other firms, the state, and other states (see Table 6.1).

2.2   Diversity of corporate crime

According to such commentators as Stephen **Box (1983)**, violations of the civil or criminal law, or of other regulatory codes, are commonly committed by large and otherwise legitimate corporations in the course of their commercial activities. The crimes of large corporations may be subdivided according to their victim, though in practice there is often considerable overlap. Let's briefly outline the main forms of victimization associated with corporate crime.

2.2.1   Offences against employees

In the drive to reduce costs, meet deadlines and at times to increase profits, companies and other public bodies may breach employment contracts and health and safety regulations at the expense of the workforce. Corporate offences against employees most commonly come to public attention when they lead to death or injury at work.

In the UK since 1965, 25,000 people have been killed at work or in major commercial disasters. According to Health and Safety Executive reports, 70 per cent of these deaths resulted from a management failure (*The Guardian*, 29 November 1999). For example, the deaths of 168 workers on the Piper Alpha oil rig in the North Sea in 1988 were subsequently attributed to the weakness of both safety regulations and their enforcement in an industry characterized by hazardous conditions and intense time pressures dictated by market forces (Clarke, 1990a; Carson, 1982). Long before the Piper Alpha fire, North Sea oil had acquired a reputation as one of the most dangerous spheres of employment in UK industry. The Piper Alpha disaster followed similar earlier incidents in the North Sea, one on Sea Gem in 1965 which led to 13 deaths, and another on the Alexander Kielland rig in Norwegian waters which led to 123 deaths. Was this a natural disaster, an accident or a crime? In attempting to answer such a question, other than in a moralistic way, several key elements to the ambiguous concept of corporate crime need to be noted. In particular, the following distinctions need to be borne in mind:

- omission vs. commission;
- intent vs. effect;
- law vs. social harm;
- criminal law vs. administrative regulation.

The implications of these distinctions will be spelt out more fully in the discussion which follows.

The burnt-out shell of the Piper Alpha oil rig in which 168 people died: a natural disaster, an accident or a crime?

2.2.2   Offences against consumers

The selling of defective products is as old as the market, but modern capitalism has greatly expanded the scope for offences against the consumer. These extend from fraudulent advertising, through inferior design, manufacture and maintenance, to the defiance of regulations designed to protect the welfare of those who purchase a particular commodity or service.

Whereas in the past the sale of adulterated bread or watered-down beer and spirits probably caused minor upsets or irritation to a small number of people, the mass marketing of defective foodstuffs or of dangerous consumer goods in modern society may have catastrophic consequences. For example, in Spain in 1987 the consumption of cooking oil contaminated with toxic chemicals killed 259 people (Croall, 1992). The sale of the Ford Pinto in the USA in the 1970s, when the company was fully aware of the car's mechanical defects, may have led to between 500 and 900 deaths (Box, 1983).

The defective manufacture and negligent operation of mass transportation systems involving air, rail, sea or road have led to numerous disasters with loss of life and serious injury to passengers. The report of the Sheen inquiry into the capsize of the passenger and freight ferry the *Herald of Free Enterprise* at Zeebrugge in March 1987, which resulted in the deaths of 154 passengers and 38 crew members, blamed the ferry owners P&O Ferries International Ltd for failing to provide a safe operating system and the assistant bosun for falling asleep on the job (Wells, 1993, pp.44–8). Though the Director of Public Prosecutions was pressed to institute a 'corporate manslaughter' prosecution, this could not be sustained, not least due to the highly complex and legally ambiguous nature of the event. Similar acts of culpable negligence were exposed as the causes of the signal failure that led to the Clapham rail disaster, which killed 35 people in 1987, and the sinking of the pleasure boat *Marchioness* as a result of a collision with another vessel on the Thames in 1989. More recently, the train crashes at Southall in 1997 and Paddington in 1999 appear to have

Paddington – a case of corporate manslaughter?

been linked to the failure of the company, Railtrack, to install the technology of the Automatic Train Protection System. However, it is important to note that none of these 'disasters' has been dealt with as a crime. Perhaps this highlights the ambiguities in play in the realm of corporate crime. Think back again to the four distinctions introduced at the end of Section 2.2.1 above.

2.2.3 Offences against the public

The potential danger to the public and the environment resulting from industrial development has grown with the scale of corporate enterprise and with the toxicity of some of the products and by-products of modern production processes. The extraction and consumption of traditional sources of energy – coal, oil, gas – has always been a dirty and dangerous business, but the accelerated pace of such activities in modern times has caused levels of pollution with global consequences. The most widely exploited alternative to fossil fuels, nuclear power, has the potential to be even more dangerous, with risks of leakage as well as toxic waste. Any corporate irresponsibility in this area, which may not in formal terms be defined as 'criminal' intent, in parallel with the potential to endanger the public and the environment, could make a lethal combination in terms of 'criminal' effect.

Bhopal, 1984: thousands died, and tens of thousands were injured following the release of toxic gases at the Indian-based factory of the US chemical corporation, Union Carbide

'Accidents' resulting from similar sets of circumstances, perhaps without the same catastrophic consequences, are always possible throughout modern industry. Disasters associated with explosive and toxic chemicals have become familiar news items. An explosion at Flixborough near Scarborough in England in 1974, for example, killed 28 people and injured another 89. The release of dioxin at Seveso in Italy in 1976 caused widespread pollution and an epidemic of disfiguring chloracne among local children.

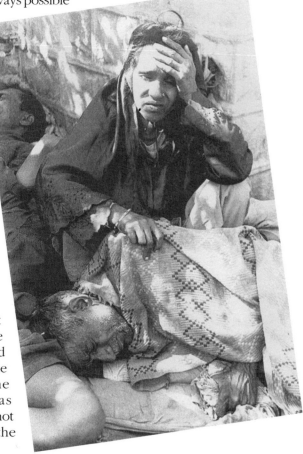

In their detailed account of the catastrophic release of toxic gases at the Union Carbide factory at Bhopal in India in 1984, Pearce and Tombs (1993, 1998) expose the poor design of the plant, its inappropriate siting near a shanty town, its inadequate safety systems, the lack of a proper emergency plan, and the generally run-down conditions that prevailed. They conclude that 'despite public commitments to health, safety and environmental protection … Union Carbide created, or allowed to develop, the conditions whereby an accident was possible'. Furthermore, the company 'had not taken the steps necessary to mitigate the effects of any accident' (1993, p.207).

2.2.4 Offences against other firms

The competitive struggle to maximize profits or to survive sometimes drives entrepreneurs to transgress various rules and regulations in order to gain advantage over their rivals. The speculative financial boom of the late 1980s provided the conditions for a wide range of sharp practices shading into overt fraud. This is the specific context in which to locate the now famous Guinness-Distillers 'affair' involving the corporate crime of insider dealing. The background to the Guinness-Distillers affair, which was exposed in 1986, was the trend for corporations in the UK to look to 'mergers and acquisitions' in the City. In takeover bids, and in the closely associated activities of 'corporate raiding' (i.e. seeking to gain control of a company by acquiring a large proportion of its stock) and 'asset stripping' (i.e. the practice of acquiring control of a company and selling off its assets for profit), all of which flourished in the 1980s, the dividing line between business and crime is one which many, not least the City's own regulatory bodies and the courts, find difficult to define. The ambiguous criminal status of such economic activities will be returned to in greater depth in Sections 4 and 5.

Guinness's takeover bid for Distillers was fiercely contested and, as Clarke observes, 'contested bids are the most prone of all to abuse, since not only is the target company resisting the bid, but there are two (rarely more) bidders chasing the shares' (1990a, p.176). To strengthen its own position in relation both to Distillers and to a rival bid from the Argyll group, Guinness spent £25 million in arranging for friends and associates to buy up its own shares and thus bolster its share price. At the same time it bought up a decisive tranche of Distillers' shares at an inflated price it could not have honoured to all the shareholders. Both these manoeuvres were considered in breach of Stock Exchange regulations and, in 1991, of the criminal law. Chief executive Ernest Saunders and two associates were convicted and received prison sentences.

2.2.5 Offences against the state

The high level of state intervention in economic life in modern society creates a range of points of contact between government officials and corporations at which corrupt practices may occur. Corporate tax evasion is probably the biggest single cause of lost revenue to the government, but it is usually dealt with by informal means and rarely comes to the courts.

Companies may also bribe government officials to secure important contracts, as the aerospace firm Lockheed did in the USA on a grand scale in the 1960s and 1970s. Firms may pay off officials in central and local government or other regulatory bodies to ignore breaches of various regulations. On the other hand, as in the scandal surrounding sales to Iraq of engineering equipment with potential military use by the British firm Matrix Churchill shortly before the Gulf War in 1990, government ministers may discreetly encourage companies to act in defiance of controls (and then try to hide behind civil servants and 'official secrecy' regulations) (Norton-Taylor, 1995; see also Chapter 7 of this volume).

Companies may cultivate close links with politicians and civil servants to secure government initiatives that are considered to be in the company's interests. The line between legitimate lobbying and corruption may be a fine one. The resignation of US vice-president Spiro Agnew in 1973, after revelations that he continued to receive the gifts from companies that he had enjoyed as governor of Maryland even after he became vice-president, indicated the extent of such practices in the USA. President Nixon granted Agnew immunity from prosecution, thus avoiding a trial in which, it was believed, similar offences by others in high places would have been exposed. Newspaper revelations in the UK in 1993 and 1994 that MPs had accepted payments for asking parliamentary questions in pursuit of various commercial interests were followed by a series of similar scandals, giving rise to widespread concern over the extent of 'sleaze' in public life and a concomitant decline in trust in political leaders.

In the UK the trend towards the privatization of formerly nationalized industries and public services in the 1980s and 1990s opened up enormous scope for bribery to secure contracts and other sorts of corruption. In January 1994 the public accounts committee of the House of Commons published 'a damning catalogue of public impropriety, fraud and mismanagement' in government departments, health authorities and newly established quangos such as the Property Services Agency, the National Rivers Authority and Civil Service Catering (*The Guardian*, 28 January 1994).

Major multinational companies have frequently combined their economic activities overseas with political interference in other countries to secure what they regard as favourable conditions for their commercial activities. This may mean acting as an agent for the foreign policy of their country of origin. Examples include the involvement of the United Fruit Company in bringing down the Arbenz government in Guatemala in the 1950s, the role played by Tiny Rowland's Lonrho company in evading sanctions against Ian Smith's white minority regime in Rhodesia in the 1960s, and the activities of the telecommunications firm ITT in undermining the Allende government in Chile in the early 1970s. However, political interference by firms is by no means confined to the Third World. There have been scandals about payments to politicians in many European countries and Japan, leading to ministerial and even prime ministerial resignations.

ACTIVITY 6.2

How would you begin to design a victim survey of corporate crime? What are the major difficulties in finding out who has been victimized?

2.3 Explaining the ambiguity of corporate crime

The above discussion has highlighted the harmful effects and consequences of activities associated with legitimate corporate bodies, whether defined in strictly legal terms as 'criminal' or not. The next key question is, given the range of victims and serious consequences of corporate crime in terms of the costs, hazards and harms outlined above, how might we explain both its relative public invisibility and the ambiguity towards it shared by many commentators and the public authorities? A number of common characteristics of corporate crime and its regulation may be identified which help to explain why such offences are regarded differently and more ambiguously by society and treated differently within the criminal justice system from more familiar forms of 'street' criminality. In particular, we may note:

- their low visibility;
- their complexity;
- the diffusion of responsibility;
- the diffusion of victimization;
- the distinctive forms of regulation surrounding these crimes.

2.3.1 Low visibility

When somebody is stabbed and deprived of their wallet while walking down the street, it will often be clear to all involved – and to a wider public notified through the media – that a crime has taken place. In the case of, for example, the Guinness bid to take over Distillers, the offences of which several Guinness executives were subsequently convicted were not at all apparent to many of those closely involved, let alone to the public at large. In the context of corporate crime and harm, the distinctions between misfortune, incompetence, malpractice and criminality may be far from obvious.

The fact that corporate crimes are carried out under the cover of normal occupational routines helps to hide them from public view. The image of respectability projected by large corporations with familiar brand name products and highly publicized commitments to charitable trusts and other good works may also disguise their transgressions of laws and regulations. As we have seen, the fine line between aggressive business tactics in a competitive market and overt criminality may in practice be a difficult one to discern, particularly by those with high personal stakes in corporate success.

low visibility

The essentially 'private nature' of corporate crime also contributes to its relative invisibility or at least its low visibility. By contrast with 'crimes of the streets', 'crimes of the suites' take place out of public view and, generally, out of the glare of publicity.

ACTIVITY 6.3

Levi (1987, p.13) has commented thus on the media's attitude to white-collar crime: 'The general relative media neglect of business crime compared with other forms of crime is explicable more by laziness, investigative cost, the invisible nature of the crime and the deviousness of its progenitors, and by the difficulty of presenting it simply in the human terms expected by mass audiences, than by any elite conspiracy to suppress it.'

Do you agree with this assessment. Try to check the empirical accuracy of Levi's thesis of media neglect of business crime by looking at which crimes are reported in your daily newspaper over the course of a week.

2.3.2 Complexity

When a house is burgled, the offence is not only transparent, it is also straightforward – one person has forcibly entered another's house and seized their property. In the case of corporate crime the offence is often more complicated, particularly in terms of the process of appropriating money or goods, which may involve numerous transactions among different agents over a considerable period of time.

Major frauds, for example, are characteristically highly complex. These cases involve large numbers of individuals (with varying degrees of awareness and culpability) and a network of companies and bank accounts engaged in interlinked deals and transfers of assets over several years. In recent decades, teams of expert investigators have spent years (and many millions) in attempting to unravel these megafrauds in the hope of pursuing prosecutions and securing the return of at least some of the misappropriated funds.

Complexity is not, however, peculiar to criminal corporations acting illicitly, but is a characteristic feature of bureaucratic organization within the modern company acting licitly. For example, the aggressively anti-state, pro-market ideology characteristic of the neo-liberalism on both sides of the Atlantic throughout the last two decades of the twentieth century, further complicated the organization of commercial activity. The withdrawal of state controls from national markets and financial systems sought to accelerate the global circulation of capital and commodities. Together with the parallel trend towards the privatization of industry and services, it also increased the scope for fraud and corruption. The deregulation of the money markets has also taken place in tandem with the development of computer and information technologies, enabling instantaneous communication and round-the-clock trading on the world's major money markets. All of these trends create greater scope for highly rewarding illicit activity of a complexity mirroring that of the system itself.

2.3.3 Diffusion of responsibility

The difficulty of pinning the blame for the crimes of the powerful on any particular individual becomes clearest when the question of culpability for a major disaster arises. For example, inquiries into responsibility for the deaths that occurred in the *Herald of Free Enterprise* and *Marchioness* disasters in the UK variously attributed blame to individual crew members on duty at the time of the incident, their commanding officers, the companies owning and operating the boats, and the regulatory authorities. Though various prosecutions were initiated against individual crew members, by the state authorities and privately by relatives of the deceased, none succeeded. It is noteworthy that, in terms of media attention and judicial procedures, the only individuals identified as potentially culpable were the crew members in charge of the boats when the incidents took place. Neither the press nor the courts identified individual company executives or members of the regulatory authorities as bearing any personal responsibility for these disasters.

diffusion of responsibility

The diffusion of responsibility for corporate crime is in part a consequence of the complex division of labour and hierarchical structure of the large firm, which makes it difficult to determine who is responsible for a particular offence. As Croall (1992, pp.12–13) argues, 'this is particularly the case with organizational offences which may involve neglect or deliberate flouting of many regulations covering health, safety, quality control, information or sales practices'. Furthermore, 'at all levels of the chain of responsibility … individual employees can deny responsibility by claiming that they were only "following orders" or that their orders were ignored'. In Ruggiero's words (1996, p.85), we have 'sins without sinners'.

The attribution of responsibility is further complicated by the fact that many corporate crimes do not result from any obvious malign intent (*mens rea* in legal terms), but rather from neglect of, and indifference to, regulations. The difficulty of proving that the corporate offenders consciously intended to inflict the harm that resulted from their actions (or failure to act) means that in law such offences can rarely be considered 'criminal'. Thus, whatever the scale of death or injury that results, the state regards such corporate wrongdoings as 'quasi' crimes committed against a vaguely defined 'public welfare', whereas 'real' crimes are directed, intentionally, against individuals (Wells, 1993, pp.5–8).

Nelken (1997, p.894) has noted that different lessons have been drawn from roughly similar materials by commentators. For example, Green (1990, p.xv) argues that white-collar crime is even more dangerous than ordinary crime, even if it is more likely to escape control. And he pays particular attention to discovering more effective ways of bringing criminal penalties to bear on this type of crime. By contrast, Clarke, whilst considering similar data, argues that there are differences between these offences and those more usually dealt with as crimes:

> Business crime, however, in the sense in which it is used here, covers a much wider range of misconduct, which may be none the less damaging and otherwise undesirable, resulting from duress, incompetence, negligence, lack of training, lack of clarity in the rules, opportunism, technical infraction, or sheer muddle-headedness, rather than calculated deceit motivated by greed.
>
> (Clarke, 1990a, p.16)

Disagreement and profoundly ambivalent messages continue to surround the nature of corporate 'crime': an ambivalence that is reflected in social science research.

2.3.4 Diffusion of victimization

diffusion of victimization

Whereas it is usually apparent when somebody has been robbed or murdered, the victims of corporate crime may not even be aware of the offence. This is most obvious in the case of company violations of anti-pollution regulations, which may affect vast numbers of people, but often (though by no means always) to a relatively small and scarcely perceptible degree. This is termed the diffusion of victimization. Thus, while the immediate local impact of the Chernobyl nuclear power station explosion in 1986 was lethally clear, its wider consequences, in terms of an increased incidence of radiation-related malignancies and other disorders over a wide area of Northern Europe, only become apparent over several decades. Periodic disasters draw public attention to the more mundane corporate neglect of environmental safeguards that is prejudicial to public health on a small scale, but is commonplace and may well result in considerable excess morbidity and mortality in the long term.

Similarly, the losses to any particular individual resulting from petty frauds perpetrated against a large number of consumers or creditors may be relatively small, even though the gain to the fraudsters may be considerable. Again, it is only the more spectacular frauds resulting in substantial losses to relatively large numbers of people that bring to public attention the fact that we all have to pay the price of more mundane white-collar crime – in higher prices, insurance premiums, taxes, etc. – as well as suffering inferior consumer goods and services.

2.3.5 Distinctive forms of regulation

The distinctive features of the regulation of corporate crime when compared with the regulation of conventional street crime are:

- greater informality and a lower risk of detection;
- a lower risk of prosecution;
- more lenient sanctions.

Let's look at each of these features more closely.

Informal regulation and the lower risk of detection

Though some of the violations we have considered above, such as major fraud, come under the jurisdiction of the criminal justice system, many corporate crimes are regulatory offences. These include violations of health and safety, environmental health, or trading standards regulations, which are monitored by a variety of statutory, non-statutory or quasi-autonomous regulatory agencies. Because of the problem of proving 'malign intent' (*mens rea*), it is difficult to pursue criminal prosecutions against individuals (and even more difficult against companies), even though their neglect or evasion of particular standards or regulations may have caused major injury or loss of life.

regulatory offences

Even in the sphere of major fraud, the 'instinct' of private enterprise for informal self-regulation – as manifested historically in the London Stock Exchange or Lloyds – remains powerful. Traditionally, companies have jealously protected their commercial independence against outside interference, even at the cost of accepting a certain level of loss through fraud or other illicit practice. Many commentators have noted the gradual and piecemeal development of legislation against fraud (Clarke, 1990a).

The problem with all informal forms of regulation is that they assume a consensus on norms and standards of business practice which, if it ever existed, no longer does. In turn, regulatory agencies are themselves highly vulnerable to strategies of collusion and subversion – just as are public police agencies.

ACTIVITY 6.4

Read the article 'Britain fails to come to grips with suspicious share deals' from *The Independent*, reproduced overleaf, which was written in the mid-1990s. Why has the Stock Exchange had such difficulty in dealing with brokers who violate its rules? How would legislation help?

Britain fails to come to grips with suspicious share deals

by Heather Connon

Any irritation on Lord Archer's part at the Department of Trade and Industry's delay in releasing its verdict on whether he insider dealt in the shares of Anglia Television would be understandable.

The transactions that aroused the Stock Exchange's suspicion occurred in January; the DTI appointed inspectors on 8 February. It took them more than five months to produce their report, which was delivered to the DTI this week. There is still no indication of when the DTI will announce the outcome.

That may seem an inordinately long time to study three transactions, establish whether Lord Archer or his associates dealt in Anglia shares, and if so whether it was because they knew something they shouldn't. Yet this inquiry was dealt with more swiftly than most such investigations – if they are started at all.

The City's attitude to insider dealing has moved on dramatically since Sir Martin Jacomb, then chairman of the stockbroker Barclays de Zoete Wedd, described it as a victimless crime in 1986. Now institutional shareholders describe it as theft – and they know that they, and the pensioners and private shareholders they represent, are the victims. Those who buy or sell ahead of price-sensitive announcements are robbing law-abiding shareholders of profits, or inflicting losses on them.

Nevertheless, many in the City believe it is still rife. There is growing frustration at the apparent inability of the Stock Exchange to track down the offenders, at the delays in the investigation process, and at the difficulty in securing convictions when cases are actually brought to court.

In the past five years, the Stock Exchange has referred 52 suspicious cases to the DTI. It is responsible for deciding whether the allegations warrant further investigation – usually done by independent inspectors. In the same period 25 of these were appointed.

These numbers are tiny compared to the number of suspicious price movements seen in the market each week.

On Wednesday, for instance, after its share price had halved to 6p in a matter of days, the property adviser de Morgan was forced to confirm bid talks had been aborted. And last week Castle Communications disclosed it was in bid talks after its shares had soared.

These cases may already be on either the Stock Exchange or the DTI's list but the City doubts it. And in any case only 52 people have been tried, and just 23 convicted, in the 34 cases brought since the legislation was introduced in 1980.

Tighter legislation, introduced by the Criminal Justice Act on 1 March, may help – or it may just lead to more confusion, since it brings far more people into the insider net.

The best place to start improving matters is probably the Stock Exchange, where a 20-strong surveillance team is responsible for monitoring suspicious trades.

'Their credibility has been destroyed', one institutional investor said, pointing to Tiphook, where Paul Myners, chairman of the fund manager Gartmore, took the rare step of publicly calling for reform of the exchange's procedures because of their lack of success. 'They have no enthusiasm for investigation – they just go through the motions'.

A growing number of people believe that responsibility for monitoring all forms of market misconduct should no longer rest with the Stock Exchange.

Indeed, the regulator, the Securities and Investments Board, in a recent paper suggested that it should take on the responsibility for market surveillance. It argues markets are becoming increasingly complex, and more international. Effective surveillance will, therefore, increasingly depend on cooperation with other market regulators, like the London International Financial Futures Exchange and the London Traded Options Market, as well as with their counterparts overseas.

The exchange insists that it has never had any problem in getting cooperation from other regulators, although some suggest surveillance staff frequently have trouble even in persuading colleagues in other departments to talk to them.

Passing the responsibility up to the SIB would put a bit more distance between practitioners and regulators, which may give it more credibility.

But it would also need the exchange's cooperation and adequate resources: the 20 surveillance staff pale into insignificance compared with the huge resources available to the Securities and Exchange Commission in the US.

That has led some to suggest that Britain should have a Government-backed SEC-style market regulator. They compare the SEC's successful $100m fine and 22-month prison sentence for Ivan Boesky with the £25,000 fine and 12 months suspended for Geoffrey Collier, the Morgan Grenfell merchant banker who is still Britain's most famous offender.

British governments, however, tend to be less than effective regulators. So others suggest that insider dealing should become only a regulatory offence, which could be dealt with by the SIB or the exchange. Punishment would be a fine and disqualification from trading.

That would speed things up – there would be no need for time-consuming DTI reports or decisions by ministers. It would also remove the stringent evidence requirements needed to secure criminal conviction.

Leaving it to regulators is half-way to accepting that it is a victimless crime, though. A better solution may be to make it a civil offence, where less weighty evidence is required. In the US, it can be either – and the SEC will focus its energy only on criminal prosecution for cases involving large sums, or where there is evidence of a series of offences.

But letting regulators punish dealers would be unpopular unless there were radical changes to the surveillance system. As information is the key, that would be a good place to start. The rules permitting disclosure of large trades to be delayed by 90 minutes, or even up to five days, keep information from the market and should be abolished.

Most people in the City will be able to tell you which stockbrokers are regularly associated with suspicious deals. Immediate publication of all trades, and who carried them out, would disseminate that information more widely.

And that goes for companies too. The less time information is kept confidential, the fewer insiders are created.

(*The Independent*, 22 July 1994)

256

The characteristic features of corporate crime make it more likely that the offender will escape detection. The character of the regulatory machinery also helps to make such offences much less risky than conventional crimes like burglary or armed robbery. The most elementary difference is that, whereas the police patrol the streets and have increasingly sophisticated methods of surveillance of *public* areas, it is difficult for anybody to see what is going on in the *private* spaces of corporate life. The corporate sector has its own private security systems and 'watchdogs' of various sorts. Indeed, the police has a team dedicated to financial crime. However, the fact that by 1985 only 538 of Britain's then 120,000 police were allocated to the Fraud Squad is a reflection of its priorities (Levi, 1987, p.14). By 1998 this had risen to 600 officers on full-time attachment to such squads (Peter Stelfox, personal communication). Regulatory agencies maintain teams of inspectors, but usually their numbers are small in relation to their responsibilities, and their powers of investigation are limited. The Health and Safety Inspectorate is a good example of a regulatory body with too few staff and too limited powers to monitor standards effectively in an area where, as we have seen, violations cause hundreds of deaths and major injuries every year. It is instructive to note that in Britain in the 1990s, factories were inspected for safety offences on average once every four years (Nelken, 1997, pp.891–2).

Regulatory agencies usually deploy a mixture of reactive and proactive investigative techniques, but the emphasis is always on securing compliance with **compliance** regulations rather than detecting offenders. Research findings indicate that regulatory bodies and their inspectors do not see themselves as 'industrial policemen' but rather view their role as that of advising and cajoling the majority of fundamentally law-abiding business people (Hutter, 1988). Consequences rather than intentions provide the key focus of their work, often resulting in the collapsing of the distinction between incompetence and deliberateness and in the dilution rather than extension of the criminal stigma. Though environmental health and trading standards inspections are always unannounced, other agencies provide advance notice of inspection. This gives companies the opportunity to tighten up their procedures and also allows them to revert to their illicit practices the following day. The close relationship between regulatory agencies and the companies they regulate thus provides ample scope for collusion if not corruption.

Lower risk of prosecution

As we have seen, the emphasis of the authorities concerned with the crimes of the powerful is on securing compliance rather than inflicting punishment. This approach is particularly clear in the sphere of tax evasion. Though such crimes are common (every year in Britain over 100,000 people make settlements with the Inland Revenue after they have been discovered fiddling their taxes), the chances of detection are low, and on detection the chances of facing criminal charges are also low (Deane, 1981).

Studies in Britain comparing the official responses to tax evasion and social security fraud reveal a dramatic difference. Whereas in 1986–87 around 8,000 social security claimants were prosecuted, the figure for tax dodgers was 459 (Cook, 1989). In dealing with social security fraud the authorities emphasize coercion, policing the poor, and deterrence by prosecuting some and intimidating the rest. By contrast, their approach to tax evasion emphasizes compliance, a concern to spare the feelings of the offender, and deterrence by exemplary prosecutions of a few. Croall (1992) suggests that the policy of reserving prosecution for a minority of more serious offences or more blameworthy offenders has a wider applicability in relation to white-collar crime. Levi (1987, p.183) also notes the low prosecution rate in relation to commercial fraud and observes that, by contrast with conventional crime, bringing criminal charges is generally regarded as the last resort in such cases.

More lenient sanctions

> Persistent offenders who steal £1 go to prison; persistent insider dealers who steal £10m pay back the money – perhaps in addition to a substantial fine – on the rare occasions that they are caught ... for the greatest things, the law provides no remedy.
>
> (Levi, 1987, p.357)

In November 1993 Roger Levitt, a City 'financial adviser' whose firm collapsed in 1990 with debts of £34 million, was sentenced to 180 hours of community service (see Chapter 1). While the leniency of this punishment provoked a public outcry, it appeared to confirm Levi's point. Elsewhere Levi observes that 'except for professional people who steal from their clients' accounts – who are almost always sent to jail – fraudsters enjoy a low rate and average length of imprisonment, and a low average size of fine and compensation' (Levi, 1989, p.106).

For Levi, the difficulty of judging whether the sentences imposed on those found guilty of commercial fraud are more lenient than those imposed on conventional criminals arises from the difficulty of making clear comparisons. Is robbing somebody of a small amount at knifepoint a more or less serious crime than defrauding them of a great deal more through the stroke of a pen? Levi concludes that 'commercial elites enjoy a structural advantage from the reporting, policing and prosecution processes, so that the practical significance of the post-conviction sentencing process, for members of the upperworld, is comparatively minor, at least at present' (1987, p.313).

ACTIVITY 6.5

The spoof letter from the police to an adolescent burglar reproduced below reflects the differential response of the criminal justice system to conventional and white-collar or corporate crime:

Dear G E Rald,

We should like to take this opportunity to inform you that on 12th of March this year you were seen entering empty handed into the private premises of Ms P C Edwards of Convent St, Folkestone, and leaving shortly afterwards with your hands full.

In our opinion, this constitutes a violation of the Theft Act 1968 subsection 32 (c) and we would be grateful if you would consider the following advice: please stop going down Convent St and entering houses without the owners' permission.

We should warn you that next March 12th another police constable will be on foot duty in Convent St, and should he notice a repetition of your behaviour, we shall have to consider the possibility of taking even more stringent action than we have on this occasion.

(Box, 1983, p.50)

List some of the key differences between the way in which the authorities seek to regulate white-collar crime and their methods for curbing burglaries.

As Box observes, there would be a public outcry if the authorities dealt with familiar types of criminality in the same way in which they approach white-collar crime. The official response to the crimes of the powerful is consistent with some of the themes we have considered above: such violations are often not regarded as 'real' crime and are not treated as such at any stage in the legal process.

Box's letter illustrates how the state tries to control white-collar crime. Such offences are commonly subject either to civil courts or to non-judicial forms of regulation, rather than being dealt with by the criminal justice system. Offenders carry a lower risk of detection and, if they are caught, less chance of prosecution. The authorities tend to seek compliance with regulations and, if appropriate, financial reparation, rather than emphasizing the pursuit of punitive sanctions. If a white-collar offender is detected, prosecuted and convicted, then it is likely that he or she will receive a relatively lenient sentence, though because of the rarity of such cases it is difficult to make comparisons with sentencing for conventional crime.

One of the moral implications of Box's ironic spoof letter in the context of his work as a whole appears to be that corporate crimes should be punished like 'ordinary' crimes. However, rather than demanding that white-collar criminals be treated like more familiar criminals, we could argue the reverse – with a greater emphasis being placed on attempts at compliance as a prelude to prosecution for 'ordinary' criminals (**Braithwaite, 1989**). However, such an argument is rarely made in criminology (Nelken, 1997, p.916), never mind in the wider public debate on criminal justice.

In Section 2 we have examined a particular sphere of rule-breaking behaviour that is often not considered criminal, either by the law or by public opinion. Much corporate and white-collar crime remains *hidden* because it is carried out by apparently respectable persons in the course of their routine commercial activities. Far from corresponding to the familiar stereotype of the criminal, many of those convicted on charges of major fraud, insider dealing or other such offences were formerly regarded as being of good character, with a stable family background and often possessing substantial means. Indeed, many such offenders have previously won recognition and success through their entrepreneurial flair. The distinction between the sort of offences they commit and the fiercely competitive activities customarily carried out by individuals and companies under the pressure of market forces appears to many to be one of ambiguous degree, rather than a question of clear-cut principle. There is, in other words, an intimate link between the marketplace and white-collar crime. The difficulty of differentiating between the pursuit of legitimate commercial advantage and rule-breaking profiteering goes some way towards explaining the differential response of the authorities and public opinion towards white-collar and 'ordinary' crime. It also helps to explain the difficulty in regulating such offences.

3   Organized crime: myths and realities

In the previous section we explored corporate crime and its ambiguous status as 'real crime'. In this section we focus attention on that 'species' of crime perpetrated by organized criminals which appears to be the pinnacle of criminality. In what follows the connections as well as dissimilarities between corporate and organized crime will be highlighted.

We noted in the Introduction to this chapter that there are popular and powerful stereotypes of the professional criminal and of the nature of criminal organizations. However, criminologists have raised some important qualifications to these stereotypes.

organized crime

Commentators such as Levi (1998) argue that organized crime is characterized by being a continuing criminal enterprise, which works rationally to make profit through illicit activities, and ensures its existence at times through the use of threats or force and the corruption of officials. The notion of organized crime as a continuing criminal enterprise is embodied in the popularly accepted definition in Europe employed by the German Federal police, the BundesKriminalAmt:

> Organized crime is the planned violation of the law for profit or to acquire power, which offences are each, or together, of a major significance, and are carried out by more than two participants who cooperate within a division of labour for a long or undetermined time span using
>
> (a) commercial or commercial-like structures, or
>
> (b) violence or other means of intimidation, or
>
> (c) influence on politics, media, public administration, justice and the legitimate economy.
>
> (quoted in Levi, 1998, p.335)

Writing about the growth of organized crime in post-communist Russia, Gilinskiy provides further confirmation of the emerging international criminological consensus around the nature of organized crime: 'Organized crime in any society involves the functions of stable hierarchical associations, engaged in crime as a form of business whilst setting up a system of protection from public control, usually by means of protection rackets and other forms of corruption' (1998, p.235).

It is difficult to estimate the extent of organized crime in the UK and elsewhere. As we saw in Chapter 1, official statistics or victim surveys do not provide us with even a starting point for estimating the extent and distribution of organized crime. That said, organized crime is big business and, like corporate crime, pursues its 'work' in many spheres and across a range of enterprises, as Table 6.2 shows.

Table 6.2   Examples of crimes often associated with organized crime

- Organizing robberies, car thefts or shoplifting where items may be stolen to order
- Selling stolen goods
- Protection rackets – in which businesses are asked to pay to 'protect' themselves from violence, arson or other forms of damage
- Organized frauds – for example, social security or excise frauds
- Long firm frauds
- The drugs market – the manufacture, distribution and sale of prohibited drugs
- The illegal arms market – obtaining and distributing prohibited arms
- The sex industry – including prostitution and pornography
- Illegal drinking clubs – selling alcohol outside normal licensing arrangements
- Providing and arranging venues for other banned or controlled leisure pursuits – for example, rave parties; boxing and wrestling bouts
- 'People trafficking' – providing transport for illegal immigrants. This can also involve employing illegal immigrants as servants or labourers and 'sex trafficking' where women are employed in the sex industry
- Arranging for the theft and sale of art works
- Organizing illegal gambling
- Arranging for the illegal disposal of industrial waste
- The manufacture, distribution and sale of counterfeit goods
- The distribution and sale of goods banned in one country to another country
- Dealing in goods subject to import controls of health and safety regulations – for example, trading in meat unfit for human consumption; frauds against the European Union
- Money laundering
- Corruption – paying law enforcers and other state agencies and politicians to avoid investigation
- The distribution and sale of goods subject to excise – for example, contraband cigarettes and 'bootleg' alcohol
- Sales frauds and the transmission of pornography via the internet
- PIN frauds

Source: adapted from Croall, 1998, p.236

ACTIVITY 6.6

Look back at Activity 6.2 (at the end of Section 2.2) and think about the main difficulties associated with trying to carry out a survey of those victimized by organized crime.

We noted at the start of this chapter that there is uncertainty over trying to answer the question of how much organized crime exists. However, this uncertainty over the extent, distribution and nature of organized crime has not meant that there is either a lack of debate or attempts to explain it in both popular and academic commentaries. In particular, this section focuses on three issues:

1   the mythologizing of organized crime;

2   reconstructing organized crime as work and rational enterprise;

3   changes in organized crime and the globalization thesis.

3.1   Mythologizing organized crime

The Godfather: mythologizing of the Mafia in the film industry

The old narrative of the mobster calls upon a well-entrenched set of stereotypes on both sides of the Atlantic. In the UK there is almost a romanticized nostalgia for the traditional underworld, supposedly characterized by shared codes of honour and pride in craft and skill. As Hobbs (1995, p.28) observes, 'if the unwritten code of the underworld ever existed, it's now as outdated as an Ealing comedy'. That noted, new stereotypes of 'Mafia'-like, 'underworld' criminal gangs continue to be manufactured and mythologized, often in highly racialized forms.

According to Michael Woodiwiss, the mythologizing of organized crime in terms of there being an alien Mafia conspiracy at work in the USA (and elsewhere) may be dated quite specifically from the immediate post-Second World War years of the Cold War:

> On 20 December 1946 Colonel Garland Williams of the Federal Bureau of Narcotics (FBN) gave Americans a new way of understanding organized crime. He announced that the Mafia 'is a very dangerous criminal organization that is being used to undermine the principles of American ideals of law enforcement.' He then elaborated: 'The organization is national in scope. [Its] leaders meet annually, usually in Florida, and there agree upon policies for the control and correlation of their various criminal enterprises.
>
> (Woodiwiss, 1993, p.1)

This idea gained in momentum in subsequent decades, eventually dominating not just American but also international perceptions of organized crime. The basis of the idea was that of an alien, implanted conspiracy (of Sicilian origins) which was centrally organized and also dominated organized crime both nationally and internationally. Block (1991) has noted that the criminological study of organized crime has been fascinated and seduced by this state-sponsored conspiracy theory. In turn, this fascination leads to a depiction of monolithic, impenetrable, culturally hermetic groups of criminals. Furthermore, this conventional theory also looks to an ethnic explanation for other examples of organized crime. We have seen, then, the recent application of the 'Sicilian', foreign conspiracy paradigm to the understanding of organized crime (especially the drugs trade) among blacks, Hispanics, Orientals and a range of culturally defined 'others'. Historically, the concept of organized crime as an alien, dangerous and unified entity was as vital to the law enforcement community in the USA as the idea of communism as an alien, dangerous and united entity was for the intelligence and foreign policy making community (Woodiwiss, 1993, p.13).

Criminologists now suggest that this dominant, 'alien conspiracy' theory is more the stuff of myth than historical and sociological reality. The Mafia conspiracy narrative, then, like the cowboy hero of the West, is the stuff of folklore. Looking at the history of Italian-American organized crime does not support the claim of there being a neat and tidy hierarchy of bosses (or 'capos') and street soldiers. Instead, there has been evidence of often savage, internecine struggle among competing groups. Again, Woodiwiss notes that there has never been an ethnically based monopoly in the drug business in the USA. Rather, there are many thousands of distribution and smuggling networks – 'decentralization characterizes the industry with a high turnover of personnel' (Woodiwiss, 1993, p.25). Furthermore, contemporary criminologists such as Hobbs (1997) argue that organized crime has a complex and all-pervasive influence on all levels of US life, not least in terms of the complex interaction between 'criminal' and 'non-criminal' worlds: 'When viewed from a perspective that regards organized crime, not as separate, exclusive, and essentially removed from normative civil society, but as one of its central props, what emerges is a loose set of power relationships that interact with both upper and underworlds' (Hobbs, 1997, p.828). Organized crime in the USA, the most powerful society in the world, is thus best viewed as what Hobbs terms a 'spectrum of enterprise' rather than an 'evil empire'. We thus find, not so much 'godfathers' presiding over a secret but unified family/society, but rather 'fluid sets of mobile marauders in the urban landscape alert to institutional weaknesses in both legitimate and illegitimate spheres' (Block, 1983, p.245).

The American and international myth of organized crime as a dark, secret and alien underworld ignores both the increasing centrality of organized criminal enterprises and activities to the 'upperworld' (see Section 5 below) and its institutional proximity to other licit enterprises. Woodiwiss concludes that 'Organized crime is an essential feature of the American social, economic and political systems, but the experts and commentators who stick to the Mafia framework manage to disguise this fact by representing it as something alien and distinct from American life' (Woodiwiss, 1993, p.27). Drawing on the research by Block, Levi adds further support to this demythologizing thesis by suggesting that organized crime in the USA is a set of shifting conditions between groups of gangsters, business people, politicians, and union leaders, normally local or regional in scope (Levi, 1998, p.338).

'alien conspiracy' theory

3.2 Reconstructing organized crime as work and rational enterprise

Researchers such as Ruggiero point out that the dynamics of organized crime for the most part involve the same elements as white-collar or corporate crime; for example, both generally manifest complex and adaptive institutional structures rather than monolithic institutional structures underscored by similar values. However, organized crime has been treated differently from corporate crime on the grounds of who commits it (that is, not respectable, high status, legitimate businessmen and experts but 'racketeers', 'gangsters' and such like): 'To paraphrase Sutherland's statement organized crime *is* also white collar crime' (Ruggiero, 1996, p.19). Hobbs's (1995) research into the careers and occupational strategies of perpetrators of organized crime – such as dealers, robbers and smugglers – also demystifies the study of serious crime groups, not least by describing them as 'commodity brokers' whose enterprise is mainly demand-led. Like successful legitimate economic enterprises, the most successful criminal enterprises are multifaceted, large-scale and adaptive to the opportunities and uncertainties of the external environment and the changing marketplace, particularly with regard to the production or circulation of illicit goods, and with successful criminals as rational actors choosing the ideal maximization of their returns. And of course most conventional organized crime faces an environment in which risk and uncertainty – the classic ingredients of entrepreneurship – are compounded by the illegal nature of its undertakings.

criminal enterprise

It is evident from the above that the routine business of criminal organizations requires an entrepreneurial structure. Remember, a key characteristic of criminal businesses is the provision of goods and services which are officially defined as illegal, thus filling the gaps left by legal agencies. They rely on the sale of commodities and they need a base for customers to access their services. Another key feature of this structure is the capacity of organized crime to mobilize labour: 'we have organized crime when activities are structured in the guise of a "collective" endeavour implying the recruitment of criminal workers and the payment to them of a wage' (Ruggiero, 1996, p.119). As a consequence, organized crime shows features of an industrial type of institution, recruiting both skilled and unskilled and increasingly casualized labour: 'It is the presence of these diverse figures holding varying degrees of professionalism and skills which should be regarded as a significant hallmark of organized crime' (Ruggiero, 1996, p.121). This institutional characteristic also implies a strict separation of planning and execution. Unlike the myth of a separate, hermetically sealed 'underworld' criminal culture, this emphasis on the economic principles at work in organized crime alerts us once more to the proximity of its characteristics to those of the 'upperworld' of business and industry. However, for serious crime groups, violence replaces the bureaucracy of normative capitalist market economies. A credible threat of violence ensures that these groups are able to maintain a position of strength in the marketplace. As Hobbs (1995, p.122) notes, 'the use of a traditional masculine strategy within the arena of the contemporary market indicates that there is a powerful sense of continuity within their inherited identities'. Here we should note the dissimilarities as well as the connections between organized and corporate crime and their perpetrators.

entrepreneurial structure

At the highest level of illegal markets, 'bigger' would seem to be best. Arlacchi's research on organized crime in Italy, for example, emphasizes the advantages over other 'firms' of the three big players in large-scale illegality in Italy (the Cosa Nostra of Sicily, the Calabrian 'Ndrangheta and the Campanian Camorra), in terms of the large economic scale of their activity, the number and expertise of their affiliates, the ability to manipulate public institutions and the complexity of their organizational structure (Arlacchi, 1998, p.206). It is also clear that much low level criminal work is relatively disorganized, casualized and increasingly fragmented, with the boundaries with legitimate business increasingly blurred, rather than tightly organized and unified because of any mythologized closed brotherhood. In Arlacchi's (1998, p.204) words, the enterprises of organized crime are 'rational economic phenomena and well-structured industries'.

3.3 Changes in organized crime and globalization

We noted above that there has been a dominant myth about, and stereotypes of, the organized criminal in the second half of the twentieth century, chiefly based on the notion of an alien criminal conspiracy associated with tightly knit secret societies. According to Hobbs (1997, p.829), recent influential populist commentaries on, and media reporting of, the threat of globalization have also been associated with the claim that there is now a 'transnational organized crime' conspiracy, often linked to the new, so-called 'Mafias' of post-communist societies and other 'alien' networks such as the Chinese Triads, Jamaican Yardies and Japanese Yakusi alongside the 'old' Italian-American Mafia. By 1998, the problem of organized crime was the top issue on the United Nations criminological agenda (Levi, 1998, p.336) and the 'emotional kick' associated with fears of 'new Mafias' has stimulated new policing initiatives such as the National Criminal Investigation Service (NCIS) in the UK and Europol in Europe. This latest revisiting of the old alien conspiracy narrative and moral panic is open to some questioning from researchers in the field, including police experts (Stelfox, 1998). Nevertheless, there is evidence of important contemporary transitions in some aspects of this category of crime – not least the adaptation to the new technology of the computer and the Internet (see the 'Law-breaking on the Web' extract from *The Independent* reproduced overleaf). Hobbs (1995, p.8) notes that the structural alterations experienced by the marketplace, such as key technological innovations in the field of electronic communications, 'have enabled those of villainous intent to launch offensives upon information, or money … that are comparable to the way the shotgun and thermic lance enabled and enhanced the practice of previous generations of thieves and robbers'. Like legitimate industry in recent years, the organized crime industry has also seen a growth of casualization and deskilling of its labour force, reflecting pressures from new competitors in illegal enterprise across the world. On the basis of his own research on drug economies in Europe, Ruggiero (1996, p.115) has noted the particularly striking growth in the hierarchical structure of illegal drugs production and distribution which he suggests is also an increasing hallmark of organized crime more generally. As a consequence of this organizational development, there is evidence of a deskilling of much criminal work at the bottom of the hierarchy. In the strict division of labour, we find economic dependence at the bottom – for example, the street level 'pusher'/

addict or the 'mule'/carrier of narcotics across borders, who are expendable labourers serving the market – whilst at the top there is a drive towards more structured and professionalized operations.

Law-breaking on the Web

Pornography

Two company bosses were convicted this summer of using their computers to publish hard-core pornography. The mastermind behind the company, Graham Waddon, 28, was said to have earned £800,000 from the scheme.

Software Piracy

An estimated third of business software in Britain is illegal, part of a £7bn annual loss of revenue to program companies worldwide.

Viruses

An estimated 200 new viruses, which are programs that can delete files from a computer's hard disk, are released every month in the United States.

Fraud

Seen as one of the big growth areas. Visa reported in April that 1 per cent of credit card transactions over the internet accounted for 47 per cent of disputes, with half of them being people denying they had ever bought the goods. There are several programs on the Internet that allow users to generate new credit card numbers, which can be used to buy goods. Old scams, such as pyramid sales and advance fee fraud, in which people are asked to pay for a non-existent service up front, have been given a new lease of life on the Internet.

Criminal Communications

Criminals are using encrypted messages to pass on secrets and instructions, such as paedophile material and extortion demands. Police are looking at using more code breakers to trace source of material.

Computer Hacking

Russian cyber criminals were able to steal $400,000 from US Citibank in 1994 by hacking into their system. Commercial espionage takes place in which corporate plans and research is stolen. Vandalism can occur when disgruntled employees, ex-employees or customers may sabotage a company's records. Pranksters have altered many sites such as in 1996 when the Labour Party's website was changed to Labour Party Sex Shop and in the same year the CIA read 'Central Stupidity Agency'.

Gambling

There are about 1,000 gambling sites, which are outside UK jurisdiction. No sign yet that British citizens are being conned, but they are believed to be rife for exploitation.

(*The Independent*, 26 October 1999)

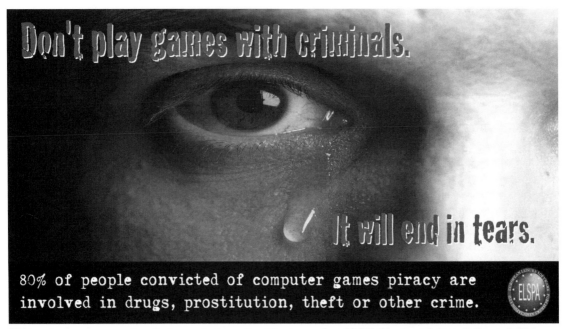

Don't play games with criminals. It will end in tears.

80% of people convicted of computer games piracy are involved in drugs, prostitution, theft or other crime.

ELSPA

'Cyber crime' and new modes of crime control: an advertising poster from ELSPA (European Leisure Software Publishers Association Crime Unit)

Hobbs (1997; Hobbs and Dunningham, 1998) has also noted that trends in the UK have seen the erosion of traditional criminal communities and their criminal progeny (such as the East End of London and its (in)famous 'gangland' families such as the Krays). Now local organized crime has mutated into forms of enterprise that should be regarded as indigenous renditions of global markets, or what has been termed 'glocal' organized crime (Hobbs and Dunningham, 1998, p.289). Hobbs insists then that most criminal enterprises are still local phenomena grounded in specific historical practices and relationships (Hobbs, 1997, p.829). But new forms of multinational partnerships have also been noted by researchers in the field of the new illegal enterprises across Europe (Ruggiero, 1996). For example, there have been initiatives to develop innovative strategies in the context of new markets via the promotional distribution of low-priced drugs (as 'loss leaders') in Eastern Europe by partnerships between established drug production and distribution networks in alliance with 'new' local networks of criminals (see Table 6.3 on the features of the illegal drugs economy across the world, and Figure 6.1 which shows the major global trafficking routes for illegal drugs).

Table 6.3 The illegal drugs business: key features of a global growth industry

1 The industry is a multi-million pound global industry.

2 It generates enormous profits which in turn necessitate 'money laundering'.

3 It is increasingly diversifying into other businesses and operating with legitimate 'fronts'.

4 There is a complex import and export trade based on illegal drugs being grown in less well-developed countries from where they are transported, often across the globe, before being imported and distributed on the 'high street'.

5 Organizationally, the business involves:
- entrepreneurs who purchase supplies from growers and organize their distribution;
- traffickers involved with transportation;
- importers and wholesalers who pass on the 'goods' to retailers ('dealers') who in turn pass on to casualized labourers ('dealers-users') or sell to consumers.

Source: adapted from Croall, 1998, p.256

Figure 6.1 The contraband trade routes: major trafficking routes of the international illegal drugs trade (Source: The Independent, 22 February 1999)

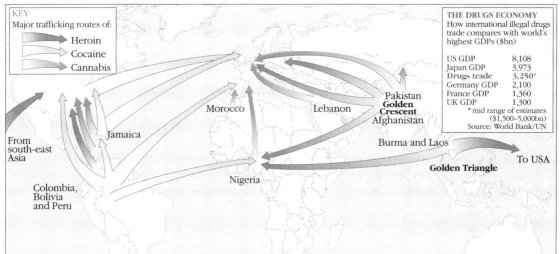

4   Crimes, markets and capitalism

> Enterprise may be positioned somewhere along a spectrum between legal and criminal, so the fluctuations of legitimate and illegitimate business appear as ambiguous and as fluid as in practice they are.
>
> (Findlay, 1998, p.139)

Despite this claim, Vicenzo Ruggiero (1996, p.45) has noted that both common sense and much established criminological analysis seem to be committed to a moral imperative whereby criminal activities must be regarded as having a completely different logic from other economically motivated activities. However, this moral imperative may be challenged when we shift our focus in the study of crime from *persons* to *events*. In other words, it is perhaps more productive to see economically motivated crimes as involving similar processes to other organized economic activities. Markets are frameworks of commercial relationships and crime is one such relationship. Crime, whether by licit or illicit enterprises, may therefore be seen as *illegal activities engaged in by business organizations in pursuit of their goal of maximizing profit and power in relatively unpredictable social, political and economic environments.*

In the 1970s and 1980s, radical criminologists sought to locate the problems of both organized and corporate crime within a wider critique of modern capitalism and the social conflicts that it generates (Pearce, 1976; Box, 1983). These authors maintained that when companies encounter obstacles to maintaining profitability by legitimate means, they resort to illicit methods of the sorts we have already reviewed. They argue that such corporate crime is an inevitable corollary of the capitalist economy. In other words, capitalism is viewed as being criminogenic.

Other radical commentators have emphasized the close relationship in general between the spirit of capitalist enterprise and corporate criminality. For Mars (1982, p.49), 'there is only a blurred line between entrepreneurality and flair on the one hand and sharp practices on the other'. When entrepreneurs are under intense competitive pressures, the boundaries between legitimate and illegitimate measures to reduce costs and maximize profits inevitably become blurred. It is also inevitable that the boundaries will be set differently by company executives keen to cut some corners, and by employees who may be obliged to work more intensively and perhaps at greater risk to health and safety. Consumers and the wider public may take a different view again, according to the nature of the enterprise and the consequences of violations of established codes of practice.

In addition, this perspective stresses the important functional role that organized crime has played in the development of capitalist economies worldwide. Luttwak (1995) reminds us of the crucial and highly complex part that local organized criminal groupings supported by US foreign policy played in the post-Second World War re-establishment and remarkable recovery of the West German, Italian and Japanese economies. He also maintains that a similar 'beneficial' process is presently playing itself out in the crypto-capitalist economies of Eastern Europe (but see Section 6 below). In Russia, for example:

Local Mafias act in many places and many ways to resist the excessive concentrations of economic power brought by government corruption, or rather by the prevalence of under the table joint ventures between Russian government officials and new private firms run by ex-officials – including the very highest officials and the very largest firms. They are, in effect, competitors which use physical force, or more often just the threat of force, usefully to offset the monopolistic market power in a still lawless economy.

(Luttwak, 1995, p.7)

As a result of the affinity between the spirit of enterprise (taking risks and developing innovative commercial activities) and a readiness to bend the often flexible and discretionary legal rules to guarantee profits, there is widespread moral ambivalence about white-collar offences. For many entrepreneurs the state and its laws are often regarded as imposing illegitimate restraints on the free operation of the sovereign laws of the market. As Benson (1985, p.588) observes, 'criminal behaviour can then be characterized as being in line with other higher laws of free enterprise'. For the typical small businessman, for example, tax evasion may not so much be viewed as an offence or a crime, but as a gesture of defiance against unwarranted state intrusions.

Once we shift the focus of our attention from the street or home to the boardroom, office or other workplace, the close association between various offences and commercial enterprise is inescapable. All forms of trade inevitably create the possibility of fraud; the greater the scale of commercial activity, the greater the scope for dishonest practices. For example, the expansion of manufacturing industry and the parallel growth of credit and the finance sector in the UK in the nineteenth-century appear to have been accompanied by a rising incidence of major frauds as well as other offences against employees, competitors, consumers and the public (Robb, 1992).

The growing bureaucratic complexity of the modern enterprise and the **bureaucratic** separation of ownership and control following the transition from family firms **complexity** to those with publicly held shares, with prices regulated through stock exchanges, have facilitated large-scale, organized, corporate crime. These developments make it impossible for the 'old-style' entrepreneur-owner to supervise and 'self-police' corporate affairs directly. The resulting division of labour makes it possible for individuals at any level of the hierarchy to engage in illicit activities. The concentration and centralization of capital into larger and larger units administered by professional managers means that the modern company offers executives the prospect of big rewards for relatively little risk, making corporate crime an attractive option for some in times of both economic expansion and recession.

Tendencies towards monopoly and periodic boom and recession in the modern era have expanded the range of corporate wrongdoing. Attempts to fix prices and thus contain competitive rivalries among a small number of large firms operating in the same market have provoked state intervention, through informal regulations or formal legislation, in an attempt to uphold the principles of the free market. Meanwhile, periods of both economic crisis and boom have intensified competitive rivalries, increasing pressures towards sharp practice and illegality.

The onset of the worldwide recession of the 1980s resulted in Western and indeed many former Communist governments pursuing a policy of deregulation, reining back state intervention and promoting market forces in all spheres of economic activity. The deregulation of the London Stock Exchange in the 'Big Bang' of October 1986 marked a decisive opening up of the City of London to international money markets. Whatever the effect of these policies in reviving industry, there can be little doubt that the relaxation of controls on the financial sector in the UK appeared to increase the scale of fraud and corruption, leading to the collapse of banks and destabilizing other institutions, such as the insurance brokers Lloyds. Periods of both recession and boom thus appear to bring different opportunities for crimes – for example, 'protective' crimes which may stop the company going out of business and 'expansive' crimes associated with growth.

Scene from the film Rogue Trader *depicting the tale of Nick Leeson and illegal activities in the world's commodities trading markets*

The close association between commerce and crime suggests that the link is not merely that enterprise offers opportunities for the unscrupulous. The market assumes equal exchange, yet it creates the possibility of unequal exchange, by fraud or deception. The most fundamental dictate of the market – 'buy cheap, sell dear' – implies a competitive pressure to gain an advantage over a rival or customer. The market itself has no means of distinguishing whether this is achieved by fair means or foul. The spectrum of practices that stretches from legitimate competition, through 'sharp practice' to overt fraud appears to be inherent in market relations. The shades of grey that we have noted in the sphere of corporate offences originate in market forces. The personal characteristics of the corporate criminal – charm, aggression, ambition, cunning, ruthlessness – are difficult to distinguish from those of the successful entrepreneur. Indeed, it is striking that many individuals convicted of major white-collar crimes – Guinness executive Ernest Saunders, US car salesman John De Lorean, Mike Miliken, the 'junk-bond king' of Wall Street – were successful businessmen before they seemingly turned to 'crime'. And of course successful criminals often become businessmen after they turn from crime.

Is capitalism as such criminogenic? Not all commentators agree with the broadly Marxist explanation outlined above. Nelken (1997, p.906) points out some problems with this viewpoint. He suggests that it predicts too much crime and may have difficulty in explaining the relative stability of economic trade within and between countries. The explanation may also have difficulty in accounting for improvements in safety and increases in the quality of goods in capitalism. Nelken also argues that the claim that all business people are 'amoral calculators' is as flawed as the idea that corporate criminals are just a few 'bad apples'.

5 'You can bank on it': connecting licit and illicit enterprises

In previous sections we have already highlighted the, at times, intimate *interconnections* between the spheres of legitimate business and political and administrative agencies and those of both corporate and organized crime. These 'close encounters of the illicit kind' are the focus of the discussion here. At times, the boundaries between the two supposedly distinct 'worlds' are as blurred in the contemporary world as they have been in the past. However, mutual services and joint enterprises between legitimate business and illicit enterprises may be more significant in the context of neo-liberal deregulation of money markets and the political 'chaos' of the post-Cold War world order (Huntington, 1998). The clearest examples of such blurring of licit and illicit boundaries of activity relate to arms trading and money laundering.

Let's first examine the example of arms trading. The illegality of arms trading may lie in the quality and quantity of arms produced which are subject to international restrictions and regulations. The black market in light armaments and second-hand weapons is largely controlled by conventional organized crime. However, the major actors in large-scale arms trading are often 'establishment' ones, such as manufacturers, politicians or army officials. It appears that the growing 'grey market' in heavy, high-technology armaments to post-communist and developing countries does not need such an uncomfortable ally as the professional criminal (Ruggiero, 1996, p.131). Indeed, the example of the 'arms to Iraq affair' in the early 1990s, in which the export of arms supplies by British manufacturers were 'encouraged' by cabinet ministers and the intelligence services despite the formal legal ban on such exports, suggests the interpenetration of political authorities and arms industry in the promotion of illegal activities without the need for involvement from organized crime (see Chapter 7 in this volume).

We have noted that criminal groups often provide services to, and act as a supplementary infrastructure for, the legal economy. But the roles can also be reversed. Corruption cases, for example, illustrate in dramatic fashion the provision of services carried out by official actors for the benefit of organized crime. However, the most important example of legitimate institutions providing services to, and acting as the crucial infrastructure for, the illegal economy lies in the crime of money laundering. Money laundering concerns the hiding and laundering of the proceeds of illegal gains. Money laundering is vital in relation to most financially motivated crime. A famous example of such money laundering in the UK was the 'Brink's-Mat' robbery case in the mid-1990s when the proceeds of the robbery were 'laundered' through unknowing London banks by a number of 'respectable' businessmen. It may also be noted that much of the wealth of Switzerland, for example, relies on the flow, not just from 'clean' money from licit profits, but also from the more 'murky' money deposited by corporate criminals (e.g. tax evasion) and corrupt politicians from across the globe (as well as from the 'dirty' money derived from criminal activities). There also appears to be a loosely-knit world system of offshore finance centres in which money laundering takes place on a massive scale. These transactions are often supported by legal professional privilege and customer confidentiality. It is likely that international networks (to varying degrees 'licit' and 'illicit') exist but their forms are subtle and complex (Levi, 1987, p.343). To take another example, commenting on the American banking system's relationship to organized crime, Senator William Proxmire has noted ironically that 'many banks are addicted to drugs money, just as millions of Americans are addicted to drugs' (quoted in Woodiwiss, 1993, p.26). More generally, it would seem that organized crime is an important source of investment capital across the USA and other advanced capitalist societies.

Mutual entrepreneurial promotion between business and organized crime has also come to the fore in studies of European Union fraud – that is, the improper use of EU funds (Clarke, 1993). The biggest abuse relates to the agricultural subsidy funds. The main commodities implicated in this fraud and abuse are olive oil, wine, cereals and beef. At its simplest, such fraud involves firms being paid subsidies for the production of vast quantities of produce that in reality do not exist (Levi and Maguire, 1998, p.185). The exact costs of such crimes are probably unknowable given their largely hidden nature and complex entanglement with legitimate use of funds, but one estimate in 1989 calculated that 10 per cent of the EEC budget was subject to fraud and abuse (Tiedeman cited in Clarke, 1993, p.175). In 1994, frauds against the funds of the EU were estimated at ECU 60 billion (around £50 billion) (Levi and Maguire, 1998, p.183). Researchers have also noted that criminal organizations in the 1990s have been working in collaboration with legitimate businesses, such as printers and supermarkets, in developing major frauds such as those against EU agricultural subsidy programmes (Nelken, 1997, p.910). Furthermore, the 'syndication of crime' – that is, the development of associations of criminal enterprises organized to undertake joint projects requiring considerable capital – is reflected at the global level in the syndication of control responses (such as the cross-border collaboration in Europe between police forces, or the United Nations' crime prevention initiatives; see Levi and Maguire, 1998).

Mutual entrepreneurial partnerships between 'respectable' business and organized crime also take place between the affluent West and developing countries across the world. For example, Ruggiero cites the case of an elaborate enterprise involving the illegal importing of, and production of, expensive consumer goods (shoes and handbags) based on the skins of a protected species, the caiman alligator. One company involved in this trade in Milan justified the illegality of their business by invoking the pressing demand for the goods they sold – an argument not dissimilar from that which could be used by illicit drug traffickers. Overall, the illegal trade in caiman alligators results in an estimated one million animals being killed each year for the shoes and bags of affluent, fashion-conscious Westerners (Ruggiero, 1996, p.79).

6 Social transformation, and the criminalization of economy and politics: a case study of Russia

We noted in Section 4 that criminal enterprise has played an important historical role in the past with regard to state formation and economic development in many societies, not least the UK and the USA. At times, there has been a seamless relationship between state-sponsored crime and the dominant socio-economic order. In the Elizabethan period in Britain, for example, state-sponsored pirates were used both to establish and maintain English colonies. Their royally-endorsed licence to plunder across the high seas was exploited to the full by the state, and the success of the pirates was rewarded in some notable cases by legitimation and an entrée into polite society (Sherry, 1986). This pattern of market exploitation, violence, incorporation and institutionalized legitimation was to be repeated in the USA in the nineteenth and early twentieth centuries, with examples of robber barons involved in criminal activities eventually established as leaders of this society (Hobbs, 1997, p.823). History thus provides us with examples of the key role played at times by organized criminal activities in national state formation in periods of major social transformation. In the context of the globalizing forces of the twenty-first century, there is evidence once again of the central role played by organized crime in attempting to control both the economic and political destinies of whole countries. Groups of criminals who commit serious crimes may even begin to constitute the state. It is a matter for debate to decide how far up the political chain one reaches in one's delineation of who are 'organized criminals'. Columbia is perhaps the most extreme example of a society whose destiny is largely bound up with the workings of the illegal drugs economy. However, it is developments in post-communist Russia which may provide the most significant example of how illicit activities, legitimate business and political authority are increasingly interwoven and indistinguishable.

6.1 'Horse without a bridle'

Russia's movement from a state-regulated command economy to that of a free-market economy has been associated with an unprecedented wave of economic and organized crime. There are estimates that 40 per cent of the money circulating in Russia by the mid-1990s was generated by illegal activity. Crimes of violence have also risen dramatically, with for example murder up from 8.5 cases per 100,000 of the population in 1985 to 21.4 cases per 100,000 in 1995 (Gilinskiy, 1998, p.253). There is a broad consensus among researchers that the particularly powerful influence of criminal groups in Russia (as in Italy) lies in their active presence in the official and political arena. Through both lobbying and direct infiltration, criminals are seemingly implicated in direct attempts to influence the government and the state. According to Gilinskiy (1998, p.237), the defining feature of organized crime in post-communist Russia lies in its involvement with, and the advantageous positions it occupies within, the culture of enterprise. Indeed, organized crime has a position of dominance in many spheres of legitimate business.

Rawlinson's (1998) research on the relationship between organized crime and the legitimate structures in the former Soviet Union is particularly important in demystifying the popular, media myth about Russia's crime problem being due to the existence of Mafia gangster gangs. The obsession with the stereotypical Slavic mobster with 'big muscles and designer suits' is, she claims, a distraction from the most critical area of centralized organized criminal activity, which is where licit and illicit business interface alongside the connections back to the old command state and its abuses. She develops a model of the process by which organized crime may over time change its relationship with the legitimate structures of society, both political and economic, from no integration or negotiation to that of proactive control over the legitimate structures of society. This model is termed the Chameleon Syndrome (see Figure 6.2). Rawlinson suggests that the situation in post-communist Russia is that of the 'proactive' stage whereby 'organized crime acts like a chameleon, blending into the very structures whose management it seeks and achieves' (Rawlinson, 1998, p.245). Again, it is argued that the proliferation of quasi-licit and illicit business practices in the developing market economy is a more detrimental force than the much publicized gangsterism of rackets and mobs. The world of 'grey' business and the tolerance of and collusion with criminal structures is thus viewed as a major threat to the social fabric. And it is a development which in part has been aided by the West's support for free-market 'shock therapy' for Russia throughout the 1990s. (See, for example, the 'disastrous' advice given by Western experts of the IMF to Russia, as reported in the article by Jonathan Steele reproduced on pages 275–6).

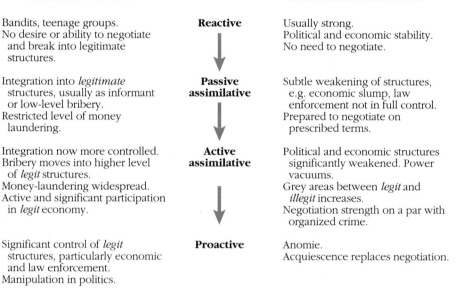

ORGANIZED CRIME		LEGITIMATE STRUCTURES
Bandits, teenage groups. No desire or ability to negotiate and break into legitimate structures.	**Reactive**	Usually strong. Political and economic stability. No need to negotiate.
Integration into *legitimate* structures, usually as informant or low-level bribery. Restricted level of money laundering.	**Passive assimilative**	Subtle weakening of structures, e.g. economic slump, law enforcement not in full control. Prepared to negotiate on prescribed terms.
Integration now more controlled. Bribery moves into higher level of *legit* structures. Money-laundering widespread. Active and significant participation in *legit* economy.	**Active assimilative**	Political and economic structures significantly weakened. Power vacuums. Grey areas between *legit* and *illegit* increases. Negotiation strength on a par with organized crime.
Significant control of *legit* structures, particularly economic and law enforcement. Manipulation in politics.	**Proactive**	Anomie. Acquiescence replaces negotiation.

Figure 6.2   The Chameleon Syndrome (Source: Rawlinson, 1998, p.244)

Russia: the biggest money launderette in the world

Jonathan Steele in Moscow

It is bad luck for the International Monetary Fund that a team of its economists should be in Moscow preparing to lend more millions to Russia just as revelations of another avalanche of unexplained capital flight hit the headlines. It may be the biggest money-launderette the world has ever seen, with estimates that at least $4,200m, and possibly as much as $10,000m, churned through the Bank of New York in little more than a year.

The IMF says there is no evidence that any of this money came from its own loans. So far, so true. But that is what money-laundering is for. The aim is to funnel cash though a variety of fronts and off-shore companies to conceal its origins. Whatever eventually emerges from the latest cash-flow mystery, the IMF cannot deny that earlier loans given to Russia's central bank were used by the bank itself for speculation on the foreign exchanges. Huge sums were routed through a shell company based in Jersey, and the profits disappeared into private Russian pockets. An auditors' report which the IMF commissioned from Price Waterhouse made that plain, and Stanley Fischer, the IMF's deputy director, recently admitted, 'we were lied to'.

On the face of it, therefore, we have a simple moral tale. Well-meaning western governments give money to budding new Russian market economists to help them make their country prosper. On the way the money is abused and somehow, billions of dollars later, it sadly transpires that the new Russian polity has turned into a kleptocracy. The country is being run by thieves.

Shocked and distressed, American media are now full of agonised articles about the apparent deception. The crisis of discovery has entered the election campaign, with the Republicans beginning to ask, 'Who lost Russia?' The answer, naturally, is the Democrats and their presidential contender, Al Gore, who chaired the so-called Gore-Chernomyrdin commission. Sitting alongside Russia's long-time prime minister, Viktor Chernomyrdin, who also happens to be one of Russia's richest new capitalists, Gore told the Russian government how to obtain the IMF's money.

Of course the real picture is not that clear. For one thing, Russia was never in any foreign government's gift to win or lose. For another, the Republicans were in power in 1991 and 1992 when the first western 'help' to post-Communist Russia was given. But the main issue is that the help did not merely consist of loans. It was advice.

If powerful kleptocrats have emerged in Russia, this is not because Russians are uniquely prone to dishonesty and corruption. It is because western advisers advocated policies which created the conditions for any rational profit-maximizer to grab, grab and grab. It only needed a single blip in New York's electricity grid in 1975 to plunge the city into darkness and spawn a thousand looters out of otherwise law-abiding citizens. The Russian economy has had eight years of slow-motion looting, for which western governments with their policy recommendations are as guilty as the Russian thieves.

Not all the western advice was taken. But on the key issues, the Russian government did what westerners urged it to do. In the first phase, when economists such as Jeffrey Sachs of Harvard university were regularly commuting to Moscow, the central recommendation was to lift all price controls. In an economy of monopolies this immediately produced hyper-inflation, a huge growth of inter-enterprise debt, an escape from money into barter, and the wiping-out of ordinary citizens' savings.

Professor Sachs, in a recent interview in the *New York Times* on his advice for handling the ailing Soviet economy in 1991, boasted 'I understood the challenge better, I think, than anybody'. That does not reflect the image he gave at a Moscow press conference at the time. He was asked how the various steps towards a market economy should be sequenced. Price liberalization, creating a stock market, privatization, giving the central bank independence, building up private banks, passing legislation to protect contracts, breaking up the monopolies – what was the right order? Blindly, Sachs replied, 'Ideally, all of them at once'.

In the mid-90s came the second strategic blunder, supported by the IMF which by this time had arrived on the Russian scene with its cash-for-policies. It allowed a handful of Russian bankers to become owners of the richest raw-material producers in return for lending the government money. Never mind the fact that these bankers had made their first millions by favoured contact with government officials rather than through any skill at picking companies which would invest in increased production or modernizing their plant. They were given the concessions to pass government money on to the regions. Instead of dispatching it immediately they speculated on the foreign currency markets and made substantial profits in a few weeks.

The third mistake was to encourage the Russian government in 1997, as a way of cutting its budget deficit, to raise money by offering government bonds with absurdly high rates of interest. It turned into a giant pyramid scheme, which many western investors entered as greedily as any Russians. The IMF found itself pouring millions in to Russia simply to protect the value of the rouble and western bankers. The bubble burst last August when the Russian government devalued, though

275

not before the biggest Russian financiers had taken their money out.

The most prominent figures in this sorry saga are not the 'red directors', as the elderly ex-Communist managers of Russia's privatized industries are often called. They are the 'young reformers' who are still touted in some quarters in the west as the country's best hope. One is Anatoly Chubais, who led the privatization process for several years and later served as Russia's contact with the IMF. Now he heads the power monopoly, United Energy Systems, and is one of Russia's super-rich.

Another 'young reformer' is Konstantin Kagalovsky, who served from 1992 to 1995 as the link man with the IMF. Now vice-president of Yukos oil, he has been in the news this month because it was through the accounts which his wife managed at the Bank of New York that millions of dollars from Russia flowed. She denies wrong-doing but has been suspended.

Ironically, shortly before the story broke, Kagalovsky had told the *New York Times* 'We now see such simple truths: that a country that is based on stealing and corruption is much less efficient than a normal society. And that the end does not justify the means. If the Communists had won the 1996 elections, I'm not sure we would be in a worse situation than now'.

That is quite an admission, but the IMF and those western economists and governments who gave Russia the wrong advice should kindly follow suit.

(*The Guardian,* 31 August 1999)

The journalist Stephen Handelman also provides some 'first-hand' accounts of the pervasive nature of the criminal enterprise in contemporary Russia. He suggests that the path followed by post-Soviet mobsters was similar to that taken by organized crime in other countries. In particular, organized crime 'took advantage of the vacuum of power to create the only working system of authority in many parts of Russia'. However, to a greater extent than Western organized crime (perhaps with the exception of Italy), Handelman contends that Russian gangs and their counterparts 'were able to exploit the institutions, structures, and civil servants of a state that was already criminalized by its previous rulers' (Handelman, 1995, p.335). Extract 6.2 depicts in a graphic way the thesis of the criminalization of Russia's political and economic order. This extract also helps explain Handelman's analogy of contemporary Russia being akin to a 'horse without a bridle'.

Extract 6.2 Handelman: 'Comrade criminal'

In the city of Tver, just north of Moscow, anyone who wanted to open up a sidewalk stand in 1994 was required to seek the permission of the local gang leader before getting a license from municipal authorities. Tver gangsters, like Konstantin Tsyganov of Yekaterinburg, rightly considered themselves the most dependable investment bankers in their city. They provided loans to young businessmen who would otherwise have found it impossible to obtain credit from government banks. The same system operated in the country at large. The principal pools of capital available for domestic investment following the Soviet collapse (other than foreign loans) were the coffers of the Communist Party and the *obshchaki*, the treasure chests of the Thieves World. The capital was channeled into commercial enterprises, banks, luxury shops, and hotels. It not only spurred the equivalent of Russia's first consumer boom but also merged bureaucrats and gangsters into a uniquely Russian form of crime boss – the comrade criminal.

'There's a big difference between the Russian mafiya and the Cosa Nostra,' Safaryan explained. 'In the West, criminal groups are involved in drugs or other kinds of illegal activities, but in our country the mafiya is involved in legal business. So most of my business friends can't avoid dealing with it.'

By 1993, organized crime allegedly accounted for between 30 and 40 per cent of the national turnover in goods and services, or about twenty billion dollars. Russian law enforcement agencies, who provided the estimate, did not explain how they arrived at the figure. This was not surprising, since no one could agree on an acceptable definition of criminal behaviour.

The effects of this development are viewed with much bleak pessimism by most expert commentators. For example, Gilinskiy (1998, p.239) contends: 'In the sphere of business and commerce, the idea of honest business practices is almost a chimera. We describe the process as one of the criminalization of the economy and of politics.' Rawlinson (1998, p.260) comes to a similar conclusion: 'We are witnessing the criminalization of politics, of the criminal justice system and of society as a whole, as organized criminal influences have become proactive, encouraged by definitional ambiguities of what constitutes organized crime and in turn, legal business.'

It is impossible to deny that, in 1990s' Russia, capitalism has triumphed over the centrally planned system. But in Handelman's terms it is 'capitalism of an older, darker model', unrestrained by legal authorities and institutionalizing a rapaciousness throughout the society: 'And it is not hard to imagine the dangers when a corruption-plagued economy the size of Russia's becomes part of the network of global trade and finance' (Handelman, 1995, p.viii).

The above discussion points to an urgent crisis for Russia in its transition to deregulated markets and capitalism. However, this is no unique case; the same tendencies are also evident anywhere where the impact of global transitions, especially economic changes, are being encountered and confronted. China, for example, also appears to be moving in the direction of rampant marketization. Indeed, the sociologist, Manuel Castells presents a bleak vision of the effects of the globalization of crime resulting in a 'lawless world' for us all:

globalization of crime

> What is new is not the pervasiveness of crime and its impact on politics. What is new is the global linkage of organizational crime, its conditioning of international relations, both economic and political, because of the scale and dynamism of the criminal economy. What is new is the deep penetration, and eventual destruction, of national states in a variety of contexts under the influence of transnational crime.
>
> (Castells, 1997, p.259)

This was the heart of Russia's crime dilemma. The tension between 'good crime' and 'bad crime' recurs throughout this book. For people like Mikhail, the would-be dentist who turned to art smuggling to finance his clinic, crime was what one did to survive. 'There are no laws protecting anyone, and the police are useless, so to tell you the truth, people are getting used to the mafiya,' Mark Melzer, manager of the boxing club in Moscow, told me in 1992. 'It's much clearer and easier to understand than anything else in our country. You know that if you pay, everything is all right. If you don't pay, then you are in shit.' Such 'clarity' at least offered comfort to the average Russian entrepreneur, who found it difficult to keep his hands clean. High taxes and red tape made it extraordinarily hard to conduct business without breaking the law. Nothing in the new Russian economy could be accomplished without a bribe. The only beneficiaries of the situation were corrupt bureaucrats and racketeers, who exploited the nation's legal chaos.

As I pursued the trail of the mafiya through post-Communist society, I kept encountering officials who honestly felt that organized crime was a necessary evil in the transition to a market economy. Unable to perceive any satisfactory way of stopping it, short of the authoritarian measures used by the former regime, many even considered some forms of illegal behaviour a productive means of eliminating the lingering monopolies of the Soviet system. It was an attractively unorthodox, but ultimately barren approach.

(Handelman, 1995, pp.335–6)

Are we, then, heading towards a world in which there is no safe place due to the 'entangled whirlwind of crime, capital and power' (Castells, 1997, p.261)? This of course may be too bleak a scenario and there are countervailing tendencies at work, not least as evidenced in the efforts of transnational institutions such as the OECD, EU and UN to regulate corruption in, and across, nations and regions.

7 Conclusion

The aim of this chapter has been to develop and extend our study of crime in general by looking at two seemingly separate spheres of rule-breaking behaviour. One sphere (corporate crime) is often not considered unambiguously criminal, whereas the other sphere (organized crime) has traditionally been demonized and pathologized as the pinnacle of criminality by agencies of social control and both expert and popular opinion. In the course of our discussion we pointed to both the range and 'serious' criminal character of corporate crime as well as its ambiguous status in terms of traditional legal definitions of crime. We also deconstructed the mythology around organized crime and highlighted its rational, entrepreneurial character. Furthermore, it has been contended throughout this discussion that there are significant points of convergence between the values and organizational dynamics underpinning corporate and organized criminal enterprises, at times making the distinction between the two untenable.

This chapter has thus challenged a number of common assumptions about the nature of the 'problem of crime'. We tend to think of crime in terms of 'ordinary', local crimes that take place on our streets and in local housing estates. And of course we cannot ignore the seriousness of this social problem. However, this chapter has also shown that we cannot ignore in the twenty-first century the increasing threat coming from international crime flows, such as environmental pollution, drugs, fraud and such like, which are the consequences of the globalization of markets. And key actors in these 'crime flows' are organized crime enterprises and corporations. Crime appears at times to be the inevitable consequence of (or depends upon) business, trading and commerce. With the increasing globalization of business and financial transactions and trends towards deregulation comes new multiple opportunities for criminal enterprise, not least the regular collaboration between 'respectable' business and 'organized' crime. Such globalizing trends certainly raise questions about the power of nation states to control crime. They may also suggest a more disorderly and dangerous world in the future.

The study of the crimes of corporate business and organized crime is politically sensitive in that it raises the question of how closely interwoven, if distinguishable at all, are the much vaunted mainstream values of legal risk-taking entrepreneurship in the marketplace and the illegal activities of organized and corporate criminals. Indeed, the difficulty of differentiating the pursuit of legitimate commercial advantage and rule-breaking profiteering goes some way towards explaining the differential response of the authorities and public opinion regarding corporate crime. Crimes of the powerful are no longer invisible but neither are they very visible in the dominant law and order agenda in nation states like the UK. We hear little from home secretaries along the lines of being 'tough on corporate crime, tough on the causes of corporate crime'. Throughout our discussion there has been a recurrent debate about what is 'criminal' and what is 'legal' in different sites and times. In turn, this debate alerts us to the discretionary powers built into the law itself, in which the latter may be a 'flexible friend' for the powerful, often reflecting and stabilizing their interests.

It is also clear that the dynamics examined in this chapter suggest that the moralistic overtones which often accompany the explanation of the crimes of the powerful may be inappropriate. As Ruggiero notes, 'Contrary to analysts adopting such overtones, these types of crime constitute neither exceptional behaviours nor social pathologies' (Ruggiero, 1996, p.155). Furthermore, the most successful organized criminals 'make it' into the legal economy. With the recognition of 'work as crime' and 'crime as work' we also move beyond the search for a specific 'cause' for criminality and instead we explore seemingly non-criminological questions and issues traditionally associated with economics and politics. Thus, when crime is examined as a business process, this alerts us to the problems of funding, technical skills, distribution mechanisms and money-handling facilities (Levi, 1998, p.343). It would seem that crime is one of the options offered to all individuals who happen to be faced with structures of opportunities arising from both legal and illegal domains. In Ruggerio's terms, 'Organized illegal activities seem less the result of poverty, underdevelopment or lack of self control than of its opposite: affluence, development and the control of resources' (Ruggerio, 1996, p.33).

Finally, the issues raised in this chapter may help us to recognize that 'the problem of crime' is both complex and intractable since it cannot be simply reducible to the activities of pathological 'outsiders', whether they be the disadvantaged 'underclass' or the street criminal, or the 'alien' gangster, 'bad apple' businessman or official. Instead, the pursuit of profit, power and control through, at times, illegal enterprise appears to be at the very heart of the institutional fabric of modern capitalist societies. More generally, our discussion forces us to consider why and how in certain social formations some harmful behaviours are legally 'selected' as criminal and others are not. This exploration in turn reveals the critical relationship between social order and social control processes in society. It also reminds us of the artificiality and contingency of all definitions of crime. This raises the issue of whether the very normality of much organized and corporate crime offers the most profound challenge to our thinking on crimes, criminals and social control.

Review questions

- Why is the analysis of corporate crime surrounded by ambiguity?
- In what ways is the crime 'industry'/business related to its legitimate counterpart?
- Are organized and corporate crimes better viewed as pathological or normal features of economic life?
- In what ways does the exploration of corporate and organized crime help us to de/reconstruct the problem of crime?
- What are the connections between the market, globalizing trends and illegal enterprises?

Further reading

Croall (1992 and 1998) and Slapper and Tombs (1999) provide a good general introduction to the subject of corporate crime in a UK context, and Nelken (1997) explores some of the continuing controversies and ambiguities in the criminological study of white-collar crime. For more detailed studies of corporate crime, it is well worth consulting some of the works of Levi (1987, 1991a and 1991b) on the financial sector, Clarke (1990a and 1990b) on business crime and insurance, and Wells (1993) on corporate liability for the consequences of disasters.

For an accessible overview of organized crime, see Hobbs (1997). Block's work is particularly important in rethinking the nature of organized crime throughout the twentieth century (Block, 1991). On the criminalization of post-communist Russia, see both Rawlinson (1998) and Handelman (1995).

The most comprehensive overview of the area covered in this chapter is Ruggiero (1996). This book is also a challenging critique of the tendency for criminologists to analyse corporate crime and organized crime as separate and distinct forms of activity. See also Ruggiero's (2000) text which provides a joint analysis of 'crimes of the street' and 'crimes of the elite'.

References

Arlacchi, P. (1998) 'Some observations on illegal markets', in Ruggiero, V. *et al.* (1998).

Benson, M.L. (1985) 'Denying the guilty mind: accounting for involvement in a white-collar crime', *Criminology*, vol.23, no.4, pp.583–604.

Block, A. (1983) *East Side-West Side: Organizing Crime in New York 1930–1950*, Newark, NJ, Transaction Books.

Block, A. (1991) *Perspectives on Organizing Crime: Essays in Opposition*, Dordrecht, Kluwer.

Box, S. (1983) *Power, Crime and Mystification*, London, Tavistock. (Extract reprinted as 'Crime, power and ideological mystification' in Muncie *et al.*, 1996.)

Braithwaite, J. (1989) *Crime, Shame and Reintegration*, Cambridge, Cambridge University Press. (Extract reprinted as 'Reintegrative shaming' in Muncie *et al.*, 1996.)

Carson, W.G. (1982) *The Other Price of Britain's Oil*, Oxford, Martin Robertson.

Castells, M. (1997) *The Power of Identity*, Oxford, Blackwell.

Clarke, M. (1990a) *Business Crime: Its Nature and Control*, Cambridge, Polity.

Clarke, M. (1990b) 'The control of insurance fraud: a comparative view', *British Journal of Criminology*, vol.30, no.1, pp.1–23.

Clarke, M. (1993) 'EC Fraud', in Pearce, F. and Woodiwiss, M. (1993).

Cook, D. (1989) *Rich Law, Poor Law: Differential Responses to Tax and Supplementary Benefit Fraud*, Buckingham, Open University Press.

Croall, H. (1992) *White-Collar Crime*, Buckingham, Open University Press.

Croall, H. (1998) *Crime and Society in Britain,* London, Longman.

Deane, K.D. (1981) 'Tax evasion, criminality and sentencing the tax offender', *British Journal of Criminology*, vol.21, no.1, pp.47–57.

Findlay, M. (1998) *The Globalization of Crime*, Cambridge, Cambridge University Press.

Geis, G. and Meier, R.F. (eds) (1977) *White-Collar Crime,* New York, Free Press.

Gilinskiy, Y. (1998) 'The market and crime in Russia', in Ruggiero, V. *et al.* (1998).

Green, G. (1990) *Occupational Crime*, Chicago, IL, Nelson Hall.

Handelman, S. (1995) *Comrade Criminal: Russia's New Mafiya*, New Haven, CT, Yale University Press.

Hobbs, D. (1995) *Bad Business,* Oxford, Oxford University Press.

Hobbs, D. (1997) 'Criminal collaboration' in Maguire, M. *et al.* (1997).

Hobbs, D. and Dunningham, C. (1998) 'Global organized crime: context and pretext', in Ruggiero, V. *et al.* (1998).

Huntington, S. (1998) *The Clash of Civilizations and the Remaking of World Order*, London, Touchstone.

Hutter, B. (1988) *The Reasonable Arm of the Law*, Oxford, Clarendon Press.

Levi, M. (1987) *Regulating Fraud: White-Collar Crime and the Criminal Process,* London, Tavistock.

Levi, M. (1989) 'Sentencing white collar-criminals', in Carlen, P. and Cook, D. (eds) *Paying for Crime*, Buckingham, Open University Press.

Levi, M. (1991a) 'Pecunia non olet: cleansing the money-launderers from the temple', *Crime, Law and Social Change*, vol.16, pp.217–302.

Levi, M. (1991b) 'Regulating money laundering: the death of bank secrecy in the UK', *British Journal of Criminology*, vol.31, no.2, pp.109–25.

Levi, M. (1998) 'Perspectives on "organized crime": an overview', *Howard Journal*, vol.37, no.4, pp.335–45.

Levi, M. (1999) 'White collar crime in the press', paper delivered at the British Criminology Conference, Liverpool.

Levi, M. and Maguire, M. (1998) 'Crime and policy in Europe', in Bailey, J. (ed.) *Social Europe,* London, Longman.

Luttwak, E. (1995) 'Does the Russian Mafia deserve the Nobel prize for economics?', *London Review of Books*, vol.17, no.15, p.7.

Maguire, M., Morgan, R. and Reiner, R. (eds) (1997) *The Oxford Handbook of Criminology* (2nd edn), Oxford, Clarendon Press.

Mars, G. (1982) *Cheats at Work: An Anthology of Workplace Crime*, London, Allen and Unwin.

McLaughlin, E. (2001) 'Key issues in policework', in McLaughlin, E. and Muncie, J. (eds) *Controlling Crime* (2nd edn), London, Sage in association with The Open University.

Muncie, J., McLaughlin, E. and Langan, M. (eds) (1996) *Criminological Perspectives: A Reader*, London, Sage in association with The Open University.

Nelken, D. (1997) 'White collar crime', in Maguire, M. *et al.* (1997).

Norton-Taylor, R. (1995) *Truth is a Difficult Concept: Inside the Scott Inquiry*, London, Fourth Estate.

Pearce, F. (1976) *Crimes of the Powerful: Marxism, Crime and Deviance*, London, Pluto.

Pearce, F. and Tombs, S. (1993) 'Union Carbide and Bhopal', in Pearce, F. and Woodiwiss, M. (1993).

Pearce, F. and Tombs, S. (1998) *Toxic Capitalism: Corporate Crime and the Chemical Industry*, Aldershot, Ashgate.

Pearce, F. and Woodiwiss, M. (eds) (1993) *Global Crime Connections: Dynamics and Control*, London, Macmillan.

Rawlinson, P. (1998) 'Russian organized crime: moving beyond ideology', in Ruggiero, V. *et al.* (1998)

Robb, G. (1992) *White-Collar Crime in Modern England: Financial Fraud and Business Morality, 1845–1929*, Cambridge, Cambridge University Press.

Ruggiero, V. (1996) *Organized and Corporate Crime in Europe*, Aldershot, Dartmouth.

Ruggiero, V. (2000) *Crime and Markets: Essays in Anti-Criminology,* Oxford, Oxford University Press.

Ruggiero, V. South, N. and Taylor, I. (eds) (1998) *The New European Criminology: Crime and Social Order in Europe*, London, Routledge.

Sherry, F. (1986) *Raiders and Rebels*, New York, Hearst Marine Books.

Slapper, G. and Tombs, S. (1999) *Corporate Crime*, London, Longman.

Stelfox, P. (1998) 'Policing lower levels of organized crime in England and Wales', *Howard Journal*, vol.37, no.4, pp.393–406.

Sutherland, E.H. (1949/1967) *White-Collar Crime*, New York, Holt, Rinehart and Winston.

Wells, C. (1993) *Corporations and Criminal Responsibility,* Oxford, Clarendon Press.

Woodiwiss, M. (1993) 'Crime's global reach', in Pearce, F. and Woodiwiss, M. (1993).

CHAPTER 7

Political Violence, Terrorism and States of Fear

by Eugene McLaughlin

Contents

1 Introduction

Chapter 6 outlined the debates concerning the relationship between crime, power and social order. This chapter extends the debate by examining the question of violent political crime, both against and by the state. We begin by locating political violence in relation to other forms of violence, and move on to address the crucial issue of the relationship between the nation state and violence. The chapter then considers how states respond to those individuals and groups who proclaim that their violence and law-breaking are motivated by 'higher' political ideals. In the sections that follow, we consider how and why only certain actions are defined as 'terrorism' and analyse what the implications of such labelling can be. In considering these issues, we begin to see how, transnationally, the monopoly of violence wielded by the nation state can be used to victimize citizens through gross human-rights violations such as torture, judicial murder, genocide and ethnic cleansing. Finally, we reflect on the emergent international criminal justice framework for the control of political violence and terror. Throughout this chapter, a central question to be considered is whether the discourses and procedures of international criminal law are able to uphold civil liberties and human rights and provide meaningful justice and reparation for those who have been the victims of state criminality.

The types of crime considered in this chapter are beginning to occupy a more central place on the criminological agenda as it is increasingly recognized that they undermine all notions of the rule of law, civil liberties and human rights.

2 Theorizing violence

A brief survey of the debates on how violence should be conceptualized indicate that criminologists need to recognize the following points as paramount. Firstly, in common with many concepts employed for both descriptive and analytical purposes, the term 'violence' lacks precision, making it difficult to define. **rhetoric of violence** Foucault (1980) holds that there is a rhetoric of violence that classifies certain behaviours, events and individuals as violent. This rhetoric produces and reproduces subjects of violence and structures 'violence' as a seemingly coherent, unproblematic 'fact'. And, yet, it could be contended that embedded in events and actions, which are perceived and understood as 'violent', are highly variable, contingent, and conflicting conceptions of social and moral order.

It might be argued that the only way to produce a precise and unambiguous definition of the concept of violence is to concentrate on the archetypal public representation: the infliction of serious or irreparable physical damage or injury instrumentally or impulsively wrought by a 'dangerous stranger' upon the body of another human being. It is perhaps this concept of violence that concerns most law-abiding citizens. However, other analysts have expanded its meaning to include the destruction of property, the threat of violence, and damaging psychological processes, such as domination, humiliation and degradation. Stanko (1998, p.3) argues that violence is 'any behaviour by an individual that intentionally threatens, attempts to inflict, or does cause, physical, sexual or psychological harm to others or to themselves. An individual may commit an act of violence or intimidation with the support of a group or even the state'. Skolnick (1969, p.5) contends that 'Less dramatic but equally destructive processes may occur well within the routine operation of "orderly" social life … indifference, inaction, and slow decay that routinely afflict the poor are far more destructive than the bomb in the night. High infant mortality rates or rates of preventable disease, perpetuated through discrimination, take a far greater toll than civil disorder'. Bourdieu (1977) agrees, arguing that we need to acknowledge the 'symbolic violence' that is continually reproduced in dominant socio-economic relations.

symbolic violence

A second key element in conceptualizing violence is the recognition that only certain categories of violence are defined as illegal and as a result subject to regulation. Acts of criminal violence normally encompass discrete events that have beginnings and ends and involve individuals who intentionally physically damage or destroy other human beings in a specific location at a specific time. Murder, assault, rape and robbery are the paradigmatic crimes of violence that hold a hegemonic position in legal discourse and public imagination; institutional or structural violence neither falls within the domain of the criminal law nor the process of criminalization (Skolnick, 1969; Bourdieu, 1977).

Third, the causes of, and solutions to, human violence have long troubled and divided the academic community. Socio-biology, anthropology, psychology, psychiatry, theology, philosophy and sociology have all made the act itself an object of study, and have also looked at the perpetrators, the victims, the motivational factors and the social and psychosocial contexts in which violence occurs. Different disciplines have presented very diverse explanations for the root causes of violent forms of human aggression. More recent research has been directed by explorations of the connections between aggression, sex and gender across time, place and culture, and there is agreement that questions of violent masculinities need to be brought to the fore and addressed (see, for example, Segal, 1990, Levi, 1997, Bowker, 1998; Dobash and Dobash, 1999; Radford *et al.*, 2000; see also Chapter 5, section 5).

Fourth, as we have seen earlier in this book (Chapter 5) and as we will in the course of this chapter, violence is not always unequivocally condemned. While it is generally perceived as a *prima facie* moral transgression that 'dehumanizes' both perpetrator and victim and decivilizes society, as Turpin and Kurtz (1997) and Whitner (1997) note, societies can exhibit ambiguous and contradictory reactions to violence. For example, popular cultural representations or simulations of violence are capable of triggering both critical artistic praise *and* moral condemnation.

Stanley Kubrick's Clockwork Orange *has remained a central reference point in the debate over the effect of violent films on young people*

285

The belief that certain categories of violence are innate to human nature has generated many attempts to explain away or justify violence, irrespective of whether or not it is legal. As we shall see in this chapter, it has been in certain instances rendered socially acceptable by various techniques of neutralization.

> In defence of violence, man has insisted that he was provoked beyond human endurance; he has stated that he was not responsible by reason of insanity; he has pointed out that he acted only in self-defence; he has claimed that honour and manhood required violent response; he has maintained that he never intended to produce the outcome that occurred; he has said that what he did was for the ultimate good of society; and he has felt, if not said, that his actions were inescapably necessary given the situation in which he has found himself.
>
> (McNeil, 1966, p.155)

2.1   Theorizing political violence

A great deal of time has been given to investigating the question of whether it is possible to distinguish between 'political' and other forms of violence. According to Nieburg (1969, p.13), the term refers to 'acts of disruption, destruction, injury whose purpose, choice of targets or victims, surrounding circumstances, implementation, and/or effects have political significance, that is, tend to modify the behaviour of others in a bargaining situation, that has consequences for the social system'. He also identifies two forms of political violence: state-sanctioned violence and internal violence against the state.

2.1.1   Nation state-sanctioned violence

Max Weber asserted that there is one characteristic above all others that marks out the form, structure and procedures of the modern state:

> Ultimately one can define the modern state sociologically only in terms of the specific *means* peculiar to it, as to every political association, namely the use of physical force ... Of course force is certainly not the normal or the only means of the state – nobody says that – but force is a means specific to the state. Today, the relation between the state and violence is an especially intimate one ... we have to say that a state is a human community that successfully claims the *monopoly of the legitimate use of physical force* within a given territory ... the right to use physical force is ascribed to other institutions or to individuals only to the extent to which the state permits it. The state is considered the sole source of the 'right' to use violence.
>
> (Weber, 1970, p.77)

The exceptional power and potency of the state, irrespective of its specific social, political or ethnic formation, spatial or temporal setting, lie in its monopolization and institutionalization of violence. Here we meet a question that should be central to criminology: why does the state claim such a unique right or privilege? To persist as a sovereign entity, the nation state must possess sufficient coercive powers to provide a security umbrella for the citizenry and, in doing so, restrain citizens from resorting to violence to resolve their own private disputes. The nation state's monopoly of violence, in the final instance, is the *de facto* foundation of internal social order (Tilly, 1985).

Nevertheless, it is important to address how specific state forms conceptualize and utilize this 'monopoly of violence'. In theory, the democratic state's custodianship of violence is regulated and can only be deployed within clearly defined parameters. Internally, nation state violence is transformed into **state violence** 'legitimate force' by being bound by the rule of law, the constitutional civil and human rights of the citizenry, and through its institutionalization in policing and military bureaucracies that are governed by operational procedures and disciplinary codes of conduct. For violence by state agencies and officials to be considered legitimate, it must only be used in the last resort and only when all avenues of rational persuasion and peaceful resolution have been exhausted. It must also be minimal in application.

Externally, the nation state's right to resort to violence is also regulated. The **legitimate** apogée of organized mass violence between states, warfare is a rule-governed **force** and ordered activity. It is framed formally by a tangle of international 'laws of war' and international humanitarian law that encompass both *when* states can resort to armed conflict (*jus ad bellum*) and *how* the actual conduct and practice of warfare (*jus in bello*) should be carried out. Significantly, 'war', a highly problematic concept in itself, is not a 'crime': it is seen as inevitable and morally justified in certain circumstances (see Hinde and Watson, 1995). All states have inalienable rights under international law to use armed force in certain exceptional 'just war' circumstances: for example, to resist aggression, protect their territory, defend their cultural and ethnic integrity and fulfil internationally recognized treaty obligations. Hence, we see that there are clearly identifiable moments when states can assert the right to kill and destroy.

There are also detailed international agreements, rules, declarations, conventions, resolutions and protocols that aim to restrain, moderate, regulate and 'civilize' the kind and degree of violence resorted to in times of war (Weschler, 1999, Roberts and Guelff, 2000). Two key humanitarian precepts underpin this particular set of laws:

1   The 'principle of distinction', which asserts that armed conflict ought to be conducted exclusively by readily identifiable combatants, and that unarmed and uninvolved civilians are not legitimate targets.

2   The 'principle of proportionality', which directs that all loss of life and damage to property should be strictly comparable to the military advantage likely to be gained.

ACTIVITY 7.1

What forms of behaviour and actions do you think are outlawed by the laws of war? For what reasons?

In the aftermath of the Hague Conventions of 1899 and 1907, the European nation states accepted in principle that certain violations of the laws of war were criminal and would incur individual responsibility. Following the end of the Second World War, the International Military Tribunal at Nuremberg (1945–46) adopted what seemed a straightforward criminal justice (rather than political or military) approach to produce a basic definition of what constitutes a war **war crime** crime. This, according to the tribunal, comprised:

- the murder, ill-treatment, torture, or deportation to slave labour or for any other purpose, of civilians of or in occupied territory; the murder, ill-treatment or torture of prisoners of war; the killing of hostages; the plunder of property; the wanton destruction of human settlements ; and devastation not warranted by military necessity.

crime of obedience

Members of the armed forces and civilians who violate these laws are considered guilty of committing war crimes and can be judged individually and, where appropriate, sanctioned by international or national courts and military tribunals. This is the case even when their actions have been ordered by a political leader or by commanding officers. Individuals accused of war crimes cannot absolve themselves of criminal responsibility by citing an official position or by arguing that they were obeying superior orders: this is defined as the 'crime of obedience'. Conversely, commanding officers are responsible for violations carried out by their troops unless they self-evidently attempted to suppress them. At a general level, war crimes are acts that retain their essential criminal nature even though they are committed by individuals in time of war and/or under orders.

crimes against humanity

Perhaps as significantly, the tribunal created two further new categories of crime. A 'crime against peace' was established to encompass the planning, preparation, initiation or waging of a war of aggression, or a war in flagrant and unjustified violation of international treaties. There was also the first formal acknowledgement of crimes against humanity in international law. These crimes were classified as the:

> murder, extermination, enslavement or deportation, and other inhumane acts committed against any civilian population, before or during the war or persecutions on political, racial or religious grounds in the execution of or in connection with any crime within the jurisdiction of the Tribunal, whether or not in violation of the domestic law of the country in question.
>
> (International Military Tribunal, 1947, vol.1, p.11)

genocide

In 1948, the United Nations (UN) re-named this as the crime of 'genocide', and stressed that it was a crime in peacetime as well as during a war to seek systematically and deliberately to eradicate, or attempt to eradicate, a national, ethnic, racial or religious group. In its Convention on the Prevention and Punishment of the Crime of Genocide, the UN defined genocide as the 'ultimate crime' and the gravest of all violations of human rights. The convention, which predated the UN Universal Declaration of Human Rights by one day, also crucially established that genocide was not a private nation-state issue but a matter of international law. Under it, states have a legal obligation not only to not commit genocide themselves but also to take appropriate action for the prevention, suppression and punishment of genocide committed by other states.

Torture of combatants, prisoners of war and non-combatants was formally prohibited by the Universal Declaration of Human Rights in 1948. There have been a succession of laws enacted throughout the world since then that also outlaw the use of torture. These include the:

- 1949 Geneva Conventions Relative to the Treatment of Prisoners of War and Relative to the Protection of Civilian Persons in Time of War.

- 1950 European Convention for the Protection of Human Rights and Fundamental Freedoms.

- 1984 United Nations Convention Against Torture and Other Cruel, Inhuman or Degrading Treatment or Punishment, which makes torture a crime triable anywhere and not only in the country in which it is committed.

- 1987 European Convention for the Prevention of Torture and Inhuman or Degrading Treatment or Punishment and a Committee for the Prevention of Torture (which has the right to visit any site within the territory of a signatory to the Convention where citizens are being detained) (see Boulesbaa, 1999).

Before we move on, it is worth pointing out that the criminal law discourse and the stress on individual – as opposed to collective – responsibility championed by the Nuremberg tribunal was deemed by many jurists to be inappropriate (Cesarani 1992; Coates, 1999). The legality of the trials was called into question because defendants were being held to account for crimes that had been created *ad hoc* and ex-*post facto*. Was it *just* that individuals could be asked to account for crimes that they didn't know they were committing? There was also unease about the prosecuting authorities' rejection of the defence of obeying orders. This raised the question of whether professional soldiers could be expected to disobey the chain-of-command and risk a military court martial. In addition, the fact that only 177 Nazis were indicted, with 25 being sentenced to death and 20 to life imprisonment, threw up as many questions as it answered. Some argued that holding these few individuals to account for the slaughter of millions could generate accusations of tokenism, scapegoating, or the conducting of show trials, transform defendants into victims and even martyrs, and perpetuate the myth that such actions resulted from the machinations of a few evil individuals rather than the logical outcome of state policies that were ideologically approved by significant sections of German society.

Survivors of Auschwitz during the first hours of the concentration camp's liberation by soldiers of the Soviet Army, 27 January 1945. Colonel Telford Taylor, US Prosecutor at Nuremberg, stated: 'Crime has been piled upon crime … until we are in danger of losing our sense of proportion. We have heard so much of mass extermination that we are likely to forget that simple murder is a capital offence' (quoted in Cesarani, 1992, p.178)

In addition, the Nuremberg tribunal gave rise to questions that post-Nuremberg tribunals would have to address:

■ What punishment could the tribunal possibly pass which could be seen as fitting retribution given the nature and sheer scale of these crimes and which would act as a deterrence to others?

■ How would the international community reform, and indeed rehabilitate, the guilty society in which the crimes occurred in order to prevent them from happening again?

■ What would be an appropriate act of communal atonement?

2.1.2 Violence against the nation state

When we move on to examine the internal use of violence against the nation state, two main issues arise: first, we have to ask whether violence can ever be seen as a legitimate means of settling political disputes or grievances. Are citizens under an a priori moral obligation to comply with the law and accept the exisiting social order – no matter how unjust or oppressive – if no means other than violence will overthrow it? Second is a question that perplexes legislators: how should the law classify and treat those who resort to violence for political reasons? In particular, should the category of political offender be formally recognized by the state?

Is there a right to resort to violence? Political theorists, such as Zures *et al.* (1999) and della Porta and Diani (1999), argue that only rational debate and compromise can resolve political grievances, and that challenging the nation state's monopoly of violence often works to compound existing injustices. They argue that direct action can give the authorities the justification to intensify authoritarian clampdowns and create a culture of coercion, thereby creating a destabilizing influence on the body politic and civil society. If this argument is developed further, it could be proposed that violence against the state can only be embarked upon when the following moral criteria are met:

1   There must be 'just cause'. This means that a fundamental injustice afflicting a significant proportion of the population must exist.

2   Violence must be a last resort. All lawful, and non-violent methods, processes of negotiation and means of protest (including civil disobedience) must have been tried and demonstrably found wanting.

3   The violence must remain only one part of a wider socio-political struggle and should be defensive or reactive rather than aggressive or proactive in nature.

4   Due deliberation must be given to limiting the extent and seriousness of the violence: the forms of violence resorted to must be strictly limited.

5   Violent strategy must always be a means to a negotiable end, and restraint must be exercised to ensure that violence does not become a nihilistic end in itself.

6   Advocates of a violent strategy must demonstrate that such a strategy can correct the injustice.

It could be argued, however, that such an 'exceptionality' conceptualization is highly problematic because it severely curtails the circumstances under which a citizenry can resort to violent protest. Resorting to violence has frequently been a powerful catalyst for change, and central, in many geographical settings, to the achievement of basic human rights and justice, a case in point being the struggle to overthrow apartheid in South Africa:

> The time comes in the life of any nation when there remain only two choices: submit or fight. That fight has now come in South Africa ... We shall not submit ... The liberation organizations have consistently followed a policy of non-violence – because we prefer peaceful change to civil war, but our patience is not endless. The government has interpreted our peacefulness as weakness but government force will no longer be met by non-violence.
>
> The choice is not ours ... It has been made for us by the government, which has answered every peaceable demand for rights and freedom with force. Umkhonto we Sizwe will be at the frontline of our defence.
>
> (Nelson Mandela in 1961, quoted in Pinchuck, 1994, pp.92–3)

We cannot explore the issue of political criminality in depth here. Nevertheless, it is essential that we touch on a few key points and consider them briefly. The first consideration is to ask how the state should act towards those who challenge its political authority and power.

Before the French Revolution, most crimes against political rulers were **political** defined as 'treason': in Roman law, they were considered crimes against sacred **criminality** authority (*lèse-majesté*). This encompassed acts of betrayal, challenges to political authority, sedition, assassination, hindrance of the official function, and usurpation, of the state's powers. Significantly, it also included conspiracy to act as well as the deed itself. Those accused of politically motivated crimes were likely to suffer gruesome public punishment (including judicially regulated torture), which was frequently much more exacting than that sanctioned against 'ordinary' criminals. As Foucault (1979) has commented, the more rational and selfless the act, the less pardonable it was deemed to be.

By the nineteenth century, however, politically motivated crime came to be redefined in Western Europe as an offence against the state (*lèse-nation*). A consequence of the change in law was that the political offender came to be viewed in certain countries as motivated neither by private avarice nor by vindictiveness but by principled considerations such as opposing autocratic regimes in the name of liberal democracy or championing the cause of nationalism:

> It may ... happen that in the course of committing these Crimes, and with a view to facilitating the commission of them, other acts are done which, in everything but the accompanying Motive, are not distinguishable from ordinary Crimes. A question, then, may be presented whether these Acts ought to be treated as (1.) ordinary Crimes, and no more nor less, regard being had only to the Intention and not to the Motive; or (2.) as merely incidents to or aggravation of the Political Offence, regard being had to the Motive, and not to the Intention; or (3.) as Acts qualified by reference both to the Intention and to the Motive, and so, as *sui generis*, being punishable on principles founded on the special views of Political expediency.
>
> (quoted in Radzinowicz and Hood, 1990, p.404)

It was the recognition that the use of violence could be politically progressive both in intent and outcome that prompted the change in official attitude towards the political offender in certain European jurisdictions. The principle that such offenders should be dealt with 'politically' rather than in accordance with the strict provisions of the criminal law found its place in several European penal codes.

> Whereas formerly, the political criminal was treated as a public enemy, he is today considered as a friend of the public good ... his criminality cannot be compared with that of the ordinary malefactor, with the murderer, the thief, etc. The criminality has not at all the same morality. It is only relative, dependent on time, place, circumstances, the institutions of the land, and it is often inspired by noble sentiments, by disinterested motives, by devotion to persons and principles, by love of one's country. In conclusion, the criminality is only passing.
>
> (quoted in Ingraham, 1979, p.35)

England faced the challenge posed by the Fenians in Ireland and the Suffragettes at home. Both groups committed acts that were clear breaches of the criminal law in the furtherance of political objectives, and during the 1860s heated parliamentary and press discussions ensued about whether the concept of 'political offender' should be explicitly acknowledged in law.

Parliamentary debate centred on whether England was deviating from international convention in treating Fenian prisoners charged with treason-felony more harshly than common criminals on the grounds that they were much more of a threat to the interests of the state. Fenian offenders informed the courts that they regarded their trials as political and that they considered their offence to be of a special character, implying in their view no criminal culpability. They proceeded to engage in a series of protests, for example, when their political **political** status went unrecognized by the courts or the penal authorities. This led to **status** further exceptional punishment by prison authorities and courts, and accompanying public protest and campaigns for a political amnesty argued that the prison authorities were trying to break, through torture, the political resolve of the Fenian prisoners (Hopper, 1984). During the passage of the 1877 Prison Act, Irish and Liberal MPs, in an effort to resolve the issue, proposed that the government establish a penal regime, similar to the *custodia honesta* prison regimes in Europe. These were run on the principle that it was not practicable to reform ideologically committed offenders.

Because of their 'direct action' tactics during the 'Women's War' (1905–10), the Suffragettes also raised the question of whether they should be treated as political offenders. One stumbling block for legislators was the Suffragettes' refusal to recognize the legitimacy of court proceedings. They asserted that they were not under any a priori obligation to accept the laws promulgated by a male political establishment and demanded that they be treated as political prisoners (Pankhurst, 1931, pp.134–5). In prison, they launched a campaign of resistance in the form of disobedience, riot and hunger strikes. In turn, they had to endure strip-searching, hosings, beatings, being placed in canvas straitjackets and solitary confinement and being forcibly fed. In an attempt to break the deadlock, Keir Hardie, then leader of the Independent Labour Party, introduced a Prison (Political Offence) bill to achieve treatment as *de facto* political offenders for Suffragettes. It was subsequently blocked by the Home Office.

The case of both the Fenians and the Suffragettes highlights why certain observers advocated treating political offenders differently from other detainees. Politically motivated offenders were seen as being beyond the grasp of the conventional criminal justice system and, indeed, posing a fundamental challenge to its very legitimacy. There was also the possibility that those who defined themselves as political prisoners could, through their resistance to the process of criminalization and representation of themselves as victims and martyrs, gain considerable public sympathy with demands for clemency or outright amnesty. By demanding that their acts be considered in terms of intention rather than in terms of the acts themselves, political offenders tested to the limit the questions: what is crime? and what is criminal justice?

Ingraham (1979), however, notes that the First World War heralded a significant change in the attitude of the European powers to political criminals. This is evidenced by the more repressive laws sanctioned to deal with them that emerged over the following decades. Most notably, European nation states returned to using the death penalty for crimes which were political in nature. Various external and internal reasons can be found for the cause of this shift in policy. First, two world wars, escalating anti-colonialist struggles and the rise of transnational ideologies of communism, anarchism and fascism re-awakened governmental anxieties about treason, espionage, sabotage, conspiracy and subversion. Second, a profound reordering of the state and civil society had taken place across Europe. The processes of governance were now democratized, political and industrial rights were recognized legally and the concurrent 'institutionalization' of political conflict occurred. Such transformations reinforced a perception that political reform could be realized gradually, through rational discourse and compromise. Finally, as Peters (1985) suggests, the identification of the state with an ethnic national community

> constituted in the early twentieth-century state a very different organism from the abstract State of the Enlightenment and its nineteenth century successors, the eclectics, classicists, utilitarians and positivists. Now the state, like the law, represented, indeed personified, a people, and it was operated according to the people's will; those who opposed it, whether ordinary criminals or political criminals, opposed the will of the people, and gradually the political criminal came to be regarded as more dangerous – and more repulsive – than the ordinary criminal.
>
> (Peters, 1985, p.120)

However, as we shall see in section 3 below, perceptions of violent crime against the state were to shift again so that, by the late twentieth century, the political criminal was now reconceptualized as the 'terrorist'.

3   Deconstructing the problem of 'terrorism'

In the course of the twentieth century, the 'political criminal' was transformed into the 'terrorist'. From the late 1960s onwards, terrorism has been elevated to **terrorism** the status of the ultimate criminal threat to world order because it has the capacity to disrupt and paralyse, on a national and transnational scale, virtually every aspect of life. According to Johnson:

Terrorism is the cancer of the modern world. No state is immune to it. It is a dynamic organism which attacks the healthy flesh of the surrounding society. It has the essential hallmark of malignant cancer; unless treated, and treated drastically, its growth is inexorable, until it poisons and engulfs the society on which it feeds and drags it down to destruction.

(Johnson, 1986, p.31)

During the 1980s and 1990s, the news media was saturated with reports of national and global 'terrorist' incidents, ringing condemnations of atrocities that were said to plumb new depths of savagery and new transnational agreements for the prevention and punishment of such inhuman acts. Very soon it was possible to provide seemingly definitive answers to the questions: what is terrorism? and who are terrorists?

ACTIVITY 7.2

Make a note of what you think are the defining features and images of terrorism. You will need to consider the following questions:

- What are acts of terrorism?

- Whom does terrorism target?

- What type of person carries out such acts?

- Which political ideologies, organizations and countries are readily associated with terrorism?

- What are the differences between those labelled as terrorists, guerrillas, freedom-fighters or political criminals?

Analyse how you have reached your conclusions. Was the news media an important source of your information?

Hogan and Walker (1989) argue that governments now use the terms 'terrorism' and 'terrorist' rather than the terms 'political violence' and 'political offenders' because the former terms have much wider moral and ideological potency. Three key points can be drawn from their analysis:

1   Terrorism is defined as violence that deliberately targets civilians who have no chance of defending themselves.

2   Terrorism is revolutionary in nature and conducted by sub-state groups.

3   Terrorists are pathologically deranged, fanatical individuals, who operate in a clandestine manner with the support of a minority of 'rogue' states who use them to advance their own geopolitical interests.

A closer examination of these defining features, nevertheless, will illustrate that any attempt to draw clear boundaries around who are the terrorists and to distinguish between terrorism and orthodox forms of warfare is far from simple. It is only by reflecting critically on its essential features that it is possible to produce an extensive reconstruction and reconceptualization of the problem of terrorism.

3.1   The targets of terrorism

Few of us are immune to the fall-out from 'terrorist' acts, whether we are direct witnesses to the carnage and devastation caused by a no-warning bomb or gun attack or if it is only as media witnesses from the other side of the world.

> I can only say to the people who committed that act of appalling violence that those children did not deserve what they went through and to those who let off that sort of bomb in that area is the most cruel and inhumane thing I have seen in my life. I only hope the people who did it will now stop. I don't want them punished for what they did. I just want them to say now that they will finish it, they will stop it and they won't do it to anybody else's children.
>
> (Victor Barker, father of 12-year-old James Barker, who died in the Omagh Bombing by the Real IRA in August 1998, *Derry Journal*, 21 August 1998, p.9)

Terrorists, according to writers such as Hoffman (1999) and Stern (1999), intend to generate shock and spread fear and insecurity by deliberately targeting innocent, defenceless bystanders. The rationale of acts of indiscriminate violence is to provoke a public awareness that if no-one in particular is the target, no-one can feel safe. Thus, the terrorist act is a form of symbolic communication designed by its perpetrator(s) to cause fear and terror in an audience much broader than the immediate victim. In addition, acts of terrorism are the most visible manifestation to a citizenry that the state has insufficient control of an integral aspect of its sovereignty – its monopoly of violence. These are the features, it could be argued, that distinguish terrorism from conventional warfare and, indeed, from the actions of freedom-fighters:

> In seeking to destroy freedom and democracy, terrorists deliberately target non-combatants for their own cynical purposes. They kill and maim defenceless men, women and children. They murder judges, newspaper reporters, elected officials, government administrators, labour leaders, policemen, priests and others who defend the values of civilized society. Freedom fighters, in contrast, seek to adhere to international law and civilized standards of conduct. They attack military targets, not defenceless citizens. Non-combatant casualties in this context are an aberration or attributable to the fortunes of war. They are not the result of deliberate policy designed to terrorize the opposition.
>
> (US President George Bush, quoted in Brogan, 1992, p.543)

However, this broad conceptualization of terrorism is deficient in several respects. First, as Taylor (1993) has noted, officially designated terrorists go to considerable lengths to deny that they primarily target civilians and, in certain instances, have apologized publicly for what they define as 'military actions' that have gone disastrously wrong. Second, they argue, in classic 'just war' tradition, that physical force is used only in so far as no other political methods are available or effective. Third, it could be argued that their violence has a specific and identifiable purpose and is measured by its likely outcome.

Conversely, accounts of conventional twentieth-century military campaigns and wars remind us that the difference between terrorist atrocities and the conduct of conventional war (irrespective of what the aforementioned laws of war stipulate) may not be so clear-cut. For instance, in 1938, Winston Churchill announced that, if war with Germany was declared, it would be no part of British policy to breach the 'principle of distinction' because:

> In the first place, it is against international law to bomb civilians as such and to make deliberate attacks upon civilian populations. That is undoubtedly a violation of international law. In the second place, targets which are aimed at from the air must be legitimate military objectives and must be capable of identification. In the third place, reasonable care must be taken in attacking those military objectives so that by carelessness a civilian population in the neighbourhood is not bombed.
>
> (quoted in Best, 1994, p.200)

However, the realities of waging total war proved much more complicated than Churchill had anticipated, especially when it was realized that adhering strictly to the rules was resulting in heavy casualties among Allied air crews. These operational difficulties led to a dramatic redefinition of what constituted a 'legitimate target': not merely military forces and installations, but also factories engaged in the manufacture of military supplies and key lines of communications. The presence of civilians would no longer rule out attacks on factories, ports, airports, railway stations, roads or dams. Moreover, if significant military installations were sited in densely populated urban areas, they could also be viewed as legitimate targets.

It was this policy shift that created the lasting controversy about the legality or otherwise of the Allies' 'saturation bombing' of German cities and the dropping of atom bombs on Japan in 1945. These are among the most significant operations of the Second World War. They hastened the end of a conflict in which the Nazis and the Japanese had broken all the laws of war and shocked the conscience of humankind by using conquered populations as slave labour; ruthessly abusing prisoners of war; massacring and mutilating non-combatants; authorizing mass rape; conducting grotesque medical experiments; and systematically murdering millions in history's greatest example of industrialized genocide. The Allied bombings were unquestionably horrific but, according to moral philosopher Michael Walzer (1977), a temporary lowering of moral and legal standards was necessary because this was the 'supreme emergency' situation. The violence deployed was for the ultimate 'good war' or just cause, namely the defence of civilization.

Nonetheless, it is also necessary that we examine where the line between war crime and non-war crime was drawn. It could be reasoned, for instance, that those responsible for masterminding and sanctioning the 'war within a war' strategy should have been held to account before a court of law for the slaughter of civilians on an unprecedented scale. In this argument, it could be contended, for instance, that Britain and the United States, like Germany, had breached the rules of war by deliberately incinerating German and Japanese cities that had no significant military or industrial installations. 'Without mercy' bombings could be viewed as being specifically calculated to terrorize and produce a stupefying effect on the morale of the civilian population. Giddens (1985, p.33) argues, for example, that: 'the atomic bombs dropped on Hiroshima and Nagasaki, were nothing more nor less than a concentrated application of terror, designed to shock Japan into surrender'. And with regard to the bombing of Germany, there is evidence to suggest that certain sections of the British war cabinet, the Air Staff Command, and even aircrews, became increasingly troubled when forced to reflect upon the possibility that they could be held to account under the international laws of war. In 1945, for example, Churchill stated:

It seems to me that the moment has come when the question of bombing of German cities simply for the sake of increasing the terror, though under other pretexts, should be reviewed. Otherwise we shall come into control of an utterly ruined land ... I feel the need for more precise concentration on military objectives ... rather than on mere acts of terror and wanton destruction, however impressive.

(quoted in Saward, 1985, p.382)

Determined efforts were made by the Allies to exclude the contentious issue of saturation bombing from the agenda of the Nuremberg war crimes tribunal by announcing that, because all sides had used such tactics, it would be impossible to enforce the rules of war. This 'closing of the books' bequeathed two notable legacies: first, it established that the victors had the right to define what a war crime was and who was and who was not a war criminal. The commission of atrocities by a defeated nation in a war precluded its civilians from claiming the status of victim in relation to atrocities committed by a victorious nation.

The second legacy was the precedent it set unintentionally. The laws of war had been broken with impunity and the principle of distinction in effect obliterated. Consequently, it would be very difficult to condemn or take punitive action against any future targeting of civilians:

Various terrorist groups have from time to time defended their indiscriminate killing of civilians by saying that they were only following the precedent established by the British in World War Two ... This is what might be called the *nemesis effect* of violating the war convention, even in a worthy cause: such a departure often returns to haunt those originally responsible for it. Others pursuing a far less just end now find it convenient and possible to wrap themselves in the mantle of legitimacy when they employ those new techniques of violence, which often are directed at the very society that originally introduced them.

(Garrett, 1993, p.200)

View from the town hall tower over the ruins of Dresden, 1945

Although assurance was given that Dresden, Hiroshima and Nagasaki were exceptional deviations from the 'norms of war', the deliberate targeting of non-combatants and the civilian infrastructure was to become the centre-piece of military strategy in the second half of the twentieth century. As we have seen, killing civilians took on its own military rationale, namely to terrorize and demoralize. Let us consider another concrete situation – the Vietnam War (1955–75). In fact, it could be argued that the whole of the Vietnam War could be defined as a 'war of terror' because American forces resorted to saturation bombing and the use of napalm, white phosphorous, 'search and destroy' missions, free-fire zones, 'body-count' operations and ecocidal chemicals. In the process 1,350,000 civilians died. As Ely (1993) notes, by the time the undeclared and illegal, and therefore unattributable, bombing of Laos (which began in 1965) ended in 1973, the United States Air Force had dropped almost 800,000 tonnes of bombs with the destructive effect of

25 Hiroshima-style nuclear explosions: it is estimated that at least 150,000 civilians were killed and tens of thousands maimed.

While the stated rationale of US military tactics in Vietnam was to obliterate the physical and social infrastructure of the North Vietnamese, it does provide evidence that the frontlining of unsuspecting civilian populations is not the sole preserve of officially defined terrorist campaigns. The all-consuming nature of contemporary warfares, in conjunction with the lethal nature of the weaponry available, means that there is the distinct possibility that 'collateral damage' – that is, mass civilian casualties – will be excessive in any officially defined war of the twenty-first century (Kaldor, 1999).

3.2   The purpose of terrorism

When we move on to consider the second aspect of what constitutes terrorism – its purpose – we are confronted with the assertion that terrorism is practised by extremist revolutionary groups and individuals committed to seizing the state or establishing a new state. This has led in the past to an emphasis on the exploits of what has been described as the 'high priests' of revolutionary terrorism: groups such as the African National Congress (ANC), Euskadi Ta Askatasuna (ETA), Hezbollah, Irish Republican Army (IRA), Islamic Jihad and Al-Qaida, the Palestine Liberation Organization (PLO), and the Tamil Tigers. However, this representation of terrorism can conflate very different political struggles and risk draining them of their political meaning and historical specificity. Furthermore, as Chomsky (1991) emphasizes, such a 'bottom-up' conceptualization fails to recognize the critical linkages that can exist between the nation state and terrorism. Indeed, according to Herman (1993), there is simply no overstating the degree to which nation states, because of their monopolization of violence, have the potential to become epicentres of terrorism. Since the mid-1990s, the US State Department has published an annual inventory of foreign states alleged to be the criminal paymasters of international terrorism. Those named on this are 'outed' for secretly providing finance, weaponry and logistical support and also for providing terrorists with a safe haven. Being designated as a terrorist state means that countries are defined as invalid for most kinds of US aid and loans from multilateral financial institutions such as the International Monetary Fund, and run the risk of trade embargoes and global freezing of assets (National Commission on Terrorism, 2000).

What is notable is that absent from the 'most wanted' list are Western and pro-Western countries who, in the 1980s' global cold war fight against communism covertly, and illegally, spent billions of dollars funding, equipping and training networks of anti-communist groupings in many parts of the world. Evidence of this can be found in groups such as UNITA in Angola, the Contras in Nicaragua, the Mujahadeen in Afghanistan and Renamo in Mozambique, who relied on terror to stage right-wing revolutions. It was also established that during the 1990s the CIA provided training and logistical support for anti-communist forces in Argentina, Chile, Guatemala, Mexico and Uruguay. Sections of the Western media have come under criticism for uncritically reproducing – often in the form of visual clichés – the official 'What is terrorism?' and 'Who are the terrorists?' storylines. As Hall has argued of 'news framing' generally:

news framing

> Some things, people, events, relationships always get represented: always centre-stage, always in a position to define, to set the agenda, to establish the terms of the conversation. Some others sometimes get represented – but always at the margin, always responding to a question whose terms and conditions have been defined elsewhere; never 'centred'. Still others are always 'represented' only by their eloquent absence, their silences, or refracted through the glance or gaze of others.
>
> (Hall, 1986, p.9)

Livingston (1994) suggests that, in the 1980s and 1990s, those groupings that did not pose a threat to or indeed those who advanced US geopolitical interests were much more likely to be categorized by the American news media as 'freedom-fighters', 'liberation movements', rebels, armed militias, guerrillas and partisans. Moreover, there was considerable bias when it came to identifying what could be defined as acts of terrorism. Livingston's research into US media representations indicates that the violent actions of pro-American or anti-communist groups, no matter how indiscriminate and horrific, were likely to be explained as being retaliatory or accidental in nature. Because these groups managed to evade the official label of terrorism, their activities attracted considerably less news media coverage and analysis. This particular media framing, which Livingston terms a 'crime of omission', has an important knock-on effect for victims of terrorist violence. The deaths of a large number of people were ignored or down-played while others, who were portrayed in the media as victims of 'terrorist' organizations, were elevated to the status of what he calls 'super-victim', with due outrage and sympathy being accorded to their suffering. Political considerations, therefore, defined victims as being worthy or unworthy of news media recognition and created a 'hierarchy of victimization'. Greenslade (1999, p.20) argues that in its coverage of the Northern Ireland conflict the British news media also constructed a 'hierarchy of death'.

crime of omission

hierarchy of victimization

> In the first rank – getting the most prominent coverage were British people killed in Britain; in the second, members of the security forces, whether army or RUC; in the third, civilian victims of republicans; including prison officers; in the fourth, members of the IRA or Sinn Fein, killed either by the security forces or loyalist paramilitaries; and in the fifth rank, garnering least coverage, were the innocent victims of loyalist paramilitaries.

ACTIVITY 7.3

Research indicates that the nation state's involvement with terror does not stop at sponsorship. In what other ways can a nation state terrorize its own citizens? Why might it do this and what might the effects be?

3.2.1 The nation state and terrorism

State terrorism can take several often interrelated forms. States, experiencing political conflict, have displayed a remarkable similarity in attempts to restore 'law and order', namely, a mixture of surreptitious negotiations and repressive strategies. Criminal justice procedures can be streamlined; core civil liberties and human rights 'temporarily' restricted or suspended; news media censorship or control imposed; and special courts established to hasten 'terrorist' detention, convictions or executions. States are also able to:

- promulgate sweeping 'emergency' legislation to extend the surveillance and investigative powers of internal security/policing agencies
- upgrade the coercive and intelligence capacity of state agencies
- establish covert counter-insurgency units to terrorize the 'terrorists' into submission.

counter-terrorism

The crucial point about counter-terror or 'balance of terror' strategies, according to Wolf (1987), is that once they are unleashed, they develop a momentum of their own and this gives rise to the possibility that those fighting terrorism eventually resort to undeclared 'dirty wars'. In many situations, for example, where counter-terrorist measures have been resorted to, state-directed or pro-state 'death squads' and militias have surfaced. These have a tendency to operate with very broad definitions of who make up the 'terrorists', the 'subversives', or the 'undesirables', and to act as judge, jury and executioner (Sluka, 2000).

In South Africa, after the collapse of the apartheid system in the 1990s, it was proven that state-sponsored death squads had been responsible for the assassination of political opponents and many of the civilian massacres in the townships and on commuter trains (The Truth and Reconciliation Commission, 1999). Throughout the duration of the Northern Ireland conflict, evidence has emerged to suggest that sections of the police and security forces had colluded with loyalist paramilitaries to target Irish Republicans (McPhilemy, 1998; Ní Aoláin, 2000).

torture

Torture is the second type of terror practised by states, and is regarded as the extreme form of individualized terror. As we noted in section 2.1.1, according to international humanitarian law and human rights conventions, torture is illegal in all circumstances. However, it remains commonplace throughout the world and, as a consequence of the lucrative global market in 'internal security' technologies and 'law-enforcement' expertise, it undergoes constant refinement and modernization (Duner, 1998; Morgan and Evans, 1999, Conroy, 2000). Extract 7.1 suggests that torture is practised by state security and policing institutions for five main reasons: information; incrimination; indoctrination; intimidation; and isolation.

Extract 7.1   Suedfeld: Why torture?

What do torturers expect to achieve? Common rationales for applying torture may be subsumed under five major headings:

1   *Information.* Torture is used to force the victim to provide factual information concerning criminal, political or military matters of which he or she is presumed to have knowledge. Perhaps the most common example is in the military field intelligence settings.

2   *Incrimination.* The goal is to force the prisoner to identify other individuals engaged in behaviours that the captor considers culpable or to confess to having engaged in such behaviours. This is frequently the goal in the torture of prisoners who

are either suspected of being part of a conspiratorial group or are being groomed for public trial.

3   *Indoctrination.* The captor wishes to establish conditions under which the prisoner will abandon previously held beliefs and attitudes and adopt others that are more acceptable to the captor. Torture is a preliminary step in bringing about a change in loyalties, as in brainwashing.

4   *Intimidation.* Torture is used to deter the prisoner and others from behaviour considered unacceptable by the captor. In many such cases, the torturer ensures that the mistreatment of the victim is publicly known, as a means of frightening

Torture transforms the victim's body into a political text. Inscribed on it is the omnipotence of the state and an all-too-visible warning for dissident groups or whole communities (Bushnell *et al.*, 1991; Rejali, 1994; Feitlowitz, 1998 and Siegel, 1998). The intention is to make the costs of political opposition or resistance too high to be contemplated.

> The state takes upon itself the right to impose, through violence, its definitions of reality and correct behaviour throughout the whole field of human action. As terror penetrates the sinews of every organization and association in social life, people are numbed into subservience and repress any independent thought or impulse to action. Life becomes pervaded by the symbols of the all powerful state and its agents and tools of repression – the political police, their weapons and prisons, and their wider cultural manifestations, all conveying the ever-present threat of violent reprisal for transgressions of all types. A culture of terror develops in which no-one is to be trusted.
>
> (Bushnell *et al.*, 1991, p.9)

Furthermore, because torture is being used to intimidate and silence the general population, innocent surrogate victims are as effective as political activists. Where nation states are at war or in conflict with sections of their own citizenry, key state agencies can be transformed into bureaucratic instruments of terror, complete with networks of clandestine torture and death centres and professionals whose specialist knowledge is utilized to keep people alive for as long as is deemed either useful or necessary:

> Although death squads and torture groups may torture victims, only states have the resources to torture systematically. States possess the financial and human resources to sustain a torture complex. Further, they can rely on support from other sectors of society to provide technical support (hospitals and mental asylums) and information (universities, unions, the criminal undergrounds).
>
> (Rejali, 1994, p.134)

The third type of state terrorism is disappearance – that is, extra-judicial arrest **disappearance** or abduction of alleged critics and opponents, usually followed by their torture, secret execution and burial. Its contemporary origins lie in the Second World

---

other potential victims. In the case of hostages and kidnap victims, torture may be used to deter attempts at rescue by indicating to the police or the victim's government that any strong action would result in additional suffering for the captive. Intimidation also includes torture as a punishment, for example, flogging or amputation as the legally mandated penalty for some crimes or torture by police and prison authorities when prisoners attempt to escape or violate regulations. Furthermore, a persuasive knowledge that political or other prisoners are subject to torture may be used to intimidate large segments of a polity into submission ...

5   *Isolation.* The goal here is to convince both the captor and the captive that they have nothing in common with the other, not even a common humanity. For the torturer, having the complete power to mistreat the prisoner instils contempt and hatred of the group to which the prisoner belongs and increases the torturer's loyalty by isolating him or her from the victimized group and even from society at large. The person being tortured, in turn, learns that the gap between omnipotent guards and helpless prisoners (and perhaps between prisoners and the world in general) is as the difference between different species. It is also a way to harden recruits ...

(Suedfeld, 1990, pp.2–3)

War when the Nazis passed a 'Night and Fog' decree throughout Nazi-occupied zones, under which anyone deemed to be a threat to security was 'ghosted' to Germany under cover of night. Despite the fact that it was made illegal under the Geneva convention of 1949, the practice re-emerged in various Latin-American states in the post-war period. There is evidence that the military across Latin America also learned from previous reigns of terror. In Argentina, for example, between 1976 and 1983 under the military dictatorship, it is estimated that between 10,000 and 30,000 people were 'disappeared' in a pre-planned 'war against terrorism':

> There would be none of the evidence of mass slaughter which followed Pinochet's seizure of power in Chile and none of the international outcry which it provoked. There would be no mass imprisonment as in Uruguay, where left-wing suspects had converted other prisoners and even prison guards to their cause, and there would be no possibility of such prisoners being released under a general amnesty only to start their campaign again, as happened in Argentina under Perón's predecessor, President Cámpora. There would be no evidence and no one would be able to prove who was responsible. The murderous campaign would be concealed from Argentina and the world.
>
> (Fisher, 1989, p.180)

General Iberico Saint Jean, governor of Buenos Aires Province, makes clear the reasoning of the Argentinian state at that time: 'First we kill all the subversives; then, their collaborators; later, those who sympathize with them; afterward, those who remain indifferent; and finally, the undecided' (quoted in Morgan, 1989, p.126). The Guatemalan authorities later studied the Argentinian approach before unleashing their death squads, boasting that they would leave no witnesses or written accounts of their actions (Schirmer, 2000).

States and governing elites can also preside over *systemic* mass murder leading to or bordering on outright genocide to realize a multitude of ideological objectives such as spreading terror among class, ethnic, religious or political enemies; redressing past victimizations; or socially engineering 'brave new worlds' (Rummel, 1995; Jonassohn, 1998).

In 1933, the Polish scholar, Raphael Lemkin proposed an international treaty that would define aggression towards national, ethnic and religious groups as an international crime. In 1944, Lemkin, who was by then an advisor to the United States war department, coined the term 'genocide' because he believed that the terms 'mass murder' and 'war crimes' were inadequate for describing and explaining what had happened in Nazi Germany. Existing criminal categories could not account for the motive for the crime, which acted on the principle that the victim is not human. Lemkin defined genocide as a co-ordinated plan to destroy the essential foundations of the life of national groups, with the aim of annihilating the groups themselves. He also contended that genocide had two phases: first, the destruction of the national pattern of the oppressed group, and, second, the imposition of the national pattern of the oppressor. What is significant is that in the original formulation physical extermination is considered the most extreme form of genocide.

The 1948 UN Convention on the Prevention and Punishment of the Crime of Genocide defined genocide as 'acts committed with the intent to destroy, in whole or in part, a national, ethnical, racial or religious group'. Genocidal acts include:

- killing members of the group
- causing serious bodily or mental harm to members of the group
- deliberately inflicting on the group conditions of life calculated to bring about its destruction in whole or part
- imposing measures intended to prevent births within the group
- forcibly transferring children of the group to another group.

The 1948 convention also outlawed conspiracy to commit genocide; attempts to commit genocide and complicity in genocide. The convention includes individual and state responsibility for acts of genocide and also imposed a general duty on all signatory states not only to punish but to prevent and suppress such acts. The convention ruled that those charged with genocide could be tried by court in the territory within which the act was committed or by a specially convened international court. To facilitate extradition proceedings between states, genocide was also decreed to be a non-political crime.

As a result of *realpolitik*, the 1948 convention settled on a more limited definition of genocide than the one coined by Lemkin. The categories of 'politically defined groups' and 'economically defined groups' were deliberately omitted from the definition as was the notion of cultural genocide (destroying a group through compulsory incorporation into a dominant culture). Furthermore, the principle of 'intentionality', which was embedded in the definition, has been criticized by human rights activists because it facilitates governments and individuals in arguing that their actions were accidental and/or unplanned (Jonassohn, 1998).

There was also considerable disagreement about the acts of mass violence that would be contained within the definition. For example, after the Indonesian invasion and annexation of East Timor in 1975, an estimated 200,000 out of a total population of 700,000 were killed. During the Khmer Rouge's reign (1975–78), between one and two million people died in the Cambodian 'killing fields' as a result of the conditions of state-initiated massacres and prison-based execution programmes. However, the international community argued that that these acts did not meet the definition of genocide laid down by the 1948 convention since both perpetrators and victims were from the same ethnic/racial background. It has been suggested that the reluctance to define these actions as genocidal also emanated from a desire not to over-use the term and thereby trivialize the nature and meaning of the Holocaust (Ball, 1999).

In 1993, the first international tribunal was established to prosecute those responsible for committing or ordering serious violations of international humanitarian law, including genocide, in the former Yugoslavia (ITY). A similar tribunal was established in 1994 for Rwanda (ITR) to investigate the murder of 800,000 people, mostly Tutsi minority by the Hutu majority (Destexhe, 1995; Gourevitch, 2000) Both tribunals had to develop rules of procedure and establish principles to define the exact criminal nature of what had happened. In August 1998, the ITR produced a landmark decision in the history of international criminal law when it found Jean Kambanda, Rwanda's former prime minister, guilty of the crime of genocide. During 2000, the ITY heard the first charges of genocide to come before it. The indictment of senior officers of the Bosnian Serb army represented a breakthrough in international criminal law because it established that there was evidence that senior politicians and military leaders had planned the massacre of thousands of Bosnian Muslims in the UN 'safe haven' of Srebrenica in 1995 (Honig and Both, 1996).

In 1998, 120 nation states signed a resolution calling for the establishment of a permanent international criminal court (ICC) that will have the power and organizational capacity to investigate and prosecute genocide, war crimes and crimes against humanity. It is hoped that the ICC will come into existence in 2002. In order to establish its credibility, the new court will have to end the 'culture of immunity' that has been a hallmark of the twentieth century and establish punishments that are deemed to be appropriate to such criminality.

ethnic cleansing

Like genocide, 'ethnic cleansing' is one of the ultimate forms of hate crime and state-sanctioned terrorism. Unlike genocide, however, the United Nations does not designate ethnic cleansing as a specific crime. It is a generic term that covers a multitude of criminal acts and breaches of the Geneva conventions. Ethnic cleansing is a governmental process in which the military and/or paramilitary representatives of a powerful and/or victorious ethnic group engage in the premeditated, methodical expulsion of other powerless or defeated ethnic groups from a specified territory. This may entail the complete destruction of a particular group or the exertion of enough pressure for the group to voluntarily leave a particular city, village or part of a country. The intention is to clear the way for the establishment of ethnically homogeneous enclaves for members of a particular group. Forms of ethnic cleansing were practised throughout the twentieth century and have been a central part of the territorial expansion or consolidation involved in the formation of many nation states. The term is most closely associated with events in Bosnia and Herzegovina between 1992 and 1995 when Bosnian Serbs used murder, destruction of property, deportation and rape to force Bosnian Muslims to flee to areas outside of Serb control and influence (Cigar and Mestrovic, 1995; US State Department, 1999). Human rights groups have campaigned for ethnic cleansing to be designated as a specific crime against humanity and brought within the remit of the ICC.

A display outside Phnom Penh burial pits for victims of Kampuchea's Khmer Rouge regime. 8,985 remains were found at this site. The iron shackles were used to bind the victims

3.3 The mind of a terrorist

'What kind of person could do such a thing?' is the question that immediately comes to mind when watching the emergency services clearing up after a no-warning 'terrorist' bomb explosion or gun attack. Many of the most influential textbooks on terrorism answer this question by asserting that the 'terrorist' is the pathological 'other' who glories in senseless violence: he or she is either criminally insane or a cold-blooded thug. In this narrative, such dysfunctional individuals cynically use politics as an outlet for their barbaric tendencies. Although it may be the case that individuals can be cited who fit the stereotype, Giddens nonetheless maintains that, at a general level:

> This sort of characterization is usually far from the truth. Most groups purporting to use violence to further their ends have a coherent philosophy about why they act as they do. Controversial though their ideas may be, these groups are not normally composed of people who claim to value violence for its own sake.
>
> (Giddens, 1989, p.368)

The classic image of the terrorist

Research by Taylor and Quayle (1994) indicates that 'terrorists' are not discernibly different in psychological terms from 'non-terrorists'.

Their research also questions whether those who are officially labelled 'terrorists' are any more 'psychopathological' than soldiers in conventional armies. It is argued that, in order to justify their murderous deeds, 'terrorists' depersonalize and dehumanize their victims, but dehumanization is also an inescapable part of military socialization generally and one of the reasons why 'guilt-free' atrocities **dehumanization** can occur (Kelman and Hamilton, 1989; Bourke, 1999). Dehumanization involves constructing mental frameworks that deny the 'enemy' their humanity by excluding them from the moral and cognitive universe. The enemy or 'other' is

> deprived of the two qualities essential to being perceived as fully human and included in the moral compact that governs human relationships: *identity* – standing as independent, distinctive individuals, capable of making choices and entitled to live their own lives – and *community* – fellow membership in an interconnected network of individuals who care for each other and respect each other's individuality and rights.
>
> (Kelman and Hamilton, 1989, p.19)

In addition, dehumanization can work to counteract moral doubts and fears. The less-than-human 'enemy' is seen to be guilty and to have precipitated her or his victimization. This process of 'enemy creation' can be taken one step **enemy creation** further if racist ideologies are mobilized. So, for example, in the 1960s, American GIs in Vietnam searched for and destroyed stereotypical 'dinks', 'gooks', 'dopes' and 'slopes'. The Serbians in the 1990s were ethnically cleansing 'gypsies', 'filth' and 'animals', while on the other side of the globe the Tutsis of Rwanda were described as 'inyenzi' (cockroaches). Once racist ideologies are mobilized, moral restraints against killing and personal responsibility can be neutralized.

Extract 7.2   Bilton and Sim: 'My Lai, Vietnam'

I went to turn her over and there was a little baby with her that I had also killed. The baby's face was half gone. My mind just went. The training came to me and I just started killing. Old men, women, children, water buffaloes, everything. We were told to leave nothing standing. We did what we were told, regardless of whether they were civilians. They was the enemy. Period. Kill. If you don't follow a direct order you can be shot yourself. Now what am I supposed to do? You're damned if you do and you're damned if you don't. You didn't have to look for people to kill, they were just there. I cut their throats, cut off their hands, cut out their tongue, their hair, scalped them. I did it. A lot of people were doing it and I just followed. I just lost all sense of direction.

I just started killing any kinda way I can kill. It just came. I didn't know I had it in me. After I killed the child my whole mind just went. It just went. And after you start it's very easy to keep on. The hardest is to kill the first time but once you kill, then it becomes easier to kill the next person and the next one and the next one. Because I had no feelings, no emotions. Nothing.

I just killed. I wasn't the only one that did it; a lot of people in the company did it, hung 'em, all types of ways, any type of way you could kill someone that's what they did. That day in My Lai I was personally responsible for killing about twenty-five people. Personally. I don't think beforehand anyone thought that we would kill so many people. I mean we're talking about four to five hundred people. We almost wiped out the whole village, a whole community. I can't forget the magnitude of the number of people that we killed and how they were killed, killed in lots of ways.

Do you realize what it was like killing five hundred people in a matter of four or five hours? It's just like the gas chambers – what Hitler did. You line up fifty people, women, old men, children, and just mow 'em down. And that's the way it was – from twenty-five to fifty to one hundred. Just killed. We just rounded 'em up, me and a couple of guys, just put the M-16 on automatic, and just mowed 'em down.

(quoted in Bilton and Sim, 1993, pp.130–1)

Kelman and Hamilton (1989, p.19), for example, argue that this process can be self-perpetuating once set in motion. Soldiers can, for example, come to view their victims in 'body-count' terms and 'are reinforced in their perception of the victims as less than human by observing their very victimization'. A disturbing illustration of this process occurred during the Vietnam War at My Lai (see Extract 7.2). On 16 March 1968, a platoon of American troops under the command of Lieutenant William Calley entered the South Vietnamese village as part of a 'counter-terrorism' mission. By the time they left four hours later, approximately 500 unarmed villagers had been killed in an atrocity that was not acknowledged publicly until late 1969.

Official dehumanization can be methodical in other respects also. Crelinsten's (1993) research on the training of state torturers shows that, more often than not, they are state employees who undergo specialist training and group socialization and who, by and large, regard their work with a degree of detachment. In essence, state-sanctioned torture becomes a form of routine activity. As Crelinsten argues:

First, the torturer is doing a *job*, he is 'doing torture'; second, he is supposed to do it well, 'mastering torture'; third, he is supposed to achieve certain results ('making them talk'), i.e., obtaining confessions, breaking the enemy's will; fourth, the central method used to achieve these results is inflicting pain ('making them hurt'); fifth, the people upon whom this pain is inflicted are defined as 'enemies'. The information, the confessions, and, ultimately, the broken people, are the end products of the torturer's work. It is these end products by which he is judged as skilled or unskilled, deserving of promotion or dismissal, considered indispensible or expendable. It is this *judgement* or *assessment* of the torturer's work that leads us to the final feature of the torturer's world: the torturer is working in an institutional context, within a hierarchy in which others, his superiors and their superiors and their superiors, decide who is an enemy, what needs to be known, and what must be done to know it.

(Crelinsten, 1993, p.40)

This quote highlights that the making of a torturer appears to have less to do with 'individual psychology' and more to do with the political and organizational contexts in which the torture is licensed to take place. Key evidence for this was provided by the experiments carried out in the 1960s by Yale psychologist, Stanley Milgram, who showed how situational pressures can induce people to carry out horrendous acts:

Two people were invited into the psychology department, ostensibly to take part in a study on learning and memory which would assess the effect of punishment on learning. One was assigned the role of 'learner' (he was in fact a confederate of the experimenter), the other that of the 'teacher'; this person was the experimental subject. The 'teacher' then saw the 'learner' being strapped into a chair in the next room and an electrode attached to his wrist. The teacher subject was then seated before an impressive shock generator and told to administer the test and apply increasing levels of shock to the learner (up to levels clearly marked 'dangerous') when he made mistakes in learning a paired series of words. Each subject was given a sample of the kind of electric shock that was about to be administered to the learner. As the experiment proceeded, the learner's cries of anguish and pleas to stop could be heard.

(Wetherell, 1996, pp.21–2)

In truth, the learner's cries were pre-recorded and no electric shocks were in actual fact being administered. However, this was unknown to the subjects and many of them were prepared to carry on and obey the experimenter, ignoring the 'victim' even when the victim *pleaded directly* to the subject to stop. In the original experiment, twenty-six out of the forty male subjects administered the highest shock level on the generator (Wetherell, p.22).

In discussing the factors that contribute to the creation of a torturer, Gibson refers to a number of studies, particularly of the Nazi regime, which make it clear there is no one 'type of person' who is likely to become a torturer:

It might be comforting to assume that torturers are, in fact, peculiar monsters who can be explained away as the sort of freaks of nature who commit mass murders in periods of insanity. However, the conclusions ... show clearly that this is not the case: They hold that, although it is true that, in some situations, deranged and sadistic individuals have committed acts of torture for pleasure, in most cases in which torture is committed at the instigation of government officials, the torturers can best be described as normal individuals. ... The conclusion of these studies is that individual personality characteristics and background information about individuals, by themselves, cannot distinguish individuals who will commit torture or other cruel acts from those who will not.

(Gibson, 1990, p.78)

So what are the situational factors that contribute to the creation of a torturer? A key aspect of torture is the emergence of programmes that train security personnel in 'interrogation' techniques. The case of Greece, under the military junta (1967–74), was researched by Haritos-Fatouros (1988).

Extract 7.3   M. Haritos-Fatouros: 'The official torturer: a learning model for obedience to the authority of violence'

Throughout the basic and advanced training of the recruits … there was systematic application of a learning model based on principles of behaviour change. Some of these are described below.

Overlearning. To teach obedience to the authority of violence and to the authority of the irrational, the method of overlearning was widely applied. Obedience without question to an order without logic was the ultimate goal. In this way, the recruits were carefully prepared to carry out orders for acts of cruelty that had little meaning for them. They were never told why a particular person was tortured or what he had done; in some cases they even ignored his name.

Dixon (1976), when describing the so-called 'bull' behaviour in the military, which includes similar but much milder forms of such training procedures, gives a different and equally plausible interpretation. Dixon believes that such procedures serve to reduce initiative and thereby increase the feeling of dependency on superiors.

Accordingly, degrading and illogical acts were forced upon the Greek servicemen. For instance some reported: 'They made us eat the grass of the camp;' 'they forced us to say love words to a lamp-post and to make love to our kit-bags and scream at the same time.' They also mentioned scenes of violence such as: 'I was forced to eat my burning cigarette;' 'we went kneeling all the way to the canteen to eat' (kapsoni treatment).

Desensitization. The servicemen were gradually desensitized to the idea of torture in two ways. First,

they had to endure torture as if it were an everyday, 'normal' act. They all described a daily routine of flogging in which they were often forced to run to exhaustion, fully equipped, and were beaten at the same time (kapsoni). This was almost a routine in the morning, before lunch, and before sleep. Recruits described the procedure as follows: 'We were forced to run while beaten until there were drops of sweat hanging from the ceiling.' Very appropriately and with insight for the ultimate aim of this training, one of the subjects reported: 'We had to *learn* to *love* pain.' The 'banality of evil' was clearly aimed at this procedure (Aronson & Mills, 1959; Wolff, 1969).

Second, a systematic technique for densensitization to the act of torture was used in order to eliminate anxiety that might accompany the torture. The intent was to turn the noxious stimulus (i.e., torture) into a neutral or even a pleasant one. This technique also served for selection purposes, particularly with reference to persons selected for the position of the prison-warder who was the chief torturer and for the positions of members of the Persecution Section.

Subjects estimated that this process resulted in the selection of 10–15 of the 100 servicemen … for the Persecution Section, which was solely responsible for providing torturers. Training in the Persecution Section included the following: The servicemen were first brought into contact with prisoners by carrying food to them and 'occasionally' were ordered to 'give the prisoner some blows.' The next step was to place them

---

Haritos-Fatouros concluded that under the right circumstances, any individual is a potential torturer (see Extract 7.3). More recently, Huggins and Haritos-Fatouros (1998) have explored the relationship between masculinity and the institutional making of torturers.

4   Rethinking the problem of 'terrorism'

ideological censure

What can we conclude from our survey of terrorism? Overall, it can be argued that terrorism is an ideological censure which, if successfully applied, can play a decisive role in forming and inflecting public understanding of complicated political conflicts. And as we have seen, it has been deployed in a highly selective manner. First, there is more likelihood that the violence of the powerless will be defined as 'terrorist' than will the violence of the nation state. Second, certain

as guards in the detention rooms where they watched others torturing prisoners; they would occasionally take part in some group-floggings. Later, they were asked to take part in the 'standing-ordeal' during which they had to beat the prisoner (on the legs mainly) every time he moved. The final step, the 'chrism' of the chief torture, i.e., the prison-warder, was announced suddenly to the servicemen by the commander-in-chief without leaving him any time for reflection.

Role Modeling. Model learning was also used. Older servicemen flogged and degraded the freshmen, in preparation for the recruits' task of torturing that was soon to follow. Older servicemen were never forced to do so, but they often used degrading remarks as negative reinforcements for the young soldiers to produce the desired effect. Similar procedures, but of much milder forms, are also reported in connection with military training in general (Dixon, 1976); they are also know among the traditional British public schools.

Reinforcement. Negative and positive reinforcement were used to maintain the behaviours of the torturers once it had been acquired. Negative reinforcers used direct or indirect threat, intimidation, and punishment. Subjects reported that no one trusted the others, and each spied upon the others. One of the subjects said that 'there were always two servicemen torturing a prisoner so that one would spy on the other and the officers spied on both, through the hole on the door of the cell.' There were direct threats to the servicemen

themselves and to their families. One of the subjects reported, for instance, 'an officer used to tell us that if a warder helps a prisoner, he will take the prisoner's place and the whole platoon will flog him. We always lived with this threat over our heads.' Another reported, 'you looked at your face in the mirror and you were afraid that it might tell on you.'

Material and social gain was used systematically as positive reinforcement. All subjects reported that the majority of the military police servicemen belonged to low socio-economic classes and that a fair percentage were village boys. Therefore, both social and material rewards were quite highly valued among them. Moreover, the fact that they belonged to a highly esteemed, highly feared, and all-powerful army corp was the strongest long-term positive reward of all, because they enjoyed many standing privileges and rights during and after completing their military service.

References:

Aronson, E., and Mills, J. (1959) 'Effect of severity of initiation on liking for a group', *Journal of Abnormal Social Psychology*, 51, 1977–1981.

Dixon, N. (1976) *On the Psychology of Military Incompetence*, London, Jonathan Cape.

Wolff, K.H. (1969) 'For a sociology of evil', *Journal of Social Issues*, 35, pp.111–25.

(M. Haritos-Fatouros, 1988, pp.1115–18)

nation states are more likely to be labelled as major centres of international terrorism or sponsors of terrorism. Such is the power of the censure that academics and journalists who have challenged the reigning orthodoxy by publishing critical analyses of terrorism, or by pointing the finger at state terrorism, have been 'unveiled' as 'fellow travellers' and accused of providing terrorists with lethal 'ideological bullets'. One example is Edward Said, professor of English and Comparative Literature at the University of Columbia, who has, because of his association with the Palestinian cause, been repeatedly denounced in the USA as a 'professor of terrorism' and charged with spilling ink to justify the terrorists' spilling of blood (Alexander, 1989). In the UK, *The Guardian* newspaper is labelled by right-wing newspaper journalists as 'pro-IRA' in its coverage of and editorial line on the Northern Ireland peace process (see Rusbridger, 2000).

This raises the central question of whether social scientists should continue to use the terms 'terrorism' and 'terrorist'. Hitchens (1986), Guelke (1998) and Oliverio (1998) argue that we should not because in doing so we are employing a polemical device that makes rational discussion of the causes of and solutions to political conflict untenable. Morgan (1989, p.33) agrees: 'The murder exists. The fear exists. The grief exists. But, yes the terrorist *is* a figment of our imagination – and more, a figment of our lack of imagination'. We can see these terms as 'explanatory fictions', and we find evidence throughout the world of officially labelled 'terrorists' becoming redefined as 'freedom-fighters' and, eventually, respected leaders of their communities or indeed nation states; and of successful 'terrorist' campaigns being redefined as national wars of liberation or independence. In Palestine, for instance, Britain eventually reached a settlement with the leaders of Irgun Zvai Leumi in 1948, the Jewish 'terrorist' organization responsible for many atrocities, including the no-warning bombing of the King David Hotel in Jerusalem in July 1946 in which over 90 people were killed (Bowyer-Bell, 1976). The founder of Irgun Zvai Leumi, Menachem Begin, was awarded the Nobel Peace Prize in 1978, almost 30 years after he was removed from the list of Britain's most wanted terrorists. The most cited examples of the late twentieth century were the 'peace processes' which transformed Nelson Mandela of the African National Congress, Gerry Adams of Sinn Fein and Yasser Arafat of the Palestine Liberation Organization from 'terrorists' into respectable political leaders. In each case, prisoners who had been processed as 'criminals' were redesignated as 'political' and released as part of the negotiations for peace.

The uncomfortable reality is that, as we have seen earlier in this chapter, a variety of political actors, nation states, sub-state groupings, and individuals are capable of resorting to terror in the pursuit of a variety of ideological objectives: 'Any understanding of terrorism that pictures governments as completely legitimate and rational and "terrorists" as completely illegitimate and irrational must be flawed. Governors and terrorists are both involved in the pathology of societies that have broken down to the point where politics has been wholly or partly replaced by violent action' (Woolacott, 1995, p.20).

5   State terrorism and the politics of justice

So far we have restricted our attention to clarifying definitional issues. In section 5, we examine how the dominant definition of terrorism operates to limit the response to state terror. During the 1980s and 1990s, Western governments assured their citizenry and the international community that there would be no hiding place for those defined and labelled as 'terrorists'. Bombings, shootings or hostage-taking by 'terrorist' groupings were followed by statements informing the public that there would be 'no deals with the men of violence', 'no surrender to extremists', and that 'terrorism will never win'. Any deviation from this fundamental principle, in the form of trade-offs, concessions or negotiations, would, it was argued, encourage other 'criminal gangs' to attempt to hold nation states to ransom (Harmon, 2000). Israel relentlessly pursued its enemies, British special forces successfully ambushed and 'neutralized' IRA active service units, and France sensationally extradited 'Carlos the Jackal' – 'the world's most wanted terror chief' – from Sudan. Strenuous efforts were made by the United States to bring to trial two Libyans accused of plotting the 1988 Lockerbie bombing, in which all the passengers aboard a Pan Am flight en route from Europe to New York were killed. In the aftermath of the 1998 bombing of its embassies in

Kenya and Tanzania, the United States also posted a $5 million reward for the capture of Osama bin Laden, leader of Al Qaida, and launched cruise missiles against his bases in Afghanistan and Sudan (Lobel, 1999). However, we now need to consider whether the same time and effort is used to apprehend and punish those who have participated in state-orchestrated or pro-state terrorist actions that are prima facie violations of national and international law.

5.1   Internal regulation and control

There are significant difficulties in attempting to call to account those responsible for safeguarding civil liberties and guaranteeing human rights in the way that non-state actors are called to account. It should be borne in mind, from the outset, that states can and do use the rule of law to deny individuals or social groups basic human rights. Nuremberg laws passed by the Nazi state, for example, stripped the Jews of their legal rights, placing them outside citizenship. Through redefining the Jews as 'non-human', the Nazi law effectively paved the way for their extermination (Finkielkraut, 1992). In addition, citizens of the Nazi state who gave shelter to Jews or aided their passage out of the country were committing criminal acts.

5.1.1   Denial and techniques of neutralization

Cohen (1993) documents how state authorities and officials accused of torture or murder can mobilize what he describes as a litany of denials for their actions:

> The standard vocabulary of official (government) denial weaves its way – at times simultaneously, at times sequentially – through a complete spiral of denial. First you try 'it didn't happen'. There was no massacre, no one was tortured. But then the media, human rights organisations and victims show that it does happen: here are the graves; we have the photos; look at the autopsy reports. So you have to say that what happened was not what it looks to be but really something else: a 'transfer of population', 'collateral damage', 'self-defence'.
>
> (Cohen, 1993, p.102; see also Cohen, 1995)

Cohen also details how state authorities and officials can deploy carefully crafted techniques of neutralization that are very similar in nature to those that **Sykes and Matza (1957)** argued are used by juvenile offenders. These are ready-made justifications which are intended to protect the accused from self-blame and the blame of others, namely: denial of responsibility; denial of injury; denial of victims; condemnation of condemners; appeal to higher loyalties. Through these discourses, the accused state authorities and officials can present themselves as more sinned against than sinning. Tomlinson (1999) argues that there are further techniques of neutralization that only nation states have the power to deploy:

techniques of neutralization

- techniques which not only deny the innocent status of victims but criminalize them
- techniques which discredit those campaigning for justice for victims of state atrocities
- techniques which distance the state from the actions of pro-state terrorist groups.

THE PROBLEM OF CRIME

ACTIVITY 7.4

Is it morally acceptable for state authorities to violate national and international law so long as they do so with good intentions? States and/or government agencies have sometimes presented a 'ticking bomb justification' argument to justify the over-riding of human rights.

> Suppose you know that some terrorists have planted a bomb somewhere. You don't know where, but you do know that it is timed to go off six hours from now, and that when it does it will kill or maim many innocent people. Suppose at that point you catch one of the terrorists. Surely you are entitled to do everything you can to get him to tell you where that bomb is, so that you can save all those innocent victims, even if it means causing a guilty man some temporary pain?
>
> (Sieghart, 1985, p.112)

What crucial factors does it ignore? Sieghart (1985, p.113) contends that this argument ignores at least four crucial factors. First, the authorities may *think* the person they have caught is a 'guilty' terrorist who knows where the bomb is, but they may well be wrong; if they are, they will be torturing an innocent person. Second, confessions made under torture are seldom reliable; more often than not the victim will say *anything* to avoid pain. Third, presumably, the authorities are trying to protect society from the 'evil' people who are attacking it. But what kind of society is it whose own government deliberately violates human rights and tortures its own people? Finally, once the authorities are willing to accept that a good end will justify their means, where will they stop? How long will it be before they are locking up people in concentration camps, or unleashing death squads in the name of 'law and order' and national security?

5.1.2 Official inquiries and criminal prosecutions

A further response that nation states routinely make to accusations of torture or murder is to appoint official judicial investigations to uncover the 'truth' of serious allegations. However, official inquiries can operate, in times of serious political and social conflict, to maintain the legitimacy of the state and preserve the 'good' name of its agencies and serve, through a process of stonewalling and bureaucratic obfuscation, to eclipse the truth rather than uncover it.

In the first years of the Northern Ireland conflict, for example, there were four major official inquiries into controversial events or incidents: the Cameron commission and the Scarman tribunal into various aspects of the 1968–69 disturbances; the Compton inquiry into allegations against the security forces of physical brutality and torture in 1971; and the Widgery tribunal into 'Bloody Sunday' when soldiers of the Parachute Regiment shot dead 14 civilians during a civil rights demonstration in 1972. Extract 7.4 provides us with a classic example of how a serious question mark hangs over their approaches, analyses and ideological balance.

The serious flaws in the Widgery tribunal were acknowledged by the British government in January 1998 when it announced that a new inquiry into 'Bloody Sunday' would be headed by Lord Saville. The announcement was the culmination of a family and community campaign which had been established in 1992 to achieve truth and justice for those killed and injured on 30 January 1972.

Extract 7.4 Boyle *et al.*: 'The failure of official inquiries'

First, the terms of reference were usually interpreted in such a way as to exclude certain broader issues from the scope of inquiry. This was particularly true of the Widgery Tribunal, which was established by a Parliamentary motion to inquire '... into a definite matter of urgent public importance, namely the events on Sunday 30 January [1972] which led to loss of life in connection with the procession in Londonderry on that day.' These terms were taken by Lord Widgery to exclude consideration of the important issues of Army/government relationships and the source of the orders for 30 January. Yet he devoted two full introductory pages to a description of the security situation in Londonderry over the previous six months, indicating the pressures under which the Army was operating. This was apparently based entirely on Army evidence. There was no similar description of the strains the people of Derry were experiencing. This one-sided approach to his terms of reference lessened the credibility of the rest of Lord Widgery's report.

Secondly, the conclusions which the various reports drew from their findings, with the possible exception of Cameron and Scarman, were not always in accord with what might have been expected from an objective assessment of those findings. The Compton Report ... based its rejection of the allegations of brutality by security forces on a thoroughly unconvincing distinction between brutality and ill-treatment. Lord Widgery made a generally favourable assessment of the conduct of the paratroops in Londonderry which it is difficult to justify in terms of the specific findings he made over the various individual incidents with which he was concerned, notably the 'reckless' shooting in the Glenfada Flats area. And in reaching even these findings Lord Widgery appeared to have placed undue credence on Army evidence and to have distrusted all other sources. It was in any event

the overall assessments of the various reports rather than the detailed findings which attracted most attention, and gave rise to the widespread feeling that the actions of the security forces were being 'whitewashed'. Assessments of this kind must remain a matter of opinion, but the Compton and Widgery reports certainly failed to persuade either the Roman Catholic community or uncommitted observers that their assessments had struck the right balance.

Thirdly, there was the question of delay. This applied primarily to the Scarman Tribunal which stretched over two whole years and finally reported nearly three years after the events into which it was inquiring. It is hardly surprising that after such a long delay the impact of the report was virtually nil in terms of restoring confidence in the impartiality of the RUC [Royal Ulster Constabulary], in so far as that was a valid finding. By that time an entirely new set of disputed incidents and allegations had taken over from those of 1969.

Finally, and perhaps most important, was the fact that no action was taken to deal with those cases in which the various reports found the security forces or individual soldiers or policemen to have been seriously at fault. The most notorious instances in this respect were the findings of ill-treatment/brutality against those involved in the arrest, detention and interrogation of some of the persons arrested in August 1971, and the finding over the Glenfada Flats incidents, in which four civilians were shot dead, that on the balance of probability 'when these four men were shot the group of civilians was not acting aggressively and that the shots were fired without justification' [H.C. 220, para. 85, April 1972]. It was widely agreed that in these cases the actions by the security forces constituted the criminal offences of assault or manslaughter, if not murder.

(Boyle *et al.*, 1975, pp.127–8)

Even if a public inquiry declares that a state-initiated atrocity has occurred, this is not the same as holding state authorities and officials to account. There is a repetitive global pattern of inquiries and investigations being aborted because of lack of proof, witnesses mysteriously withdrawing their evidence or disappearing, evidence disappearing or being altered, charges not being pursued beyond a certain point and defendants being acquitted either at the original trial or on appeal. In the rare instances when officials are found guilty, human rights organizations, such as Amnesty International and Human Rights Watch, argue that the punishments meted out are rarely commensurate with the crimes committed. Normally, those involved can present their own version of what happened or claim that their only crime was obedience in carrying out orders, and many states, irrespective of the Nuremberg tribunal ruling, seem to sympathize with and to a degree accept this particular plea. Let us go back to the My Lai massacre. Despite the indisputable evidence of an official cover-up, only 25 soldiers were charged and only one – Lieutenant Calley – was court-martialled. Although Calley was found guilty and sentenced to life imprisonment, he spent three days in a military jail before being transferred to house arrest and quickly paroled. Throughout the trial, Calley pleaded the 'crime of obedience':

> I was ordered to go in there and destroy the enemy. That was my job on that day. That was the mission I was given. I did not sit down and think in terms of men, women and children. They were all classified the same, and that was the classification that we dealt with, just as enemy soldiers … *I felt then and I still do that I acted as I was directed, and I carried out the orders that I was given and I do not feel wrong in doing so.*
>
> (quoted in Bilton and Sim, 1993, p.335, emphasis added)

Equally significantly, Ernest Medina, Calley's superior officer was acquitted.

The issue of 'crimes of obedience' raises important moral and philosophical questions. What are the implications of an individual pleading the 'crime of obedience' and, if found guilty, serving the kind of sentence finally served by Lt Calley. What of the individual's superiors who gave the orders? Under what other circumstances might there be an apparent reluctance or inability to hold perpetrators of gross human rights violations to account?

My Lai massacre scene: bodies of women and children lie on the road leading out of My Lai village, March 1968

Prosecution difficulties can persist in countries where an oppressive regime has given way to a democratic one that has irrefutable evidence of monumental human rights violations. The crucial issue for successor governments is how to confront and explicate the crimes of the past committed by 'intimate enemies'. There are very few situations in which the transfer of political power is unproblematic and very few new governments are in a position to prosecute and punish without having to consider the political consequences. Political realism tends to prioritize the restoration of social order over justice and this requires a certain national amnesia if it is to succeed. To facilitate the difficult and lengthy process of peace-making and reconciliation and the healing of wounded societies, to prove impartiality, avoid further bloodshed, placate still powerful security machines and establish the political stability necessary for the transition to be successful, compromises are accepted. A considerable re-embroidering of the past can take place in which 'everyone' was guilty of 'something' and 'we must learn to forget'; *de jure* or *de facto* amnesties and pardons are declared which exonerate specific categories of offences, along with promises that there will be no 'witch hunts' or mass prosecutions for past crimes (Cohen, 1995). Leaders of the old regime may also be allowed to go into political exile or fade into the political background. This is, in effect, a form of *decriminalization* and human rights groups argue that it benefits employees of the former state the most. And, as Walsh has argued, this airbrushing and attempted forgetting of history may not work: 'What seems beyond doubt, though, is that unsettled and unforgotten grievances do not simply go away. They rankle, divide and remain nearly impossible to put to rest. Amnesties can help wipe the slate clean, but more times than not, the blood stains, like those on Lady MacBeth's hands, cannot be so easily scrubbed into invisibility' (Walsh, 1995, p.29).

As an illustration of this, let us consider what happened after the military rulers were dislodged in Argentina in 1983. A National Commission on Disappeared People (CONADEP) was established and, as Fisher (1989) and Guzman Bouvard (1994) have detailed, it faced considerable difficulties in trying to establish what had happened during the military's rule. It gathered 50,000 pages of evidence from survivors and families but elicited little information from the military itself. Eventually, five of the nine military leaders brought to trial were convicted and sentenced to prison terms, but the nature of the crimes with which they were charged made court proceedings extremely difficult:

> As in Nazi-occupied territories, the Argentine phenomenon of *disappearance* constituted a form of state sponsored torture that unleashed terror not only on the *disappeared* but also on society as a whole. It was a crime with no legal recourse. After the fall of the junta, when the military trials were trying those responsible for the Dirty War, many of these people could not be sentenced for murder because there were no bodies as evidence and no laws that covered this practice. *Disappearance* means just that: no proof remains of the whereabouts or the death of a person, who has lost his or her legal and social identity.
>
> (Guzman Bouvard, 1994, p.41)

After 1986, in an attempt to neutralize the threat of a military coup, a series of presidential decrees effectively brought the accounting to a halt. The *Ley de Punto Final* (a 'full stop' law) held that, after April 1987, no more claims of human rights violations against the military would be heard by the courts. This was followed by the passing of an even more significant 'law of due obedience', which absolved all soldiers and officers beneath the rank of colonel of responsibility for virtually any actions they had committed in the 'war against subversives'. Tarnopolsky (1994) estimates that around forty officers could still have been tried for serious human rights abuses when President Raul Alfonsin, facing more political problems, including rumoured military coups, announced a general amnesty. In 1988, his successor, Carlos Saul Menem, an outspoken opponent of the amnesty while running for political office, changed his mind when he was elected. In 1990, he pardoned the five senior military officers already sentenced, together with 280 other members of the armed forces – which

The Mothers of the Disappeared: hundreds of women (many wearing the symbolic white headscarf) march in the Plaza de Mayo in Buenos Aires, demanding that the government reveal what happened to the thousands of people who disappeared during the 'dirty war' in Argentina

meant that all crimes committed during the 'war against subversives', for which prosecutions were still outstanding after the passing of the laws of 1986 and 1987, had now been pardoned (Cohen, 1995, p.30). Opponents of this amnesty, however, continued to campaign for information on the whereabouts and fate of the thousands of people who had 'disappeared', and in 1994 the wall of military silence began to crumble when ex-naval officers publicly admitted that: 'the navy had used torture as a "tool" in the fight against subversion' and that 'so-called "task groups" that were engaged in the clandestine operations of the "dirty war", including torture and extrajudicial executions, were an intrinsic part of the navy's operations' (Amnesty International, 1995, p.60). These admissions, however, did not lead to due public acknowledgement or reparation for past atrocities. Despite renewed efforts by the international human rights community to bring those responsible for the 'Dirty War' to account for their actions, the Argentinian government insists that it is better to draw a line over the past (Koonings and Krujit, 1999).

5.2 External regulation and control

Those concerned about particular states or those who are not satisfied with the outcome of official state investigations can, in theory, seek international intervention or request independent human rights bodies to examine abuses. These bodies, established in the post-war period, have, in principle, altered the relationship between the individual and the state by formally recognizing inviolable universal human rights and enhancing the ability of the individual to place the state in the role of defendant in order that it will be held accountable for its actions. Being publicly named and shamed before an international audience may, at the very least, embarrass states and governments and force them into doing something about their human rights record. However, it is very difficult for any of these international avenues to deliver substantive justice, even in the most obvious cases where human, civil or legal rights have been flouted on a mass scale. As Weiss *et al.* (1994, pp.162, 166) argue: 'Since 1948, the central problem has not been the abstract codification of norms; the problem has been in marshalling sufficient political will to deal with concrete violations of internationally recognized human rights … In other words, human rights treaties are widely accepted in law and widely violated in practice'. The international community has been reluctant to act decisively against human rights violations crimes committed during armed conflict. There are many complex legal and political reasons for the reluctance to get to grips with this problem, most of which are tied up with the fact that the decisions and actions of the relevant international bodies are determined by its member states.

The European Convention on Human Rights, backed up by a Commission and Court (in Strasbourg), obliges those states who are signatories to it to respect basic rights and freedoms of their citizenry. However, the rights and freedoms contained in the convention are not absolute. Most of the time, they are qualified by get-out clauses such as except 'in the interests of national security, public safety' and 'territorial integrity'. These qualifications mean that there is ample space for states to derogate legally from the Convention. However, many would argue that it is precisely during national emergencies that citizens need added international protection from the state, rather than allowing the state to do as it sees fit. What is more, the European Commission on Human Rights, the body that deals with the majority of complaints and petitions, has also been accused of adopting a cumbersome 'conflict-management' approach to state violations, by (a) attempting to achieve 'friendly' settlements; (b) being more concerned to prevent future recurrences rather than punishing past actions; or (c) being unwilling to apportion blame and guilt.

If we consider the nature of the United Nations, we find a law-enforcement entity whose competence and jurisdiction is compromised by the fact that it is first and foremost a forum of states and does not have its own military, police, prisons or judiciary, and furthermore by the process of highly politicized 'protect-your-own' voting by states. Despite the various supranational conventions and laws of war and human rights mentioned previously, non-interference in the internal affairs of sovereign states has been the fundamental guiding principle of the United Nations since the Second World War. Kuper (1981) argues that this 'radical non-interventionist' principle has effectively blocked the United Nations from responding effectively to massacres verging on outright genocide during this time. It is worth keeping in mind that, when the United Nations Declaration of Human Rights was adopted in 1948, many states did not sign it and those that did declared that the principles were not legally binding. The United Nation's interventions, irrespective of the seriousness of the situation, have generally been restricted: (a) to areas in which the consent of the territorial states in question has been secured or where all semblance of governance has collapsed; and (b) to providing humanitarian aid to alleviate and soften the suffering of civilian populations. As a result, transparently criminal states have not been held to account except when violations have concurred with the political interests of one of the geopolitical blocs. In addition, many states reject interference from a Western-dominated 'human rights' international community, which they regard as operating with double standards, and complain that a handful of powerful states have enjoyed a considerable degree of the *de facto* indemnity from systematic scrutiny of their human rights record.

It was not until 1994 that the United Nations established, at the Hague, an 'International War Crimes Tribunal for the former Yugoslavia' (ITY), the first since the Nuremberg and Tokyo Trials, to try those accused of serious breaches of the Geneva convention and crimes against humanity. Progress was seriously hindered, however, because there was little prison accommodation for suspects, and the initial budget could not cover the 'nuts and bolts' of a thorough investigation.

Moreover, given that the conflict was ongoing, few believed that the ITY would succeed in bringing those who had planned and overseen war crimes, caused breaches of the Geneva convention or invoked genocide to trial. The Serbians, the key suspects, refused to co-operate with it, denying that atrocities had ever happened and arguing that the ITY was biased. In addition, those states and international bodies seeking a negotiated solution to the conflict needed the co-operation of people – like President Slobodan Milosevic of Serbia, the Bosnian Serb leader, Radovan Karadzic and his military leader General Ratko Mladic – who had been identified as major war criminals. It also became clear that intentionality and direct culpability would be difficult to prove because the majority of prosecutions would be dependent on witnesses and very little documentary evidence was available. In May 1999, the ITY finally made a symbolic breakthrough when, in the context of NATO's bombing of Yugoslavia, Slobodan Milosevic was indicted for war crimes in Kosovo. This made him the first serving political leader

US State Department 'Wanted' poster for Milosevic, Karadzic and Mladic

Up To $5 Million Reward

Wanted

For crimes against humanity

Slobodan Milosevic
President of the Federal
Republic of Yugoslavia

For genocide and crimes against humanity

Radovan Karadzic

Ratko Mladic

Milosevic, **Karadzic**, and **Mladic** have been indicted by the United Nations International Criminal Tribunal for the Former Yugoslavia for crimes against humanity, including murders and rapes of thousands of innocent civilians, torture, hostage-taking of peacekeepers, wanton destruction of private property, and the destruction of sacred places. **Mladic** and **Karadzic** also have been indicted for genocide.

To bring **Milosevic, Karadzic,** and **Mladic** to justice, the United States Government is offering a reward of up to $5 million for information leading to the transfer to, or conviction by, the International Criminal Tribunal for the Former Yugoslavia of any of these individuals or any other person indicted by the International Tribunal.

If you believe you have information, please contact the nearest U.S. embassy or consulate, or write the U.S. Department of State, Diplomatic Security Service at:

REWARDS FOR JUSTICE
Post Office Box 96781 • Washington, D.C. 20090-6781 U.S.A.
email: mail@dssrewards.net • www.dssrewards.net
1-800-437-6371 (U.S.A. Only)

to be charged with this range of criminal offences (as we indicated in section 3.2.1). The International Criminal Tribunal in Rwanda (ITR) had similar difficulties in establishing its credibility and impartiality. The ITR had to develop appropriate rules of procedure, define the 'criminal' nature of a genocide that claimed 800,000 mainly Tutsi Rwandans, and establish mechanisms to obtain reliable testimony. It was also beset by a lack of funding and accusations of mismanagement, corruption and incompetence. However, between 1998 and 2000 the ITR produced a series of historic rulings when it found senior members of the Rwandan political regime guilty of genocide, rape and sexual violence, breaches of the Geneva conventions and crimes against humanity.

6   The emergent regime of global security and conflict resolution

A critical question for the twenty-first century is whether and how state violence can be controlled or eliminated. As we have made clear, there are no simple or straightforward answers to the problem. Campaigning groups such as Human Rights Watch, Amnesty International and the Independent Commission on International Humanitarian Issues argue that strong and resolute steps can be taken to make the protection of human rights and civil liberties an integral part of national and global governance. This means embedding nation states in a web of legal duties and responsibilities that will make them accountable to international bodies and thus locate the rights of the individual and civil society *above* the interests of the state. According to the human rights community, all states should be forced to demonstrate, through independent monitoring and evaluation, that international human rights conventions are formally recognized in and ratified by their legal systems. Citizens must also be made aware of their internationally guaranteed human rights and civil liberties and have substantive means of redress. The organizational and operational sub-cultures which generate powerful pressures on members to conform, irrespective of whether the conformity is right or wrong, must also be challenged. Through institutional democratization and the use of rewards and sanctions, the 'crimes of obedience' syndrome can be broken.

Human rights groups also argue that the international community should develop effective preventative policies by establishing early-warning systems and risk-assessment patterns and typologies based upon the lessons learnt from previous crisis situations. Reactive strategies which concentrate only on helping the victims and survivors should be regarded as a policy failure. A central part of a proactive strategy would be studying why some nation state formations are more prone to criminal activity than others. It is also vital that state killers and indeed 'killer states' be subject to criminal prosecution to help establish confidence in an international rule of law. If prosecutions do not take place, a clear message is relayed to states and officials that serious crime pays.

A result of the deliberations of the war crime tribunals for the former Yugoslavia and Rwanda and the Pinochet case in the UK is that we may be moving closer to the mainstreaming of a human rights discourse and an international criminal justice paradigm where:

1   The principle of 'command responsibility' will be reinforced.

2   Pleas made on the grounds of: obeying higher authority, following military orders; national security, or acting under 'emergency' legislation will be inadmissible.

3   Human rights violations will not be cloaked by statutes of limitation.

4   Suspected war criminals will not be excluded from amnesty decrees or allowed refugee status or a right to political asylum.

5   A nation state's 'right' to assert the right of derogation, or to insert blanket 'exceptional circumstances' clauses into international human rights legislation will be outlawed.

In March 2000, General Augusto Pinochet left the UK for Chile after seventeen months of legal deliberations which finally established that former heads of state are not immune from prosecution for war crimes against humanity

6   A legitimate and effective permanent international criminal court will be established which will be independent of global political bodies and be empowered to pursue, across state borders, those who have committed human rights violations.

7   Laws covering organizational criminal liability and individual responsibility for organizational conduct will be strengthened.

However, Alvarez (1999) argues that we need to be aware of the limitations of the international criminal justice paradigm because it privileges a highly formal 'top-down' legalistic approach to crimes of the state. By contrast, Alvarez argues that we also need to pay close attention to what he defines as the 'hate crime perspective' articulated by many first-hand accounts of atrocities in various parts of the world. These accounts foreground the need to understand the complex role that race, ethnicity and religion play in triggering the most serious human rights violations. The international criminal justice paradigm tends to play down the significance of such non-legal factors, preferring to focus on the 'unproblematic' legal 'facts' of a specific war crime. The history behind such conflicts also tends to be ignored. Alvarez argues for an approach that recognizes that societies and communities are struggling to come to terms with acts of violence that have inverted their moral universe and that 'these are crimes of *hate* as well as of states' (p.482). Instead of over-reliance on war tribunals staffed by international personnel, the United Nations should concentrate on re-establishing the credibility and impartiality of local police, prosecutors and courts:

> While international tribunals need to be kept as an option of last resort, good faith domestic prosecutions that encourage civil dissensus may better preserve collective memory and promote the mollification of victims, the accountability of perpetrators, the national (and even international) rule of law, and national reconciliation. The didactic functions of war crimes trials may best be furthered locally, through thousands of indictments and trials that truly resonate within a culture and whose lessons do not seem to be imposed, in top-down fashion, by the international community. Properly mediated by international law (and where necessary), local criminal accountability helps to restore the rule of law where it matters most – at the local level, where all of us live.

(Alvarez, 1999, pp.482–3)

Although Alvarez does not discuss it, his local approach to justice in societies devastated by atrocities would necessitate the establishment of truth and reconciliation commissions (TRCs). Since 1974, over twenty of these commissions have been established with different degrees of success in various parts of the world (see Extract 7.5). To date, the most important TRC is the one that existed in South Africa from 1996–98 and produced a 3,500 page report encompassing the different histories of apartheid. The TRC was established under the Promotion of National Unity and Reconciliation Act to hear evidence of gross human rights abuses committed by all sides in the war for and against apartheid (1960–93). It was given powers to grant immunity from prosecution to perpetrators who agreed to full disclosure. The assumption behind the TRC was that establishing 'what really happened' would facilitate national unification and reconciliation in a society emerging from violent conflict. This was deemed to be particularly important because the political deal brokered between the ANC and the apartheid regime ruled out the possibility of using the criminal justice system to prosecute and punish those guilty of human rights violations. Post-apartheid, there would be no war crimes tribunals or 'victors' justice' in South Africa (Asmal, 2000).

The case of the South African TRC illustrates how difficult it is for traumatized societies to balance 'truth', 'reconciliation' and 'justice'. The harrowing testimony given to it also demonstrated both that the 'past' is an inextricable part of the 'present' and 'future' and that 'reconciliation' is a traumatic process, not an end point. The TRC achieved a number of different things: it managed to empower victims and survivors through memorializing their testimonies of loss and pain, and enabled survivors to confront perpetrators. It facilitated the cross-examination of the motives and explanations of perpetrators, and allowed the falsely accused to clear their names. It also allowed a conclusion to be given for unfinished stories and ensured that society was confronted with facts that the powerful would prefer to remain hidden. Finally, it gave victims and survivors the chance to grieve publicly.

In terms of 'justice', however, the TRC was less effective. It has been suggested that the quality of 'the truth' presented to the TRC is open to question, because those giving testimony had very different understandings of 'what really happened'. Gillian Slovo (1998), in her account of meeting the state agents responsible for the murder of her mother, Ruth First, the anti-apartheid campaigner, in a university in Mozambique in 1982, argues that the supporters of the apartheid regime were attempting to use the TRC to rewrite South Africa's history. In this revisioning, all meaning was reversed: the Afrikaners were also 'victims', they had also been 'de-humanized'; no one side had the monopoly on suffering, their loss and sorrow needed to be acknowledged; and guilt and responsibility needed to be shared:

> And reconciliation? Well, if our experience is anything to go by, then there is none. But then reconciliation was never really aimed at individuals like us. It was an attempt to move a whole society to a better future. Maybe it will work. Maybe those men will fail in their attempt to change the record. Maybe in its own way the Commission, like Nuremberg, will offer some real accounting for history.
>
> As for me, the whole experience remains raw and troubling.
>
> (Slovo, 1998, p.16)

Extract 7.5   Sider: 'Learning to heal the wounds from the past'

Since 1996, dozens of mass graves have been exhumed on the initiative of local communities through Guatemala. In a country where over 50,000 individuals were 'disappeared', for many people – both Mayans and Ladino – exhumations hold out the hope of finding a body to mourn.

Teams of forensic scientists, linked to NGOs and the Catholic Church, have worked to identify victims, and provide details of the massacres, which took place in the early Eighties. These exhumations are an integral part of the truth-telling process in Guatemala. They constitute both an acknowledgement of the victims, and a reaffirmation of their living relatives, allowing for a reconstruction of their cultural universe. They also represent a highly concrete form of evidence of military violence – an 'objective truth', and a direct condemnation of impunity.

Exhumations and commemorations do not equate with punishment of those responsible for the abuse. Many people in Guatemala are now demanding both judicial sanctions against perpetrators, and economic compensation for their victims: yet given political and legal constraints, and the sheer scale of the repression, they are not likely to secure either. Un-met calls for compensation could potentially be a source of political conflict in the future. Perhaps the best that can be hoped for, in terms of reconciliation, is an agreement between people to reconcile their difference by non-violent means.

Truth-telling processes necessarily start with victims' testimonies, but can also extend to include the perpetrators of violence. The REMHI initiative, like the South African TRC, aimed to give perpetrators of violence a space to give their testimony. A number did come forward, although the majority of accounts were from victims.

Determining degrees of complicity and culpability in widespread human rights' abuse is a problematic and much-debated question. Yet, in Guatemala, where huge number of peasants were forced to kill each other by the army during the counter-insurgency war, many of the material authors of atrocities are also victims themselves. Many of these people in the areas I worked remained unable to tell their stories, fearing retribution, both from the military (for breaking the complicity of silence) and from their victims.

Some appeared to be in denial, unable to confront the enormity of what they had done.

But what of the principal intellectual and material authors of the counter-insurgency violence? In the absence of any 'amnesty for truth' deals of powers of subpoena on the part of the truth commissions, the experience throughout Latin America has shown that it takes years for military officers responsible for human rights abuse to come forward and tell their story. Most never do, and remain convinced that their actions were justified in the prevailing ideological and political context. This has undoubtedly constituted a weakness of post-conflict reconciliation in the region (only in exceptional cases, such as Chile, have leading members of the transition government acknowledged official responsibility for abuses).

However, even in the case of South Africa, where the TRC can demand testimony in exchange for amnesty, it has not attempted to secure repentance on the part of those guilty of abuses. The question remains as to what extent a new moral community can be built in the absence of recognition of guilt and a serious desire to change by perpetrators.

In Latin America, official processes of remembering have generally not been tied to judicial processes, and have tended not to individualise guilt (name names). Nonetheless, as the Chilean truth and reconciliation commissioner, Jose Zalaquett, has pointed out, they are an official means to try and reconstitute moral and political orders by particular ways of remembering the past.

In this sense, official truth-telling exercises are part of a transitional renegotiation of the normative values, or moral community, of the nation-state. In Guatemala, the continuing power and influence of the military has resulted in a limited mandate for the commission, and a difficult and restricted atmosphere within which to discuss the past.

In addition, despite the efforts made to reform the judicial system as part of the peace process, it remains largely incapable of sanctioning even current abuses of human rights, thereby perpetuating impunity and fear. In such an environment, it is unrealistic to expect that the truth commission alone will significantly strengthen the rule of law.

(Sider, 1998)

7 Conclusion

This chapter has provided an overview of forms of crime and criminality that present a challenge to mainstream criminological and popular representations of the crime problem and complicate discussions of key criminological concepts such as 'violence', 'dangerousness', 'risk', 'security' and 'victimization'.

Criminological examinations of violence need to be expanded to incorporate analysis of how violence is embodied and embedded in the practices of state agencies legally mandated to use coercive force. This entails making the study of the most significant political invention of Western modernity – the nation state – once more a central part of the criminological enterprise. It is critical that criminologists research how, in various parts of the world, nation states can become sites of insecurity and risk where the monopoly of violence is deployed in an illegal manner. Complex processes of post 'cold war' globalization have brought about the fracturing or disintegration of nation states, unleashing new forms of post-nation state violence in the process. This violence has also triggered a redefinition of the position of the nation state in an unfolding framework of international governance and regulation, and an institutionalization of the idea of transnational peacekeeping and policing operations.

The discussion of 'terrorism' as an ideological censure provides further illustration of why criminologists need to continue to pay attention to the discursive processes by which criminal definitions are constructed and realized, and the normative distinctions that flow from these definitions. It has given insight into what is denied, repressed and trivialized by dominant definitions, and shows how criminalization processes can be contested by those subjected to such labelling and become constitutive of identities of resistance. Examining the notion of 'terrorism' as ideological censure also gives us some understanding of the techniques that can render state terrorism invisible. At the beginning of the twenty-first century, such is the ideological potency of the dominant concept of 'terrorism' that it is being applied across a multiplicity of actions and motivations, e.g. 'eco-terrorism', 'bio-terrorism', 'cyber-terrorism', 'hyper-terrorism' and so on. Although critical criminologists have attempted to reconstruct the concept so that it can be applied to the actions of the state, in many ways this works to reinforce and consolidate the official discourse. It may be more appropriate to use the replacement discourses of 'political violence' or 'political crime'.

Criminologists need also to consider the implications of the emergence of a global criminal justice paradigm. As was indicated above, at the beginning of the twenty-first century in certain parts of the world, the nation state and law and order have all but collapsed with post-modern civil wars being conducted by 'disorganized' irregular forces, mercenaries and paramilitary groupings. It looks as if violence will continue to play a critical role in the birthing of new nation states who may then make efforts to claim sovereignty over their internal affairs and assert their right to non-interference from international policing bodies. However, it is becoming increasingly difficult for nation states to sustain this position. The deliberations of the UN's war crimes tribunals for the former Yugoslavia and Rwanda have bolstered the case for the establishment of an independent international court of justice that will act as an effective counter balance to national criminal justice systems, and the institutionalization of human rights into the domestic law and governmental practices of nation states.

However, we are left with the vexed issue of whether the international criminal justice paradigm can deliver both good governance and 'justice'. There are a number of impediments to this. First, there is considerable difficulty in tackling the political realities of these post-modern conflicts and notions such as 'race', 'ethnicity', 'culture' and 'nationalism', which are the drivers of many of these conflicts. Second, the ability of the international criminal justice system to control such violence is limited because the emphasis is on controlling war crimes *after* they occur. Third, the spotlight remains on individuals rather than collectivities, and, lastly, there are difficulties in establishing and guaranteeing the court's political independence.

The limitations of a criminal justice approach to the problem of crime are well known to criminologists. Indeed, this is what has provoked the search for alternatives that focus on crime prevention. In the area of state crime and human rights violations, there is a pressing need to assess whether the principles of conventional crime prevention could apply. Would it be possible for the international community to develop an effective risk-assessment system which can provide early warning of a nation state's criminal propensities? This could be achieved through analysing the racial, ethnic and cultural tensions that are built into a nation state's formation, assessing the degree to which human rights and civil liberties conventions are operationalized, and measuring the degree of democratic control of the military and police.

Finally, criminologists need to study truth commissions and the complex politics associated with remembering, truth-telling, anger, forgiveness and justice. The lesson that is being learned from various parts of the world is that without establishing some form of consensus about what has happened and *why*, there is little chance of communal and/or individual reconciliation, and the institutionalization of reconciliation is an essential part of any meaningful long-term peace-making.

Review questions

- Why is it so difficult to produce an adequate definition of 'violence'?
- Can torture be justified?
- What are crimes of obedience?
- 'How we define the problem of terrorism has major ramifications for how we propose to deal with it'. Discuss.
- Why do truth commissions raise fundamental questions about the relationship between politics and justice?

Further reading

The literature on political violence, terrorism and crimes of the state is expanding beyond **Cohen's (1993)** pathbreaking analysis of its relevance to criminology. In terms of the issues highlighted in this chapter, Whitner (1997) provides an interesting overview of the emplacement of violence in society. Anthropological and historical perspectives on the relationship between states, state-formation and illegal practices are provided by McC.Heyman (1999). Oliverio (1998) covers many of the key themes on the study of terrorism developed in this chapter. In Duner (1998), leading authorities assess the prospects for the eradication of torture. Sluka (2000) presents a series of essays on the phenomenon of state-sponsored death squads. The multi-volume South African Truth Commission (1998) is required reading for those trying to work through the pros and cons of such an approach to peace making. The significance of crimes of obedience is explored by Kelman and Hamilton (1989).

Acknowledgements

In writing this chapter, we are indebted to Stanley Cohen, professor of criminology at the London School of Economics, for a series of influential seminars on human rights and crimes of the state, given by him in London and Milton Keynes during 1994. We are also very grateful to the assistance provided by Fiona Harris on working through the literature on torture.

References

Alexander, E. (1989) 'Professor of terror', *Commentary*, vol.88, no.2, pp.49–50.

Alvarez, J.E. (1999) 'Crimes of state/crimes of hate: lessons from Rwanda', *Yale Journal of International Law*, vol.24, no.2, pp.365–84.

Amnesty International (1995) *Amnesty International Report 1995*, London, Amnesty International.

Asmal, K. (2000) 'Truth, reconciliation and justice: the South African experience in perspective, *Modern Law Review*, vol.63, no.1, pp.1–24.

Ball, H. (1999) *Prosecuting War Crimes and Genocide: The Twentieth Century Experience*, University Of Kansas Press.

Best, G. (1994) *War and Law Since 1945*, Oxford, Clarendon.

Bilton, M. and Sim, K. (1993) *Four Hours in My Lai: A War Crime and its Aftermath*, New York and Harmondsworth, Penguin.

Boulesbaa, A. (1999) *The UN Convention on Torture and the Prospects of Enforcement*, Dordrecht, Kluwer Books.

Bourdieu, P. (1977) *Outline of a Theory of Practice*, Cambridge, Cambridge University Press.

Bourke, J. (1999) *An Intimate History of Killing: Face to Face Killing in Twentieth Century Warfare*, London, Granta Books.

Bowker, L.H. (1998) *Masculinities and Violence*, London, Sage.

Bowyer-Bell, J. (1976) *Terror out of Zion*, New York, St Martin's Press.

Boyle, K., Hadden, T. and Hillyard, P. (1975) *Law and State: The Case of Northern Ireland,* London, Martin Robertson.

Brogan, P. (1992) *World Conflicts: Why and Where They Are Happening*, 2nd edn, London, Bloomsbury.

Bushnell, P.T., Shlapentokh, V. and Vanderpool, C.K. (1991) *State Organized Terror*, Boulder, CO, Westview.

Cesarani, D. (1992) *Justice Delayed: How Britain Became a Refuge for Nazi War Criminals*, London, Heinemann.

Chomsky, N. (1988) *The Culture of Terrorism*, Boston, MA, South End Press.

Chomsky, N. (1991) *Pirates and Emperors: International Terrorism in the Real World*, New York, Black Rose Books.

Cigar, N. and Mestrovic, S.G. (1995) *Genocide in Bosnia: The Policy of Ethnic Cleansing*, Austin, Texas AM University Press.

Coates, T. (1999) *Judgement at Nuremberg*, London, Stationery Office Books.

Cohen, S. (1993) 'Human rights and crimes of the state: the culture of denial', ***Australian and New Zealand Journal of Criminology***, **vol.26, no.1, pp.87–115. (Extract reprinted in Muncie** ***et al.*****, 1996.)**

Cohen, S. (1995) 'State crimes of previous regimes: knowledge, accountability, and policing the past', *Law and Social Inquiry*, vol.20, no.1, pp.7–50.

Conroy, J. (2000) *Unspeakable Acts, Ordinary People: The Dynamics of Torture*, New York, A.A. Knopf.

Crelinsten, R.D. (1993) 'In their own words: the world of the torturer', in Crelinsten, R.D. and Schmid, A.P. (eds) (1993) *The Politics of Pain: Torturers and Their Masters*, Leiden, Center for the Study of Social Conflicts.

della, Porta, D. and Diani, M. (1999) *Social Movements: An Introduction*, Oxford, Blackwell.

Destexhe, A. (1995) *Rwanda and Genocide in the Twentieth Century*, New York, New York University Press.

Dobash, R. and Dobash, E. (1999) *Changing Violent Men*, London, Sage.

Duner, B. (1998) (ed.) *An End To Torture: Strategies For Its Eradication*, New York, St Martin's Press.

Ely, J.H. (1993) *War and Responsibility: Constitutional Lessons of Vietnam and its Aftermath*, Princeton, NJ, Princeton University Press.

Feitlowitz, M. (1998) *A Lexicon of Terror: Argentina and the Legacies of Terror*, Oxford, Oxford University Press.

Finkielkraut, A. (1992) *Remembering in Vain: The Klaus Barbie Trial and Crimes Against Humanity*, New York, Columbia University Press.

Fisher, J. (1989) *Mothers of the Disappeared*, London, Zed.

Foucault, M. (1979) *Discipline and Punish: The Birth of the Prison*, Harmondsworth, Penguin.

Foucault, M. (1980) *Power/Knowledge*, Brighton, Harvester Wheatsheaf.

Garrett, S.A. (1993) *Ethics and Airpower in World War Two*, New York, St Martin's Press.

Gibson, J.T. (1990) 'Factors contributing to the creation of a torturer', in Suedfeld, P. (ed.) *Psychology and Torture*, New York, Hemisphere.

Gill, J. (1998) 'I don't want them punished, I want them to stop', *Derry Journal*, 21 August, p.9.

Giddens, A. (1985) *Nation State and Violence*, Cambridge, Polity.

Giddens, A. (1989) *Sociology*, Cambridge, Polity.

Gourevitch, P. (2000) *We Wish To Inform You That Tomorrow We Will Be Killed*, London, Picador.

Greenslade, R. (1999) 'Out of the spotlight,' *The Guardian*, 1 July, p.20.

Guelke, A. (1998) 'Wars of fear: coming to grips with terrorism', *Harvard International Review*, vol.20, no.4, pp.44–7.

Guzman Bouvard, M. (1994) *Revolutionizing Motherhood: The Mothers of the Plaza de Mayo*, Wilmington, DE, Scholarly Resources.

Hall, S. (1986) 'Media power and class power', in Curran, J., Ecclestone, J., Oakley, G. and Richardson, A. (eds) *Bending Reality: The State of the Media*, London, Pluto.

Haritos-Fatouros, M. (1988) 'The official torturer: a learning model for obedience to the authority of violence', *Journal of Applied Social Psychology*, vol.18, no.13, pp.1107–120.

Harmon, C.C. (2000) *Terrorism Today*, New York, Cass Books.

Herman, E.S. (1993) 'Terrorism: misrepresentations of power', in Brown, D.J. and Merrill, R. (eds) *Violent Persuasions: The Politics and Imagery of Terrorism*, Seattle, WA, Bay Press.

Hitchens, C. (1986) 'Wanton acts of usage', *Harpers*, September.

Hoffman, B. (1999) *Inside Terrorism*, London, Victor Golancz.

Hogan, G. and Walker, C. (1989) *Political Violence and the Law in Ireland*, Manchester, Manchester University Press.

Honig, J.W. and Both, N. (1996) *Srebrenica: Record of a War Crime*, Harmondsworth, Penguin.

Hopper, K.T. (1984) *Elections, Politics and Society in Ireland 1832–1885*, Oxford, Clarendon.

Ingraham, B.L. (1979) *Political Crime in Europe*, Berkeley, CA, University of California Press.

International Military Tribunal (1947) *Trial of the Major War Criminals*, Nuremberg.

Johnson, P. (1986) 'Terrorism' in B. Netanyahu (ed.) *Terrorism: How the West can Win*, London, Weidenfeld and Nicolson.

Jonassohn, K. (1998) *Genocide and Gross Human Rights Violations*, Plymouth, Transaction Books.

Kaldor, M. (1999) *New and Old Wars*, Cambridge, Polity Press.

Karnow, S. (1983) *Vietnam*, London, Century.

Kelman, H.C. and Hamilton, V.L. (1989) *Crimes of Obedience,* New Haven, CT, Yale University Press.

Koonings, K. and Kruijt, D. (1999) *Societies of Fear: The Legacy of Civil War, Violence and Terror in Latin America*, London, Zed Books.

Levi, M (1997) 'Violent Crime' in M. Maguire, R. Morgan and R. Reiner (eds*) The Oxford Handbook of Criminology*, Oxford University Press.

Livingston, S. (1994) *The Terrorism Spectacle,* Boulder, CO, Westview.

Lobel, J. (1999) 'The use of force to respond to terrorist attacks', *Yale Journal of International Law*, 24, 2, pp.537–57.

McNeil, E.B. (1966) 'Violence and human development', *Annals of the American Academy of Political and Social Science*, no. 364, pp.152–65.

McPhilemy, S. (1998) *The Committee: Political Assassination in Northern Ireland*, New York, Robert Reinholt Publications.

McC.Heyman, J. (1999) (ed.) *States and Illegal Practices*, New York, Berg.

Morgan, R. (1989) *The Demon Lover: On the Sexuality of Terrorism*, London, Methuen.

Morgan, R. and Evans, M.D. (eds) (1999) *Protecting Prisoners: the Standards of the European Committee for the Prevention of Torture in Context*, Oxford, Oxford University Press.

Muncie, J., McLaughlin, E. and Langan, M. (eds) (1996) ***Criminological Perspectives: A Reader***, **London, Sage in association with The Open University.**

National Committee on the Terrorism (2000) *Report of the National Committee on Terrorism*, Washington DC, United States State Department.

Ní Aoláin, F. (2000) *The Politics of Force: Conflict Management and State Violence in Northern Ireland*, Belfast, Blackstaff Press.

Nieburg, H.L. (1969) *Political Violence*, New York, St Martin's Press.

Oliverio, A. (1998) *The State of Terror*, New York, SUNY Press.

Pankhurst, E. (1931) *The Suffragette Movement*, London, Longman.

Peters, E. (1985) *Torture*, Oxford, Basil Blackwell.

Pinchuck, T. (1994) *Mandela,* Cambridge, Icon Books.

Radford, J., Friedberg, M. and Harne, L. (2000) *Women, Violence and Strategies for Action*, Milton Keynes, Open University Press.

Radzinowicz, L. and Hood, R. (1990) *The Emergence of Penal Policy*, vol.5 of *A History of English Criminal Law*, Oxford, Clarendon.

Rejali, D.M. (1994) *Torture and Modernity,* Boulder, CO, Westview.

Roberts, A. and Guelff, R. (2000) *Documents of the Laws of War*, Oxford, Clarendon.

Rummel, R.J. (1995) *Death by Government: Genocide and Mass Murder Since 1900*, Plymouth, Transaction Publishers.

Rusbridger, A. (2000) 'Sound and fury signifying, well, not much,' *The Guardian*, 13 March 2000, pp.4–5.

Saward, D. (1985) *'Bomber' Harris*, London, Sphere Books.

Schirmer, J. (2000) *The Guatemalan Military Project–A Violence Called Democracy*, University of Pennsylvania Press.

Segal, L. (1990) *Slow Motion: Changing Masculinities, Changing Men*, London, Virago. (Extract reprinted as 'Explaining male violence' in Muncie *et al.*, 1996.)

Sider, R. (1998) 'Burying the Past: Justice, forgiveness and reconciliation in politics', *The Independent*, 28 September.

Siegel, J.T. (1998) *A New Criminal Type in Jakarta: Counter-Revolution Today*, Duke University Press, Durham, NC.

Skolnick, J. (1969) *The Politics of Protest*, New York, Ballantine.

Slovo, G. (1998) 'Evil has a human face', *The Guardian*, 31 October, pp.8–16.

Sluka, J.A. (2000) (ed.) *Death Squad: The Anthropology of State Terror*, Philadelphia, University of Pennsylvania Press.

Stanko, E. (1998) *Taking Stock: What Do We Know About Violence?*, Swindon, Economic and Research Council.

Stern, J. (1999) *The Ultimate Terrorists*, Boston, Harvard University Press.

Suedfeld, P. (ed.) (1990) 'Torture: A brief overview', *Psychology and Torture*, New York, Hemisphere.

Sykes, G.M. and Matza, D. (1957) 'Techniques of neutralization', *American Sociological Review*, vol.22, no.6, pp.664–70. (Extract reprinted in Muncie *et al.*, 1996.)

Tarnopolsky, N. (1994) 'Argentina: fight barbarism from a wall of memory', *International Herald Tribune*, 15 December, p.4.

Taylor, J.G. (1999) *East Timor: The Price of Freedom*, London, Zed Books.

Taylor, M. and Quayle, E. (1994) *Terrorist Lives*, Washington, Brassey's.

Taylor, P. (1993) *States of Terror: Democracy and Political Violence*, Harmondsworth, Penguin.

Taylor, P. (2000) *Loyalists*, London, Bloomsbury Books.

Tilly, C. (1985) 'War making and state making as organised crime', in Evans, P.B., Rueschemeyer, D. and Skocpol, T. (eds) *Bringing the State Back In*, Cambridge, Cambridge University Press.

Tomlinson, M. (1999) 'State killings and the Northern Ireland conflict: Strategies of denial and struggles for justice,' British Criminology Conference, Liverpool, July.

Truth and Reconciliation Commission (1999) *Report of the Truth and Reconciliation Commission*, London, Macmillan.

Turpin, J. and Kurtz, L.R (1997) *Web of Violence*, Bloomington, Indiana Press

U. S. Department of State (1999) *Erasing History: Ethnic Cleansing in Kosovo*, Washington DC, U.S. Government.

Vulliamy, E. (1995) 'In times of trial', *The Guardian*, 31 October, pp.6–7.

Walsh, J. (1995) 'Can justice ever be done?', *Time*, 22 May, pp.28–33.

Walzer, M. (1977) *Just and Unjust Wars*, New York, Basic Books.

Weber, M. (1970) *From Max Weber: Essays in Sociology* (trans. and ed. H.J.H. Gerth and C.W. Mills), London, Routledge.

Weiss, T.G., Forsythe, D.P. and Coate, R.A. (1994) *The United Nations and Changing World Politics*, Boulder, CO, Westview.

Weschler, L. (1999) 'International humanitarian law: an overview' in Guttman, R. and Rieff, D. (eds) *Crimes of War: What the Public Should Know*, London, W.W. Norton and Co.

Wetherell, M. (ed.) (1996) *Identities, Groups and Social Issues*, London, Sage/ The Open University.

Whitner, B. (1997) *The Violence Mythos*, New York, SUNY Press.

Wilson, J.Q. (1983) *Thinking about Crime*

Wolf, J.B. (1987) *Anti-Terrorism Initiatives*, New York, Plenum Books.

Woolacott, M. (1995) 'Three sides to every story', *The Guardian*, 2 September, p.20.

Zures, S, Kurtz, L.R and Asher, S.B (1999) (eds) *Non Violent Social Movements*, Oxford, Blackwell.

Acknowledgements

Grateful acknowledgement is made to the following sources for permission to reproduce material in this book:

Text

Chapter 1: Pearson, G. (1983) *Hooligan: A History of Respectable Fears*, Macmillan Press Ltd, reproduced with permission of Palgrave; 'Levittating the laws', *The Guardian*, 27 November 1993, © Guardian Newspapers Ltd 1993; Davies, N. (1999) 'Revealed: how police fiddle crime figures', *The Guardian*, 18 March 1999, © Guardian Newspapers Ltd 1999; Brummer, A. (1993) 'Crime in the City', *The Guardian*, 1 July 1993, © Guardian Newspapers Ltd 1993; Lewthwaite, J. (1992) 'The "killer" mistress who was at lover's wedding', *The Sun*, 7 July 1992, © News International Ltd, 7 July 1992; Curran, F. (1994) 'You're mad not bad', *Daily Star*, 10 December 1994, Express Newspapers plc; Scraton, P. and Chadwick, K. (1991) 'The theoretical and political priorities of critical criminology', in Stenson, K. and Cowell, D. (eds) *The Politics of Crime Control*, Sage Publications Ltd; Young, J. (1986) 'The failure of criminology: the need for a radical realism', in Matthews, R. and Young, J. (eds) *Confronting Crime*, Sage Publications Ltd; Travis, A. (1998) 'Crime "crisis" based on myth', *The Guardian*, 6 January 1998, © Guardian Newspapers Ltd 1998. **Chapter 2:** Christie, A. (1965) *At Bertram's Hotel*, HarperCollins Publishers Ltd, © Agatha Christie Ltd 1965; from *Cop Killer* by Maj Sjöwall and Per Wahlöö, trans. from the Swedish by T. Teal, copyright © 1975 by Random House, Inc., reprinted by permission of Pantheon Books, a division of Random House, Inc.; Mosley, W. (1993) *White Butterfly*, W.W. Norton & Co., Inc., copyright © 1992 by Walter Mosley, reproduced by permission of Serpent's Tail; Forrest, K.V. (1993) *Murder by Tradition*, HarperCollins Publishers Ltd., also by permission of the Naiad Press Inc. **Chapter 4:** Park, R.E., Burgess, E.W. and McKenzie, R.D. (1925) *The City*, The University of Chicago Press, Introduction © 1967 by The University of Chicago. All rights reserved; Davis, M. (1990) *City of Quartz*, Verso. **Chapter 5:** Segal, L, *Slow Motion* © 1990 Lynne Segal, reprinted by permission of Rutgers University Press and Virago Press Ltd; Byrne, J. (1994) *When Home is Where the Hurt Is*, BBC Radio Two Social Action Team and the Women's Aid Federations; Wainwright, M. (1999) 'Domestic violence on trial in new court', *The Guardian*, 3 June 1999, © Guardian Newspapers Ltd 1999. **Chapter 6:** Connon, H. (1994) 'Britain fails to come to grips with suspicious share deals, *The Independent*, 22 July 1994; Bennetto, J. (1999) 'Law-breaking on the Web', *The Independent*, 26 October 1999; Steele, J. (1999) 'Russia: the biggest money launderette in the world', *The Guardian*, 31 August 1999, © Guardian Newspapers Ltd 1999; Handelman, S. (1995) *Comrade Criminal: Russia's New Mafiya*, Yale University Press. © 1995 by Stephen Handelman. **Chapter 7:** Bilton, M. and Sim, K. (1992) *Four Hours in My Lai*, Penguin Books, © Michael Bilton and Kevin Sim, 1992. All rights reserved; Haritos-Fatouros, M. (1988) 'The official torturer: a learning model for obedience to the authority of violence', *Journal of Applied Social Psychology*, 18, 13, copyright © by V.H. Winston and Sons, Inc. All rights reserved; Boyle, K., Hadden, T. and Hillyard, P. (1975) *Law and State: The Case for Northern Ireland*, Martin Robertson, © Kevin Boyle, Tom Hadden and Paddy Hillyard, 1975; Sider, R. (1998) 'Learning to heal the wounds from the past', *The Independent*, 29 September 1998.

Figures

Figure 1.1: Audit Commission (1999) *Safety in Numbers: Promoting Community Safety*, © Audit Commission 1999; *Figure 1.2*: Henry, S. and Lanier, M.M. (1998) *Essential Criminology*, Westview Press; *Figures 1.3, 1.4*: Barclay, G.C. and Tavares, C. (1999) *Digest 4: Information on the Criminal Justice System in England and Wales*, Home Office Research and Statistics Department, © Crown Copyright is reproduced with the permission of the Controller of Her Majesty's Stationery Office; *Figure 1.5*: Hall, S., Clarke, J., Critcher, C., Jefferson, A. and Roberts, B. (1975) *Stencilled Occasional Papers: Newsmaking and Crime*, January 1975, © Centre for Contemporary Cultural Studies; *Figure 1.6*: adapted from Wilson, D. and Ashton, J. (1998) *What Everyone in Britain Should Know About Crime and Punishment*, Blackstone Press Ltd; *Figure 1.7*: Wilkins, L.T. (1964) *Social Deviance*, Routledge, also reproduced by permission of Prentice Hall, Inc.; *Figure 1.8*: Muncie, J. (1987) 'Much ado about nothing', *Social Studies Review*, 3 (2), November 1987, Philip Allan Publishers; *Figures 3.1 and 3.2*: Beattie, J.M. (1974) 'The pattern of crime in England 1660-1800', *Past and Present*, 62, February 1974, © World Copyright: The Past and Present Society, 1974; *Figure 3.3*: Sharpe, J.A. (1984) *Crime in Early Modern England, 1550–1750*, Longman Group Ltd; *Figure 4.1*: Park, R.E., Burgess, E.W. and McKenzie, R.D. (1925) *The City*, The University of Chicago Press, Introduction © 1967 by The University of Chicago. All rights reserved; *Figure 4.2*: Davis, M. (1994) *Beyond Bladerunner: Urban Control: The Ecology of Fear*, Pamphlet 23, Open Magazine Pamphlet Series, © Mike Davis, 1992, 1994; *Figure 6.1*: Coyle, D. (1999) 'The contraband trade routes', *The Independent*, 22 February 1999; *Figure 6.2*: Rawlinson, P. (1998) 'Russian organised crime, moving beyond ideology', in Ruggiero, V., South, N. and Taylor, I. (eds) *The New European Criminology, Crime and Social Order in Europe*, Routledge.

Tables

Table 1.2: Mirrlees-Black, C., Budd, T., Partridge, S. and Mayhew, P. (1998) *The 1998 British Crime Survey, England and Wales*, Home Office Statistical Bulletin, Issue 21/98, © Crown Copyright is reproduced with the permission of the Controller of Her Majesty's Stationery Office; *Table 1.3*: Braithwaite, J. (1989) *Crime, Shame and Reintegration*, Cambridge University Press; *Table 1.5*: Hough, M. and Mayhew, P. (1983) *The British Crime Survey: First Report*, © Crown Copyright is reproduced with the permission of the Controller of Her Majesty's Stationery Office; *Tables 6.1, 6.2*: Croall, H. (1998) *Crime and Society in Britain*, Addison Wesley Longman.

Photographs/Illustrations

p.12: © Alex MacNaughton; *p.30 (left)*: Mary Evans Picture Library; *p.30 (bottom)*: *Illustrated London News*; *p.30 (right)*: reproduced with permission from Young, P.M. (1968) *A History of British Football*, Stanley Paul; *p.33*: Commission for Racial Equality; *p.46*: Curran, F. (1994) 'You're mad not bad', *Daily Star*, 10 December 1994, Express Newspapers plc; *p.48*: Sean Smith/*The Guardian*; *p.52*: front page of *Daily Mirror*, 18 May 1964, © Mirror Syndication International;

p.77: LWT Productions Licensing & Marketing/courtesy of Mr David Suchet; *p.85*: Kobal Collection/Warner Brothers; *p.92*: © Granada Television Ltd, reproduced with the kind permission of Ms Helen Mirren, Ms Liza Sadovy and Mr Tom Bell; *p.100*: BBC copyright photograph, reproduced with the kind permission of Ms Siobhan Redmond; *p.102*: from *Evil Under the Sun*, a Columbia-EMI-Warner film, Ronald Grant Archive; *pp.105, 114, 133*: © The British Museum; *p.132*: Mary Evans Picture Library; *p.155*: Guildhall Library, Corporation of London/photo: Geremy Butler Photography; *p.166*: Aerofilms; *p.193*: Hulton Deutsch Collection; *p.206*: Women's Aid Federation (England) Ltd; *p.213*: Pam Isherwood/Format; *p.219*: Howard Davies/Save the Children Fund; *p.224*: *(a)* © the estate of Franki Raffles/courtesy of Edinburgh District Council Women's Unit, Zero Tolerance Division; *(b)* © the Association of London Authorities. The Zero Tolerance logo is copyright of the estate of Franki Raffles; *(c)* Women's Aid Federation; *p.230*: © The European Campaign Against Domestic Violence for The European Commission, Brussels; *pp.241, 247, 249*: Popperfoto/Reuter; *p.248*: Peter McDiarmid/*The Independent*; *p.262*: © Paramount/Kobal Collection; *p.266*: © David Burrell/Blueprint Marketing Services; *p.270*: © Pathe/The Ronald Grant Archive; *p.285*: © Warner Bros (Courtesy Kobal); *pp.289, 304*: Popperfoto/Reuter; *p.297*: AKG London; *p.305*: Pacemaker Press International Ltd; *p.314*: Associated Press. Photo from *LIFE* Magazine, © 1969 Ronald L. Haeberle; *p.316*: Popperfoto/UPI; *p.318*: Associated Press/US State Department; *p.320*: Chris Bournoncle/Agence France Presse.

Index